THE BṚHAT SAṀHITĀ OF VARĀHA MIHIRA

SRI GARIB DASS ORIENTAL SERIES NO. 43

THE BṚHAT SAṀHITĀ OF VARĀHA MIHIRA

TRANSLATED INTO ENGLISH WITH NOTES

By

N.C. IYER

SRI SATGURU PUBLICATIONS
DELHI—INDIA

Published by :
SRI SATGURU PUBLICATIONS
a Division of
INDIAN BOOKS CENTRE
40/5, Shakti Nagar
Delhi-110 007
(INDIA)

Second revised edition : Delhi, 1987.

I.S.B.N.—81-7030-094-0

Printed in India at :
Kiran Mudran Kendra
A-38/2, Maya Puri, Phase I,
New Delhi 1100064.

Preface

India has long continued to be the centre of attraction not only in respect of its wealth and civilization but in that of its intellectual advancement. To it converged, as to a common focus, the eyes of foreigners from the earliest period of the world's history. It was the one fountain of knowledge from which issued streams to water distant lands of ignorance at every point of the compass, now yielding abundance of intellectual harvest. Time was when Indian wisdom shone resplendent, and, from its eminence, dazzled the eyes of distant nations—distant geographically and distant chronologically,—illumined every corner of the intellectual horizon and served as a beacon, lighting the paths of erring travellers. History is puzzled in its attempt to reach the data of Āryan civilization. Antiquarians are at logger-heads in their conclusions touching the age of Āryan learning.

Now it is well known that Āryan learning dates from the remotest antiquity. The Aryans have cultivated almost every department of knowledge. As the art of printing was unknown a large proportion of Āryan literature has been washed into oblivion by the mighty ways of time. Not a few remain,

"Like stranded wrecks the tide returning hoarse
To sweep them from our sight".

unless rescued from their fate. But most of the Hindus, of the present day, can not use the books themselves.

The public can therefore do much if their eyes could only be opened to the importance of the subject, Most of the English knowing natives hardly know what these books treat of. I have many a time astonished young Collegians and graduates by quoting from Hindu astronomers and mathematicians, and they were surprised to find that the Āryans knew what the Europeans know forgetting that these sciences were taken to the west from here.

Now it has come to my knowledge that in many Hindu families whole libraries, for want of inspection, are now being feasted on by moths and white ants and large quantities have already been emptied into the dustbins, the dccay having gone too for. English education, like Aaron's rod, appears to have devoured up every other education and it has spread now throughout the land.

In the humble hope that the progressing ruin might be in a measure retarded, it is proposed to tell the present Indian generation, in the language in which they *will all* and can all hear that, if they would exert a little, they might rescue from ruin a vast amount of splendid Aryan literature: As the pro-perity of a nation depends on its literature, the public are requested to for into societies for the collection and preservation of Āryan works.

Contents

		Page
	Preface	v
	Introduction	xii
Chapters		
1.	Introductory	1
2.	The Astrologer	3
3.	On the Sun	12
4.	On the Moon	17
5.	On Rāhu	22
6.	On Mars	38
7.	On Mercury	41
8.	On Jupiter	44
9.	On Venus	54
10.	On Saturn	60
11.	On Comets and the Like	64
12.	On Camopus	73
13.	On the Urṣa Major (The Constellation of the Seven Sages)	78
14.	Division of Globe	81
15.	Stellar Rulership	87
16.	On the Planets	91
17.	On Planetary Conjunctions	96
18.	On the Moon's Conjuctions with the Planets	107
19.	On Planetary Years	109

Chapters		Page
20.	On Planetary Meetings	113
21.	On the Rain Clouds	115
22.	Rain Support Days	122
23.	On Rain	123
24.	On Rohiṇī Yoga	125
25.	Svāati Yoga	132
26.	On Āṣāḍhi Yoga	134
27.	On the Winds	137
28.	On Immediate Rain	139
29.	On Flowers and Planets	143
30.	On Twilight Hours	148
31.	Glow at the Horizon	153
32.	On Erathquakes	154
33.	On Meteors	159
34.	On Halos	163
35.	On the Rainbow	167
36.	On the Cloud Castles	169
37.	On Parhelion	170
38.	On Dust Storms	171
39.	On Thunderbolts	172
40.	On Vegetable Horoscopy	173
41.	On commodities	175
42.	On the price of Commodities	177
43.	On Indra's Banner	179
44.	On the Lustration of Arms	188
45.	On the Wagtail	192
46.	On Portents	195
47.	Mutley Miscellany	208

Chapters		Page
48.	On Royal Bath	217
49.	On Cron Plate	226
50.	On the Sword	227
51.	On Limbs	229
52.	On Pimples	237
53.	On House-Building	239
54.	On under Currents	255
55.	On Gardening	269
56.	On the Building of Temples	281
57.	On Durable Cements	284
58.	On Temple Images	286
59.	On entry into the forest	293
60.	On the fixing of the Images in temples	295
61.	On the features of Cows and Oxen	298
62.	On the features of the Dog	300
63.	On the fertures of the Cock	301
64.	On the features of the Turtle	302
65.	On the features of the Goat	303
66.	On the features of the Horse	305
67.	On the features of the Elephant	306
68.	On the features of the Man	308
69.	On the Five great men	322
70.	On the features of the Women	327
71.	On Injuries to Garments	331
72.	On Chamara	334
73.	On Umbrellas	335
74.	On the praise of women	336

Chapters		*Page*
75.	On Amiability	339
76.	On Spermatic Drugs and Medicines	341
77.	On Perfume mixtures	346
78.	On Sexual Union	358
79.	On Cats and Seats	363
80.	On Diamonds	368
81.	On Pearls	371
82.	On Rubies	375
83.	On Emeralds	377
84.	On Lamps	378
85.	On Tooth-Brush	379
86.	Omen through Birds and Beasts	381
87.	On the circle of Horizon	392
88.	On Ominous cries	398
89,	On Ominous Connected with the Dog	404
90.	On the cry of the Jackal	408
91.	On Omens connected with wild animals	410
92.	On Omens connected with the Cow	411
93.	On Omens connected with the Horse	412
94.	On Omens connected with the Elephant	414
95.	On the Cawing of the crow	416
96.	Supplementary to Omens	424
97.	On Effective Periods	427
98.	On the Constellations	430
99.	On Lunar Days and Half Lunar Days	433
100.	On Marriage Lagnas	435
101.	The Moon in The Asterisms	436

Chapters | *Page*

102.	On the Division of the Zodiac	439
103.	On Marriages	440
104.	On the Effects of Planetary Motions	443
105.	On the Worship of the Stellar Deity	454
106.	Conclusion	456

Introduction

Varāha Mihira was a native of Avanti and the son of Ādityadāsa who was an astronomer and from whom he received his education as he himself tells us in his Bṛhat Jātaka (Chapter XXVI Verse 5). The data of his birth is involved in obscurity. It is the practice of all the Hiudu astronomers to give this information in their works on astronomy; but unfortunately Varāha Mihira's work on astronomy, known as the Panchasidhāntika, is now lost beyond all hope of recovery. The popular notion is that he was one of the 12 gems of the Court of Vikrāmarka. Now Vikrama Era, as we find from the Hindu calendar, dates from 56 B.C. whereas Varāha Mihira is considered so have flourished in the sixth century after Christ. So the Vikrāmarka of the first century before Christ must be different from the Vikrāmarka of the 6th century after Christ, unless we go to the length of believing that Vikramarka reigned, according to the Hindu legend, for a thousand years. We are not without parallel instances in the Christian Bible in which Enos is said to have lived 905 years, Cainan 910 years, Seth 912 years, Adam 930 years, Noah 950 years, Jared 962 years and Methusala 969 years ; and yet poor non-biblical Vikrāmarka is grudged a comparatively small matter of 500 years.

Now A.D. 505 is considered by some to be the date of Varāha Mihira's birth and by others to be that of his Panchasidhāntika, and A.D. 587 is thought to be the data of his death. It is also said that Varāha Mihira has quoted from Āryabhatta; that Āryabhatta was born in 476 A.D. and that this circumstance goes to prove that the dates given above are probably not incorrect. We shall now examine how far these dates are supported by evidence to be obtained from Varāha Mihira's own works—a circumstance which, curiously enough, appears to have escaped the attention of even such eminent scholars as Colebrook, Davis, Sir William Jones and others:

In verse 2 of Chapter III of his Bṛahat Saṁhitā, Varāha Mihira says:—

"At present the Solsticial points coincide with the beginning Karkataka (Sign Cancer) and with the beginning of Makara (Sign Capricornus)."

This amounts to saying that the Vernal equinox, which is midway between the Solstices (90° from coincided was at the commencement of Meṣa (Sign Aries) *i.e.* coincided with the Star Revati where the fixed Hin du Zodiac commences. The precession of the equinoxes was known to the Hindus long before it was known to the Europeans, although Hindu astronomers are not agreed as to the nature of its course—some asserting that it oscillates on both sides of the star Revati while others that it makes a complete revolution round the heavens, a point about which even European astronomers have not arrived at any conclusion. Now this point is at present about 20° to the west of the star Revati. Its annual rate of motion is known and increment in the rate is also know; so that by a process of simple calculation we can arive at the period when the point must have coincided with the star Revati. Now unfortunately, the exact distance between Vernal Equinox and the star Revati is not known, and cannot be determined from observation as the star (which the Hindu astronomers say was on the ecliptic) appears some how to have disappeared. Mr. Kero Latchmana Chatrai M.A. of Poona has adopted a star, known as the Zeeta Piscium (which however is not on the ecliptic) as the Revati of the Hindus. According to him the Āyanamsam, (the distance between the vernal Equinox and the star Revati), on the fisst January 1883 was 18° 14′ 20″. According to the late Mr. C. Reghunathachariar of Madras, (after him, Messrs. Vencateswara Deekshitar and Sundereswara Srouthy of Southern India) and Mr. Bapu Deva Sastry of Benares, the Āyanamsam on the 1st January 1883 was 22° 2′ 39″ and 21° 58′ 29″ respectively. But as these lengths have been arbitrarily assumed they may be dismissed as deserving of no consideration in this place. I have discovered it to be 20° 24′ 15″ on the above date and my discovery rests on the Druva Nāḍi, a work of Satyachariar, a great astronomer. For particulars of his disputed question the reader is referred to my artiele on the Hindu Zodiac published in the April (1883) issue of Theosophist.

Now we will calculate Varāha Mihira's time from the lengths of the Ayanamsam as adopted by Mr. K.L. Chatrai and as discovered by me. The question is one of Arithmetical progression. We will suppose,

a=rate of motion of Vernal Equinox when it coincided with the star Revati.

d=the annual increment in the rate.

l=the last term or rate of motion on the first January 1883.

s=the sum of the terms or the length of the Ayanamsam.

n=number of terms or number of years required.

We have the following series:

$a,\ a+d,\ a+2d,\ a+3d,\ldots\ldots\ldots a+(n-1)d.$

$\therefore\ l=a+(n-1)d. \qquad \therefore\ a=l-(n-1)d.$

$$s=(+l)\frac{n}{2}=\left\{l-(n-1)\ d+l\right\}\frac{n}{2}.$$

$$=\left\{2l-(n-1)\mathrm{d}\right\}\frac{n}{2}.$$

$\therefore\ 2s=(2l+d)n-dn^2.$

$\therefore\ dn^2-(2l+d)n+2s=0.$

$$\therefore\ n=\frac{2l+d\pm\sqrt{(2l+d)^2-4.\ d.\ 2s.}}{2d.}$$

where l= 50.″. 00024.

d=20° 24′ 15″ or 18° 14′ 20″.

Substituting these values, we get n=14,66 and 4,17,368 years, or=1310 and 4,17,523 yeart, before first January 1883 where the bigger figures may be rejected as they refer to the position of the vernal Equinox in its second revolution. So that Varāha Mihira's time is found to be either 1882 - 1466= 416 A.D. or 1812—13 0=572 A.D., according to me or Mr.

K.L. Chatrai respectively. Now it is true that 572 A.D. is in support of the supposed dates, above given, of Varāha Mihira's birth and death. But I cannot bring myself to believe that Zeeta piscium was the Revati of the Hindus, for this simple reason, that it is not on the ecliptic. Several stars of comparatively less importance, stated by the Hindu astromomers to be on the ecliptic are found to be so when examined with the aid of modern astronomical instruments. It is therefore unreasable to suppose that Hindu astronomers could have blundered in describing the position of the star Revati. As regards the difficulty that Varāha Mihira has quoted from Ārya Bhaṭṭa—which quotation must be in his Panchasidhāntika now lost—it is not improbable that the quotation is from Vṛdharya bhatīam.

It may be remarked here that when, in his work on Saṁhitā, Varāha Mihira refers to the position of the planets in the several signs of the zodiac, he refers to the fixed zodiac of the Hindus commencing from the star Revati and not to the shifting zodiac of the wastern astronomers which always commences at the moving vernal Equinox.

The whole book is one huge attempt to interpret the language of Nature and ascertain its bearing on the fortunes of men and nations. Where the lapidary discovers a diamond, the simple negro finds a piece of glass; where the botanist discovers a simple with valuable properties the farmer sees a thistle. Nature has been found to speak in a thousand ways at every moment of time and the Hindus from the eariiest times have learnt to hear and understand her language. This language, the modern scientific world, *at present* ignores, and with the simplicity of a negro or a farmer can even afford to to laugh at the supposed ignorance of the Hindus. "What is truth? asked jesting Pilate, but would not wait for an answer". They have not the patience to try and see what amount of truth there is in the Hindu interpretation of Nature's language.

We will take a few instances: 1500 years ago Varāha Mlhirā (who only quotes the opinion of writers that went before him) said that solar spots indicate famine in the land. This was found to be the case during the famine of 1876—77.

Again it is generally known that all India observe anxiously the course of the moon with respect to the four stars of the 10th constellation (*Magha*) when the sun is in the sign Aquarius i.e. from about February 10 to March 10, with a view to ascertain the future agricultural prospects of the land: the market price of food-grains is at once lowered or raised according as the moon's course lies to the south of the four stars or more and more to the north of the southernmost star. It is also stated that if the moon should pass to the north of all the four stars the world would be at an end.

Now astronomers know very well that *ordinarily* the moon will never pass to the north of all the four stars. I may also remark here that in the famine of 1876-77 the moon's course lay between the northern most star and the one next to it. We will cite one more instance.

Hindu astronomers say that if Saturn should enter the constrilation of Rohiṇī (4th) the world would be at an end. The story is that the astronomers of Daśaratha's court announced to the prince the dreaded entry of Saturn into the said constellation that the prince at once flew in the air and stood before Saturn in his orbit resolved to stop his course; that Saturn, pleased with the prince's boldness, promised never more to enter the circle. Now, astronomical calculations show that *ordinarily* Saturn will never enter the said circle, —a circumstance which shows that the story is simply intended to cover an astronomical truth. It is a well-known fact that recently Saturn approached the circle within a degree from it but did not enter it.

In justice to the wisdom of the ancient Hindus, who, for ages, continued their observation and tabulation of the phenomena of nature, the public will do well to give each matter a patient trial and see what amount of truth there is in each and not follow the wisdom of Alexander the Great who, unable to untie the Gordian knot, chose to cut it, In the course of this work the reader will find that the author refers to several phenomena which, within the limited experience of the modern scientific world might appear improbable. True wisdom consists in patient investigation and not in hasty rejection.

It is humbly hoped that, if this book were carefully studied and its truths practically examined, the material prosperity of the world would be vastly improved.

CHAPTER 1

Introductory

1. Glory be to the Sun who is the author and the Soul of the Universe, the ornament of the firmament and who is enveloped in a thousand rays of the color of molten gold.

2. Having correctly examined the substance of the voluminous works of the sages of the past, I attempt to write a clear treatise neither too long nor too short.

3. What means the notion that the works of the Ṛṣis are sound and not so the works of men? In cases where the matter refers to no mantra, what is there to choose between, when the meaning is the same because the words are different?

4. If Brahma has declared "Kśhititanaya divasa varo naśubhakrit"[1] and man "Kuja dinamaniśtam"[1] what is there to choose between the work of man and that of a Deva?

5. Having examined the vast works that have proceeded from writers from Brahma downwards, I purpose to write a brief work embodying the substance of the same. The task is a pleasing one to me.

6. There was darkness (chaos) in the beginning. Then came water (into existence). On it (floated) a gold colored egg, the (divine) seed consisting of the Earth and the Firmament from which there arose Brahma, the creative agent with the sun and moon for his eyes.

7. Kapila[2] says that the Universe had its origin in pradhana[3]; Kanātha[4] in drivya[5] and the like; a few[6] in kāla (time); others[7] in Svabhāva (nature); and some[8] in Karma.

8. Enough of this (subject of Cosmogony) on account of its vastness. If this question were discussed; it would swell very much in length. The subject I have now to treat of is the Aṅgaviniścaya (Saṁhitā) section of Jyotiṣ Śāstra.

9. Jyotiṣ Śāstra treats of many different subjects and consists of three sections. The sages call the whole by the general name of Saṁhitā. This[9] section which treats of the motions of

the planets is called the Taṅtraśāstra (Astronomy). Another section is the Horāśāstra (Horoscopy). The third section is known as the Aṅgaviniscayaśāstra (Saṁhitā or natural astrology).

10. In my work on Astronomy, I have treated of the heliacal rising and setting of the planets as well as their retrograde and re-retrograde motions and the like. In my work on Horoscopy I have fully treated of nativity, of *yātrā* and of marriage.

11. In the prerent treatise, I have rejected questions and re-questions, historical narrations, unimportant planetary phenomena and all that is useless; and I purpose to speak clearly only of the vital truths of the several subjects treated of.

REFERENCES

1. Both the phrases mean that Tuesday is an inauspicious day though expressed in different words.
2. Kapila was the author of the saṅkhya Philosophy.
3. Pradhana is a due proportion of the three guṇas Satwa, Raja and Tama.
4. Kanātha, also called Kānātha, which term literally means the atomgiver i.e. the founder of the atomic theory.
5. Drivya: these are nine: earth, water, air, fire, ākāś, Kāla [time], dik [direction], ātmā [the soul], and manas the mind].
6. A few: these are the Pauraṇikas.
7. Others: these are the Lokayatikas.
8. Some: these are the Mīmāṁsakas.
9. The Śloka is evidently quoted from Varāhamihira's work on Astronomy, known as the Pañcasiddhāntika which appears to have been lost.

CHAPTER 2

The Astrologer[1]

We shall now proceed to give a brief description of (the qualifications of) a Jyotiṣaka. He must be of noble birth and of agreeable appearance; meek, truthful and without jealousy; of proportional limbs; of joints well built and of good growth; have no physical defects; be of fine hands, feet, nails, eyes, chin, eteth, ears, forehead, eye-brows and head; of fine physique and of high, sonorous voice.

Generally speaking do not virtues and voices follow the body?

The Virtues: He must be of cleanly habits, able, noble-minded, eloquent and of originality and imagination; must possess a knowledge of place and time; be meek and without nervousness must be difficult of conquest by his fellow students; must be able and devoid of vices; must be learned in matters of expiatory ceremonies, of Hygeine, of Occult Magic and of ablutions; must be a worshipper of the Devas and an observer of fast and penance; must be of remarkable genius and capable of solving any difficulties save in matters of direct divine interference; and finally, he must be learned in astronomy, natural astrology (Saṁhitā) and horoscopy.

In Astronomy: He must have studied the works of Puliśa Romaka, Vasiṣṭha, Sūrya and Pitāmaha; he must have a correct, knowledge of a *Yuga* (43,20,000 Solar years), *Varṣa* (a solar year), *Ayana* (6 solar months), *Ruthu* (2 solar months), *Māsa* (a solar month), *Pakṣa* (15 solar days), *Ahorathra* (a solar day), *Yama* (one-eighth of a solar day), *Muhurta* (one-thirtieth of a solar day), *Nāḍī* (one-sixtieth of a solar day or 24 seconds), *Pinadi* (one sixtieth of a Nāḍī or 24 minutes), *Prāṇa* (4 seconds) *Truti* (33,750th of a second) and parts of a *Truṭi* and other divisions of time and also of divisions of space.

He must have a clear knowledge of the Causes of *Solar*,

Sāvana,[2] *Siderial* and *Lunar* months as well as of *intercalary lunations* and *intercalary days*.

He must have a knowledge of the beginning and end of *Śaśtyabda* (a cycle of 60 years), *a yuga* (5 years), *Varśa* (a year), *Māsa* (a month), *Thina* (a day) and *horā* (an hour) and of their lords.

He must know the solar and other divisions of time, their similarity and dissimilarity and must be capable of propounding the fitness or unfitness of each for particular purposes: these divisions of time are, of Man, of Devas, of Jupiter, of Pithris, of Star (Siderial) of the Sun (solar), of the Moon (lunar), of the Earth (terrestrial), and of Brahma.

If the methods of calculation given in the five Astronomical works mentioned above should produce different results he must be able to calculate correctly the places of the sun and planets by actual observation (by means of shadow and water level and with the help of Astronomical instruments) of the termination of their *ayana* (northward and southward course), of their being due east to the observer after rising and of their altitude at any time.

He must know the reason for the correction required for the conversion of the heliocentric into geocentric longitude and vice versa; the causes of the ayana of the sun and planets and of their slow and rapid movements at different times.

In solar and lunar eclipses, he must be able to calculate the times of the commencement and end of the eclipses, the places of first and last contact, the magnitude and duration of the eclipse; in total eclipses, he must be able to calculate the time between middle eclipse and the beginning or end of total phase, (this period being technically known as Vimarda). He must also know the color of the eclipsed lunar disc. He must be able to calculate before hand the times of the Moon's conjunction with the planets as well as of planetary conjunctions.

He must know the length, in yojana (5 miles), of the daily motion of each planets in its orbit and of the orbit itself, and generally the length, in yojana, in every case.

He must know the Earth's revolutiou round the sun and its rotation round its axis; its shape, size and the like; the latitude of a place and its complement; the nature of the hour circle; the *chara dala kala* [the difference between 6 hours and half a day], the times of the rising of the Zodiacal signs. He must also be able to calculate time from shadow and shadow from time and to convert longitude into right ascension and right ascension into longitude.

He must be able to meet objections and questions in clear and distinct language and must be capable of explaining the science in its purity in just the same way as separating the pure gold [from all dross] and making it capable of retaining its value when submitted to the touch stone, to the fire and to the hammer.

How can one, who is incapable of entrapping others with a hard question or of answering any that is put to himself or of explaining his views to his students, expect to become an astronomer?

The fool whose exposition is at variance with the text and whose illustration is opposed to such exposition is not unlike one who addressing Brahma as Pārvatī (Goddess) begins his praise by recounting the vices of a prostitute.

The predictions of one, who knows astronomy well, who is able to calculate the exact Lagna with such helps as the shadow, water and astronomical instruments and who is well versed in horoscopy will never fail.

Viṣṇuguptā says "flying with the speed of the wind, one might find it possible to cross to the ocean's opposite shore; but a non-Ṛṣi can never, even mentally, reach the opposite shore of the vast ocean of Jyotiṣśāstra."

And in horoscopy[4] the Jyoutiṣaka must know such divisions of space as *rāśi* (a sign of Zodiac or a space of 30°), *horā* (15° or half a sign), *drekkana* (10° or one third of a sign), *Navāṁśa* (3°20′ or one ninth of a sign), *Dvādaśāṁśa* (2°30′ or one twelfth of a sign), *Triṁśāṁśa* (1° or one thirtieth of a sign), and their strength or weakness considered horoscopically; he must know the horoscopic strength of the planets with respect to their *dik*[5] (direction), *stana*[6] (place), *Kāla*[7] (time), *Cheshta*[8] (motions, conjunctions and the like).

He must know the temperament of the planets and the parts of the body lorded over by each; the mineral division of each; the caste, sex and authority of each and the like; he must be able to state, from the time of conception or birth of a person, particulars connected with these occasions so as to insure belief; he must be able to say in what cases a child will die in infancy, and to calculate the period of one's existence, he must be able to divide one's life into planetary divisions and sub-divisions; he must be able to use the *aśtakavarga*[9] Tables to a given horoscope. He must know how[10] the several *Raja*, *Cāndra*, *Dvigraha*, and *Nābhasa* yogas affect the fortunes of men. He must also know how the fortunes of men are affected by the position and look of planets. He must be able to calculate the cause of one's death and discover his future life.

He must be able to discover auspicious periods for marriages and the like.

In *yātrā*[11] he must know the fitness or unfitness of a *tithi* [lunar day], *vāra* [week day], *Karana*, *Nakṣatra*, *Muhūrta*, and *lagna* [a sign of zodiac] and *yoga* for particular purposes. He must be able to interpret natural gestures and dreams;[12] he must be able to state when a prince ought to start for battle to secure success in war; he must be learned in rules relating to ablutions and sacred fire ceremonies in honor of the planets and offerings to evil spirits; he must be able to interpret phenomena connected with such sacred fires and with elephants and horses while mounting the same.

He must be able to interpret the language and gestures of fighting men and the like; he must be learned in the *Śadguṇa*[13] and *upāya*[14] policies; he must be able to predict the success or failure of an undertaking; he must be able to interpret omens; he must have a knowledge of favourable halting places for the King's army; he must be able to interpret the color of ceremonial fires; he must know when to employ the minister, spies, messengers and forest men; he must be able to give directions touching the capture of the enemy's fortress.

On all the above subjects, works of learned men exist. The predictions of one to whom the truths of the science appear as if spread before his eyes, written on his mind and planted in his breast will never fail.

A true Astrologer is also one who has thoroughly mastered the Science of Saṁhitā.

It treats[15] of the motions of the sun and planets; of their size, color, rays, brilliancy and shape and changes in the same of their disappearance and reappearance; of their courses and deviations therefrom; of their retrograde and re-retrograde motions; of their conjunction with the stars and of their places among the stars and the like.

It treats of the effects of *Agastya chara*[16] and *Saptarṣi chara*[17] on particular parts of India, corresponding to particular portions of the ecliptic; of the stellar divisions of every substance, animal and plant, and of their increase or decrease according to the motion of the planets among the stars; of the formation and interpretation of various figures presented by the planets when meeting together; of planetary conjunctions; of planetary years; of monsūniś indications of the weather; of the moon's conjunction with *Rohiṇī* (4th constellation), *svātī* (15th constellation) and the two *Āṣāḍhas* (20th and 21st constellations), on particular week days of the month of Āṣāḍha and of predicting the nature of the coming weather and crops from the same.

It treats of the prediction of immediate rain from surrounding phenomena; of judging the nature of the future crops from the growth of plants and flowers; of the halos round the sun and moon; of lines of clouds crossing the solar disc at rising and setting; of the winds; of meteoric falls; of false fires; of earthquakes; of the red sky immediately before sunrise and after sunset; of the fanciful shapes of clouds; of dust storms; of thunderbolts; of the price of food grains; of gardening.

It treats of *indradhvaja*,[18] of the rainbow and of architecture; of the prediction of events from casual words and gestures and from the cawing of crows; of the formation of Zodiacal circles for purposes of horary astrology.

It treats of the prediction of future events from phenomena connected with the deer, the dog and the motions of the wind; of the construction of temples, towers and palaces; of the casting of images and of founding the same; of the growth of plants and trees; of under currents; of certain annual ceremonies to be performed by princes for success in war.

It also treats of the prediction of events from the flight of the *kanjana* (a small black bird—the gracular religiosa) and from the appearance of various abnormal phenomena, of expiatory ceremonies; of miscellaneous planetary phenomena; of *ghrita kambala*;[19] of the royal sword; of patta;[20] of the features of a house cock, a cow, a sheep, a horse, an elephant, a man and a woman.

It also treats of the treatment of women; of moles in the body; of injuries to shoes and clothes; of hairy fans; of walking sticks; of beds and seats; of lamplight; of tooth brush and the like.

Generally, the determination of the fortunes of men and princes depends on matters enumerated above and changing every moment. It therefore behoves a prince to employ astrologers solely upon this work. As it is impossible for a single astrologer to observe and determine all the phenomena occurring day and night, the task must be assigned to four competent and well paid astrologers; one of them is to observe the east and south-east; another the south and southwest; a third the west and north-west; and the fourth the north and north-east. For the fall of meteors and the like is sudden in its nature and the determination of one's fortunes depends on the shape, color, gloss, size and the like of these falling bodies and upon how they approach or cross planets and stars.

And Bhagavan Garga says:—

7. That prince meets with ruin who does not support a Jyotiṣaka well versed in all the Divisions and Subdivisions of Saṁhitā and in Horoscopy and Astronomy.

8. Even men who, having conquered their passions and cut asunder all ties of family, live in woods, desire to question a learned Jyotiṣaka regarding their future.

9. As is the night without a lamp and the sky without the sun, so is a prince without a Jyotiṣaka and he gropes his way in the dark.

10. If there were no Jyotiṣakas, the *muhūrtas*, the *tithīs*, the *nakṣatras*, the *ruthus* and the *ayanas* would go wrong.

11. It therefore behoves a prince who loves success, fame, wealth, happiness and renown to secure the services of a learned Jyotiṣaka.

12. He who loves prosperity ought not to live in a country devoid of a Jyotiṣaka. He (the Jyotiṣaka) forms as it were the eye of the land and where he dwells, sins exist not.

13. A learned Jyotiṣaka not only escapes hell but (after death) goes to the Brahma loka and obtains salvation.

14. That Brāhmiṇ Jyotiṣaka who has mastered both the text and the purport of the entire science deserves to be respec-

ted and fed first on occasions of *Śraddhā* and he purifies the party of diners.

15. Even the Mlechas and the Yavanas (Greeks) who have well studied the science are respected as Ṛṣis. Such being the case, if the Jyotiṣaka should happen to be a Brahmin, who will deny him respect?

16. A pretentious Jyotiṣaka whose knowledge of the science has been picked up from what has occasionally fallen on his cars ought not to be consulted.

17. He who, not having studied the science, passes for a Jyotiṣaka is a sinner and a disgrace to society.

18. He who ridicules the words of a Jyotiṣaka, as well as the person who sneers at the science itself, will suffer miseries in the hell of darkness.

19. To question an ignorant man is not unlike begging of a clod of earth at the gate of a city for a gift: whatever is truth will finally triumph.

20. One that, after the occurrence of an event, pretends that his prediction already meant so much, and one that wanders away from the subject as well as the person who is proud, having only an imperfect knowledge of the subject shall be rejected by a prince.

21. He who well knows the horā, the gaṇita and the Saṁhitā śāstras ought to be respected by the prince who loves victory and admitted into his court.

22. That service, which a single Jyotiṣaka, having a knowledge of place and time can render to a prince, cannot be rendered to him by a thousand elephants or by four thousand horses.

23. The evils of bad dreams, of sad thoughts, of ill omens and of evil deeds and the like will vanish immediately one hears of the moon's motion among the stars.

24. Neither the father nor the mother nor the relations nor friends of a prince will desire so much *his* well being and that of his subjects as a true Jyotiṣaka.

REFERENCES

1. One who is versed in Saṁhitā, Astronomy and Horoscopy.
2. 30 times the interval from sunrise to sunrise.
3. Vide ślokas 23 and 24 Chapter VIII.
4. Here follow a number of technical terms which might appear forbiding to persons not conversant with the subject.
5. Mercury and Jupiter have *dik bala* when situated in one of there signs, Mesha (Aries), Simha (Leo) and Dhanus (Sagittarius), technically known as the eastern signs. The Sun and Mars have it if in one of the three signs, Vṛṣabha (Taurus), Kanyā (Virgo), Makara (capricornus) known as the Southern Signs. Saturn has it in one of the three signs, *Mithūna [Gemini]*, *Tulā* (*Libra*), *Kumbha* (*Aquarius*) known as the western signs. Venus and the Moon have it if in one of the three signs, *Kataka* (*Cancer*) *Vriṣcika* (*Scorpio*) and *Mīna* (*Pisces*) known as the northern signs.
6. A planet has *Stana bala* if he is in his own sign, in a friendly sign, in his ucha sign or in his own *navāṁśa* or drekkana.
7. The Moon, Mars and Saturn have *Kalabala* at night, Mercury has it at all times, the other planets during the day, the malefic planets in the waning moon and the benefic ones in the waxing moon. A planet has also *Kalabala* in his year, month, day and hour.
8. The sun and moon have *cheshta bala* when in one of the six signs from *Makara;* the other planets have it when retrograde, when in conjunction with the Moon, or when in their greatest brilliancy. In conjunctions the northern planets have it.
9. The object is to discover from the positions of the planets in one's nativity how the planets affect one's fortunes as they pass through the several zodiacal signs.
10. These are particular positions of the planets.
11. This literally means journey—evidently royal marches and forms a section of horoscopy.

12. To ascertain the King's fortunes in war, the practice was to direct the minister, the astrologer and the priest to sleep in the Temple and then to interpret their dreams.

13. These are six—1. *Sandhi* or reconciliation with the enemy. 2. *Vigraha* or open battle. 3. *Yana* or proceeding to battle or other strategic movement 4. *Āsana* or stopping in the capital 5. *Dvayidham* or of two enemies to join one with a view to defeat the other 6. *Āsrya* or submission.

14. These are four 1. *Sama* or reasoning with. 2. *Dāna* or gift. 3. *Bheda* or bringing about dissension among the enemies. 4. *Daṇḍa* or punishment.

15. The following is by no means an exhaustive list of the subjects treated of.

16. Heliacal rising of canopus.

17. Heliacal rising of the Bear.

18. This refers to the erection of a flag staff on occasions of certain annual ceremonies performed by princes.

19. A certain ceremony of ablution on the occasion of a sovereign's coronation.

20. A gold ornament for the forehead.

CHAPTER 3

On the Sun

1. At one time, the Sun's southward course commenced on his reaching the middle of Āśleṣā (the ninth constellation) and its northward course on its reaching the beginning of Dhaniṣṭhā (the twenty-third constellation, the Delphin of European Astronomers). This must have been the case as we find it so recorded in ancient books.

2. Whereas at present the one course of the sun commences at the beginning of Cancer, and the other at the beginning of Capricornus. That it is so, and different from what it was at one time can easily be ascertained from actual observation as follows.

3. Either from observing some distant point in the horizon where the sun rises or sets or from observing the ingress or the egress of the end of shadow of a perpendicular rod placed at the centre of a big horizontal circle (the change in the sun's course can be detected.)

4. If the Sun should change his course before reaching *Makara* (*Capricornus*) he will bring evil on the west and south; and if he should do so before reaching *Kataka* (*Cancer*), he will bring evil on the north and east.

5. The Sun when he changes his course from north to south and when in his usual condition will bring on prosperity and increase of crops; but when he undergoes a change either in his usual course or in his usual appearance[1] he causes fear to mankind.

6. Even on other than new-moon days the Ketu named Tvaṣṭa eclipses the solar disc. Then seven princes and their subjects will perish by the sword, by fire and by famine.

7. The dark spots, also known as Ketus, the sons of Rāhu are *Thamara*, *Kīlaka* and the like, and are 33 in number. How they affect the earth depends upon their color, position and shape.

8. If these spots should appear on the solar disc, mankind will suffer miseries; if on the lunar disc mankind will be happy; but if they take the shape of a crow, a headless human body, or a weapon, mankind will suffer even though the spots should appear on the moon.

9. When the spots appear on the solar disc the waters will get disturbed; the sky will be filled with dust; high winds capable of breaking down the tops of mountains and of trees, will carry pebbles and sand along their course.

10. The trees will fail to yield in their appropriate seasons birds and animals will appear to be burning; there will be an appearance of false fire all round; and lightning and earthquake will afflict mankind.

11. If there should appear on the solar disc Ketus[2] other than the thirty-three already mentioned, or spots pikelike in shape the effects of these and of solar eclipses are the same as those assigned to them in the Chapters [V and XI] on Rehuchara and Ketuchara.

12. The princes of the countries in which the spots are visible will be afflicted with miseries.

13. Even Ṛṣis, reduced to mere skeletons by starvation, giving up their pious course of life, with fleshless infants in their arms.

14. Deprived of their property by highway men, with long sighs, closed eyes, emaciated bodies, and with their sight dimmed with the tears of sorrow will proceed with difficulty to other lands.

15. Men, reduced to mere bones and ashamed to beg will be harrassed both by their own princes and by the princes of other lands. Some will begin to speak disparagingly of the character and deeds of their own sovereign.

16. Even though there should be indications of good rain, the clouds will yield little rain; the rivers will fall and [food] crops will be found [only] here and there.

17. If the spots should be of the shape of a rod the prince dies; if of the shape of a headless body mankind will suffer from disease; if of the shape of a crow they will suffer from robbers; and if of the shape of a pike, they will suffer famine.

18. If the solar spots should be of the shape of the emblems of royalty such as *Chhatra* [umbrella], *Dhvaja* [flag staff] and

Chamara [hairy fan] and the like, the reigning prince will be dethroned and a foreign prince will begin to reign. If the spots should appear like sparks of fire, like the smoke and the like, his subjects will suffer.

19. A single spot will bring on famine; if two or more spots should appear, the reigning prince will die; if they should appear white, red, yellow or black then the Brahmins, the Kṣatrias, the Vaiśyas or the Śūdras will suffer respectively.

20. Only those parts of the earth will suffer in the corresponding parts of which on the solar disc the spots happen to appear.

21. If, when the rays are turned away from the earth the color of the sun be that of copper the commander-in-chief dies; if it be green or yellow the king's son dies; if it be white the royal chaplain dies.

22. If the sun be variegated in color or of the color of smoke there will be either immediate rain or mankind will suffer from robbers and from weapons.

23. If in *Śiśira* [February, March] the sun be of copper color or red black, if, in *Vasanta* [April, May], blue crimson, if, in *Grīṣma* [June, July], slightly white and of gold color, if, in *Varṣā* [August, September], white.

24. If, in *Śarat* [October, November], of the color of the centre of the lotus, if, in *Hemanta* [December, January], of blood color, mankind will be happy.

If, in *Varṣā* [August, September], the rays of the sun be soft, mankind will be happy even though the sun should be of any of the colors mentioned above.

25. If, in *Varṣā*, when the rays are sharp, the sun be white then the Brahmins, if of blood color the Kṣatrias, if yellow the Vaiṣyas, and if black the Śūdras will perish. If, as said above, the rays be soft, mankind will be happy.

26. If, in *Griṣma*, the sun be of blood color mankind will be afflicted with various fears;

If, in *Varṣā*, he be black there will be drought on the Earth;

If, in *Hemanta* he be yellow there will be immediate fear from disease.

27. If the solar disc should be crossed by the rainbow the

princes of the land will be at war with one another. If in winter the disc be clear there will be immediate rain.

28. If in *Varṣā* the color of the sun be that of the flower *Śirīṣa* (Mimosa flexuosa) there will be immediate rain; if the color be that of the peacock's plume there will be no rain for 12 years to come.

29. If, *then* the sun be black there will be fear from worms and reptiles; if it be ashy pale there will be fear from foreign princes; if the sun should appear with a hole that prince will perish in the star[3] of whose nativity the sun then happens to be.

30. If at other times than rising or setting the sun be of the color of the blood of a hare there will be war in the land; if he should appear like the moon, the reigning prince will be killed and a foreign prince will succeed immediately.

31. If the sun should appear like a pot; he brings on hunger and death; if he should appear broken, the reigning prince dies; if without rays, mankind will be afflicted with fears; if like a gate, then the capital city, if like an umbrella then the country, will perish.

32. If the sun should appear like a flag staff, or a bow, or quivering or of sharp rays he will bring on wars; if there should appear black lines on his disc the reigning prince will die by the hand of his own minister.

33. If, at rising,[4] the sun should be crossed by the fall of an aerolite, or thunderbolt, or by lightning, the reigning prince will die and a foreign prince will succeed.

34. If, for several days, there should appear a halo round the sun both at rising and seeting or if the sun should, at such periods, be of blood color, the reigning sovereign will be dethroned and a foreign prince will succeed.

35. If at rising and setting the sun should be hid by clouds of the shape of implements of war, he will bring on strife; if these clouds should appear like a deer, a buffalo, a bird, an ass or a young camel, mankind will be afflicted with fears.

36. The planets, when subjected to the hot rays of the sun are freed from their impurities just as gold is purified by the action of the fire.

37. If the halo should be to the north of the sun there will be rain; if to the south there will be wind; if on both sides there will be fear from floods; if above the sun (towards the meridian)

then the king, if below it (towards the horizon), then his subjects, will perish.

38. If the sun should be of blood color when in mid-heaven, or if he should appear red by a dust storm the reigning prince will die.

39. If the sun should be either black or a mixture of black and other colors and if birds and animals should fearfully howl towards night-fall, mankind will perish.

40. If the solar disc should be of clear appearance and not irregular in shape if its rays be pure, wide and far-reaching and if the disc should be stainless mankind will enjoy prosperity.

REFERENCES

1. The recent phenomenon of the blue or green rayless sun is an instance.
2. This term in applied both to comets and to solar spots.
3. The star of a person is that constellation in which the moon is at the time of his birth.
4. Or setting, according to commentator.

CHAPTER 4

On the Moon

1. The Moon is always below (nearer to the Earth than) the sun. It is spherical in shape. One half of it is always illumined by the light of the sun, while the other half is dark owning to its own shadow, just like a pot placed in the sun.

2. The rays of the sun falling on the watery moon remove the darkness of the night (on Earth) just in the same way as light reflected from a mirror (placed in the sun) removes the darkness (from) within a room.

3. The moon after quitting the place (direction) of the sun becomes illumined by the sun from below and she then also rises after the sun.

4. Thus the lunar disc appears more and more illumined day by day by the sun according to her change of place, just in the same way as the western half of a pot becomes gradually illumined by the sun in the afternoon.

5. If the moon should pass to the south of *Jyeṣṭhā*[1] (the 18th constellation), *Mūla* (the 19th constellation) and the two *Āṣāḍhas* (20th and 21st constellations) she destroys seeds, creatures in water and forests; and there will also be fear from fire.

6. If the moon should pass to the south of *Viśākhā* (the 16th constellation) and *Anurādhā* (the 17th constellation) she will bring on evil. If she should pass through the middle of *Maghā* (the 10th constellation) or of *Viśākhā* (the 16th constellation) she will bring on prosperity.

7. In the six lunar mansions beginning from Revatī (the 27th) the stars are towards the east; and in the twelve beginning from *Ārdrā* (the 6th) they are in the centre; and in the nine beginning from *Jyeṣṭha* (the 18th) they are in the west of the several mansions; and the moon's conjunction with the several lunar mansions is said to take place when the moon is in the middle of these mansions.

8. If[2] the two horns of the moon should appear but slightly raised and far from each other presenting the appearance of a boat, she brings trouble on the sailors but prosperity on mankind at large.

9. If the northern horn of the moon should be higher than the other by one-half, the moon appearing like a plough, plough-men will then suffer. They and their prince will be friendly and there will be prosperity in the land.

10. If the southern horn should be higher than the other by one half, the appearance of the moon is also said to be plough like but of evil consequences. The ruler of Southern India will die and his army will engage in war.

11. If, on the first lunar day after newmoon, both horns should be alike and of equal height, there will be the same prosperity and rain throughout the month as on such first lunar day. If the moon appear like a rod, the cattle will suffer and the sovereign will rule with a severe rod.

12. If the moon should appear like a bow, there will be war in the land, and those will succeed whose places lie in the direction of the bow-string. If the moon should appear stretched from North to South presenting the appearance of a carriage pole there will be earthquake (within that month).

13. If, when the northern horn is a little higher than the other and bent aside, the southern horn is straight like a carriage pole, pilgrim parties will suffer and there will be no rain.

14. If one of the horns should appear higher than the other and bent down at the end, cows will suffer.

15. If the horns should together appear like a circle then the provincial rulers will have to quit their places.[3]

16. If the northern horn should be higher than the southern one otherwise than as stated already, the crops will flourish and there will be good rain. If the southern horn should be similarly higher there will be famine and fear in the land.

17. If, to any person who observes on the first lunar day after new-moon, the moon should appear of only one horn, or if one of the horns should appear bent downwards or if she appear like a full moon (when in reality such is not the case) the person dies.[5]

18. Having thus described the shape of the moon we next proceed to describe her size (generally); if the moon should

appear small there will be famine, and if big, prosperity, in the land.

19. If the middle of the moon should appear small, there will be hunger in the land and princes will be afflicted with cares. If the middle should appear big she will cause prosperity and plenty.

20. If she should appear broad, she will increase the prosperity of the princes; if she should appear big there will be happiness in the land, and if small, there will be abundance of that grain which men like most.

21. If, during the waxing moon, Mars should be eclipsed by a horn, the border (Mlecha) princes as well as wicked rulers will suffer; if Saturn should be so eclipsed there will be fear from weapons and from hunger; if Mercury should be so eclipsed there will be drought and famine in the land; if Jupiter should be so eclipsed eminent princes will suffer; and if Venus, the minor princes will suffer. As regards the waning moon the subject has been elsewhere treated.

22. If Venus should be eclipsed by the lunar disc the people of Magadha, the Yavanas, the Mlechas, men of Pulinda (a barbarous tribe), the Nepalese, the Bhṛṅgis, and the Marwaris, the men of Cutch and of Surat, the Madras, the Pāñcālas, the Kekayas, the Kulūtakas and the men of Uśīnara (Kandahar) will suffer miseries for 7 months.

23. If Jupiter should be eclipsed by the lunar disc the men of Gāndhār, of Souvīraka,[7] of Sindh and of Kīra, the rulers of the Drāviḍa countries and Brahmins as well as food grains and mountains will suffer for ten months.

24. If Mars should be so eclipsed the rulers of Traigartas (Lahore) and of Mālavas, with their fighting men in their cars, the chiefs of Kulinda, the rulers of Śibis, of Oudh, of Kuru (Delhi), of Mathsia and of Śukti will suffer for six months.

25. If Saturn should be eclipsed by the lunar disc, the ministers of Yaudheya, the Kouravas, the Arjunas as well as the men of the eastern countries will suffer miseries for ten months.

26. If Mercury should be so eclipsed the men of Magadha, of Mathurā and those on the banks of the river Veṇā will suffer miseries while the rest of the land will enjoy the happiness of Krithayuga.

27. If the moon should be eclipsed by Ketu[8] she will destroy prosperity, health and plenty. Artisans will perish, and thieves will suffer greatly.

28. If while the moon is eclipsed, she be crossed by the fall of a meteor, that prince will die in the star of whose nativity the moon then happens to be.

29. If the lunar disc be of ashy color, of sharp rays or red, or rayless, or red black, or appear broken there will be fear of hunger, of war, of disease and of robbers.

30. If the lunar disc should appear white and of the color of the snow, of Kunda,[9] of Kumuda[10] and of crystal he brings prosperity on the land.

31. If the disc of the moon that regularly waxes and wanes should appear white resembling the color of the kunda flower or that of the stem of the lotus or if the moon's course or disc or rays should suffer no irregular change there will be prosperity in the land.

32. During the waxing moon the Brahmins, the Kṣatriyas and mankind at large will prosper; and during the waning moon they will suffer miseries. The increase of prosperity will commence after the new-moon and of adversity after the full moon.

REFERENCES

1. The Moon can never pass, the commentator adds, to the south of the four stars mentioned in the text *ordinarily* and that wherever the phenomena described in the text clash with astronomical calculations they should be treated as *abnormal*.
2. The author now proceeds to state certain unusual appearances of the moon.
3. In all the above cases the observation is to be made on the first or second lunar day and these unusual phenomena will produce evil only when they clash with the calculated phases of the moon and not otherwise. It is therefore the duty of a almanac publishers to give beforehand the phases of the moon for the information of the public.

4. The author now proceeds to state certain ordinary phenomena.

5. This evidently refers to some optical illusion consequent on the diseases of the eye. I know of an old gentleman who for the last ten months sees a double sun and a double moon. It follows from this that some at least of the abnormal appearances of the sun and moon may not in probably be the result of optical illusions affecting mankind more or less.

6. A country to the North West of Hindustan Proper.

7. Probably the Suirs inhabiting the Country on the west of the Indus.

8. This refers to the lunar eclipse when the moon is in the descending node.

9. A Species of white flower.

10. do do

CHAPTER 5

On Rāhu[1]

1. Some say that *Rāhu*, the *asura*, though his head was cut, dies not but lives in the shape of a planet having tasted of ambrosia.

2. That he has a disc like the sun and moon and as that disc is black it is invisible when in the sky except on the occasion of eclipses in virtue of a boon from Brahma.

3. Others say that he resembles a serpent in shape with his head severed from his tail; a few that he is bodiless, that he is mere darkness and that he is the son of Siṁhikā.

4. Now, if he has a body or be simply a head with a regular motion in the ecliptic, how comes it that he eclipses the sun and moon when they are 180° from him ?

5. If his motion be not subject to fixed laws, how comes it that his exact place is ascertained; how comes it that he never eclipses by the part of his body between his head and tail.

6. If being of the shape of a serpent he eclipses with his head or with his tail, how comes it that he does not hide one half of the heavens lying between his head and tail.

7. If, as some say, there be two Rāhus, when the moon is eclipsed by one of them at rising or setting how comes it we see the sun in the opposite point uneclipsed by the other Rāhu of equal motion ?

8. The truth is that in her own eclipse, the moon enters the shadow of the earth, and in that of the sun, the solar disc. Hence the lunar eclipse does not commence at the western limb nor the solar at the eastern limb.

9. Just as the shadow of a tree neither continues in the same direction nor of the same length, so changes the shadow of the earth, night after night owing to the revolution of the sun.

10. When the moon, whose course is always from west to

east, is due opposite to the sun swerving neither much to the north nor to the south, she enters the shadow of the earth.

11. The moon, moving from the west, hides the solar disc from below just like a cloud; and the solar eclipse varies differently in different countries according to the different degrees of visibility of the eclipsed disc.

12. What eclipses the moon is bigger than the moon; what eclipses the sun is smaller than the sun. Hence in semi-lunar and semi-solar eclipses the luminous horns are respectively blunt and sharp.

13. Thus the causes of the eclipses have been stated by learned astronomers; that Rāhu does not cause the eclipses is the truth of the śāstras.

14. "May you be satisfied by the gifts and fire offerings (of men) on the occasion of the eclipses" is the boon bestowed on Rāhu by the command of Brahma.

15. On the occasion of the eclipses, Rāhu's presence is recognized and he is worshipped; and the moon's ascending node is termed Rāhu and her course (north or south) is ascertained astronomically with respect to such node.

16. It is impossible to determine eclipses by other means than those described above; even on other than new or full moon days, the luminaries may be eclipsed abnormally—by comets and the like.

17. It is wrong to say that there can be no eclipse unless five planets are in conjunction and it is equally wrong to suppose than on the previous Aṣṭamī (Eighth lunar) day the coming eclipse and its properties can be ascertained by examining the appearance of a drop of oil on the surface of water.

18. The magnitude of the solar eclipse is determined by means of the moon's parallax (in latitude); the points (on the disc) of the commencement and termination of the eclipse are determined by means of both parallax and angles;[2] the times of the commencement and termination of the eclipse by means of the time of new moon. The details of the process of calculation are given by me in my work on Astronomy.

19. Commencing from the time of creation, Brahma is the lord over the new and full moon periods of the first six months; the Moon is the lord over those of the second six months; Indra over those of the third six months; Kubera over those of

the fourth six months, Varuṇa over those of the fifth six months; Agni over those of the sixth six months and Yama over those of the seventh six months; and so on—the cycle being repeated over and over again.

20. If Brahma should be lord as stated above, cows and Brahmins will prosper; there will be health and happiness in the hand; and crops will thrive.

If the moon should be the lord, the effects will be those described above; also, learned men will suffer and there will be drought.

21. If Indra should be the lord, the princes will be at war with each other, the crops of Śarat (October and November), will perish and there will be no prosperity in the land.

If Kubera should be the lord, rich men will suffer in their wealth but there will be prosperity in the land.

22. If Varuṇa should be the lord, princes will suffer; the rest will be happy and crops will flourish.

If Agni should be the lord, there will be good crops, and there will also be health, freedom from fear and abundance of water.

23. If Yama should be the lord, there will be drought, famine, and total blight of crops; in the next parva mankind will be afflicted with misery, hunger, death and drought.

24. If the eclipses should occur before the calculated times, there will be miscarriage of pregnancy and wars in the land; if they should occur after the calculated times, flowers and fruits will perish and there will be fear in the land and blight of crops.[3]

25. I have described, as above, the effects of the occurrence of eclipses either before or after the calculated times in accordance with the ancient śāstras; but the calculation of a really learned Astronomer will at no time fail.

26. If there should be both lunar and solar eclipses in one month,[4] princes will suffer both from dissensions among their own army and from wars.

27. If the eclipse should occur at rising or setting, the crops of Śarat (October and November) will perish and princes will suffer. In total eclipses if the eclipsed sun or moon should be subject to malefic planetary influence there will be deth and famine in the land.

28. If the sun and moon should begin to be eclipsed when only half risen, deceitful men will suffer as well as sacrificial rites. If they should be eclipsed when in the first section[5] of the firmament, those that live by fire and virtuous Brahmins will suffer as well as men belonging to one of the holy orders.

29. If they should be eclipsed when in the second section of the firmament, ryots, heretics, merchants, the Kṣatriyas and commanders of the army will suffer. If when in the third section, artisans, the Śūdras, the Mlechas and ministers will suffer.

30. If when in mid-heaven, the central provinces will suffer, but there will be happiness over the land and the price of food grains will fall. If when in the fifth section, herbivorous animals, ministers and house hold inmates will suffer as also the Vaiśyas.

31. If they should be eclipsed when in the sixth section of the firmament, women and the Śūdras will suffer; if when setting, robbers and the border Mlechas will perish. Those will be happy in whose section the eclipse terminates.[6]

32. If the sun and moon should be eclipsed when in their *uttara ayana* (northward march), the Brahmins and the Kṣatriyas will suffer; if when in their *dakṣiṇa ayana* (southward march) the Vaiśyas and the Śūdras will suffer. If the eclipse should commence at the northern, eastern, southern, or western point of the disc, the Brahmins, the Kṣatriyas, the Vaiśyas or the Śūdras will suffer respectively.

33. If the disc should be eclipsed at one of the corners,[7] the Mlechas, persons proceeding to battle and those who live by fire[8] will perish; if the southern limb should be eclipsed aquatic creatures as well as elephants will die; and if the northern limb should be eclipsed cows will suffer.

34. If the eastern limb should be eclipsed there will be abundant rain; if the western limb should be eclipsed, farmers and servants will suffer and seed grains will be destroyed.

35. If the sun and moon should be eclipsed when in the sign of Aries (Meṣa),[9] the Pāñcāla, the Kaliṅgas,[10] Śūrasenas, soldiers the people of Kāmboja,[11] of Odhra,[12] of Kirāta[12] and persons who live by fire will be afflicted with miseries.

36. If the sun or moon should be eclipsed when in the sign of Tanrus (Vṛṣabha), shepherds, cows, their owners and eminent men will suffer miseries.

37. If they should be eclipsed when in the sign of Gemini (Mithūna), chaste women, princes, powerful petty chiefs learned men, people living on the banks of the Jumnā and the rulers of Balhika and Matsia with their subjects will suffer miseries.

38. If they should be eclipsed when in the sign of Cancer (Kataka) the Ābhīras, the Śabaras,[14] the Pallavas, the Mallahs, the Matsyas, the Kurus,[15] the Śakas,[16] the Pāñcālas and the Vikalas[17] will be afflicted with miseries and food grains will be destroyed.

39. If the sun and moon should be eclipsed when in the sign of Leo (Siṁha) hill men, prince like people possessed of a single military force,[18] princes and forest and forest men will suffer miseries. If they should be eclipsed when in the sign of Virgo (Kanyā), crops, poets, writers and singers will suffer and the rice fields of Aśmaka, and Tripura[19] will be destroyed.

40. If they should be eclipsed when in the sign of Libra (Tulā), the people of the extreme border lands on the West, the people of Sindh, the trading classes, and the people of Broach will be afflicted with miseries. If when in the sign of Scorpio (Vṛṣika), the people of Udambara, of Matra,[20] of Cola and of Yaudheya will all suffer miseries along with soldiers armed with poisoned weapons.

41. If they should be eclipsed when in the sign of Sagittarius (Dhanuṣ), mininsters, fine horses, the Videhas, the Mullas, the Pāñcālas. Physicians, merchants and persons skilled in the use of destructive weapons will perish. If when in the sign of Capricornus (Makara), fishes, the families of ministers, the candalas, skilled magicians and physicians and old soldiers will perish.

42. If they should be eclipsed when in the sign of Aquarius (Kumbha), hill men, men of western countries, carriers, robbers, shepherds, serpents, worthy men, lions, citizens and the people of Barbara will perish. If when in the sign of Pisces (Mīna), the products of the sea beach and of the sea, men of respectability, and of learning and persons that live by water will suffer.[21]

Also those provinces will be affected which correspond to particular lunar mansions in which the eclipses happen to occur as, will be explained in the Chapter (14) on Division of Globe (Kūrma Vibhāga).

43. Solar and Lunar eclipses are of ten kinds and they are technically known as 1. *Savya*, 2. *Apasavya*, 3. *Lehana*, 4. *Grasana*, 5. *Nirodha*, 6. *Avamardana*, 7. *Ārohaṇa*, 8. *Āghrāta*, 9. *Madhyatama*, 10. *Tamontya*.[22]

44. If the eclipse should commence on the left side of the disc, it is technically known as Savyagrasa: the earth will then be flooded with water and there will be joy and freedom from fear. If it should commence on the right side of the disc, it is technically known as Apasavyagrasa: mankind will suffer from their rulers and from robbers.

45. If the solar or lunar disc should be just dimmed by darkness all round which disappears immediately, the eclipse is technically known as Lehana (licking) Grasa: all creatures will be happy and the earth will be flooded with water.

46. If a third, or a fourth, or one half of the disc should be eclipsed, it is technically known as Grasana (seizing with the mouth) grasa—partial eclipse: the wealth of prosperous princes will suffer diminution and prosperous countries will be afflicted with calamities.

47. If the eclipse should, commencing at the edge, travel inwards and remain there for a time of the shape of a dark ball, it is technically known as Nirodha (blocking up) grasa: all creatures will be happy.

48. If the eclipse should be a total one and continue so for a time, it is known as Avamardana (tormenting) grasa: the then chief provinces will suffer and the then chief rulers will be afflicted with miseries.

49. If immediately after the termination of the eclipse, the disc should be re-eclipsed[23] (by comets and the like), it is technically known as Ārohaṇa (climbing) grasa: the princes will be at war and there will be fear in the land.

50. If a small portion of the disc should be so slightly eclipsed as to resemble a mirror covered with the vapor of hot breath, the eclipse is known as Āghrāta (smelling) grasa: there will be good rain in the land.

51. If the middle of the eclipsed disc should be dark while the disc continues bright all round, the eclipse is known as Madhyatama (centrally dark) grasa—annular eclipse: the Central Provinces[24] will be afflicted with miseries, mankind will suffer from stomach pain and there will be fear in the land.

52. If all round the disc, the darkness be thick, and in the middle, it is slight, the eclipse is technically known as Antyatama (terminally dark) grasa: the crops will be injured[25] and mankind will suffer from robbers.

53. If the eclipsed disc should appear white, there will be prosperity and plenty in the land, but the Brahmins will suffer; persons who live by fire will be afflicted with miseries.

54. If the disc should appear yellow, there will be increase of disease in the land and crops will suffer. If the disc should appear of gold color, swift footed animals and the Mlechas will suffer and there will be famine in the land.

55. If the disc should be of the color of the sky at dawn of day, there will be famine and drought and birds will suffer. If red-black, there will be prosperity and plenty in the land but slight rain.

56. If the disc be of the color of the pigeon or of blood color or of the color of gold or yellow-black, mankind will suffer from starvation. If again the disc be black or as said above, of the color of the pigeon, the Śūdras will suffer from disease.

57. If the eclipsed disc should appear yellow resembling the lunar in color, the Vaiśyas will perish and there will be prosperity in the land. If the disc should appear to be burning there will be fear from fire; if it should resemble gold color, there will be wars in the land.

58. If the disc should appear black resembling the color of the stem of Dūrvā grass (agrostis linearis) or yellow, there will be much death in the land. If of the color of the flower Pāṭala (Bignonia Suaveolenis)—trumpet flower—there will be fear from lightning.

59. If the eclipsed disc be of the color of red dust, the Kṣatriyas will suffer and there will be no rain. If of the color of the rising sun, of lotus, of the rainbow, there will be suffering from weapons.

60. If Mercury should see the eclipsed disc, honey and oil will become scarce; princes will suffer. If Mars should see the eclipsed disc there will be war in the land and fear from fire and robbers.

61. If Venus should see the eclipsed disc, crops will be injured and mankind will be variously afflicted. If Saturn should

see it, there will be drought and famine in the land and fear from robbers.

62. These evil effects, resulting from planetary look at the eclipsed disc, apply as well to the time of termination of the eclipse as to its commencement. If Jupiter, a beneficent planet, should also see the eclipsed disc, the evils described will vanish in just the same way as the flame of fire dies out when water is poured over it.

63. If during the eclipse, there should occur tempests, meteoric falls, duststorms, earthquakes, universal darkness, of thunderbolt, the eclipse will re-occur after six, twelve, eighteen, twenty-four, thirty, or thirty-six months respectively.

64. If Mars should be eclipsed by Rāhu,[26] the people of Avantī, those living on the banks of the Kāverī and the Narmadā and haughty princes will be afflicted with miseries.

65. If Mercury should be so eclipsed, men living between the Ganges and the Jumnā, on the banks of the Sarayū and in the country of Nepal, those living about the east sea and on the banks of the Sona will suffer and women, princes, soldier, boys and men of letters will perish.

66. If Jupiter should be so eclipsed, learned men, kings, ministers, elephants and horses will perish and persons living on the banks of the Indus and in the northern countries[27] will suffer calamities.

67. If Venus should be so eclipsed, the people of Dāśeraka, of Kekaya, of Yaudheya and of Āryāvarta and the Śibī will suffer; women and ministers will be afflicted with miseries.

68. If Saturn should be so eclipsed, the people of Maru, of Puṣkara[28] and the Saurāṣṭra, the minerals, the low classes inhabiting the Arbuda hills, and the hillmen of Gomanta and Pāriyātra will perish immediately.

69. If the solar or lunar eclipse should fall in the lunar month of Kārtika,[29] persons who live by fire, the Magadhas, the eastern princes, the Kosalas,[30] the Kalmāṣas, the Śurasenas and the people of Varanasi will suffer miseries; the ruler of Kaliṅga with his ministers and servants and the Kṣatriyas will perish but there will be prosperity and plenty in the land.

70. If the eclipses should fall in the lunar month of Mārgaśīrṣa,[31] the people of Kashmir, of Oudh and of Puṇḍra[32] will suffer ministers; quadrupeds will perish, men of the western

countries and Somayajīs[33] will suffer calamities; there will be good rain and prosperity and plenty throughout the land.

71. If the eclipses should fall in the lunar month of Pauṣa[34] the Brahmins and Kṣatriyas will suffer; the people of Sindhu, the Kukuras[35] and the Videhas will perish; there will be slight rain and fear of famine in the land.

72. If the eclipses should fall within the lunar month of Māgha,[36] persons noted for filial duty, the descendants of Vaśiṣṭha, men acting up to the Vedic principles, elephants and horses will suffer distress; the people of Vaṅga,[37] of Aṅga,[38] and of Varanasi will be afflicted with miseries; and there will be rain suited to the wants of the ryots.

73. If the eclipses should fall in the lunar month of Phālguna,[39] the people of Bengal, of Aśmaka, of Avantī and the Mekalas will be afflicted with disease; dancers, food crops chaste women, bow-makers, the Kṣatriyas and ascetics will also suffer.

74. If the eclipses should fall in the lunar month of Caitra[40] painters, writers, singers, prostitutes, men learned in the Vedas and dealers in gold, the people of Puṇḍra, of Orissa, of Kekaya and of Aśmaka will suffer distress and there will be good rain throughout the land.[41]

75. If the eclipses should fall in the lunar month of Vaiśākha[42] cotton, gingelly and beans will be injured; the Ikṣvāku,[43] the Yaudheyas, the Śakas and the Kaliṅgas will suffer but there will be prosperity over the land.[44]

76. If the eclipses should fall in the lunar month of Jyeṣṭha,[45] the Brahmins, the Queens of the reigning sovereign, crops rain, large gatherings of men, beautiful persons, the Sālvas and the Niśadas will suffer.

77. If the eclipses should fall in the lunar month of Āṣāḍha[46], wells, wet fields and rivers will become dry; dealers in roots and fruits, the people of Gāndhāra, of Kashmir, of Pulinda and of China will perish; and there will be abundance of rain.

78. If the eclipses should fall in the lunar month of Śrāvaṇa,[47] the people of Kashmir, of Pulinda and of China, the Yavanas, the Kurukṣetra, the Gāndhāras and the people of Madhyadesh (Central Provinces), the horses of Kāmboja and the

crops of Sindh will perish; the rest of mankind will enjoy prosperity and will be happy.

79. If the eclipses should fall in the lunar month of Bhādrapada[48] the people of Kaliṅga, of Bengal, of Magadha and of Sindh, the Mlechas, the Survīras, the Daradas[49] and the Śakas will perish; pregnant women will miscarry but there will be prospesity over the land.

80. If the eclipses should fall in the lunar month of Āśvina[50]. the people of Kāmboja, of China, the Yavanas, surgeons, the Vāhlīkas and the people living on the banks of Indus, together with the physicians of Ānarta and of Puṇḍra and the Kirātas[51] will perish, but there will be prosperity in the land.

81. Lunar and solar eclipses terminate in ten ways technically knows as 1. *dakṣiṇa hanu*, 2. *vāma hanu*, 3. *dakṣiṇa kukṣi*, 4. *vāma kukṣi*, 5. *dakṣiṇa pāyu*, 6. *vāma pāyu*, 7. *sañchardana*. 8. *jaraṇa*, 9. *madhyavidaraṇa*, 10. *antavidaraṇa*.[52]

82. If the lunar eclipse should terminate at the south eastern point of the disc, the termination is technically known as *dakṣiṇa hanu* (right jaw): crops will perish; facial disease will afflict mankind; princes will suffer; and there will be good rain.

83. If the lunar eclipse should terminate at the North eastern point of the disc, the termination is known as vāma hanu (left jaw); the king's son will be afflicted with fears; there will be facial disease and wars, but prosperity over the whole land.

84. If the lunar eclipse should terminate at the southern point of the disc, the termination is known as Dakṣiṇa Kukṣi (right abdomen): the king's son will suffer and the enemies in the south may then be defeated in wars.

85. If the lunar eclipse should terminate at the northern point of the disc, the termination is technically known as Vāma Kukṣi, (left abdomen): pregnant women will miscarry and crops will suffer to some extent.

86. If the lunar eclipse should terminate at the South Western and North Western points of the disc, the terminations are known as Dakṣiṇa Pāyu (right anus) and Vāma Pāyu (left-anus) respectively: there will be diseases of the genital organs in the case of both terminations, and the Queens of reigning sovereigns will suffer in the case of the latter.

87. If the lunar eclipse should commence and terminate at the eastern point of the disc,[53] the termination is known as Sañchardana (vomiting): there will be prosperity and joy in the land and food crops will flourish.

88. If it should commence at the eastern point and terminate at the western point of the disc, the termination is known as Jaraṇa (decaying): mankind will be afflicted with hunger and with wars; where then will they go for protection?

89. If the middle of the eclipsed disc should first begin to clear, the termination is known as Madhya Vidaraṇa (central opening): there will be anger at heart and prosperity over the land but not much rain.

90. If the edge should first begin to clear all round, while there is darkness in the centre, the termination is known as Anta Vidaraṇa (terminal opening): Madhyadesa or Central Provinces will suffer, and the crops of Śarat will be injured.

91. These terminations of the lunar eclipse apply to those of the solar eclipse, the only difference being that where the East has been referred to in the former, it must be taken to mean the West in the latter.[54]

92. If, within seven days from the termination of an eclipse there should occur a duststorm, mankind will suffer from destruction; if there should occur a fall of snow there will be fear from disease; if there should occur an earthquake, the chief rulers will die.

93. If within the said period, there should occur any meteor's fall, the ministers will die, if clouds of various hues should appear, mankind will suffer from various fears; if clouds should begin to roar, there will be miscarriage of pregnancy, if lightning should appear, rulers and tusked animals will suffer.

94. If within seven days from the termination of an eclipse, there should appear a halo round the Sun or Moon, there will be disease in the land; if there should be an appearance of false fire about the horizon mankind will suffer from rulers and from fire; if there should be a storm, there will be fear from robbers.

95. If there should appear either a rainbow, or a comet club-like in shape, people, afflicted with hunger, will suffer from foreign yoke; if there should be either planetary conjunctions or cometary appearances princes will be at war with one another.

96. If there should occur a fall of good rain within the said period, there will be prosperity in the land and the evils described above will disappear.

97. If on the new-moon day immediately succeeding a lunar eclipse, there should occur a solar eclipse, there will be dissensions among men and discord between husbands and wives.

98. If, on the contrary, there should occur a lunar eclipse on the full moon day immediately succeeding a solar eclipse, the Brahmins will perform various sacrificial rites and mankind will be happy.

Note:—It may be some relief to the monotony of what has preceded to append here a description of certain ceremonies for the expiation of the evil effects of the eclipses.

In lunar eclipses those persons will suffer in the sign of whose nativity in which the Sun was, the moon happens to be eclipsed.

Again, if an eclipse should occur in the sign in which the Sun was in one's nativity, then the persons on his father's side will suffer; if in the sign in which the Moon was in one's nativity then the persons on his mother's side will suffer.

Again that person will also suffer in whose Lagna[55] or Nakṣatra the sun or moon is eclipsed.

If the eclipse should occur in the 19th constellation from that in which the moon was in one's nativity the person will be afflicted with miseries, if he should fail to perform the requisite expiatory rites: it therefore behoves a person to avert the evil effects of an eclipse by gifts, by fire ceremonies, by the worship of the Devas, by japa and by (eclipse) ceremonial ablutions.

He should get a serpent made of gold or flour and present it to Brahmins on the day of the eclipse. He shall then recite the *mṛttyuñjaya* and other well known mantras. As all the devas are present on the occasion of an eclipse, mantras or japas ought not to be recited or performed while the eclipse progresses but only when the eclipse begins to decline and terminate, through, during the former period new mantras may be learnt. As regards the ablutions above referred to, we quote from Matsyapruaṇa:

That person, in the lagna of whose nativity an eclipse occurs, ought to bathe in the water purified by mantras and by drugs as prescribed below. On the occasion of the eclipse he shall adore four Brahmins with garlands of white flowers and each white sandal paste; he shall fix four pots in four place near each other and he shall bring earth from places frequented by elephants, by horses, by chariots and by cows and from art-hills and from before the entrance to the palaces of kings as well as from deep waters, and throw the earth into the water pots, he shall also put into the water *panchangavya*[56] jewels, yellow pigment, lotus, the conch shell, white sandal paste, mustard seed, ariconuts, the fragment root of the plant Andropogon Muricatus and the resin *bdelism* (exudation of the Amyris Agallowchum); he shall then broke the devas into the pots. The Brahmins shall then say about.

"May all the seas, rivers, and other waters come into these pots for the purification of our Master".

The Brahmins shall then invoke, by their respective mantras, the devas presiding over the eight points of the compass. They shall also invoke into the pots the deities presiding over all creatures and things, with or without motion, in the three worlds as well as Brahmā, Viṣṇu and the Sun. They shall also chant verses from the Rik, Yajus and Sāma Vedas. The pots also shall have threads tied round their necks and adorned with white flowers and white paste. The master shall then be bathed with the charmed waters after bathing the master shall present cloths and cows to Brahmins and worship his favourite gods. At the commencement of the eclipse the Brahmins shall tie, over the master's head, a cloth containing bits of the five precious gems and a gold plate with mantras inscribed in it. The gold plate shall then be presented to the Brahmins.

He who bathes as prescribed above will not only be purified from the evil effects of an eclipse but will gain the higher worlds.

REFERENCES

1. The moon's node, i.e., one of the two points where the moon's or bit cuts the ecliptic.

2. Technically known as Akṣ̣avalanam and Ayanavalanam.

3. The commentator is of opinion that these irregular phenomena must be *utpata* (abnormal) in their nature.
4. This is taken to mean the thirteenth or intercalary lunar month in the opinion of Vyāsa who in his Mahābhārat (Bhīṣma Parva) refers to the actual occurrence of such eclipses in an intercalary month when dissuading Duryodhana from engaging in war; and Garga is also of the same opinion.
5. Out of the six sections of the visible hemispherical vault.
6. The commentator adds that if an eclipse should both commence and terminate in one and the same section there will be both suffering first and happiness next.
7. N.E., S.E., S.W., or N.W.
8. e.g. Smiths, potters and the like.
9. Cf. the fixed Hindu Zodiac.
10. Kaliṅga: a district on the Coromaṇḍal coast extending from below Cuttack to the vicinity of Madras.
11. Kāmboja: probably the Combodia of Cochin China.
12. Odhra: the northern part of Orissa.
13. Kirāta: a degraded mountain tribe.
14. Śabaras: a wild mountain tribe.
15. Kurus: people of the District of Delhi.
16. Śakas: probably the descendents of the Tartars and Scythians who invaded India.
17. Vikalas: a warrior tribe.
18. Single military force: Cavalry, or Infantry or the like.
19. Tripura: The modern Tippera.
20. Matra: a country to the N.W. of Hindustan.
21. Such a string of apparently incoherent ideas might appear inexplicable to person ignorant of Astrology in which all objects, animate and inanimate are divided into planetary, stellar, zodiacal and other div isions.
22. These terms are explained in the subsequent stanzas; some of them have to English equivalents,

23. This, the commentator adds, must be abnormal.

24. According to Manu the country to the east of Vinasana: (the modern Panipat) to the west of Allahabad, to the north of the Vindhya mountains and to the South of the Himalayas.

25. These injuries, known as Eeti badha, are six: excessive rain, drought, rats, grass hoppers, birds, foreign invasion.

26. The eclipsed or eclipsing lunar or solar disc as the case may be.

27. Northern countries: a river, probably an imaginary geographical line, is stated to run from the N.E. to the S.W. of India and countries to the North and West of this line are known as the Northern and the Western countries and those to the East and South of it, as the Eastern and the Southern countries.

28. Puṣkara: a celebrated place of pilgrimage now called Pokur 5 miles from the city of Ajmer.

29. Kārtika: October-November, when the full moon is in the asterism of Kṛttika.

30. Kosala: the Modern Oudh.

31. Mārgaṣīrṣa: November-December, when the full moon is in the asterism of Mṛgaśīras.

32. Puṇḍra: the modern Bengal and Bihar.

33. Somayajees: those who have tasted of the juice of the *soma* plant in the sacrificial rite known as Somayaga.

34. Pauṣa: December-January, when the full moon is in the lunar mansion of Puṣya.

35. Kukuras: a branch of the Yadavas.

36. Māgha: January-February, when the full moon in the constellation of Maghā.

37. Vaṅga: East Bengal.

38. Aṅga: Bengal Proper near Bhagulpur.

39. Phālguna: February-March, when the full moon is in the asterism of Phalgunī,

40. Caitra: March-April when the full moon is in the Constellation of Citrā.

41. Immediately after the eclipse, the Commentator adds.

42. Vaiśākha: April-May, when the full moon is in the lunar mansion of Viśākhā.

43. Ikṣvāku: a warrior tribe.

44. To the end of the year, adds the Commentator.

45. Jyeṣṭha: May-June, when the full moon is in the asterism of Jyeṣṭhā.

46. Āṣāḍha: June-July, when the full moon is in the constellation of Āṣāḍhā.

47. Śrāvaṇa: July-August when the full moon is in the constellation of Śravaṇa.

48. Bhādrapada: August-September, when the full moon is in the lunar mansion of Bhādrapada.

49. Darada: a country bordering on Kashmir.

50. Āśvina: September-October, when the full moon is in the constellation of Aśvinī.

51. Kirātas: a barbarous mountain tribe.

52. These terms are explained in the subsequent stanzas.

53. This, the Commentator adds, must be utpata (abnormal) in its character.

54. The commentator adds, as a corollary from the above, that such direction as S., N., N.W. and N.E., in the case of the Lunar eclipse should be taken to men N., S., S.E., and S., W., in the case of solar eclipse.

55. Lagna: that particular sign of the zodiac which is cut by the eastern horizon at the time of one's birth.

56. Panchagavya: a mixture of the cow's milk, curd, butter, urine and dung.

CHAPTER 6

On Mars

1. The retrograde motion of Mars is of five kinds known technically as 1. *uṣṇa*, 2. *aśrumukha*, 3. *vyāla*, 4. *lohitanana and* 5. *nistrimsa musala*.[1]

2. If Mars should begin to retrograde from the 7th, 8th or 9th constellation from that in which he reappears[2] after his conjunction with the Sun, such retrograde motion is technically known as *uṣṇa*: when Mars should reappear after his next conjunction with the Sun, persons who live by fire will be afflicted with disease.

3. If Mars should begin to retrograde from the 10th, 11th, or 12th constellation from that of his reappearance, such retrograde motion is known as *aśrumukha*: when Mars should reappear after his next conjunction with the Sun, juice will be injured and there will be disease and drought.

4. If he should begin to retrograde from the 13th or 14th constellation from that of his reappearance, such retrograde motion is known as *vyāla*: when he should disappear before his next conjunction with the Sun, wild boars and fierce animals will be afflicted with distress.

5. If Mars should begin to retrograde from the 15th or the 16th constellation from that of his reappearance, such retrograde motion is known as *Rudhirānan*: at the time of such reappearance mankind will be afflicted with disease in the face and will produce fears, but there will be prosperity in the land.

6. If he should begin to retrograde from the 17th or the 18th constellation from that of his reappearance such retrograde motion is known as *Asimusala;* when Mars is in his retrograde motion, bands of robbers will be afflicted with disease and there will be drought and wars in the land.

7. If Mars should reappear in the constellation of Pūrvphalgunī (sacred to Bhaga) or in that of Uttaraphalgunī (sacred

to Aryama), retrograde in the constellation of Uttarāṣāḍha (sacred to Visvedeva), and disappear in the constellation of Rohiṇī (sacred to Brahma), he will afflict the three worlds with miseries.

8. If Mars, after his reappearance in the constellation of Śravaṇa, should retrograde in that of Puṣya, anointed monarchs will be afflicted with miseries ; those countries and those persons will suffer in whose Nakṣatra, Mars should begin to reappear.[3]

9. If Mars should pass through the middle of the constellation of *Maghā* and retrograde back through the same, the ruler of the Pāṇḍya country will perish and mankind will suffer from wars and drought.

10. If Mars should, after cutting through the constellation of Maghā, approach the middle of Viśakhā, there will be famine in the land ; if he should cut through the constellation of Rohiṇī, there will be fearful deaths in the land.

11. If Mars should pass to the south of the constellation of Rohṇī, rulers will suffer, prices will rise and there will be little rain; if Mars should appear enveloped in smoke or with a pointed flame, the people of Pariyatra[4] will perish.

12. If Mars should pass through the constellations of Rohṇī, Śravaṇa, Mūla, Uttara Phalgunī, Uttarāṣāḍha, Uttarabhādrapada and Jyeṣṭah, he will destroy clouds charged with rain.

13. If Mars should pass through the constellations of Śravaṇa, Maghā, Punarvasu, Hasta, Mūla, Pūrvabhādrapada Aśvinī, Viśākhā and Rohṇī there will be prosperity in the land.

14. If Mars should appear with a large and clear disc or red like the flower of Kiṁśuka (Butea Frondosa) or of Aśoka (Jonesia Asoka Roxb) or of clear and fine rays or like molten gold or if he should pass through the northern path,[5] rulers will be happy and there will be prosperity in the land.

REFERENCES

1. These terms are explained in the subsequent stanzas.
2. Mars is said to disappear when within 17 degrees from the Sun and to reappear when beyond it.

3. For the Nakṣtra of a country *vide*. Chap. on Division of Globe

4. Pariyatra : the central or the western portion of the Vindhya chain which skirts the province of Malwa.

5. Northern path : according to Girga, the nine constellations from Bharaṇī to Maghā constitute the Northern path; the nine from Pūrvaphalgunī to Mūla constitute the middle path and the nine from Pūrvāṣāḍha to Aświnī constitute the Southern path.

CHAPTER 7

On Mercury

1. Mercury never reappears[1] after his conjunction with the sun without upsetting the existing order of things : he causes fear from flood, from fire and from storms and paralizes trade by abnormally enhancing or lowering the price of food grains.

2. If Mercury should cut through the constellations of Śravaṇa, Dhaniṣṭhā, Rohinī, Mṛgasīras, and Uttarāṣāḍha, sacred respectively to Viṣṇu, Ashtavasu, Brahmā, the Moon and Visvedeva, his disc appearing to rub against those of the stars, he causes drought and disease in the land.

3. If Mercury should cut through the five constellations from Ārdrā to Maghā, mankind will suffer from wars, from hunger, from disease and from drought.

4. If he should cut through the six constellations from Hasta, his disc appearing to rub against those of the stars, cows will suffer, the price of liquid substances and of juice will rise, but there will be abundance of food grains in the land.

5. If he should cut through the constellations of Uttaraphalagunī (sacred to Ariyama, the Sun), of Kṛttikā (sacred to Agni, the fire), of Uttarabhādra and of Bharaṇī (sacred to Yama), all living creatures will be afflicted with disease in blood, in flesh, in bones and the like.

6. If he should cut through the constellations of Aświnī (sacred to the Aświnī Devas), of Sataya (Sacred to Varuṇa), of Mūla and Revati, tradesmen, physician, boatmen, creatures of water and horses will suffer.

7. If he should cut through one of the constellations of Pūrvaphalgunī and Pūrvāṣāḍha and Pūrvabhādra mankind will suffer from hunger, from wars and thieves and from disease.

8. In Paraśara's work on Astronomy, Mercury has seven courses assigned to him; they are technically known as

1. Prakṛtā, 2. Vimiśrā, 3. Saṁkṣiptā, 4. Tīkṣṇā, 5. Yogāntā 6. Ghorā, and 7. Pāpā.

9. If Mercury should pass through the constellations of Svātī, Bharaṇī, Rohiṇī, and Kṛttikā, sacred, respectively to Vāyu, to Yama, to Pitāmaha and to Agni, his course is technically known as Prākṛtā. If he should pass through the constellation of Mṛgaśiras, Ārdrā, Maghā, Āśleṣa, sacred respectively to the Moon, to Śiva, to the Pritris and to the serpent, his course is known as Misragati.

10. If Mercury should pass through the constellations of Puṣya, Punarvasu and the two Phalgunīs, his course is known as Saṁkṣiptā. If he should pass through the constellations of the two Bhādrapadas, of Viśākhā, of Aświnī and of Revatī, his course is known as Tīkṣṇā.

11. If Mercury should pass through the constellations of Mūla and the two Āṣāḍhas, his course is known as Yogāntā. If such course should lie through the constellations of Śravaṇa, Chitrā, Dhaniṣṭhā and Śatabhiṣaj, it is known as Ghorā.

12. If Mercury should pass through the constellations of Hasta, Anurādhā, Jyeṣṭhā, sacred respectively to the Sun, to Mittra and to Indra his course is known as Pāpā. We now proceed to state the periods, in days, of the effects of Mercury's reappearance in, and course through, particular lunar mansions.

13. The effects of the Prākṛtā, and other courses of Mercury described above, will last respectively for 40, 30, 22, 18, 9, 15 and 11 days.

14. When Mercury is in his Prākṛtā course, there will be increase of health, of rain and of crops, and there will be prosperity in the land. If he should be either in his Saṁkṣiptā or Miśrā course mankind will be partly happy and partly miserable. When in his remaining four courses, Mercury brings on adversity.

15. According to Devala, the effects of the *Ṛjvī* (direct) the *Ativakrā* (over retrograde), the *vakrā* (retrograde) and the *vikalā* (of irregular rate), motions of Mercury will last respectively for 30, 24, 12 and 6 days.

16. When Mercury is in his *Ṛjvī* course, mankind will be happy; when in his *ativakrā* course he will destroy wealth;

when he is in his *vakrā* course there will be wars in the land; and when he is in his *vikalā* course mankind will be afflicted with free and disease.

17. If Mercury should, after his conjunction with the Sun, reappear in the month of Āṣāḍha or Śrāvaṇa or Vaiśākha, or Magha, there will be fear in the land; but if he should be in his *course* in those months there will be happiness in the land.

18. If Mercury should so reappear in the month of Kārtika of Aśvina, there will be wars in the land, and mankind will suffer from robbers, from fire, from disease, from flood and from hunger.

19. When Mercury should disappear, the chief towns in the land will be besieged by enemies, but when he reappears the siege will be raised. According to some writers, the latter occurs only when Mercury reappears as an evening star; and learned writers also say that the chief rulers will also get an accession of territories.

20. If Mercury should be of the color of gold or of a parrot or if it should resemble the hue of the Sasyaka[2] gem, or if his disc should appear glossy or big in size, mankind will be happy; but if otherwise, they will be afflicted with miseries.

REFERENCES

1. Mercury disappears when within 14 degrees from the Sun and reappears beyond that distance; but when retrograde, the limit is only 12 degrees.
2. Sasyaka : a species of precious stone colored like the inner fruit of a co-coa nut; perhaps an opal.

CHAPTER 8

On Jupiter

1. The years of Jupiter take their names from the several Nakṣatras in which he reappears[1] after his conjunction with the Sun; and these names are identical with the names of the lunar months.

2. These years beginning from Kārtika follow, each, two stars beginning from Kṛttikā ; but the fifth, the eleventh and the twelfth years follow, each, three Nakṣatras.[2]

3. In the Kārtika year of Jupiter, cart drivers, persons that live by fire, and cows will be afflicted with miseries ; there will be disease and wars in the land ; flowers of blood and of yellow color will thrive.

4. In the Mārgaśīrṣa year of Jupiter there will be drought, and crops will be injured by animals, by rats, by grass hoppers and by birds ; there will be disease in the land and rulers will be at strife even with their friends.

5. In the Pauṣa year of Jupiter mankind will be happy ; princes will cease their enmity to one another ; the price of food crops will become cheap doubly or tribly and there will be an increase of ceremonies to secure special benefits.[3]

6. In the Māgha year of Jupiter there will be an increase, of respect to fathers ; all creatures will be happy, health and rain will prevail over the land ; the price of food grains will fall ; and mankind will be more friendly than ever.

7. In the Phālguna year of Jupiter there will be prosperity, rain, and crops, here and there ; women will suffer miseries ; thieves will become powerful and rulers tyrannic.

8. In the Caitra year of Jupiter there will be slight rain good food, and happiness ; rulers will become mild ; leguminous grains will increase and fair men will suffer miseries.

9. In the Vaiśākha year of Jupiter princes with their subjects will be virtuous, fearless, and happy ; men will engage in sacrificial rites and there will also be growth of crops.

10. In the Jyeṣṭha year of Jupiter the chief men of every caste, of every family, of every opulent class and every village as well as princes and learned men will suffer miseries ; and grains excepting Kaṅgu[4] and pod grains will suffer.

11. In the Āṣāḍha year of Jupiter there will be crops here and there and drought in other places, mankind will not be very happy ; and rulers will be afflicted with cares.

12. In the Śrāvaṇa year of Jupiter mankind will be happy and crops will thrive and ripen well ; wicked men and impostors will suffer their followers.

13. In the Bhādrapada year of Jupiter the produce of creepers will thrive as well as the first crops ; but the second crops will fail and there will be prosperity in some places and fear here and there.

14. In the Āśwayuja year of Jupiter the rainfall will be incessant, mankind will be happy and prosperous ; all living creatures will grow strong and food supply will be abundant.

15. When Jupiter passes through the northern path[5] there will be health and happiness in the land ; when he passes through the southern path the reverse of these will be the case ; and when he passes through the middle path there will be neither much of the former nor much of latter.

16. If, in one year, Jupiter should pass through a space of two stellar divisions, there will be prosperity in the land ; if he should pass through two and a half of such divisions there will not be much of it ; and if at any time, he should pass through over two and a half of these divisions crops will be injured.

17. If the disc of Jupiter should appear of the color of fire, there will be fear from fire: if yellow, there will be disease in the land ; if dark-blue, there will be wars; if green, suffering from thieves, and if of blood color, suffering from weapons.

18. If the disc of Jupiter should appear of the color of smoke there will be drought ; if it should be visible during day, rulers will perish and if it should appear large and clear at night, mankind will be happy.

19. The Nakṣatras, Rohiṇī and Kṛttikā, form the body of the Vatsara Puruṣa,[6] the two Āṣāḍhas form his navel, Ayalya forms the heart and Maghā, the heart-bladder ; when benefic planets pass through these, there will be happiness in the land ; if malefic planets should pass through the body, there will be suffering from fire and winds ; if they should pass through the navel, there will be suffering from starvation; if they should pass through the heart-bladder, roots and fruits will suffer, and if they should pass through the heart, crops will perish.

20. Multiply by 11 the number of past solar years from the time of the Śaka prince (Śālivāhana), and take 4 times the product ; to it add 8589, and divide the sum by 3750.

21. Add the quotient to the said number of solar years from the time of the Śaka prince, and divide the sum by 60; the remainder represents the number of years by which Jupiter has advanced in his cycle of 60 years ; (call it J.); divide this remainder by 5, the quotient will give the number of yugas preceding the currents yuga of Jupiter calculated from *Viṣṇu* (the name of the first of Jupiter's 12 Yugas, each consisting of 5 years); and the remainder will give the years by which Jupiter has advanced in his current Yuga.

22. Divide J (Jupiter's years) by 12 and multiply the remainder by 9 and divide the product by 4 ; the quotient will represent the number of Nakṣatras, calculated from *Dhaniṣṭhā*, passed over by Mean Jupiter and the remainder the number of Navamsas passed over by him in the next *Nakṣatra*.

Note:—We will now explain the principles involved in the calculations contained in the three preceding stanzas : A *kalpa* contains 1000, Chatur Yugas; in a *kalpa*, according to Ariyabhaṭṭa the number of siderial revolutions or years of the *Sun* is 4,32,00,00,000; and the number of siderial revolutions of Jupiter is 364224000; but as each revolution contains 12 years, the number of Jupiter's years in the same period is 4,37,06 88,000, in other wards, in a Chatur yuga.

No. of Solar years : No. of Jupiter's years : : 43,20,000 : 43,70,688

: : 1875 : 1897

or : : 3750 : 3794, to suit

ourselves to the figures in the text. So that for every 3,750 solar years we get 3,750+44 years of Jupiter ; therefore a solar year$=1+\frac{44}{3750}$ years of Jupiter.

We will now find out the number of years by which Jupiter had advanced in the Kaliyug at the commencement of the Śaka era, it being known that the number of solar years during the said period is 3179. We have the following proportion, 3750 : 3794 : : 3179 : *x*, years of Jupiter required.

$x = \frac{3794 \times 3179}{3750} = 3216\frac{1126}{3750}$, the number of years of Jupiter from the commencement of the Kaliyug to the comencement of the Śaka era.

Now it is known that Kaliyuga commenced in the year Vijaya (the 27 year from Prabhava, which is the first year in a cycle of 60 years of Jupiter).

Therefore $3216\frac{1126}{3750}+26$ or $3242\frac{1126}{3750}$, being divided by 60, the remainder will give the particular year of Jupiter (in his cycle of 60 years) from Prabhava at the time of the commencement of the Saka era and this remainder is $2\frac{1126}{3750}$ which is the 3rd year or the year *Śukla* of the cycle.

Now $2\frac{1126}{3750} = \frac{8626}{3750}$.

Coming down to the period subsequent to the commencement of the Śaka era we have, as already stated,

$1 : 1\frac{44}{3750}$: : *No.* of past Solar years : *x*, *No.* of past Jupiter's years.

$$\therefore x = \left.\begin{matrix}\text{No. of past}\\ \text{Solar years}\end{matrix}\right\} + \frac{44 \times \text{No. of past Solar years.}}{3750.}$$

Adding to this the $2\frac{1126}{3750}$ or $\frac{8626}{3750}$ years which elapsed from the beginning of Prabhava to the time of the commencement of the Śaka era we get,

$$\left.\begin{matrix}\text{No. of past}\\ \text{Solar years}\end{matrix}\right\} + \frac{44 \times \text{No. of past Solar years}}{3750} + \frac{8626}{3750}$$

$$= \left.\begin{matrix}\text{No. of past}\\ \text{Solar years}\end{matrix}\right\} + \frac{44 \times \text{No. of past Solar years} + 8626}{3750}$$

when this is divided by 60 the remainder will give the year of Jupiter in his cycle of 60 years commencing from Prabhava ; call this remainder J.

Now as there are 12 yugas (each of 5 years) in a cycle of 60 years J, being divided by 5, the quotient will give the number of yugas that have elapsed from the first yuga of *Viṣṇu* and the remainder the number of years by which Jupiter has advanced in the current yuga. (For the names of these yugas *vide* stanza 23).

This brings us to the end of Stanza 21. Stanza 22 aims at discovering the particular lunar mansion or Nakṣatra in which Jupiter might happen to be at any given time : Time taken by Mean Jupiter to go over a sign of Zodiac is called a year of Jupiter.

Therefore a number of such years will represent the number of signs gone over by Mean Jupiter during the time. In 12 such years Mean Jupiter makes a circuit of the heavens. Now the year Prabhava commences when Jupiter enters (or re-appears according to commentator) in the constellation of *Dhaniṣṭhā* in the month of Māgha, and Mean Jupiter takes 12 years from Dhaniṣṭhā to it again. If therefore J were divided by 12, the remainder will show the number of years taken by Mean Jupiter to go over the number of lunar mansions lying between Dhaniṣṭhā and the particular lunar mansion in which Jupiter might happen to be at the given time. Call this remainder R. As stated above, R, which represents the number of years, also represents the number of Zodiacal signs. Now as each sign contains $2\frac{1}{4}$ lunar mansions the number of lunar mansions required (from Dhaniṣṭhā) $= 2\frac{1}{4} \times R = \frac{9}{4} R$. This brings us to the end of Stanza 22.

It will be observed from the above that the figure given in stanza 20 is 8589 and not 8626. The fact is that in our process we adopted Aryabhaṭṭa's figure, there being a difference of opinion among Hindu Astronomers regarding the number of the siderial revolutions of Jupiter in a kalpa. For instance: Bāṣkaracārriar gives it as 364 226 455 against

364 224 000 of Aryabhaṭṭa. But what we want is Varāhamīhira's figure. As his Astronomical work, Panchasindhāntika, is now lost we cannot give it exactly; but calculating backwards from the figure 8589 appearing in the text, we find the number of siderial revolutions of Jupiter, according to Varāhamihira to be 364 190 000. This is probably the correct figure.

23. The twelve yugas of Jupiter's cycle are known as belonging to the Devas 1. *Viṣṇu*, 2. *Jupiter*, 3. *Indra*, 4. *Agni* (fire), 5. *Tvaṣṭa*, 6. *Ahirbudhnya*, 7. *The Pitris*, 8. *Vaśvedeva*, 8. *Soma* (the moon), 10. *Indrāgni*, 11. *Aśvinideva*, 12. *Bhaga*.

24. The five years of each known as 1. *Saṁvatsara*, 2. *Parivatsara*, 3. *Idāvatsara.*, 4. *Anuvatsara*, 5. *Idvatsara*. These are sacred respectively to 1: *Agni* (fire), 2. *Arka* (the Sun), 3. *Chandra* (the Moon), 4. *Prājapati* (the Creater), 5. *Rudra* (the Destroyer).

25. Generally in every yuga, there will be good rain in the first year[7] and at the beginning[8] of the second year; excessive rain in the third year; moderate rain at the end (of the rainy season) of the fourth year; and slight rain in the fifth year.

26. In the first four yugas there will be prosperity in the land; in the next or middle four there will not be much of it; and in the last four mankind will suffer miseries.

27. When Jupiter reappears at the beginning of the constellation of Dhaniṣṭha in the month of Māgha, the first year of the cycle of 60 years of Jupiter known as *Prabhava* commences. In it all creatures will be happy.

28. In the same year there will be drought in certain places and suffering from storm and fire; the crops will be injured; phlegmatic maladies will afflict mankind; nevertheless mankind will be happy.

29. The next year is known as *Vibhava* the third as *Śukla*, the forth as Pramoda, and the fifth as Prajāpati : in each of these years mankind will be happier than in the next preceding year.

30. In the same four years there will be good growth of the *Sali*[9] crop, of sugarcane, of barley and other crops in

the land; mankind will be freed from all freed and they will live at peace, in happiness and without the vices of the Kaliyuga.

31. The five gears of the second yuga are known as 1. *Aṅgira*. 2. *Śrīmukha* 3. *Bhāva* 4. *Yuvan* and 5. *Dhātā*. Of these, during the first three years mankind will enjoy happiness and during the last two they will not enjoy much of it.

32. In the first three of the above five years there will be abundance of rain and mankind will be freed from fears and anxieties; in the last two years the rainfall will be moderate but disease and wars will afflict mankind.

33. The five years of the third yuga sacred to Indra are known as 1. *Īśvara*, 2. *Bahudhānya*, 3. *Pramāthin*, 4. *Vikrama* and 5. *Vṛṣa*. In the first two years mankind will enjoy the happiness of Kritayug. In the year *Pramāthin* they will feel miserable but in the years *Vikrama* and *Vṛṣa* they will again be happy.

35. The first year of the fourth yuga is known as *Ohitrabhānu;* in it mankind will be happy. The second is known as *Subhānu*. In it mankind will be neither happy nor miserable; there will however be disease in the land but no deaths in consequence.

36. The next year is known as Tāraṇa; in it there will be abundance of rain. The next is known as Pārthiva; in it crops with thrive well and mankind will be happy. The fifth year is known as *Vyaya*; in it amorous sensations will prevail over the land.

37. The first year of the next yuga sacred to *Tvaṣṭā* is known as *Sarvajit*. The next year is known as *Sarvadhārin*. The next three years are *Virodhin*, *Vikṛta*, and *Khara*: in the second of these, mankind will be happy and they will be afflicted with fears in the other years.

38. The five years of the next yuga are 1. *Nandana* 2. *Vijaya*, 3. *Jaya* 4. *Manmatha* 5. *Durmukha*: during the first three years there will be happiness in the land; in *Manmatha* mankind will feel neither happy, nor miserable and in the year Durmukha they will feel miserable.

39. The years of the seventh yuga are 1. *Hemalamba*, *Vilambi*, 3. *Vikāri*, 4. *Śarvarī* and 5. *Plava*.

40. In the first of these years crops will generally be injured and there will be storm and rain; in the second year crops will not grow in abundance and the rainfall will not be much; in the third year mankind will be afflicted with fears and there will be much rain; in the fourth year there will be famine; in *Plava*, the fifth year, there will be prosperity in the land and also much rain.

41. The first year of the next yuga sacred to Viśvedeva is *Śobhakṛt*; the next year is known as *Subhakṛt*; the third is *Krodhi*; and the remaining years are known as *Viśvavāsu* and *Parabhava*.

42. During the first two years mankind will be happy; during the third they will feel exceedingly miserable and during the last two years they will be neither happy nor miserable; but in the year Parabhava there will be fear from fire and suffering from weapons and from disease; the Brahmins and cows will also suffer.

43. The first year of the ninth yuga is *Plavaṅga*, the next year is known as *Kīlaka*, the third is known as *Soumya* and the last two years are known as *Sādhāraṇa* and *Rodhakṛt*; of these, during the years Kīlaka and Soumya mankind will be happy.

44. In the year *Plavaṅga* mankind will suffer much; in *Sādhāraṇa* there will be slight rain and crops will suffer; in the fifth year there will be a variety of rainfall and crops will thrive.

45. The first year of the yuga sacred to *Indrāgni* is known as Paridhāvi ; the remaining years are *Pramādi*, *Ānanda*, *Rakṣasa* and *Anala*.

46. In the year Paridhāvi the Madhayadesa will suffer the ruling princes will perish, there will be slight rain and fear from fire, in the in the year *Pramādi* mankind will be disposed to be however villagers will be at strife; red flowers and red seed will be destroyed.

47. In the next year mankind will be happy. In the year *Rakṣasa* and *Anala* there will be deaths and decay in the bank is Rakṣhasa again the summer crops will thrive and

in *Anala* there will be fear from fire and much suffering in the land.

48. The five years of the eleventh yuga are 1. *Piṅgala*, 2. *Kālayukta* 3. *Siddhartha* 4. *Raudra*, 5. *Durmati*. In the first year there will be much rain and fear from thieves and mankind will suffer from consumption of the lungs and the Asthmatic complaints.

49. In the year *Kālayukta* mankind will suffer from various evils but in *Sidhārtha* they will be happy in more ways there one. In the year *Raudra* mankind will suffer much and than will be loss and ruin in the land. In *Durmati* there will be moderate rain.

50. In the twelveth yuga sacred to god Bhaga, the first year is known as *Dundubhi*, the crops will thrive well. The next year is known as *Udgāri*; in it the ruling sovereigns will perish and there will not be good rain.

51. The third year is known as *Raktakṣa*; in it there will be fear from the attack of tusked animals, and mankind will suffer from disease. The fourth year is known as *Krodha*; in it there will be anger in the land and countries will be ruined in consequence of internal strife.

52. The last year of the last yuga is *Kṣaya*; there will then be much rain in the land; the Brahmins will be afflicted with fear and farmers will prosper. The Vaiśyas and Śūdras will be happy as also persons that deprive others of their property. Thus have been described briefly the effects of the sixty years of Jupiter's cycle.

53. If the disc of Jupiter be full of pure rays and large and appear of the color of white jasmine or white water lily or crystal and if he does not suffer by occultation by or conjunction with, other planets and when he is in his good courses mankind will be happy.

REFERENCES

1. Jupiter disappears when within 11 degrees from the Sun and reappears beyond that limit.

2. Thus, when Jupiter reappears,
In Kṛttika or Rohiṇī his year is known as.........Kārtika,

In Mṛgaśiras or Ārdrā ... ...Mārgaśirṣa

* * * *

In Pūrvuphalgunī or Uttaraphalgunī or Hasta ...Phālguna

* * * *

In Śatabiṣaj or Pūrvaproṣṭapada or Uttaraproṣṭapada
Proṣṭapada

In Revatī or Aśwati or Bharaṇī Āswayuja

3. Such ecomonies are known as Poushtika Karma, the cor-relative of this being Sanuha Karma, which aims at the removal of existing evils—the two together go by the name of Naimittika (purposive) Karma, whose cor-relative again is Nitya Karma i.e. ceremonies, the daily observance of which is enjoined by the Śāstras.
4. Kaṅgu : a kind of Panic seed, Panicum Italicum, several varieties of which are cultivated and form articles of food for the poor.
5. These paths have already been explained.
6. Vathsara Puruṣa : the 12 years cycle of Jupiter personified.
7. In the four months from August to November according to the commentator.
8. Of the rainy season—August and September, according to the commentator.
9. Sali : a species of rice.

CHAPTER 9

On Venus

1. The ecliptic is divided into nine divisions known as *Vīdhis* (paths). According to some each division consists of three constellations beginnig from Aświnī : these divisions are technically known as 1. *Nāga* (serpent), 2. *Gaja* (elephant), 3. *Airāvata* (the divine elephant or serpent), 4. *Vṛṣabha* (bull), 5. *Go* (cow), 6. *Jaradgava* (old ox), 7. *Mṛga* (deer), 8. *Aja* (ram), 9. *Dahana* (fire).

2. According to others the Nāga Vīdhi consists of the constellations of *Swātī*, *Bharaṇī* and *Kṛttika*; the Gaja Vīdhi of the three constellations from *Rohiṇī* the Airāvata Vīdhi of the three from *Punarvasu*; the Vṛṣabha Vīdhi of the three from *Maghā*; the Go Vīdhi of *Aświati*, *Revatī* *Pūrvabhādrapada* and *Uttarabhādrapada*.

3. The Jaradgava Vīdhi consists of the three constellations from *Śravaṇa*; the Mṛga Vīdhi of the three from *Anurādhā*; the Aja Vīdhi of *Hasta*, *Viśākhā*, and Citrā; and the Dahana Vīdhi consists of the two constellations Pūrvāṣāḍha and Uttarāṣāḍha.

4. Of the nine Vīdhis the first three are known as the northern Vīdhi; the next three as the central Vīdhis and the last three as the southern Vīdhis. Again in the case of each three the first is known as the northern Vīdhi, the second at the central Vīdhi and the last as the Southern Vīdhi.

5. According to some the position of a Vīdhi follows that of the *Yoga Tārā* (chief star) of the particular constellation; so that if the star should be on the north if the ecliptic, the Vīdhi is known as the northern one; if on the ecliptic, it is known as the central one and if on the south of the ecliptic, it is known as the southern one.

6. According to others the nine constellation from *Bharaṇī* form the northern Vīdhi or path, the nine from *Pūrvaphalgunī*

form the central path and the nine from *Pūrvāṣāḍha* form the Southern path.

7. If writers on Jyotiṣaśāstra should disagree it is not for me to determine the correct view; I have only to state the views here of several authors.

8. If Venus should either disappear or reapear[1] in a northern Vīdhi there will be prosperity and happiness in the land; if in a central Vīdhi there will not be much of either; and if in a southern Vīdhi mankind will be afflicted with miseries.

9. If Venus should disappear or reappear in the several Vīdhis beginning from the northernmost one the condition of the world will respectively be 1. very excellent, 2, excellent, 3. good, 4. fair, 5. moderate. 6. tolerable, 7. poor, 8. very poor, 9. miserable.

10. The four constellations from Bharaṇī are known as the first *maṇḍala* (circle or division). If Venus should reapper in it there will be prosperity in the land; the people of *Vaṅga* and of *Aṅga*, the Mahiṣas, the Vāhlikas, and the Kaliṅgas will be afflicted with fears.

11. If Venus, who so reappears in the said circle, should be crossed by a plant, the rulers of the *Bhadrāśva*, of the *Aswas* of the Śūrasena and of the Yaudheyas and of *Koṭivarṣa*[2] will perish.

12. The four constellations from *Ārdrā* form the second Maṇḍala or circle; if Venus should reappear in it, the rainfall will be moderate and the growth of food crops will also be moderate; the Brahmins will suffer, especially those who are wicked.

13. If Venus who so reappears in the said circle, should be crossed by a Planet, the Mlechas, foresters, persons that live by dogs, the hill-men of Gomanta and Gonarda, the Chandalas, the Śūdras and the people of Videha will become wicked and lawless.

14. The five constellations from Maghā from the third maṇḍala : if Venus should reappear in it, crops will suffer; there will also be suffering from hunger and robbers. Chandalas will prosper and there will be an intermingling of castes.

15. If Venus, who so reappears in the said maṇḍala, should be crossed by a planet, shepherds, hunters, the Śūdras, the Puṇḍras, the border Mlechas, the Śūlikas, forestdwellers, the Draviḍas and persons who live close to the sea will be afflicted with miseries.

16. The three constellations form Swāti form the fourth maṇḍala; if Venus should reappear in it, mankind will be free from fear; the Brahmiṇṣ and Kṣatryas will prosper and friends will turn into enemies.

17. If Venus, who so reappears in the said maṇḍala, should be crossed by a planet, the chiefs of the hunters will perish; the Ikṣvākus, the border Mlechas, the people of Avantī and of Pulindas and the Sūrasenas will also perish.

18. The five constellations from Jyeṣṭha form the fifth maṇḍals, if Venus should reappear in it, the people of Kashmir, the Aśmaka, the Matayas, those living on the banks of the cāruḍevī and in the country of Avanti will suffer from hunger, from thieves and from disease.

19. If Venus who so reappears in the said maṇḍala should be over powered by a planet. the Ābhīras, the Dsaviḍas. the Ambaṣṭhas the Trigartas, Sourāṣtras, the people of Sindhu and of Sauvīrakas and the ruler of kāśī will perish.

20. The six constellations from Dhaniṣṭhā form the sixth maṇḍals, if Venus should reappear in it there will be wealth and prosperity in the land and cows will thrive and crops will be abundant but fear in certain places.

21. If Venus, who so reappears in the said maṇḍala, should be crossed by a planet, the Sulikas, the people of Candahar and of Avantī will be afflicted with miseries. The Videha will perish. The servants of the border Mlechas and of the Yavanas will prosper.

22. If Venus should reappear or be cossed by a planet in the western portion of the maṇḍalas beginning from Swātī and from Jyeṣṭha or in the eastern portion of the maṇḍala beginning from Maghā, there will be happiness in the land; in all the other maṇḍalas the effects will be the same as those already described wherever Venus might happen to reappear or be them crossed.

23. If Venus should be visible before sunset there will be fear in the land; if visible throughout the day, mankind will suffer from hunger and from disease; if visible at midday in conjunction with the moon, the king's army and capital city will suffer.

24. If Venus should pass through the constellation of Kṛttikā, the Earth will be so much enundated with water as to make its surface even.

25. If Venus should pass through the constellation of Rohiṇī, Earth will assume the same appearance of death and devastation as if she was going through the ceremony of Kāpāla for the expiation of the sin of murder.

26. If Venus should enter the constellation of Mṛgaśiras, juice and crops will suffer; if she should enter the constellation of Ārdrā, the people of Kosala and of Kaliṅga will suffer and there will be abundance of rain.

27. If Venus should enter the constellation of Punarvasu the people of Aśmaka and of Vidarbha will become lawless. If Venus should enter the constellation of Puṣya, there will be good rain; singing and dancing parties will suffer.

28. If Venus should enter the constellation of Āśleṣā, there will be much suffering from serpents; if Venus should pass through the constellation of Maghā, elephant keepers or ministers will suffer and there will be abundance of rain.

29. If Venus should pass through the constellation of Pūrvaphalgunī, hill men and the people of Pulinda will perish and there will be abundance of rain; if she should pass through the constellation of Uttaraphalgunī, the people of Kuru, of Jāṇgala and of Pāñcāla will perish, and there will also be rain.

30. If she should pass through the contellation of Hasta, the Kouravas, and painters will suffer; there will be no rain; well-diggers and birds will suffer. If she should enter the constellation of Citrā, there will be good rains.

31. If she should enter the constellation of Swāti, there will be much rain; servants, merchants and boatmen will become wicked and lawless. If she should enter the constellation of Viśākhā, there will be good rain and tradesmen will suffer.

32. If she should enter the constellation of Anurādhā, rulers

will be at strife; if she should enter the constellation of Jyeṣṭha, the chief rulers will suffer; if she should enter the constellation of Mūla, physicians that deal in medicinal plants will suffer. In each of these three cases there will be drought in the land.

33. If Venus should enter the constellation of Pūrvāṣāḍha, the creatures of water will suffer; if she should enter the constellation of Uttarāṣāḍha, diseases will increase. If she should enter the constellation of Śravaṇa, diseases of the ear will afflict mankind. If she should enter the constellation of Dhaniṣṭhā, heretics will suffer.

34. If Venus should enter the constellation of Śatabhiṣaj, drunkards or dealers in liquor will suffer; if she should enter the constellation of Pūrvabhādra, gamblers will suffer as well as the Kouravas and the Pāñcāla, and there will be rain in the land.

35. If Venus should enter the constellation of Uttarabhādhrapada, fruits and roots will be injured; if she should enter the constellation of Revatī, travellers will suffer; if she should enter Aświnī, horsekeepers will suffer and if she should enter Bharaṇī, hillmen and the Yavanas will suffer.

36. If Venus should either reappear or disappear in the 8th, 14th, or 15th lunar day of the waning moon, the Earth will be flooded with water.

37. If Jupiter and Venus should be opposite to, that is 180° apart from, each other and if they should be at the same time due east and west of each other, mankind will suffer from disease, from fears and from sorrow, and there will be no rain.

38. If the course of Jupiter, Mercury, Mars and Saturn should just precede that of Venus, mankind, elephants and magicians will be at strife among themselves; storms and deaths will afflict mankind.

39. Friends will cease to be friends; the Brahmins will cease to perform religious ceremonies properly; there will be no rain; and mountains will be riven asunder by thunderbolts.

40. If the course of Saturn should just precede that of Venus, the Mlechas, cats, elephants, asses, buffaloes, black grains, hogs, barbarians, the Śūdras and travellers in the south will suffer by diseases of the eye and by windy disorders.

41. If the course of Mars should just precede that of Venus, mankind will suffer from fire, from weapons, from hunger, from drought and from thieves; all the creatures and objects of the north will suffer and the sky will be filled with fire, lightning and dust.

42. If the course of Jupiter should just precede that of Venus, he will destroy objects that are white, the Brahmins, cows and temples; the east will suffer; there will be a fall of hail from the clouds and diseases of the neck; the crops of Śarat will thrive well.

43. If the course of Mercury should just precede that of Venus, and if Mercury should then have either disappeared or reappeared, there will be rain in the land; diseases and bilious jaundice will afflict mankind; the crops of Grīṣma will flourish; ascetics, persons who have performed sacrificial rites, physicians, dancers or wrestlers, horses, the Vaiśyas, cows, rulers in their chariots and all yellow objects will perish and the west will suffer.

44. If Venus should be of the color of fire, there will be fear from fire; if of blood color, there will be wars in the land if of the color of burnished gold, there will be disease; if green, there will be asthmatic complaints; if ashy-pale or black, there will be drought in the land.

45. If Venus should be of the color of coagulated milk, of the white water lily, or of the moon, or if her course be direct, or if she should be the successful planet in conjunctions, mankind will enjoy the happiness of Kritayuga.

REFERENCES

1. Venus disappears when within 10 degrees from the Sun and reappears beyond that limit.
2. Koṭivarṣa : the city of Devikote in the Coromandel Coast.

CHAPTER 10

On Saturn

1. If the disc of Saturn should appear glossy and if his course should lie through the constellations of Śravaṇa, Swāti, Hasta, Ārdrā, Bharaṇī, or Pūrvaphalgunī, the Earth will be covered with water.

2. If his course should lie through the constellations of Āśleṣā. Śatabhiṣaj, Jyeṣṭha, there will be prosperity in the land but slight rain; if his course should lie through Mūla, mankind will suffer from hunger, from weapons and from drought. We will now proceed to state the effects of Saturn's course through each of the 27 constellations.

3. If the course of Saturn should lie through the first constellation of Aświnī, horses, horse-keepers, poets, physicians and ministers will perish. If it should lie through the constellation of Bharaṇī, dancers, players on musical instruments, vocal singers, low people and deceitful men will perish.

4. If his course should lie through the constellation of Kṛttikā, persons that live by fire and commanders of armies will perish; and if througt Rohiṇī, the people of Kosala, of Madra, of Varanasi and of Pāñcāla and carriage drivers will suffer.

5. If the course of Saturn should lie through the constellation of Mṛgaśīrṣa, the people of Vatsa,[1] the officiating priests in sacrificial rites as well as the persons that perform them, reverend men and the people of Madhyadesa will suffer miseries; if through Ārdrā, the people of Pārata, and of Ramaṭha, oil mongers, washermen and thieves will suffer.

6. If the course of Saturn should lie through the constellation of Punarvasu, the Pāñcāla, the border Mlechas and the people of Surat, of Sindh and of Souvīraka will suffer miseries; if his course should lie through the constellation of Puṣya,

bell ringers, criers the Yavanas, tradesmen, deceitful men and flowers will suffer.

7. If the course of Saturn should lie through the constellation of Āśleṣā, the creatures of water and serpents will suffer; if through the constellation of Maghā, the Bāhlīkas, the Chinese, the people of Gāndhāras, of Śūlika and of Pārata, the Vaiśyas, store houses and merchants will suffer.

8. If his course should lie through the constellation of Pūrvaphalgunī, juice sellers, prostitutes, virgins and the Maharashtras will suffer miseries; if through Uttaraphalgunī, kings, ascetics, jaggery, salt, water and the town of Takṣaśilā in the Punjab will suffer.

9. If the course of Saturn should lie through the consellation of Hasta, barbers, mill-men, thieves, physicians, weavers, elephant keepers, prostitutes, the Kosalakas, and garland makers will suffer.

10, If the course of Saturn should lie through the constellation of Citrā, women, writers, painters, various utensils will suffer; if through Swāti, the people of Magadha, reporters, messengers, charioteers, mariners, dancers and the like will suffer miseries.

11. If the course Saturn should lie through the constellation of Viśākhā, the Trigartas, the Chinese and the Kulūtas, saffron, shel-lac, crops, every thing of bright, red or crimson color will suffer.

12. If the course of Saturn should lie through the constellation of Anurādhā, the Kulūtas, the Taṅgaṅas[2] and the Khasas, the people of Kashmir, ministers, drivers, and bell-ringers will suffer and friends will turn into enemies.

13. If the course of Saturn should lie through the constellation of Jyeṣṭhā, the king's chaplain, the king's favorites, valients soldiers, and mixed crowds of men of different castes will suffer; if through Mūla, the people of Varanasi, of Kosala and of Pāñcāla, fruits, medicinal plants and soldiers will suffer.

14. If his course should lie through the constellation of Pūrvāṣāḍha, the people of Aṅga; of Vaṅga, of Kosala, of Girivraja[3] of Magadha, of Puṇḍra, of Mithilā and of Tāmralipti[4] will suffer miseries.

15. If the course of Saturn should lie through the constelation of Uttarāṣāḍha, the people of Daśārṇa,[5] the Yavanas, Ujjayinī barbarians, the people of Pāryatra, and the Kunty-bhojas will suffer.

16. If the course of Saturn should lie through Śravaṇa public officials, the chief Brahmins, physicians, and priests and the people of Kaliṅga will suffer miseries. If his course should lie through Dhaniṣṭhā the ruler of Magadha will become triumphant; and treasury officers will prosper.

17. If the course of Saturn should lie through the constellations of Śatabhiṣaj and Pūrvabhādra, physicians, poets, drunkards or those that deal in liquor, tradesmen and ministers, will be afflicted with miseries; if it should lie through the constellation of Uttarabhādra, dancers, travellers women and gold will suffer.

18. If the course of Saturn should lie through Revatī, the servants of the reigning sovereigns, the people of Krouchadvipa,[6] the crops of Śarat, barbarians and the Yavanas will suffer.

19. If, while Saturn is in Kṛttikā, Jupiter should be in the constellation of Viśākhā, mankind will then become very wicked. If both the planets should be in one and the same constellation the chief towns will suffer.

20. If Saturn should appear variegated in color, birds will perish; if yellow, there will be fear from hunger; if of blood color, there will be wars in the land and if of ashy color, mankind will be very much at strife.

21. If Saturn should appear as bright as the cats' eye gem or pure or of the color of the bana (a black flower) or Atasī[7] flower, mankind will be happy. Whatever may be the color of Saturn, the persons who or objects which correspond to the particular color will suffer.[8]

REFERENCES

1. Vatsa : name of a country ; its chief town is Kousumbha.
2. Taṅgaṇas : name of a people in the upper part of the valley of Sarayu.

3. Girivraja : name of the capital of Magadha.
4. Tāmralipti : name of a people near the western mouth of the Ganges.
5. Daśārṇa : name of a people living south east of Madhya-desa in the centre of Hindustan.
6. Krouchadvipa or Krouncha : mountain or part of the Himalayan range situated in the eastern part of the chain on the north of Assam.
7. Atasī : common flax bearing a blue flower.
8. e.g : if white the Brahmins, if red the Kṣatriyas, if yellow the Vaiśyas, if black the Śūdras and if blue the Chandalas will suffer.

CHAPTER 11

On Comets and the Like

1. Having examined the treatises of Garga, Parāśara, Asita, Devala and many others on Ketus[1], I now proceed to give a clear account of the same.

2. The reappearance or disappearance of the Ketus is not subject to astronomical calculations. The Ketus are of three kinds--celestial, etherial and terrestrial.

3. Ketus are luminous appearances resembling fire but without the power to consume objects—the glow worm, certain phosphorescent appearances, gems, precious stones and the like excepted.

4. The etherial Ketus appear in flag staffs, implements of war, houses, trees, horses, elephants and the like. The celestial Ketus appear in stellar regions and the terrestrial ones appear in pits and low grounds in the surface of the Earth.

5. Some writers[2] say that the Ketus are 101 in number; others[3] say that they are 1,000 in number; Nārada says that there is but one Ketu which appears in various shapes at various times.

6. Whether there is one Ketu or many, the effects to be described are various and these effects depend on their reappearance or disappearance (at particular times and places) their positions, the heavenly bodies with which they might appear to be in contact and on their colors.

7. The effects will last for as many month as the number of days during which the Ketus continue to be visible; if visible for months, the effects, will last for years[4]. The effects will commence after three weeks from such appearances.

8. Generally if the luminous body or comet be small clear, glossy, straight, transient, white and visible either immediately after their appearance or some time afterwards there will be health and happiness in the land.

9. If it be the opposite of these, or of the shape of the rainbow or with two or three tails, mankind will not be happy.

10. The Ketus or comets that resemble garlands, gems and gold are named Kiraṇa Ketus and are 25 in number; they have tails and appear in the East and in the West; they are the sons of the Sun, and when they appear, princes will begin to be at strife.

11. The Ketus that are of the color of the parrot, of fire, of Bhandhu Jīvika[5] flower, of Shel-lac or of blood are the sons of Agni (fire) and appear in the South-East; they are 25 in number; when they appear mankind will be afflicted with fears.

12. The Ketus or coments whose tails are bent and which are of sharp rays and black are the sons of Yama; they are 25 in number; they appear in the South; when they appear there will be deaths in the land.

13. The Ketus or comets that appear like a mirror, are round in shape without tails but with rays and looking like oil or water are the sons of the Earth; they are 23 in number, and appear in the North-East; when they appear mankind will be afflicted with fear and hunger.

14. The Ketus or Comets that appear bright like the moon, silver, snow, white jasmine and the white water lily are the sons of the moon; they appear in the North and are 3 in number; when they appear mankind will be happy.

15. The single Comet possessing three tails and three colors is named Brahmadaṇḍa and is the son of Brahma; it appears anywhere; when it appears the world will come to an end.

16. Thus have been stated briefly 101 Ketus and we will now proceed to state clearly the 1,000 Ketus already referred to.

17. The Comets that appear in the North and North East are 84 in number; they are the sons of Venus; they have large, white and shining discs and when they appear mankind will not be happy.

18. The comets that appear glossy, with rays and double tailed are 60 in number; they are the sons of Saturn; they appear anywhere and are named Kanaka Ketus; when they appear mankind will feel very miserable.

19. The Comets which are white, of single disc, without tails and glossy are named Vikaca Ketus and are the sons of Jupiter. They are 65 in number; they appear in the South and when they appear mankind will not be happy.

20. The Comets that are neither very bright nor clearly visible to the naked eye, and that are long and white are named Taskara Ketus; they are the sons of Mercury, they appear any where and are 51 in number; when they appear mankind will feel miserable.

21. The Comets which are of the color of blood or fire and with three tails are named Kauṇkuma Ketus : they are the sons of Mars and are 60 in number; they appear in the North and when they appear minkind will feel miserable.

22. The Ketus that appear as spots in the solar and lunar discs are 33 in number. They are named as Tāmasa and Kīlaka Ketus. They are the sons of Rāhu. Their effects have been stated in the Chapter on the Sun (vide stanza 7. Ch. 3.)

23. The Comets that resemble the flaming fire or a garland are 120 in number. They are the sons of Agni and are named Viśvarūpa Ketus. When they appear there will be fear from fire.

24. The Comets that are dark-red in color, without disc, presenting the appearance of *Chamara*[6] and with scattered rays are named Aruṇa Kutus. They are the sons of Vāyu (the wind) and are 77 in number; when they appear mankind will feel miserable.

25. The Comets that resemble clusters of stars are named Gaṇaka Ketus; they are 8 in number and are the sons of Prajā-pati. Those that are oblongular[7] in shape; are 204 in number and are the sons of Brahma.

26. The Comets that resemble clusters of bomboo canes and that are as bright as the moon are named Kaṅka Ketus; they are the sons of Varuṇa and are 32 in number. When they appear mankind will suffer miseries.

27. The Comets that resemble a headless trunk are named Kabandha Ketus ; they are the sons of Yama and are 96 in number ; and are without discs ; when they appear there will be much fear all over the Earth.

28. The Comets that are white possessing a single disc

are 9 in number ; they appear in the four corners. Thus we have given an account of 1,000 Ketus. We shall now give a few particulars connected with them.

29. Vasā Ketu is a comet which lies with its head towards the North ; it is of large size, glossy, and appears in the west. When it appears there will be immediate[8] deaths in the land but prosperity in the end.

30. Hasti Ketu resembles the Vasā Ketu; but if it appears of sharp rays, there will be fear in the land. Śastra Ketu also resembles the Vasā Ketu is glossy and appears in the West; and when it appears, there will be wars and deaths in the land.

31. Kapāla Ketu is visible on new-moon days; its tail is of the color of smoke : its course lies through the eastern half of the visible hemisphere; when it appears mankind will suffer from hunger, death, drought and disease.

32. Raudra Ketu is a comet resembling the dagger's end and is of a dull red color; it appears[9] in the South-East and travels through a third of the sky and produces the same effects as the Kapāla Ketu.

33. Cala Ketu is a comet which appears in the West with a tail an inch in length pointing to the South ; as it proceeds more and more towards the North, it increases in length.

34. After touching the Ursa Major or the Pole star, or the constellation of Abhijit, it turns back and after travelling one half of the sky disappears in the South.

35. When this Ketu appears, the country between Allahabad and Ujjain, the forests near Ajmer, the north, the country of Devika and Madhyadeśa will perish.

36. The other countries will also suffer in several places from disease and from famine; the effects described will last for 10 months according to some and for 18 months according to others.[10]

37. Śweta Ketu is a comet which appears in the East about midnight with its tail pointing to the South. Ka Ketu is a comet of the shape of a carriage pole and appears in the West. Both the above Ketus are seen simultaneously for 7 days.

38. If both should appear glossy, there will be prosperity and happiness in the land; if the Ka Ketu should be visible for over 7 days, there will be much suffering from wars for ten years.

39. The Śweta Ketu is of the shape of the twisted hair and of a dull and disagreeable aspect; it travels through a third of the sky and then retraces its steps. When it disappears it leaves only a third of mankind as survivors.

40. Raśmi Ketu is a comet possessing a tail slightly colored like smoke; it appears in the constellation of Kṛttikā. The effects are the same as those assigned to Śweta Ketu.

41. Dhruva Ketu is a comet possessing no fixed course color or shape and appears anywhere in the heavens, in the sky and on Earth. When it appears glossy, mankind will be happy.

42. To those whose death might be near this Ketu appears in the several divisions of the King's army, in houses, in trees, in hills and in house hold utensils.[11]

43. Kumada Ketu is a comet of the color of the white water lily. It appears in the west with its tail pointing to the east and is visible only for a night. When it appears there will be unprecedented happiness in the land for a period of ten years.[12]

44. Maṇi Ketu is a comet which appears for only 3 hours occasionally; it possesses an invisible disc and appears in the West; its tail is straight and white and it resembles a line of milk drawn from a human breast.[13]

45. There will be happiness in the land from the very time of its appearance for four and a half months; reptiles and venomous creatures will come into existence.[14]

46. Jala Ketu is a comet which appears in the west with a raised tail; it is glossy, when it appears there will be prosperity in the land for 9 months, and the world will be freed from all miseries.

47. Bhava Ketu is a comet visible only for a single night and in the East, possessing a small disc; it is glossy; the tail is bent like that of a lion.

48. There will be unprecedented happiness in the land for as many months as the number of hours for which it con-

tinues to be visible; if it should be fearful to look at fatal diseases will afflict mankind.

49, Padma Ketu is a comet white like the stem of the lotus. If it appears only for a night there will be joy and happiness in the land for 7 years.

50. Āvarta Ketu is a comet of a red color; it appears in the West at mid-night with its tail pointing to the South and it is glossy. There will be happiness in the land for as many months as the number of Kṣaṇas (Four minutes) for which it continues to be visible.

51. Saṁvarta Ketu is a comet which appears in the West in the evening with a tail of the color of smoke and copper, extending to a third of the sky and resembling the sharp end of a dagger; it is fearful to look at.

52. Princes will suffer in wars for as many years as the number of hours for which it continues to be visible. Those persons will also suffer in the star of whose nativity the comet appears.

53. Omitting the benefic comets we shall proceed to state the several princes who will perish according as the malefic comets either dim with their tails the stars of the various constellations or appear to be in contact with the same.

54. If the stars of the constellation of Aśvinī should be dimmed by the tails of or appear to be in contact with, malefic comets the ruler of Aśmaka[15] will perish ; if the stars of Bharaṇī should be so dimmed or in contact with malefic comets, the ruler of Kirātas will perish ; if those of Kṛttikā, the ruler of Kaliṅga will perish ; and if those of Rohiṇī, the ruler of Śūrasena will perish.

55. If the stars of the constellation of Mṛgaśiras should be dimmed by the tails of or appear to be in contact with malefic comets, the ruler of Uśīnaras will perish ; if those of Ārdrā, the ruler of the people subsisting by the products of water will perish; if those of Punarvasu the ruler of Aśmaka will perish ; and if those of Puṣya the ruler of Magadha will perish.

56. If the stars of the constellation of Āśleṣa should be dimmed by the tails of or appear to be in contact with malefic

comets, the ruler of Asika will perish; if those of Maghā, the ruler of Aṅga will perish; if those of Pūrvaphalgunī, the ruler of Pāṇḍya will perish; if those of Uttaraphalgunī, the ruler of Ujjain will perish; and if those of Hasta, the ruler of Dandaka[16] will perish.

57. If the stars the constellation of Citrā should be dimmed by the tails of or appear to be in contact with malefic comets, the ruler of the Kurus will perish; if those of Swātī the rulers of Kāśmīr, Kāmboja will perish.

58. If the stars of the constellation of Viśākhā should be dimmed by the tails of or appear to be in contact with the malefic comets, the rulers of Ikṣwāku and of Alakā will perish; if those of Anurādhā, the rulers of Puṇḍras will perish; if those of Jyeṣṭhā the chief emperor will suffer.

59. If the stars of the constellation of Mūla should be dimmed by the tails of or appear to be in contact with malefic comets, the ruler of Āndhra and of Madra will perish; if those of Pūrvāṣāḍhā the ruler of Varanasi will perish; if those of Uttarāṣāḍhā, the rulers of Yaudheyaka, of Arjunāyana, of Śibis and of Cedi will perish.

60. If the stars of the constellation of Śravaṇa should be dimmed by the tails of or appear to be in contact with the malefic comets, the ruler of Kekaya will perish; if those of Dhaniṣṭhā, the ruler of Punjab will perish; if those of Sataya the ruler of Ceylon will perish; if those of Pūrvabhādra, the ruler of Bengal will perish; if those of Uttarabhādra, the ruler of Naimiṣa will perish; and if those of Revatī the ruler of Kirāta will perish.

61. If the tails of the comets should be crossed by the fall of meteors there will be happiness in the land; if there should be fall of rain at the time of the appearance of a comet mankind will be exceedingly happy; but the people of Cola and of Afghans as well as the white-men and infidels and the Chinese will suffer.

62. The rulers of the countries to which the bent tails of the comets point, of the countries in the direction of which the tails of the comets extend and of the countries corresponding to the several constellations (as described above) with whose

stars the comets might appear to be in contact, will triumph over their enemies and be happy.

Note :—Compare, with the above, what modern science has to say on the subject of comets :

"What then is a comet according to the latest scientific researches ? The spectroscope has pretty will solved the query. It consists, first, of a more or less solid nucleus on fire, blazing and glowing; second, of vast masses of incandescent gas, constituting the luminous head; third, solid materials, constituting the tail, which are ponderable, which reflect the Sun's light and are carried along by the influence of the nucleus; fourth, an immense prolongation of the tail in the nature of attenuated volumes of gas. The solid materials of a comet, it is believed, consist of stones and sand, particles ground by ceaseless attrition. The proof of this is the concession of most astronomers that meteoric showers are shreds and patches of cometic matter, dropped from the tail, and these meteors are stones. The genesis of comets is found to be in the explosion of planetary bodies, a theory not without good scientific authority."

"Arago estimates that there are 17,000,000 of these fiery wanderers within the orbit of Neptune, and Lambert regards 500,000,000 as a moderate estimate for those in the Solar System. All the astronomers agree that they are scattered through space as profusely as the fish in the seas. The Orbit of the Earth is overwhelmed in a fine net work of cometary orbits, and our globe is like a lost child in a forest full of wild beasts."

REFERENCES

1. Ketus : This term is defined by the Author in stanza 3, and is made to include Comets, meteors falling stars, solar and lunar spots and the like luminous bodies.
2. Parāśara for instance.
3. Garga for instance.
4. The Commentator says : From 1 to 24 days of visibility the effects will last from 1 to 24 months. From 25 to 30

days of visibility, for two years ; if visible for $2\frac{1}{2}$ months for instance, the effects will last for $2\frac{1}{2}+1\frac{1}{2}$ or 4 years.

5. Bhandhujīvika : Pentapetes Phoenicea—a plant with a red flower which opens at mid-day and withers away the next morning at sunrise.

6. Chamara : the bushy tail of the Bos Grunniens.

7. Garga says triangular.

8. On the day of appearance according to commentator.

9. About the constellation of Āṣāḍhā according to commentator.

10. For 8 years according to Parāśara and Garga.

11. According to Parāśara it is seen in trees, mountains, bamboos, China rose, roads, implements of war, jewels, chariots, elephants, camels, beds seats, vessels and the like. The number of these Ketus is 10, 21, 60, or 100 in the opinion of several writers.

12. Vridha Garga says that this happiness cannot be an unmixed one : according to him, cometary appearances never fail to produce evils.

13. This and several other comets can be very well identified by a look into the Map of comets published by Europeans.

14. According to Parāsara if the comet continues to be visible for over 3 hours serpents, mongooses and the like will come into existence.

15. Most of these countries have been already explained. The rest wherever they can be identified, will be explained as we proceed.

16. Dandak : name of a district in the Dekhan between the Narmadā and Godāvarī rivers which in the time of Ramachandra was a forest and celebrated as a place of pilgrimage.

CHAPTER 12

On Canopus[1]

1. The mighty ocean whose, waters, when swallowd by Agastya, exhibited gems that eclipsed the splendor of the crowns of the Devas, and rocks broken by the action of the sharks on them and thus presented an appearance beautiful, though without water.

2. It also exhibited hills with trees, corals and gems and the scene was rendered picturesque by serpents that issued from the rocks.

3. It exhibited whales, water elephants and rivers and gems scattered over its bed, and though deprived of water, presented an appearance splendid as Devaloka.

4. There were also seen, moving to and fro, whales, pearl oysters and conch shells, and the sea altogether looked like a summer lake with its moving waves, water lilies and Swans.

5. Its huge white waves looked like clouds; its gems looked like stars; its crystals looked like the Moon; and its long bright serpents bearing gems in their hoods looked like comets and thus the whole sea looked like the sky.

6. Hear now the effects of the heliacal rising of Canopus, a star sacred to Agastya who suppressed the Vindhya mountains whose soaring heights obstructed the course of the Sun; to which the pictured robes of the Vidyādhara females leaning for support on their lords' arms and flying aloft in the sky formed beautiful flowing flags: whose caves were the abodes of lions which, having drunk of the perfumed blood of elephants in rut had their mouths covered with bees that looked like so many black flowers, and from which caves issued rivers; whose summits appeared to score the starry vault; whose rocks were full of buzzing bees scared by the violent pulling of flower trees by wild elephants and were also the abodes of hyenas; of bears,

of tigers and of monkeys; through which lay the secret course of the Rāvī which appeared to embrace its bosom with the affection of a mistress; and in whose forests dwelt the Devas and also Brahmin recluses, some subsisting on water, some on roots, some on the air and some altogether without food.

7. When the star Canopus reappears after its conjunction with the Sun, waters muddled by their contact with the earth will resume their original clearness just in the same way as the minds of the Sadhus naturally recover their original purity after contact with the wicked.[2]

8. The autumn is attended by the Chakravaka[3] on both its sides (i.e., beginning and end); in it is heard the music of the swan; and its opening is marked by the beautiful red sky; in all these respects the season resembles a women with a rising bosom, sounding jewels and betel colored mouth.

9. Again in the season of autumn will be found the blue and white lotus growing side by side, hovered over by beautiful lines of bees, tender creepers adding beauty to the scene; the season therefore resembles a charming woman with blue eyes, fair face, black hair and thin brows.

10. As if to view the beauty of the pure disc of her lord the Moon, the summer lake opens at night her red lotus buds —her eyes—of soft petals in which lie concealed the black bee serving as the pupil of the eye.

11. The Earth, by means of her arms, the waves, adorned by the lotus, the Swan, the ruddy goose and the water crow appears to welcome the appearance of Agastya with her offerings of gems, abundant flowers and fruits.

12. The poisonous and hot waters poured down by cloud-covered serpents by order of Indra become pure and fit for use on the re-appearance of the Star Canopus.

13. The very thought (meditation) of the sage Agastya is calculated to wash off one's sins; his praise (worship) must be capable of doing more. For the benefit, therefore, of princes,[4] I will now speak of the rules of the *Arghya* (offering) to be presented to Agastya as stated by the Ṛṣis.

14. The time of reappearance of the Star Conopus is different in different places; and it is for the learned Astronomer

to ascertain these times for given places. In the Town of Ujjain the star reappears when the sun just begins to enter the 24th digree of the sign Leo.[5]

15. When the darkness of the night should just begin to be broken by streaks of red light from the eastern horizon, princes, previously prepared[6] for the purpose, ought to offer their *Arghyam* to Agastya by pouring it on the earth in the direction of the Star Canopus rising in the South East as will be pointed out by the Astronomer.

16. The offering to be made by princes in honor of Agastya shall consist of the fragrant flowers of the season, of fruits, of precious stones, of gold cloths, of cows, of bulls, of well cooked rice, of sweet-meats, of curdled milk, of colored rice, of perfumed smoke and fragrant paste.

17. A prince making this offering, with a truly devout spirit, on every occasion of the reappearance of the Star Canopus for 7 years will be freed from disease, will triumph over his enemies, and will become the Sole ruler of the Earth.

18. A Brahmin making this offering to the extent of his ability will become learned in the Vedas and will be blessed with a wife and children; a Vaiśya doing the same will get cows; and a Śūdra doing it will get wealth, and all the four will be freed from disease and become virtuous.[7]

19. If the disc of the Star Canopus should present a disagreeable appearance, there will be disease in the land; if yellow there will be drought; if of the color of smoke cows will suffer; if of unsteady light mankind will be afflicted with fears; if white red they will suffer from hunger and from starvation; and if of very small disc the chief Towns will be surrounded by the enemy.

20. If Canopus should appear of the color of silver, of crystal, or brilliant there will be prosperity in the land, and mankind will be free from fear and disease.

21. If Canopus should be crossed by meteoric falls or by comets mankind will suffer from hunger and death. When the sun enters the constellation of Hasta, Canopus re-appears, and when he enters the constellation of Rohiṇī, Canopus disappears.[8]

REFERENCES

1. Canopus : This star is sacred to Agastya who is said to have drunk off the ocean and suppressed the heights of the Vindhya mountains. The first 5 stanzas, curiously enough are devoted to a description of the beauties of the sea on the occasion of the former feat, and the 6th stanza which is written in Dandaka metre is devoted to a description of the beauties of the Vindhya mountains on the occasion of the latter feat. The language is highly rhetorical.

2. The rhetorical beauty in this stanza consists in a certain *Sleśa* (double meaning) contained in the term *Ku Samayoga*, which means both contact with the earth and contact with the wicked.

   The next three stanzas describe the beauties of the autumn which commences with the reappearance of Canopus.

3. Chakravaka : the ruddy goose commonly called the Brahmani duck.

4. The commentator adds that this offering is equally binding on all men, and forms part of man's Nityakarma. In Viṣṇu Rahasya we find Viṣṇu addressing Agastya as follows : he who fails to worship thee by the offering of Arghya shall lose in your favor the effects of a year's *Punnyakarma* he who worships thee shall enjoy wealth and prosperity in Śweta Dwipa (Vaikuṇṭha.)

5. Leo : The word in the text is Agatasya Kanyam, which literally means before the Sun enters the sign of Virgo, but which the commentator takes to mean being in Leo. Vide Note to stanza 21.

6. Previously prepared : by fasting and performance of Agastya pūjā, according to commentator.

7. According to Matsyapurana, the offering must be made 7 times on some morning before dawn within 7 days from the reappearance of Canopus. According to some other authority the offering should be continued for 17 years, and must be accompanied in the case of the first three

classes of men by the singing of Vedic hymns. For detailed account of the ritual connected with the ceremony the reader is referred to Bhaviṣyapurāṇa and to a work entitled Danamala.

8. The statement in the text amounts to this : Canopus reappears when the sun enters the 17th degree of the sign Virgo and disappears when the sun enters the 11th degree of the sign Taurus. This the commentator says cannot be *ordinarily*, and is besides opposed to what has been stated in stanza 14th. According to commentator the author has quoted in the last stanza the opinion of Parāśara which is only an instance of *Utpata*. It cannot be otherwise ; for canopus is situated at the end of the sign Gemini which is 70° from Hasta and only 50° from Rohiṇī :—

According to some canopus reappears on the 8th lunar day or on new-moonday of the waning moon of the month of Asvayuk (Tulā and Vṛscika). This is opposed to actual observation and must be regarded as Utpata.

Again in Viṣṇu Rahasya Vachana it is stated that canopus reappears when the Sun enters Hasta ; but this as well as what Bṛhaspati says, the commentator regards as being true for the Northern countries.

CHAPTER 13

On the Ursa Major or The Constellation of The Seven Sages

1. The Seven Sages form as it were a garland of the white lotus to lady North or look like her smile or seem to be her lords.

2. Or by the direction of her lord the Pole star, lady North, appears to dance round as the Seven Sages move in their course. I begin to treat of these stars adopting the views of Vṛddha Garga.

3. During the reign of Yudhiṣṭhira[1] 2520[2] years before the commencement of Vikrama Śaka the Seven Sages were at the constellation of Maghā (Regulus).[3]

4. The Sages take a period of 100 years to go over each of the 27 Asterisms.[4] They rise in the North East and are accompanied by the chaste Arundhanti, the consort of Vasiṣṭha.[5]

5. The eastern most of the group is Bhagavan Marīci ; the next to him is Vasiṣṭha ; the next is Aṅgirasa and the next two are Atri and Pulastya.

6. The next in order are the Sages Pulaha and Kritu. The Chaste Arundhati closely attends her husband the sage Vasiṣṭha.[6]

7. If the Sages should be crossed by meteoric falls, thunderbolts, or comets, or if they should appear dim or without rays or of very small disc, they will cause misery and suffering to the persons and objects they severally represent ; but if they should appear big or bright there will be happiness and prosperity.

8. If Marīci should be affected as described above the Gandharvas, the Devas, the Asuras, skilled magicians and

physicians, the Yakṣas, the Nāgas and the Vidyādharas will also be afflicted.

9. If Vasiṣṭha should be crossed by meteoric falls or otherwise affected, the Scythians, the Yavanas, the Daradas, the Pāratas, the people of Kāmboja and the Ṛṣis of the forests will suffer ; but if Vasiṣṭha should appear bright, he will cause happiness.

10. If Aṅgiras should be affected as described above, men of knowledge, men of acute intellect and the Brahmins will be afflicted ; if Atri should be so affected the products of the forests and of water, seas, and rivers will suffer.

11. Along with Pulastya will suffer the Rākṣasas, the Piśacas, the Asuras, the Daityas and the Nāgas. Along with Pulaha will suffer roots and fruits, and along with Kratu will suffer sacrificial rites and persons performing them.

REFERENCES

1. Yudhiṣṭhira, otherwise known as Dharmaputra, the eldest of the Pandus who flourished at the end of the Dvāpara-yuga.
2. 2526, i.e. nearly 4,500 years ago. The reader will note that at this early period at least, if not earlier still, the Hindus were noted for their knowledge of Astronomy and that they had recognized the motions of the tars, speaks highly of their powers of observation.
3. Regulus : vide last note to the next stanza.
4. An Asterism is 13°.20′ of the ecliptic : at the rate of 100 years each the Sages take 2,700 years to make a circuit of the heavens.
5. The Sages are said to be in that constellation of the ecliptic with which the western most two either rise at Lanka (equator) or culminate at the meridian. In Viṣṇu Puraṇa it is stated that when the observation was made at one time, the two Sages were found in Maghā. The Puraṇa

also states that when the Sages should reach the constellation of Pūrvāṣāḍhā passing over a space of 10 asterisms in 1015 years the Nandas will reign.

6. Vasiṣṭha, as already observed, is the last star but one. What is pointed out as Arundhati near Vasiṣṭha is not the real Arundhati ; she is declared in the Śāstras to be a Sūkṣṇa Tārā (telescopic star) very close to Vasiṣṭha.

CHAPTER 14

Division of Globe[1]

1. The countries of the Earth beginning from the centre of Bhāratavaraṣa and going round the East, South East, South, etc., are divided into 9 divisions corresponding to the 27 lunar asterisms at the rate of 3 for each division and beginning from Kṛttikā.

2. The Constellations of Kṛttikā, Rohiṇī and Mṛgaśiras represent the Madhyadesa or central division consisting of the countries of Bhadra, Arimeda, Māṇḍavya, Sālwa, Nīpa, Ujjihāna, Maru, Vatsa, Ghoṣa, the countries bordering on the Jumnā and the Sarswatī, the countries of Matsya, Mādhyamika.

3. Madhurāka, Upajyotiṣaka, Dharmarani, Śūrasena, Gouragrīva, Uddehika, Pāṇḍu, Guda Aśvattha, Pāñcāl.

4. Sāketa, Kaṅku, 'Kuru, Kālakoṭi, Kukura the Pāriyātra mountains, Oudumbara, Kapiṣṭhala, Gajahvaya.

5. The constellations of Ārdrā, Punarvasu and Puṣya represent the Eastern division consisting of the mountains of Añjana, of Vṛṣabha, of Dhvaja, of Padma, and of Mālyavānt the countries of Vyāghramukha, Suhma, Karvaṭa, Candrapura, Śūrpakarṇa.

6. Khasa, Magadha, Sibiragiri, Mithilā, Samataṭa, Udra, Aśvavadana, Danturaka, and, farther-east Jyotiṣa, Lauhitya, Kṣirasamudra, the land of the Canibals.

7. The Eastern Ghauts, the countries of Bhadragondaka, Pauṇḍra, Utkala, Kaśī, Mekala, Ambaṣṭha, Yekapada, Tāmraliptika, Kosalaka and Vardhamana.

8. The constellations of Āśleśa, Maghā and Pūrvaphalgunī represent the South Eastern division consisting of the countries of Kosala, Kaliṅga, Vaṅga, Upavaṅga, Jaṭharāṅga Śūlika, Vidarbhas, Vatsa, Āndhra, Cedi, Ūrdhvakaṇṭha.

9. The islands of Vṛṣa, of Nālikera and of Carma; the countries of Vidarbharaga and other countries in the Vindhya mountains, of Tripurī, Śmaśrudharas, Hemakuḍya, Vyālagrīva, Mahāgrīva.

10. Kiṣkindha, Kaṇṭakasthala, Niṣāda, Purika, Daśārṇa Nagna, Parṇa and Śabara.

11. The constellations of Uttaraphalgunī, Hasta and Citra represent the Southern division consisting of the countries of Ceylon, Kālānjana, Saurīkīrṇa, Talikaṭa, the mountains of Giri, Nagara, Malaya, Dardura, Mahendra and Mālindya and the countries of Broach.

12. Kaṅkaṭa, Tunkana, Vanavāsi, Śibika, Phaṇikara, Koṅkaṇa, Ābhīra, Akara, the river Veṇā, the countries of Avanti, Daśapura, Gonarda, Kerala.

13. And Carnata; the forest of Mahāṭavi, the mountain of Chitrakūṭa, the countries of Nasikya, Kolla, Giri, Cola Krauñchadvīpa and Jaṭādhara, the river Kāveri and the mountain of Ṛṣyamūka.

14. The islands of Vyduryadvīpa, Sankhadvīpa, Muktadvīpa, Trivaricharadvipa and Dhurmapattanadvipa; the countries, of Gaṇarājya, of Kṛṣṇa, Velluru, the Peśika,, Śūrpa and Kusumanaga mountains.

15. The forest of Tumbavana, the country of Kārmaṇeyakas, the South sea, the countries of Tāpasāśrama, Ṛṣikas, Kāñcī, Marucīpaṭṭana, Ceryā, Ārya, Siṁhala, Ṛṣabha.

16. The Town of Baladeva, the forest of Daṇḍakā, the countries of Temingilasana, Bhadra, Cutch, Kunjaradhari and Tāmraparṇī.

17. The contellations of Swatī, Śākhā and Anurādhā represent the South-Western division consisting of the countries of Pahlava, Kāmboja, Sindhu, Souvīra, Vaḍavāmukha, Arava, Ambaṣṭha, Kapila, Nārīmukha, Ānarta.

18. Pheṇagiri, Yavana, Makara, Karṇaprāveya, Pāraśava, Śūdra, Barbara, Kirāta, Khaṇḍa, Kravya, Āsīā, Ābhīra, Cañcūkas.

19. Hemagiri, Sindhukalaka, Raivataka, Surāṣṭra Bādara, Dravida and Maharnava.

20. The constellations of Jyeṣṭhā, Mūla, and Pūrvāṣāḍhā perresent the Western division consisting of the five moun-

tains of Maṇimat, Meghavat, Vanaugha, Kṣurārpaṇa and Astagiri and the countries of Aparāntaka, Śāntika, Haihaya, Praśastadri, Vokkāṇa.

21. Punjab, Ramatha, Pārata, Tārakaṣiti, Jṛṅga, Vaiśya, Kanaka, Śaka and the rude Mlecha countries in the west.

22. The constellations of Uttarāṣāḍhā, Śravaṇa, and Śraviṣṭa represent, the north western division consisting of the countries of Māṇḍavya, Tuṣāra, Tālahala, Madra, Aśmaka, Kulūta, Lahada, Stīrājya, Nṛsiṁha, Vanakha.

23. The rivers the Veṇumatī, the Phalguluka and the Guluha, and the countries of Marukaccha and Carmaraṅga whose people possess a single eye, single lock, a long neck, a long face and long hair.

24. The contellations of Śatabhiṣaj, Pūrvabhādrapada, Uttarabhādrapada represent the Northern division consisting of the six mountains of the Kailāsa, the Himālayas, the Vasumat, the Dhanuśmat, the Krouñca and the Meru and the countries of the North Kurudesa, Kṣudramīna.

25. Kaikaya, Vasāti, Yāmuna, Bhogaprastha, Arjunāyana, Āgnīdhra, Ādarś, Antadvīpi, Trigarta, Turagānana, Śvamukha.

26. Keśadhara, Cipiṭa, Nāsika, Dāseraka, Vāṭadhāna, Śaradhāna, Taxilā, Puṣkalāvata, Kailāvata, Kāṇṭahdhāna.

27. Ambarāvata, Madraka, Malava, Paurava, Kachhāra, Daṇḍapiṅgalaka, Māṇahala, Hunas, Kohala, Śītaka, Maṇḍavya, Bhūtapura.

28. Gāndhāra, Yaśovati, Hematāla, Rajanya, Khacara, Gavya, Yaudheya, Dāsameya, Śyāmāka, and Kṣemadhūrta.

29. The constellations of Revatī, Svātī and Bharaṇī represent the North-Eastern Division consisting of the countries of Merukanaka, Naṣṭarājya, Paśupāla, Kīra, Kasmir, Abhisāra, Darada, Taṅgaṇa, Kulūta, Sairindhra, Vanarāṣtra.

30. Brihmapura, Dārvada, Amara, Vanarājya, Kirāta, China, Kauṇinda, Bhalla, Paṭola, Jaṭāsura, Kunaṭa, Khasas, Ghoṣa, Kucīkas.

31. Yekacarana, Anuvisva, Suvarṇabhū, Vasudhana, Diviṣṭha, Paurava, Ciranivasana, Trinetra, Muñjadri and Gandharva.

32. If the nine divisions of the 27 constellations from Kṛttikā should suffer from the presence of malefic planets[2] in them, the rulers of Pāñcāl, Magadha, Kaliṅga.

33. Avantī, Ānarta, Sindhu, Souvīra, Hārahoura, Madra and Kuṇinda will respectively suffer miseries.

Note:—The following list is from Parāśara.

The chief mountains are 7. The chief rivers are 40. The chief oceans are 4. The number of smaller rivers flowing into seas is 6,000.

The chief countries are 99. The number of peninsulas is 10 ; of Sandy deserts is 8 ; of deep lakes 80 ; of islands 80. The number of rivers whose course is westwards is 5,000.

According to Vikrama Siṁha the three constellations from Kṛttika form the womb, the Naval and the heart of lunar Zodiac ; the three from Āndra form the neck, face and so forth going round as before, so that Oudh, Mithila, Konliki, Gaya, Patna, Apichatra as far as Allahabad are in the womb of the lunar Zodiac ; Bengal, Utkala, Kaliṅga and Magadha are in the head ; Vengi, and Kousala are in the right food ; Siṁhala, Malaya Kañci and Kiśkinda are in the right side: Kashmir is in the left side, Kuru, Nepal and China are in the left foot.

REFERENCES

1. Division of Globe : The geographical divisions of the Earth and of India particularly, corresponding to the various stellar divisions along the ecliptic. The object is to discover which of the countries of the earth will suffer when planetary and the like celestial phenomena occur. The Chapter therefore is a useful one, though it may not be found to be interesting study to the general reader. It may be used as a geographical dictionary of reference when necessary. A few more geographical terms occur in Chapters XVI and XVII. For convenience of reference it is proposed to give an alphabetical list of the

more important terms occurring in the three Chapters at the end of Chapter XVII with the modern names given opposite to each.

2. These are the Saturn, the Sun, Mars, Rāhu and Ketu according to commentator.

List of the Star with their Longitude and Latitude

No.	Name of the chief star	Star compared	Longitude A.D. 660 °	′	Latitude °	′
1	Kṛttikā	η Tauri, Alcyone	39	58	4	1 N.
2	Rohiṇī	α Tauri, Aldebaran	49	45	5	30 S.
3	Mṛgaśiras	λ Orionis	63	40	13	25 S.
4	Ārdrā	α Orionis	68	43	16	4 S.
5	Punarvasu	β Gemini Pollux	93	14	6	39 N.
6	Puṣya	δ Cancri	108	42	0	4 N.
7	Āśleṣā	ε Hydrae	112	20	11	8 S.
8	Maghā	α Leonis, Regulas	129	49	0	27 N.
9	P. Phalgunī	δ Leonis	141	15	14	19 N.
10	U. Phalguni	β Leonis	151	37	12	17 N.
11	Hasta	δ Corvi	173	27	12	10 S.
12	Citrā	α Virginis Spica	183	49	2	2 S.
13	Swātī	α Bootis, Arcturus	184	12	30	57 N.
14	Vikśāhā	ι Librae	211	0	1	48 S.
15	Anurādhā	δ Scorpionis	222	34	1	57 S.
16	Jyeṣṭhā	α Scorpionis, Aritares	229	44	4	31 S.
17	Mūla	λ Scorpionis	244	33	13	44 S.
18	P. Āṣāḍha	δ Sagittarii	255	32	6	25 S.
19	U. Āṣāḍha	ρ Sagittarii	262	21	3	24 S.
20	Abhijit	α Lyrae, Vega	265	15	61	46 N.
21	Śravaṇa	α Aquilae. Atair	281	41	29	19 N.
22	Dhaniṣṭhā	β Delphini	296	19	31	57N.
23	Śatabhiṣaj	λ Aquarii	321	33	0	23 S.
24	P. Bhādrapada	σ Pegasi	333	27	19	25 N.
25	U. Bhdārapada	λ Pegasi and Andremedae	349	8	25	41 N.
26	Revatī	ξ Piscium	359	50	0	13 S.
27	Aświnī	β Arietis	13	56	8	28 N.
28	Bharaṇī	35 Arietis, α Musca	26	54	11	17 N.

CHAPTER 15

Stellar Rulership

1. Those who are born on the lunar day of Kṛttikā will delight in white flowers, will perform sacrificial rites, will be skilled magicians and metaphysicians, will be diggers, barbers, Brahmans, potters, priests or astromers.[1]

2. Those who are born on the lunar day of Rohiṇī will be devout men, merchants, rulers, rich men, Yogis, drivers, or men possessed of cows, cattle and the animals of water, farmers and men possessed of wealth derived from mountain produce.

3. Those who are born on the lunar day of Mṛgaśiras will delight or deal in perfumes, dress, pearls, flowers, fruits precious stones, wild beasts, birds and deer ; will be Somayajis or singers ; will be lascivious ; will be good writers or painters.

4. Those who are born on the lunar day of Ārdrā will delight inkilling, torturing, lying, in adultery, thieving, cheating and tale-bearing ; will deal in pod grains, black magic, sorcery and exorcism.

5. Those who are born on the lunar day of Punarvasu will be noted for truthfulness, generosity, cleanliness, respectable decent, personal beauty, sense, fame and wealth ; they will also be merchants, dealing in excellent articles, will be found of service and will delight in the company of painters and sculptors.

6. Those who are born on the lunar day of Puṣya will be dealers in barley, wheat, rice, sugar-canes and in the produce of the forest ; will be either ministers or rulers will live by water ; will be sadhus and will delight in sacrificial rites.

7. Those who are born on the lunar day of Āśleṣā, will be dealers in perfumes, roots, fruits, reptiles, serpents and

poison ; will delight in cheating others of their property ; will be dealers in pod grains ; and will be skilled in medicine of every sort.

8. Those who are born on the lunar day of Maghā will be possessed of wealth, grains and store-houses ; will delight in frequenting hills and in the performance of religious rites ; will be merchants ; will be valient ; will take animal food and will be female haters.

9. Those who are born on the lunar day of P. Phalgunī will delight in dance, in young women, in music, in painting, in sculpture and in trade ; will be dealers in cotton, salt, honey and oil and will be for ever in the enjoyment of the vigor of youth.

10. Those who are born on the lunar day of U. Phalgunī will be mild, cleanly, modest, heretical, generous and learned ; will be dealers in grains ; will be wealthy, virtuous and in the company of princes.

11. Those who are born on the lunar day of Hasta will be thieves, dealers in elephants, charioteers, chief ministers, painters, merchants and dealers in pod grains ; learned in the Śāstras and of bright appearance.

12. Those who are born on the lunar day of Citrā will be dealers in jewels, precious stones, fine cloths, writers and singers, manufacturers of perfumes, good mathematicians weavers, surgeons, oculists and dealers in Rajadhanya.[2]

13. Those who are born on the lunar day of Svātī will delight in keeping birds, deer, horses ; will be grian merchants dealers in beans ; of weak friendship ; weak, of abstemious habits and skilled tradesmen.

14. Those who are born on the lunar day of Viśākhā will grow trees yielding red flowers and red fruits ; be dealers in gingelly seeds, beans, cotton, black gram and chick peas and worshippers of Indra and Agni.

15. Those who are born on the lunar day of Anurādhā will be valient ; heads of parties ; fond of the Company of Sādhus, keep vehicles and grow every species of crop.

16. Those who are born on lunar day of Jyeṣṭhā will be valient, of good descent, wealthy, famous ; disposed to cheat

others of their property, fond of travelling, rulers of provinces or commanders of armies.

17. Those who are born on the lunar day of Mūla will be druggists, heads of men, dealers in flowers, roots, fruits and seeds ; will be rich and will delight in garden work.

18. Those who are born on the lunar day of P. Āṣāḍha will be of gentle manners; found of sea-voyage, truthful, cleanly and wealthy ; will delight in earth work ; will be boatmen ; will be dealers in fruits and flowers of water.

19. Those who are born on the lunar day of U. Āṣāḍha will be chief ministers or wrestlers ; will keep elephants and horses, will be religious ; will be men of principle ; soldiers ; happy and of bright appearance.

20. Those who are born on the lunar day of Śravaṇa will be cunning, of active habits, efficient workmen, bold, virtuous, god-fearing and truthful.

21. Those who are born on the lunar day of Dhaniṣṭhā will be shameless, of weak friendship, haters of women, generous, rich and free from temptation.

22. Those who are born on the lunar day of Śatabhiṣaj will be fishermen or dealers in fish and hogs ; washermen ; dealers in wine and birds.

23. Those who are born on the lunar day of P. Bhādra-pada will be thieves, shepherds, torturers ; wicked, mean, and deceitful ; will possess no virtues ; will neglect religious rites and will be successful in fight.

24. Those who are born on the lunar day of U. Bhādra-pada will be Brahmins, performers of sacrificial rights ; will be generous, devout, rich and observant of the rules of the holy orders ; will be heretics, rulers, dealers in rice.

25. Those who are born on the lunar day of Revatī will be dealers in water flowers, salt, gems, conch shells, pearls, creatures of water, pregnant flowers and perfumes ; they may also be boat-men.

26. Those who are born on the lunar day of Aśwanī will keep horses,will be commanders of army ; physicians, servants, dealers in horse, riders, tradesmen or masters of horses.

27. Those who are born on the lunar day of Bharaṇī

will deal in precious stones, will be flesh eaters, will be wicked men ; will delight in acts of killing and torturing ; will be dealers in pod grains ; will be of low descent or weak minded.

28. The constellations of P. Phalgunī, P. Āṣaḍha, P. Bhādrapada and Kṛttikā belong to the Brahmin class ; those of Puṣya, U.Phalgunī, U. Āṣāḍha and U. Bhādrapada belong to the Kṣatriya class ; those of Revatī, Anurādhā, Maghā and Rohiṇī belong to the Śūdra class.

29. The constellations of Punarvasu, Hasta, Abhijit and Aświnī belong to the Vaiśya class ; those of Mūla, Ārdrā, Swātī and Śatabhiṣaj belong to the butcher class.

30. The constellations of Mṛgaśiras, Jyeṣṭhā, Citrā and Dhāniṣṭhā belong to the serving class; those of Āśleṣa, Viśākhā, Śravaṇa and Bharaṇī belong to the lowest or Chandala class.

31. That constellation in which the Sun and the Saturn might happen to be together or through which Mars might happen to pass or in which the retrograde motion of a planet might lie or in which a lunar or solar eclipse might take place or through which the moon might pass.

32. Will bring misery to the persons and objects it represents. If on the other hand the constellation should be free from any such affection the same persons and objects will prosper.

REFERENCES

1. Of courses one and the same person connot be all thes though several characters might belong to him.

2. Rajadhanya: a kind of rice—Panicum Frumentaceum.

CHAPTER 16

On the Planets

1. The Sun presides over the people of the Western half of the Narmadā, of the countries on both banks of the Sone, of Orissa, Bengal, Suhma, Kaliṅga, Balhika, Śaka, Yavana, Magadha, Śabara, Eastern parts of Jotiśapura, China and Kamboja.

2. Over the people of Mekala, Kirāta, Viṭaka, the outer and inner mountains, Pulinda, the eastern half of Draviḍa and the east bank of the Jumnā.

3. Over the people of the Cāmpā city, the Udumbaras, the citizens of Kauśāmbī, of Cedi, of Kaliṅga in the forest of the Vindhya mountains, of Puṇḍra, of Golāṅgūla, of Śrīparvata and of the town of Vardhamana.

4. And over the people living on the banks of the Ikṣumatī. He also presides over hill men, quick-silver, deserts, shepherds, seeds, pod grains, bitter flavor, trees, gold, fire, poison, persons successful in battle.

5. Over medicines, physicians, quadrupeds, farmers, kings, butchers, travellers, thieves, serpents, forests and renowned and cruel men.

6. The Moon presides over citadels fortified by hills or by water, over Oudh, Broach, the sea, the city of Rome, the country of Tukhara, dwellers in forests, the islands of Taṅgaṇa, Hala and Strīrājya in the big seas.

7. She presides over sweet juice, flowers, fruits, water, salt, gems, conch shells, pearls, creatures of water, paddy, barley, medicinal plants, wheat, Somayajis, kings attacked in the rear, and Brahmins.

8. She also presides over fine, white horses, charming young women, commanders of armies, articlet of food, clothes, horned animals, the Rakṣasas, farmers and *srouties*.[1]

9. Mars presides over the people residing in the west half of the countries on both banks of the Sone, the Narmadā and the Beas; over those residing on the banks of the Nirvindhyā, the Vetravatī, the Siprā, the Godāvarī and the Venā.

10. The Ganges, the Payoṣṇi, the Mahānadi, the Indus, the Mālati and the Pīrā; he also presides over the country of Uttarapāṇḍya, the Mahendra, the Vindhya and the Malaya mountains and the Coladesa.

11. The Draviḍas, the Videhas, the Āndhras, the Aśmakas, the Bhāsāpuras, the Koṅkaṇas, the Mantriṣikas, the Kuntalas, the Keralas, the Daṇḍakas, the Kāntipuras, the Mlechas and the mixed races.

12. He also presides over Nasik, Bhogavardhana, Virāṭa, the countries bordering on the Vindhya mountains and over the people living on the banks of the Tāptī and the Gomatī.

13. He presides over citizens, farmers, chemists, fireman, soldiers, forest men, citadels, chief towns, butchers, sinners, haughty men.

14. Kings, children, elephants, fops, infanticides, shepherds, red fruits, red flowers, corals, commanders of armies jaggery, wine and cruel men.

15. Over store houses, Agnihotries, metal mines, the Sakhyas in red robes, the Budhists, thieves, rogues, persons harboring deep hatred and glutto.

16. Mercury presides over the western half of the Louhitya river, the Indus, the Gogra, the Gambhīrakā, the Ratha,[2] the Ganges and its tributary the Kauśikī. He also presides over the countries of Videha, and Kamboja.

17. The eastern half of Muttra, the Himālayas the Gomanta and the Citrakūṭa mountains, Sūrat, people living on table lands, on the surface of water, in valleys and in mountains.

18. Over persons possessing a knowledge of the laws of drink, of mechanics, of music, of writing, of gems, of color and of perfumes; he also presides over painters, grammarians, mathematicians, physicians, sculptors.

19. Spies, jugglers, infants, poets, rogues, tale bearers, black-magicians, messengers, hermaphrodites, buffoons, sorcerers, and conjurers.

20. Over sentinels, dancers and dancing masters; over ghee, gingelly and other oils; over seeds, over bitter flavor, over observers of religious ceremonies, over chemists and mules.

21. Jupiter presides over the eastern part of the Indus, the western half of Mathurā, the countries of Bharata, and Souvīra the town of Srughna. the province of Udicya, the Vipāśā and the Śatadru rivers, the countries of Ramaṭha, Sālva.

22. Trigarta, Pourava, Ambaṣṭha, Pārata, Vāṭadhāna Yaudheya, Śarasvata, Arjunāyana, one half of Matsya;

23. Over elephants, horses, priests, rulers, ministers, marriages and health; over mercy, truthfulness, cleanliness, religious observances; over learning, gifts and charity;

24. Over citizens, richmen, grammarians, Vedic students, sorcerers, lawyers, the ensigns of royalty—the umbrella, the flag staff, the Camara and the like;

25. Over Saileyika,[3] mansi[4] tahara,[5] kuṣṭha,[6] kuick silver, salt, beans, sweet flaver, wax and coraka.[7]

26. Venus presides over the town of Taxila, the countries of Mārtikāvata, Bahugiri, Gāndhāra, Puṣkalāvataka Prasthala, Malwa, Kaikaya, Daśārṇa, Uśīnara and Śibi.

27. Over the people living on the banks of the Vitastā, the Irāwatī and the Candrabhāgā; over chariots, silver mines elephants, horses, elephant drivers and rich men.

28. Over perfumes; flowers, perfumed paste, gems, diamonds, ornaments, lotus or conch shells, beds, bridegrooms, young men, young women, objects tending to provoke lustful desires and persons that eat good and sweet meals;

29. Over gardens, waters, voluptuaries and lewed men; over fame, comfort, generosity, beauty, and learning; over ministers, merchants, potters, birds and triphalā.[8]

30. Over simple silk; colored silk, flannel cloth, white silk, rodhra,[9] patra,[10] coca,[11] nutmeg, agaru.[12] voca[13] pippili[14] and sandal.

31. Saturn presides over the countries of Ānarta, Arbuda, Puṣkara, Sūrat, Ābhīra, Śūdra, Raivataka, countries through which the river Saraswatī passes as an under ground stream and the western countries.

32. Over the natives of Kurukṣetra, the town of Somnat,

and persons born on the banks of the Vidiśā, the Vedasmṛtī and the Mahī; over wicked men, uncleanly men and men of the lowest class; over oil monggers, weak men and persons not possessing virility.

33. Over binders, bird hunters, impure men, boatmen, or fishermen, ugly men and old men; over dealers in hogs, chiefs of tribes, men of weak resolution, hill men, barbarous mountain tribes and over poor men.

34. He also presides over pungent flavor and bitter flavor; over chemistry; over widows, serpents, thieves, buffaloes, asses, camels, beans, leguminous seeds and Niśpava.[15]

35. Rāhu presides over hill men, mountain peaks, outer and inner caves, the Mlechas, the Śūdras, persons subsisting on dogs and jackals, spear men the countries of Vokkans and Aśwamukha and persons physically deformed.

36. He also presides over the most wicked in the family, over torturers, ungrateful men, thieves, persons who are untruthful, uncleanly and ungenerous; over ass-riders, duelists, persons of easily irritable temperament, infants in the womb and Chandalas.

37. Over notorius sinners, fops, Rakṣasas, excessive sleepers, all sentient beings and wicked persons; over black gram and gingelly seed.

38. Ketu presides over mountains, fortified cities, the con tries of Pahlava, Sweta Huna; Cola, Afghans, deserts, China, and the land of the Mlechas; over rich men, men of note, men of industry and valor;

39. Over men coveting the wives of others, men prying into the secrets of other men, haughty men, ignorant men, sinners and persons found of victory.

40. If at the time of re-appearance, a planet should appear bright, of large disc and in his natural condition, not crossed by thunderbolts, meteoric falls or dust storms and not suffer in conjunction with other planets or if he should be in his house or in his ucchakṣetra or if he should be within site of a benefic planet, he will bring prosperity to the persons and objects persided over by him.

41. If on the other hand be should appear otherwise than

as described above, the same persons and objects will suffer miseries and people will also suffer from wars and from diseases and kings will be afflicted with sorrow.

42. Though free from enemies, princes will suffer from the intrigues of their sons or ministers. Their subjects, suffering from drought, will quit their native cities and resort to new towns and mountains.

REFERENCES

1. Srouty, a person skilled in the knowledge of the rules relating to sacrificial rites.
2. Ratha : is the Gundak according to Kaśyapa.
3. Saileika : benzoin or storax.
4. Mansi : otherwise known as Jatamansi, a medicinal grass—Cyperes, stoloniferess.
5. Tahara : the plant Casia Tora :
6. Kuṣṭha : a medicinal plant used as a remedy for the disease called Takman—Costus.
7. Coraka : the husk of cardamom.
8. Triphalā : the three fruits—the three myrobalans, the fruits Terminalia Cebula. T. Bellerica, and Phyllan thus Emblica, or the three fragrant fruits of nutmeg, arecanut and cloves; or the three sweet fruits of grape, pomegarnate and date.
9. Rodhra : the tree Symplocos Racemosa having yellow leaves.
10. Patra : the leaves of Cinnamon.
11. Coca : the bark of Cinnamon.
12. Agaru : Agallochum, Amyris Agallocha.
13. Vacha : a kind of aromatic root (according to some orris root.
14. Pippili :—long pepper—Piper longum.
15. Niśpava : a species of pulse—Phaseolus Raaditus.

CHAPTER 17

On Planetary Conjunctions

1. Astronomers are able to predict by calculation before hand the times and nature of planetary conjunctions. I have treated of this subject in my astronomical work, Pañcasiddhāntika[1] basing my theories on the Sūrya Siddhānta.

2. The planets all revolve in the sky and their orbits of motion lie one above the other. When seen from this great distance, the planets seem to move on one even surface.

3. The conjunctions of the planets are of 4 sorts known technically as 1. *Bheda,*[2] 2. *Ullekha,*[3] 3. *Aṁśumardana,*[4] 4. *Asavya,*[5] according as the planets are more and more distant from each other, as stated by Parāśara and other Ṛṣis.

4. If the planets should be in Bheda conjunction there will be drought in the land ; friends and persons of great families will turn into enemies ; if the planets should be in Ullekha conjunction there will be wars in the land, and princes will quarrel with their enemies ; but there will be abundance of good food.

5. If the planets should be in Aṁśuvimarda conjunction, kings will be at war and mankind will suffer from weapons, from disease and from hunger ; if they should be in Apasavya conjunction, rulers will be at war with one another.

6. The Sun when in mid heaven is known as an *Ākranda* planet ; when in the East he is known as a *Poura* planet and when in the West he is known as a *Yāyi* planet. Mercury, Jupiter and Saturn are always known as *Poura* planets. The Moon is always known as an Ākranda Planet.

7. Ketu, Mars, Rāhu and Venus are known as Yāyi planets. The planet that suffers defeat[6] in conjunction will cause suffering to the objects it represents ; but if triumphant, the objects will prosper.

8. If a Poura (citizen) planet should suffer defeat in conjunction with another Poura planet, citizens and rulers will suffer. Also if a Yāyi (marching to war) planet should suffer defeat in conjuction with another Yāyi planet or if an Ākranda (setting up a war cry) planet should suffer defeat in conjunction with another Ākranda planet or if either a Poura or Yāyi planet should suffer defeat in conjunction with a Yāyi or a Poura planet respectively the objects represented by the planet which suffers defeat will suffer miseries.

9. That planet is said to suffer defeat in conjuction, which might happen to be the Southern one, or of disagreeable appearance or of unsteady light or which might begin to retrograde immediately after conjunction or which might appear to be of small disc or which might be eclipsed by the other planets or which might undergo a change of nature or appear dim or of ugly appearance.

10. If the planet should appear otherwise than as described above, he is deemed to be the triumphant planet and that planet in conjunction which might appear of large, bright, shining disc is deemed triumphant though he might be the southern planet.[7]

11. If both planets should be equally bright, large and shining, the conjunction is known as *Samāgama*—mere meeting as opposed to a meeting in fight. In such cases there is a mutual liking between the planets—and hence also between the persons and objects they represent; but if both planets should be otherwise, the same persons and objects will perish.

12. In cases where it might be doubtful whether the conjunction of two planets is a conjunction in fight or a mere meetting, it is also doubtful whether princes will prosper or suffer.

13. If Mars should suffer defeat in his conjunction with Jupiter, the Bāhlīkas, travellers and persons that live by fire will suffer; if he should so suffer in his conjunction with Mercury the Śūrasenas, the Kaliṅgas and the Sālvas will suffer.

14. If Mars should suffer defeat in his conjunction with Saturn, townsmen will prosper but country people will suffer; if he should so suffer in his conjunction with Venus, storehouses, the Mlechas and the Kṣatriyas will suffer.

15. If Mercury should suffer defeat in his conjunction with

Mars, trees, rivers, ascetics, the people of Aśmaka, the people of the North, sacrificial rites and the Dīkṣitas performing them will suffer much.

16 If Mercury should suffer defeat in his conjunction with Jupiter, the Mlechas, the Śūdras, thieves, rich men, the people of Trigarta and those of mountainous countries will suffer and there will also be Earth-quakes.

17. If Mercury should suffer defeat in his conjunction with Saturn, boatmen, soldiers, creatures of water, rich men and pregnant women will suffer; if he should so suffer in his conjunction with Venus, there will be fear of injury from fire and crops, clouds and travellers will suffer.

18. If Jupiter should suffer defeat in his conjunction with Venus, the people of Kuluta, of Kandahar, of Kaikaya, of Madra, of Sālva, of Vatsa and of Bengal will suffer; crops and cows will perish.

19. If Jupiter should suffer defeat in his conjunction with Mars, the people of Madhyadesa and princes will suffer and cows will perish; if he should so suffer in his conjunction with Saturn, the people of Arjunāyana, of Vasati, of Yaudheya, of Śibi and the Brahmins will perish.

20. If Jupiter should suffer defeat in his conjunction with Mercury, the Mlechas, truthful men, armed soldiers and Madhyadesa will suffer; also the various persons and objects presided over Jupiter will suffer.

21. If Jupiter should suffer defeat in his conjunction with Venus, travellers and eminent men will perish. The Brahmins and the Kṣatriyas will be at war and there will be no rain.

22. The people of Kosala, Kaliṅga, Bengal, Vatsa Matsya Madhyadesa and Śūrasena and hermaphrodites will suffer great miseries.

23. If venus should suffer defeat in his conjunction with Mars, the chiefs of armies will perish and princes will be at war; if Venus should so suffer in his conjunction with Mercury, the people of mountainous countries will suffer; milk will be injured and there will be slight rain.

24. If Venus should suffer defeat in his conjunction with saturn, the chiefs of tribes, soldiers, the Kṣatriyas and creatu-

res of water will suffer; the several objects and persons presided over by Venus will also suffer in addition.

25. If Saturn should suffer defeat in his cohjunction with Venus, the price of food grains will rise and snakes and birds will suffer. If he should so suffer in his conjunction with Mars, the people of Taṅkaṇa, of Northern circars, of Orissa, of Varanasi, and of Bāhlīka will suffer.

26. If Saturn should suffer defeat in his conjunction with Mercury, the people of Bengal, tradesmen, birds, animals and snakes will suffer; if he should so suffer in his conjunction with Jupiter, women will be happy; buffaloes and the Scythians will suffer.

27. Thus have been described the special effects of the defeats of Mars, Mercury, Jupiter, Venus and Saturn in their conjunctions, each, with the other planets. To these effects must be added the effects resulting to the several objects and persons presided over by the several planets. These will suffer in proportion to the extent of defeat of the planets presiding over them.

List of Indian Geographical terms alphabetically arranged with their modern names given opposite to each.

A

Abdhinagari, Dwaraka (the old).
Ahicchatra, Ahicchatter.
Ajameetham, Ajmere.
Akasagunga, Mandakinee.
Alakanunda, Alaknunda.
Amarakantaka, Omerkantak.
Ambashta, Lahore (District).
Amritasaras, Amritsur.
Anartam, Kattywar.
Anarthanagaree, Dwaraka (the old).
Andhananagarum, Vegi; Vengi.
Anga, Bengal proper near Bhagalpur.
Angadapuri, Shahabad (in Oude).
Angadeeya, Shahabad (in Oude).
Angadesa, Bhagalpur (the District).
Angapuri, Bhagalpur (the town).
Antarvedi, Gangetic Doab.
Apaga, Apaga (a stream).
Aratta, Gujerat (province) in Punjab.
Arbuda, Aboo.
Aryavarta, Northern India.
Ashmaka, Travancore.
Asi, Asi (river).
Asmaka, Bhira (Purana)?
Atreyi, Atrae (river).
Avantayah, Malwa (Western).
Avanti, Ujjain.
Avantipuram, Vantipur.
Ayodhya, Oude (the town).

B

Baleswaram, Balasor.
Balhika, Balk.
Bhadra, Badra.
Bhagirathee, Hooghly; Ganges.
Bharatavarsha, India.
Bharukaccha, Baroach.
Bheema, Beema.
Bheemarati, Beema.
Bhogavati, Bagmati.
Brahmaputra, Brahmaputra.
Brahmasarah, Brahmasarus.
Brahmayoni : Brahmajuin (a hill).
Brihmavarta, India Upper.
Brindavana, Brindabun.

C

Chaityakagiri, Ratnagiri.
Champa, Bhagulpur (the town).
Chandra, Chenab.
Chandrakanta, Chandpur.
Chandrika, Chenab.
Charmanvati, Chumbul.
Chattagrama Chittagong.
Cheena, China.
Chintarathya, Chindinthura.
Chitra, Chittaur.
Chitrakuta, Chitrakote.
Chitropala, Chittaur.
Cholamandala, Coromandal.

D

Dakshinamanasam, Dakshinamanas.
Dakshinapatha, Southern India.
Damaliptam, Tumlook.
Damodara, Damudar.
Darada, Dard (the country).
Darduragiri, South Eastern Ghauts.
Darapuram, Dholpore ?
Dasapura, Part of Malwa or Bundel Kund.
Dasarna, Dasan (river or country).
Daseraka, the Great Desert.
Devagiri, Deogir or Dowlatabad.
Devahrida, Deverkunda.
Devikodham, Dinajpore (Southern),
Dhara, Dhar.
Dharmapattanam, Sahet Mahet?
Dharmapuram, Dharmapur.
Dharmaranyam, Dharmrun.
Drishtadvate, Cagar.
Dushpara, Chenaub.
Dwaravali, Dwaraka (the old).
Dwarika, Dwaraka (the old).

G

Gadagrama, Gargaon.
Ghandhinagarum, Kanouj.
Ganarajya, Name of an Empire in the South of India.
Gandaka, Ganda (District).
Gandaki, Gandak.
Ganga, Ganges.
Gangadri, Gangotree.
Gangadvara, Hurdwar.
Gandara, Eastern Afghanistan.
Gharghara, Gogra.
Ghardhara, Cagar.
Girivrija, The Capital of Magada.
Girivrijam, Rajgir.
Godavaree, Godavaree.
Gokarna, Rameswaram.
Gomatee, Gumtee.
Gorathagiri, Silagiri.
Govardhana, Gobardhan.
Gouda, Bengal (Northern).
Gourapuri, Gaur.
Goujara, Gujerat (Province) in Punjab.

H

Haimavater, Ganges.
Harikeliya, Bengal (Eastern).
Hariprasthan, Delhi (town).
Hataka, Ladak (province).
Hemakuta, A mountain to the north of the Himalayas.

Hemanta, Hema,
Hiranvate, Ramaganga.
Hiranyabahu, Sona (river).
Hiraryavnha, Sona (river).
Hradinee, Jhelum (river).

I

Indraprastham, Delhi (town).
Induja, Nerbudda.
Indumatee, Kaleemudee (Eastern).
Indumatee, Chenaub?
Iravati, Ravee.

J

Jalundhara, Jullunder Doab.
Jambavaka, Jumna.
Janhavee, Ganges.
Janmabhumi, India (Northern).
Jina Chakri, India (Northern).
Jaypura, Jaipur.
Jyotirathee, Johila.

K

Kaccha, Chashak (the plain).
Kacchara, Cachar.
Kalanjara, Calinjar.
Kalindapuram, Karnapur.
Kalindee, Jamna.
Kalinga, A District in the Coromandal coast (Ganjam District).
Kalinganagari, Rajmahendri.
Kalyanam, Calian.
Kalyanee, Kalianee.
Kamarupa, Kamroop.
Kampilyam, Kampil.
Kanakhalam, Kankhal (village).
Kanakhal, Khankhal (the mountain).
Kanchipuri, Conjevaram.
Kannada, N. Canara.
Kanyakubjam, Kanouj.
Kapee, Cabul (river).
Kapisa, Cossy (a river in Midnapur.)
Kapisee, Opian.
Kapishtalam, Kaithal.
Kaseepuree, Varanasi.
Kashmira, Kashmir.
Kataka, Cuttack.
Kaveri, Cauvery (river).
Keekadha. Behar (Southern).
Keera, Kashmir.
Kela, Canara.
Kerala, Malabar.
Ketakapuram, Kaira.
Khagi, Kakpur.
Khatwangi, Panchagunga.
Khunamusha, Khunomush.
Kolahalagiri, Brahmajiuin (a hill).
Kolapuram, Colapore.
Konkana, Konkan.
Kosala, Oude (the province).
Kosee, Kosi.
Kousambi, Kosam.
Konsikee, Coosi.
Kousikee Kacchah, Purnea (the District).
Kramarajyam, Kamraj.
Krishna Venee, Krishna.
Kritha Kousika, Hyderabad (Western).
Krouncha, a mountain on the North of Assam.
Kulata, Kulu (the district).
Kumala, Gomul.
Kumarika, Comarin.
Kundinam, Bidar?
Kuntala, Hyderabad (S. Western).
Kuru, Delhi.
Kurujangalam, Merut (the division).
Kurukshetra, Panipat.
Kusasthalam, Kanouj.
Kusasthalee, Ramnagar?
Kusavate, Ramanagar.
Kusumapuram, Patna.

L

Ladha, Ahmedabad District.
Lakshanavati, Gaur.

Lalitapattanam, Lalitputtam.
Lampaka, Lamghah.
Langalinee, Naglaudi.
Lanka, an island in the Equator.
Lavana, Looni.
Loharam, Lahor.
Louhitya, Brahmaputra.

M

Madhumatee, Sind (a river in (Kashmir).
Madhupuram, Madhupur.
Madhura, Madura.
Madhyadesa, Central India.
Madra, Bhutan.
Madradesa, Rechma Doab (lower).
Madrishmati, Bheragur.
Magadha, Behar (South).
Magadhi, Pancham.
Mahakosee, Kosi.
Mahanadi, Phalgu.
Maharashtra, Hyderabad (West).
Mahapadmasaras, Walur Lake.
Mahee, Myhe.
Maheesura, Mysore.
Mahendragiri, Eastern Ghauts.
Mahodayam, Kanouj.
Mahotsvapuram, Mahobia.
Malada, Shahabad.
Malawa, Malwa.
Malayachala, Southern Ghauts.
Malayavara, Malabar.
Malinee, Bhagulpur (town).
Malinee, Paisunee.
Mallabhumi, Bankora.
Mallasthanam, Multan.
Malyavan, a mountain to the East of Mount Meru.
Mandakini, Paitan.
Manimantha, Salt Range.
Manipuram, Manipore.
Manjula, Manjira.
Marava, the Great desert.
Marucaccha, Baroach.
Mathura, Muttra.
Matsyadesa, Jeypore.
Mayapura, Mayapur.
Mekala, Omerakantak (the mount).
Mekaladrija, Nerbada.
Mekalakanya, Nerbada.
Mithila, Tirhut.
Modagiri, Moongyr.
Modapuram, Madawar?
Mohanee, Mehanee.
Murala, Kalindi.

N

Nagapattanam, Negapatam.
Nairanjina, Nilajan (a torrent).
Nalasetu, Adam's bridge.
Nanda, Alakanunda.
Nandinee, Oude (the town).
Nasikya, Nasik.
Nawadweepa, Naddea.
Neelachala, Nilachal (a hill).
Nepala, Nepal.
Nicchavi, Tirhut.
Nirvindhya, Parwati (West).
Nishada, the Bhil Country.

O

Oudhra, Northern Orissa.

P

Padmakshetra, one of the four sacred districts in Orissa.
Padmapura, Pampur.
Padmavati, Cuttack?
Padmavati, Pudma.
Pampa, Pannair?
Panchami, Panchan.
Panchanada, Punjab.
Panchavati, Nassik.
Panchapam, Punjab.
Panjagaram, Panna.
Parasika, Persia.
Parna, A Brahmin settlement between the Jamna and the Ganges.
Parnasa, Punnass, Punch (village).

Pariytatra, The central or western portion of the Vindhya mountains.
Pataliputra, Patna.
Patishtanam, Paitan.
Pattanam, Pattun.
Peetaseela, Hyderabad (in Sind).
Phalguh, Phalgu.
Phenagiri, A mountain on the north of the river Indus.
Pinakini, Pennar (river).
Poorvagunga, Nerbada.
Pondanya, Badaon.
Prabhasan, Pattan Somanath.
Pragjyotisha, Kamroop?
Pragjyotishapuram, Gauhati.
Prasthala, Pattala.
Prathudakam, Pehoa.
Prayaga, Allahabad (Province).
Preta kuta, Preta kula (Gaya).
Punahpuna, Punpun.
Pundra, the modern Bengal and Behar.
Pundravardhana, Pundua.
Punnyabhumi, Northern India.
Purania, Purnea (town).
Puri, Puri.
Purvambudhi, Bay of Bengal.
Pushkaram, Pokur.
Pushpapuram, Patna.

R

Radha, Western Bengal.
Raivataka, Girinar.
Rajagriham, Rajgar.
Rajamahendri, Rajamahendri.
Rajapuri, Rajoari.
Ramagunga, Ramgunga.
Ramahrida, Kurukshetra (the lake)?
Reva, Nerbada.
Rikshaparvata, Satpura mountains.
Rishigiri, Udayagiri (near Rajgur).
Rishikulya, Rishikulia.
Rodrana, Adams' peak.
Rohitam, Rohtak.
Ruma, Lake of Samber.
Rungapuram, Rangpore.

S

Sayadri, Siadree.
Sahyadri, Western Ghauts.
Saka, the country of the Scythyans.
Sakalam, Sangla,
Sakambhari, Samber.
Saketa, Ayodhya.
Salatura, Lavor.
Samanaswasa, Jumna.
Samasthale, Gangetic Doab.
Sankasyam, Sankesa.
Saprayoga, Hugra.
Saradanda, Choya, Chittang.
Saravati, do. do.
Sarayu, Sarju, Gogra.
Sarpika, Sai.
Satadru, Satlej.
Sayyanavat, Kurukshetra (lake)?
Seetakundam, Seetakund, near Moongir.
Setubundha, Adam's bridge.
Sibika, A district in Kashmir.
Simhala, Ceylon.
Sindhu, Sind (a river in Kashmir).
Sindhudesa, North Western Punjab.
Sirisham, Sirisa .
Sivi, Jetch Doab, (Lower).
Sitadru, Satlej.
Somodbhava, Nerbada.
Sona, Son.
Soudhadesa, Soonda (District).
Soudhapuram, Soona (town).
Sourandhra, Sarhind.
Sourashtra, Gujirat, Kattiwar.
Souveera, Jetch Doab (Upper).
Sowastha, Swat (District),
Sowasthavam, Swat (town).
Sowasthavee, Swat (river).
Sravasti, Sahet Mahet?
Srihatta, Sylhet.
Sreekshetram, Puri.
Srirungapattanam, Seringapatam.

Srighnu, Sug.
Sthanuteertham, Thaneswar.
Suhma, Western Bengal.
Sundarivana, Sunderbans.
Surapuram, Sopur.
Surasena, Muttra, (Province).
Suriakunda, Dekshinamanas.
Surparakum, Supa.
Swarnagramam, Sunargaon.
Swarnalee, Maudakinee.
Swarnarekha, Subunrakha.
Syandika, Sai.

T

Takhara, Tartary.
Tahkapuram, Taki (Punjab).
Talakotam, Talicut.
Tamalika, Tumlook.
Tamralipta, Tumlook.
Tamraparni, Tamarabari.
Tangana, Name of a people in the Upper part of the valley of Sarayu.
Tapatee, Taptee.
Tapee, Taptee.
Tilinga, Hyderabad (East).
Tirabhukti, Tirhut.
Tiryaksrota, Ravee?
Trigarta, Lahore.
Trigartam, Tehara.
Trilinga, Hyderabad (East).
Tripathaga, Ganges.
Tripuri, Tewar.
Trisrota, Ganges.
Tungabhadra, Tumbudra.
Tungavena, Tunga.
Turushka, Turkestan.

U

Uda, Orissa.
Udayagiri, Udayagiri in Orissa.
Udumbara, Cutch.
Ugra, Canara.
Ujayantha, Girinar.
Ujjayini, Ujjain.
Uluka, Kulu (District).
Upahalaka, Hyderabad (South West).
Urasa, Rush.
Useenara, Jetch (doab) Lower.
Ushkapuram, Uskara.
Utkala, Orissa.
Uttaramanasam, Uttaramanus (in Gaya).

V

Vahika, Punjab.
Vairadham, Bairat.
Vaisanti, Besara.
Vaitarani, Baitarinee.
Valabhi, Babri.
Vanaganga, Banganga.
Vanamalinee, Dwaraka (the old).
Vanavasi, Soonda (the District).
Vanga, East Bengal.
Vanjula, Manjira.
Varada, Baroda Murda.
Varahagiri, Baibargiri.
Varahamula, Barmula.
Varanasi, Benares.
Varana, Barna.
Varanavata, Allahabad.
Varanavatam, Baraon.
Vardhamana, Burdwan.
Varendra, Bengal (North).
Varnakulum, Warangal.
Varnava, Bunnoo.
Varnu, Kurum (the river).
Varunee, Kaleenadee (West).
Vatadhanam, Batnair.
Vatsadesa, Allahabad.
Vatsapattnam, Kosam.
Vedasruti, Sot, Suti.
Vedavati, Vadawatee.
Veerabhumi, Birbhum.
Vena, Wurna.
Venasangaga, Sanglee.
Vetravati, Betwa.
Vidarbha, Hyderabad (West)? Berar; Bidar?

Vidasmriti, Sot; Suti.
Videha, A District in the province of Behar (Ancient Mithila). The modern Tirhoot.
Vidiśa Bhilsa.
Vidyanagaram, Bijoynagar.
Vihara, Behar (Town).
Vikramapuram, Bikrampur.
Vindhayachala, Vindhaya mountains.
Vipasa, Beas.
Vipulagiri, Bipulgiri.
Viratanagaram, Bairat.
Visala, Ujjain.
Vishnupati, Ganges.
Vitastha, Jhelum.
Vouanya, Badaon.
Vrishabha, Viga?
Vyavaharagiri, Baibargiri.

Y

Yagapura, Yajpore.
Yaganapura, Yajpore.
Yamuna, Jamna.
Yamunadri, Jumunatri (peaks).
Yasohara, Jessore.
Yuyupuram, Tripan.

REFERENCES

1. Pañcasiddhāntika : The public will be exceedingly glad to hear that two copies of this splendid work on Astronomy, long supposed to have been lost, have been purchased by the Bombay Government and that G. Thibaut Phil. Dr. assisted by Pundit Suddhakara is preparing an edition and an English Translation of the work.

2. Bheda : this conjunction occurs when the disc of one of the planets appears eclipsed by that of the other planet.

3. Ullekha: this occurs when the disc of the one appears to rub against the disc of the other.

4. Aṁśumardana : this occurs when the light of the one mixes with the light of the other.

5. Asavya : this occurs when the planets are distinctly apart from each other.

6. Planetary conjunction, is known in Hindu Astronomy as Yuddha (fight) ; when a planet in conjunction, is to be deemed as suffering defeat or as triumphant, the author describes further on.

7. The commentator states, as a corollary to the above, that a planet in conjunction which might appear of small disc

or dim must be deemed to suffer defeat though he might be the northern planet.

Again as Venus is ever bright, he is generally the successful planet in conjunctions whether he happens to be the northern or southern planet according to Sūria Siddhānta and Pulisa Siddhānta.

CHAPTER 18

On the Moon's Conjunction with the Planets

1. If the moon should pass to the north of the constellations (wherever possible) and of the planets, her course is known as Pradakṣina (course from left to right). She will then cause prosperity to mankind; if on the other hand the moon should pass to the south of the stars and planets she will cause misery.

2. If the moon should pass to the north of Mars, powerful mountaineers will triumph in fight; the Kṣatriyas with their armies that march out for battle will prosper and crops will be abundant.

3. If the moon should pass to the north of Mercury, citizens will triumph in fight; crops will flourish; there will be mutual attachment among men and the royal treasuries will be full.

4. If the moon should pass to the north of Jupiter, citizens, Brahmins, the Kṣatriyas, learned men, acts of virtue and charity, the people of Madhyadesa will prosper and mankind in general will be happy.

5. If the Moon should pass to the north of Venus, treasuries, elephants and horses will flourish; bow-men that march out for fight will triumph and crops will prosper.

6. If the Moon should pass to the north of Saturn, the rulers of citizens will triumph in fight and the Scythians, the Bāhlīkas, the people of Sindh, the Pahlawas, and the Yavanas will be happy.

7. Generally if the Moon, suffering in no way, should pass to the north of the constellations and planets, the objects and persons presided over by them will prosper; if she should pass to their South, the same objects and persons will suffer miseries.

8. In other words the effects described, when the course of the Moon lies to the north of planets and stars will be reversed when her course lies to the south of such planets and stars. Thus have been described the effects to the Moon's conjunction with stars and planets. The conjunctions of the Moon with the stars and planets are not conjunction in fight but are mere meetings *known technically* as *Samāgamas*.

CHAPTER 19

On Planetary Years[1]

1. If the sun should be the lord of the year, month or day, there will be crops here and there, the forests will be full of wild, carnivorous animals seeking for prey; springs will yield but little water; rivers will fall; and diseases and medicine will not gain much in strength.

2. The heat of the sun will be felt intolerable even in the dewy season; clouds though resembling mountains in size will not yield much rain; the sky will be full of heavenly bodies of lost luster; ascetics and cows will be afflicted with miseries.

3. Princes will range over the land in military order with proud elephants, horses foot soldiers and other strength, armed with bows, swords, cudgels, and engaged in attacking countries as they march.

4. If the moon should be the lord of the year, the sky will be filled with clouds moving like mountains and of the color of black cobra, collyrium or the bee and filling the whole Earth with water and the sky with the roar of thunder.

5. The tanks will appear beautiful by the presence, in them, of the lotus and the white lily, the groves will be full of flower trees rendered charming by the humming of black bees. Cows will yield abundance of milk, and will thrive; and wives will please their husbands by acts of love for ever.

6. There will be an abundant growth of wheat, rice, barley and other grains and also of excellent sugar-cane; the towns and mines will flourish; the surface of the Earth will be marked by the construction of raised brick works over the sites of sacrificial rites, the sky will be filled with the sound of Vedic hymns chanted by persons engaged in such rites; and the Earth will be under the protection of good rulers.

7. If Mars should be the lord of the year there will be fear from destructive fires gaining in strength by the winds that blow

over them and consuming villages, towns and forests; mankind will suffer from the attacks of robbers, and there will be heard everywhere cries of distress and there will also be loss of property and cattle.

8. Though gigantic clouds might float together in the sky, they will yield little rain. Crops, even though they might be grown in wet places, will become dry and if they happen to grow and ripen at all, they will be cut and carried away by robbers.

9. Rulers will little attend to the protection of their subjects; bilious complaints will afflict mankind; there will also be deaths from snake bites and corps will suffer blight or be otherwise injured.

10. If Mercury should be the lord of the year, the arts of jugglery and sorcery will thrive; rogues will prosper; towns and villages will flourish; musicians, writers, mathematicians and persons skilled in the use of arms will abound in the land and rulers will exchange rare and valuable gifts.

11. Mankind will be truthful; Vedic studies will flourish; criminal courts will administer justice according to the code of Manu; there will be found students of the higher mataphysics—Yoga Vidyā and Brahma Jñāna—in many places seeking their way to Salvation and there will also be found students of Logic and the like sciences.

12. Buffoons, messengers, poets, children, hermaphrodites, makers of perfumes, *and* persons living on banks, over waters and in mountains will prosper; medicinal plants will thrive.

13. If Jupiter should be the lord of the year, the sound of Vedic hymns chanted aloud by Brahmins in sacrificial rites will fill the sky, cause distress to the enemies of the rites, and bring to the minds of the Devas that partake of the offerings.

14. Abundance of excellent crops will mark the Earth, large numbers of elephants, horses, cows and foot-soldiers will thrive; there will be an increase of wealth; mankind will be happy under the protection of just rulers and the Earth will assume an appearance quite as bright as the starry heavens.

15. The sky will be full of various huge clouds yielding

abundance of rain; crops will thrive and there will be prosperity in the land.[2]

16. If Venus should be the lord of the year, rice crops and sugar-canes will flourish, low grounds will be filled with rain water, tanks will appear beautiful on account of the lotus growing in them; and the Earth will assume an appearances quite as charming as a lady be-decked with jewels.

17. Rulers will achieve success in war; the sky will be filled with the sound of the joy of triumph from the soldiers of the army; all good men will be happy and wicked men will dwindle and perish; towns and villages will thrive and the Earth will be under the protection of just rulers.

18. The spring season will be marked by husbands frequently imbibing delightful honey (wine) in the company of their wives; pleasant music from the flute and the lyre will oft delight the ear and mankind will partake of their meals in company with visitors, friends and kinsmen and the god of love will revel in triumph.

19. If Saturn should be the lord of the year, the land will suffer from wicked men, bands of robbers and big wars; cows will perish; wealth will disappear; there will be heard the cries of people mourning for the death of their kinsmen in civil strife; severe epidemics will break out and afflict people.

20. Clouds will be dispersed by winds; trees will suffer from disease; the sky will be filled with dust concealing from view the discs of the Sun and Moon; tanks will became dry and rivers will fall.

21. Crops found growing here and there will perish for want of water; and in other places they will thrive only when fed by the slight rain sent down by Indra.

22. Generally if the Lord of the year should appear of small disc or dim or in his Neecha house or if he should suffer defeat in conjunction, he will not produce all the evil effects assigned to him. If he should be otherwise, the effects will be good. If a year already known to be a bad one (vide Ch. on Jupiter) should also be found bad under this Chapter, there will be an increase of adversity; if found good in both ways then, an increase of prosperity; if found to be both good and

bad, there will be a mixture both of prosperity and adversity.

REFERENCES

1. The rule is that the planet in whose week day the new-moon falls in the lunar month of Caitra is the regent of the year which then commences. This Chapter is written in beautiful Sanscrit.
2. The above are special effects for Jupiter ; to these must be added the effects described for the year in the Ch. on Jupiter.

CHAPTER 20

On Planetary Meetings[1]

1. People living in that quarter of the earth will suffer from weapons, from hunger and from other miseries in which direction a planet reappears after, or disappears by, its conjunction with the Sun.[2]

2. If when the planets meet so as to form a circle, a bow, a triangle, a rod, a citadel, a lance or a Vajrayudha[3] mankind will suffer from starvation, from drought and from war.[4]

3. The rulers of *those* parts of the earth will suffer from foreign invasions and be dispossessed of their countries by foreign princes which correspond to the quarters of the heavens in which the several planets are seen to meet as described above towards night fall.[5]

4. The objects and persons represented by the several asterisms in which the planets happen to meet will suffer; but if the discs of the planets should be bright and apart from one another there will be happiness in the land.

5. Planetary meetings are of five sorts known technically as 1. *Saṁvarta*, 2. *Samāgama*, 3. *Sammoha*, 4. *Samāja*, 5. *Sannipāta* 6. *Kośa*. We will now define these and state their effects.

6. If, in a single sign, Poura planets and Yāyi planets should meet together to the number of 4 or 5, the meeting is known as Saṁvarta. If either Rāhu or Ketu should join them the meeting is known as Sammoha.

7. If, in a single sign, there should meet either Poura planets or Yāyi planets, in either case the meeting is known as Samāja. If when Saturn and Jupiter meet, some other planets should join them, the meeting is known as Kośa.[6]

8. The meeting of a planet which reappears in the west with another planet which reappears in the east, after their con-

junction with the Sun is known as Sannipāta. If the meeting planets should suffer no change in their nature and should appear bright and of large size, the meeting is known as Samāgama. There will then be prosperity in the land.

9. The effects of the Saṁvarta and Samāgama meetings are indifferent—i.e. there will be neither much of prosperity nor much of adversity; the effects of the Sammoha and Kośa meetings are disastrous in their character; in the Samāja meeting there will be an equal degree of prosperity and adversity; and in the Sannipāta meeting, mankind will be at war with one another.

REFERENCES

1. This refers to the apparent geometrical Figures formed by the meeting of planets.
2. This accords with the opinion of Kaśyapa.
3. Vajrayudha : a three edged weapon narrow at the middle and broad at both ends.
4. Kaśyapa says that if the planets meet in other than certain well known figures mankind will be happy.
5. Lines drawn from Madhyadesa and from the Zenith to the eight points of the compass will divide both the Earth and the sky into eight equal parts and the Madhyadesa will correspond to mid-heaven.
6. This accords with the opinion of Badarayana ; but according to Parāśara if when Jupiter and one or two other planets meet, Saturn should join them, the meeting is known as Kosa.

CHAPTER 21

On the Rain Clouds[1]

1. As food is the support of life and food depends upon rain, it is important to discover the laws of rain by any means.

2. I will now proceed to state these laws in accordance with the views of Garga, Parāśara, Kāśyapa, Vatsa and others on the subject.

3. The predictions of an astronomer who pays exclusive attention, both day and night to the indications of rain afforded by pregnant clouds, will as little fail of success as the words of Ṛṣis.

4. What science can possibly excel, in interest, the science relating to the prediction of rain, by a thorough study of which one though ignorant in other matters passes for a great astrologer in this Iron Age.

5. Some[2] say that the days of the appearance of the pregnant clouds immediately follow the bright half of the lunar month of Kārtika—October and November. This view is not however in accordance with the views of many writers on the subject. We therefore will give here the views of Garga and others.

6. The days on which clouds are to be deemed pregnant commence from the day when the Moon reaches the Asterism of P. Āṣāḍha[3] on any of the lunar days from the first, of the bright half of the lunar month of Mārgaśirṣa—November and December.

7. If pregnant clouds appear when the Moon is in a certain Asterism the delivery of rain will fall 195 days after,[4] when the Moon will be in the same Asterism.

8. Clouds conceiving during the bright half will be delivered during the dark half of a lunar month and clouds conceiving during the dark half will be delivered during the bright half. Also clouds conceiving during the day will be delivered at

night and clouds conceiving at night will be delivered during the day; also clouds conceiving in the twilight of the morning will be delivered in the twilight of the evening and clouds conceiving in the twilight of the evening will be delivered in the twilight of the morning.[5]

9. Clouds that conceive in the bright and dark halves of the month of Mārgaśirṣa—November and December and in the bright half of Pauṣa—December and January—will be delivered of rain respectively in the dark half of Jyeṣṭha—May and June—and in the bright and dark halves of Āṣāḍha—June and July; but the fall of rain in these cases will only be moderate; and clouds that conceive in the dark half of Pauṣa will be delivered of rain in the bright half of Śrāvaṇa—July and August.

10. Clouds that conceive in the bright half of Māgha—January and February,—will be delivered of rain in the dark half of Śrāvaṇa and those that conceive in the dark half of Māgha will be delivered in the bright half of Bhādrapada—August and September.

11. Clouds that conceive in the bright half of Phālguna—February and March—will be delivered of rain in the dark half of Bhādrapada and those that conceive in the dark half of Phālguna will be delivered in the bright half of Āświna—September and October.

12. Clouds that conceive in the bright half of Caitra—March and April—will be delivered of rain in the dark half of Āświna and those that conceive in the dark half of Caitra will be delivered in the bright half of Kārtika—October and November.[6]

13. Clouds that conceive in the East will be delivered in the west and clouds that conceive in the west will be delivered in the east. The same rule holds with regard to the other directions and also with respect to the winds that appear both at the times of conception and delivery.[7]

14. If gentle and agreeable winds blow from the north, north east and east, if the sky should be clear, if the Sun and Moon should appear surrounded by bright, white, thick halos;

15. If the clouds should appear huge; bright, dense, or

shaped like a needle or a sword and red, if the sky should appear dark as the crow's egg, if the Moon and Stars should appear white;

16. If the twilight should be marked by the rainbow, by the low rumbling roar of thunder, by lightning, by the mock sun or parhelion, if it be of agreeable appearance, if groups of birds and animals should sound sweet music from the north, north east and east;

17. If the planets should appear of large bright disc, if their course should lie to the north of the constellations, if they should be free from abnormal affections, if the trees should grow well and be free from disease; if men and cattle should be happy;

18. These are indications of a healthy pregnancy; and in such cases the clouds will yield abundance of rain. We will now proceed to state the indications of a healthy pregnancy of rain clouds in the several seasons of year.

19. In the months of Mārgaśirṣa and Pauṣa, if the sky should appear very red just before sun-rise and just after sunset; if the clouds should appear surrounded by halos; if the month of Mārgaśirṣa should be found to be very cold and if the fall of snow should be excessive in the month of Pauṣa;

20. In the month of Māgha, if strong winds should blow, if the discs of the Sun and Moon should be dimmed by the fall of snow, if at rising and setting the Sun should be hid by clouds and it be then exceedingly cold;

21. In the month of Phālguna if strong and violent winds should blow, if fine clouds should be found marching from place to place, if broken or imperfect halos should appear in the sky, if the sun should appear of the color of gold or red;

22. In the month of Caitra if the sky should be marked by winds, clouds, rain and halos; in the month of Vaiśākha if there should be rain, lightning and thick clouds, in all these cases it may be concluded that the pregnancy of the clouds is a healthy one.

23. If the pregnant clouds should be of the color of pearls or silver or of the color of the bark of the Tamāla[8] tree or of

the blue lotus or of collyrium, they will yield abundance of rain.

24. If the pregnant clouds should be exposed to the hot rays of the sun, if they should be accompanied by gentle winds and appear as if covered by drops of rain, they will yield abundance of rain.

25. If the appearance of the pregnant clouds should be marked by meteoric falls, by thunder bolts, dust storms and the appearance of mock fires about the horizon; or if at the time of such appearance, clouds should present the shape of cities and towers and if spots should appear in the solar disc or if there should be planetary conjuctions at the time; or,

26. If there should be a shower of blood, if halos or rainbows should appear in the sky, if there should be a solar or lunar eclipse at the time, in all these cases the pregnancy will miscarry.

27. If the symptoms of a healthy pregnancy assigned for the several seasons of the year should fail, the pregnancy will miscarry and the clouds will yield little or no rain.

28. Clouds that conceive when the Moon is in the asterisms of P. Bhādrapada, U. Bhādrapada, P. Āṣāḍha and U. Āṣāḍha and Rohiṇī will yield abundance of rain.

29. Clouds that conceive when the Moon is in the asterisms of Śatabhiṣaj, Āśleṣa, Ardrā, Swātī and Maghā will yield rain continuously for several days unless the pregnancy should have suffered in any of the ways stated above.

30. Clouds that conceive when the Moon is in any one of the five asterisms referred to in the last stanza in the six months from Mārgaśirṣa to Vaiśākha, will yield rain respectively for 8, 6, 16, 24, 20, and 3 days continuously.[9]

31. If either the Sun or Moon should be attended by a malefic planet at the time of conception, the subsequent rainfall will be marked by hail, thunder, and fish. If, on the other hand, either the Sun or Moon should be attended by or within view of a benefic planet at the time of conception the rainfall will be abundant.

32. If there should be fall of heavy rain at the time of conception, the pregnancy will miscarry and there will be no

rain. This will be the case only when the quantity of rainfall exceeds one-eighth of a *Droṇa.*[10]

33. If, owing to adverse planetary influences, the pregnant clouds should fail to yield rain at the seasons described, they will do so at the period of the next conception and in such a case the rain will be marked by a shower of hail.

34. If milch animals should remain unmilked for a long period, the milk will become solidified; so, the rain which the clouds fail to yield at the proper season becomes congealed after a time in the sky.

35. If a healthy pregnancy should be established in the five ways given below (vide stanza 37), the rainfall will extend to 100 Yojanas (500 miles) all around. If one of the five indications be wanting, the extent will be reduced to one-half; if two should be wanting, to one-fourth, and so forth.

36. If the pregnancy should be marked by all the five indications, the quantity of subsequent rainfall will be a Droṇa; if in such a case the rain should be attended by strong winds, the quantity will only be 3 *Āḍhakas*[11]; if by lightning, the quantity will be 6 āḍhakas : if then the sky should be over cast by clouds, the quantity of rainfall will be 9 Āḍhakas; if there should be the roar of thunder then 12 āḍhakas of rain will fall.

37. The signs of a healthy pregnancy are winds, rain, lightning, roar of thunder and the appearance of clouds at the time of conception; in such a case the subsequent rain fall will be abundant; but if the rain fall should be excessive at the time of conception, there will only be a poor drizzling shower during the rainy season.

This Chapter enables us to determine before hand the time, duration, place, extent, quantity and quality of rain fall. As rain is a subject of vital importance, the value of a foreknowledge of the agricultural prospects of the country can never be over estimated. The several civilized Governments will therefore do well, having a due respect for the wisdom of the ancient Hindu Sages, to call upon their Meteorological departments to study this Chapter and Chapters 22 to 28 and submit a report on the future prospects of the land, by way of testing the truth of the statements above made. Government Astronomers may also be directed to submit similar reports on the future condition of the Earth and of mankind at large, judging from the various phases of the Moon, courses and conjunctions of the planets, the appearance of comets and so forth. This appears to us to be a wiser mode of governing the country than being taken by surprise by the actual occurrence of famine and drought and than trying to move Heaven and Earth to redress their miseries—not unlike the Turk Athlete who, unable to anticipate the impending blow of his adversary, raises his weapon in its direction only after it has fallen heavily every time.

REFERENCES

1. The main idea in this Chapter is that clouds that appear in certain seasons of the year are to be deemed as pregnant clouds and that they yield rain at particular times and places.
2. Some : Siddhasena and men of his School.
3. P. Āṣāḍha *or* the first quarter of U. Āṣāḍha according to commentator.
4. i.e. fully 7 months after, as the siderial period of the Moon is exactly 27 days, 7 hours, 43 minutes, 11.4 seconds. This Stanza enablas us to determine the very day of the occurrence of rain.
5. The Commentator adds : clouds conceiving at mid-day will be delivered at mid-night and *vice versa*. In all these cases the interval between conception and delivery is of course 195 days. This stanza enables us to determine the very hour of the occurrence of rain fall.
6. These stanzas enable us to determine the particular fortnight of the fall of rain.
7. This stanza enables us to determine the direction of the fall of rain.

8. Tamāla : a tree with a very dark bark and with white blossoms—Xantho chymus Pictorius.

9. This enables us to determine the duration of rain.

10. A Droṇa is equal to 200 phalas. The stanza implies that the measurement should be made by means of a rain gauge which ought to be a circular vessel with a mouth, a cubit in diameter.

11. Āḍhaka : *āḍhaka* is one fourth of a droṇa or 50 phalas.

CHAPTER 22

Rain Support Days

1. The four days commencing from the eighth day in the light half of the month of Jyeṣṭha—May and June—are known as Vāyu Dhāraṇa Days, that is, days from the winds that blow on which the nature of the health of the pregnancy of the rain-clouds might be determined. If the winds should be gentle and agreeable and then, if the sky should be covered by fine, bright clouds, there will be good rain.

2. But if, in the said light half of Jyeṣṭha, there should be a fall of rain in the four days when the Moon passes through the asterism of from Swātī to Jyeṣṭha, there will be rain in the rainy season—from Śrāvaṇa to Kārtika—August to November.

3. If the four Dhāraṇa days should be exactly alike in their indications, there will be happiness in the land; if different from one another, there will be misery, and there will also be fear from robbers; we have the recorded opinion of Vaśiṣṭha to the same effect.

4. If on the Dhāraṇa days the Sun and Moon should be covered by wet clouds attended by lightning and dust storm, there will be good rain.

5. If on the Dhāraṇa days the sky should be marked by beautiful lightning alternately appearing in opposite benefic quarters, every species of crop will thrive.

6. If on the same days there should fall a shower of rain attended by dust storm or if children should in play blow through their mouths or birds sing or play in the dust or in water; if the halos round the Sun and Moon should appear bright and not much disfigured there will be rain and all crops will thrive.

7. If on the Dhāraṇa days, the clouds should appear beautiful and collected together with their course from left to right, there will be immediate rain and such rain will be exceedingly useful to the crops.

CHAPTER 23

On Rain

1. Judging from the rain that falls on the days when the Moon passes from the asterism of P. Āṣāḍha to that of Mūla in the lunar month of Jyeṣṭha and after the full-moon, an astronomer should predict the agricultural condition of the country as well as the quantity of rain-fall in the coming rainy season.

2. Falling rain should be collected in a vessel with a circular mouth, a cubit in diameter and the collected rain should be measured with a vessel whose capacity is an Āḍhaka, which is equal to 50 phalams.[1]

3. There will be continuous rain for as many days of the Moon's course from P. Āṣāḍha onwards (in the rainy season) as the number of asterisms, through which when the Moon passes, a shower of rain occurs just marking the Earth, from the same asterism of P. Āṣāḍha in the lunar month of Jyeśṭha, or there will be rain for as many days as the number of rain drops sticking to the edge of the blades of grass The quantity of subsequent rain-fall can also be ascertained from such rain.[2]

4. Some writers say that the subsequent rain-fall will be confined to the spot where the first shower falls; others say that the extent of the subsequent rain-fall will be 10 Yojanas—50 miles—all round; but according to Garga, Parāśara and Vasiṣṭha the extent is 12 Yojanas.

5. If there should be rain when the Moon passes through certain asterisms from P. Āṣāḍha to Mūla in the lunar month of Jyeṣṭha then there will also be rain when the Moon passes through the same asterisms in the rainy season. If there should be no rain in the month of Jyeṣṭha, there will be no rain in the rainy season.

6. If there should be a fall of rain when the Moon passes through the asterisms of Hasta, P. Āṣāḍha, Mṛgaśīras, Chitrā, Revatī, and Śraviṣṭha in the month of Jyeṣṭha, there

will fall 16 droṇas of rain in the coming rainy seoson. If there should be a fall when the Moon passes through Śatabhiṣaj, Jyeṣṭhā, and Swātī, in the month of Jyeṣṭha, the subsequent rain-fall will be 4 droṇas. If there should be a fall when the Moon passes through Kṛttika, the quantity of subsequent rain-fall will be 10 droṇas.

7. If there should be a fall of rain when the Moon passes through Śravaṇa, Meghā, Anurādhā, Bharaṇī and Mūla, the quantity of subsequent rain-fall will be 14 droṇas. If when through P. Phalgunī, the quantity will be 25 droṇas; if when through Punarvasu, the quantity will be 20 droṇas.

8. If there should be a fall of rain, when the Moon passes through the asterisms of Viśākhā and U. Āṣāḍha in the lunar month of Jyeṣṭha; the quantity of subsequent rain-fall will be 20 droṇas; if when through Āśleṣa, the quantity will be 13 droṇas; if when through U. Bhādrapada, U. Phalgunī and Rohiṇī, the quantity will be 25 droṇas.

9. If there should be fall of rain when the Moon passes through the asterisms of P. Bhādrapada and Puṣya in the lunar month of Jyeṣṭha, the quantity of rain-fall in the coming winter will be 15 droṇas; if when through Aświni, the quantity will be 12 droṇas; if when through Ārdā it will be 18 droṇas. In all the above cases the subsequent rain-fall depends upon the asterisms remaining unaffected by comets, meteors and the like from the month of Jyeṣṭha to the rainy season.

10. If the asterisms should suffer by the meeting together in them of the Sun, Saturn and Ketu (descending node of the Moon) or by the course of Mars through them or by meteoric falls, comets or planetary conjuctions, there will be neither rain nor prosperity in the land; but if benefic planets should pass through the asterisms or if the asterisms should remain unaffected in any of the ways described above mankind will be happy.

REFERENCES

1. Parāśara defines an Āḍhaka to be the capacity of a vessel with a circular mouth 20 inches in diameter and whose depth in 8 inches.
2. If such first shower should be excessive there will be no rain in the rainy season.

CHAPTER 24

On Rohiṇī Yoga[1]

1. The grove of Mount Meru was rendered agreeable by the humming of bees sipping honey from the flowers of trees growing between rocks of gold, by the sweet music of birds at play and by the melodious voice of the Sylvan fairies.

2. It was in such a grove of Mount Meru—the abode of the Devas—that Nārada communicated to Bṛhaspati the laws of Rohiṇī Yoga; the same laws have since been taught by Garga, Parāśara, Kāśyapa and Maya to numbers of their disciples.

3. Having examined these truths I propose to write a brief treatise on the same adopting the same views.[2]

4. It is part of an astronomer's duty to examine the weather indications on the day when the Moon passes through the asterism of Rohiṇī in the dark half of the lunar month of Āṣāḍha-June—July—and to predict scientifically the future condition of the land.

5. The astronomer should be able to determine before hand the time of the Moon's entry into the asterism of Rohiṇī. I have treated of this subject in my work on astronomy. The astronomer must base his conclusions on the nature of the effects of Rohiṇī yoga, on the size, gloss, color and course of the Moon and by the appearance of any comets or fall of any meteors at the time.

6. The astronomer shall choose a suitable station immediately to the North-east of his town, shall spend[3] 3 days in the worship of fire,[4] shall draw out a figure of the constellations with the planets in them and shall worship it with flowers, perfumed smoke and by gifts and sacrifices.[5]

7. He shall also prepare a raised platform, cover it with Kusa grass and place in the four points—N. E. S. and W.—

four pots[6] filled with water, precious stones and medicinal herbs, covering the mouths with tender leaves.

8. He shall then procure every species of seed, charm them by means of the Mahāvrita Mantra (referred to in the Adharvana Veda,) wet them with water rendered pure by contact with gold and kusa grass and gently put them layer over layer in a broad mouthed central pot and shall perform homa in honor of the Gods Vāyu (the wind), Varuṇa (rain), and Soma (the Moon.)

9. He shall, beforehand, ascertain and mark out the several points of the compass and, planting vertically a flag staff—the stick being straight and thrice the length of the cloth which shall be thin, fine and of black color—he shall ascertain the direction of the wind at the time when the Moon enters the asterism of Rohiṇī.

10. He shall divide the day on which the Moon enters the asterism of Rohiṇī into 8 equal parts (of 3 hours each) commencing from sun-rise—the parts representing severally the eight fortnights of the four months of the rainy season from Śrāvaṇa to Kārtika; and he shall determine on which month or fortnight and how long there will be rain judging from the direction and duration of the wind. If the wind should blow from left to right there will be prosperity in the land; if it should blow in some fixed direction, people living in that direction will be happy.[7]

11. After the Moon has passed through Rohiṇī, the astronomer shall examine the seeds; those that bear sprouts will thrive well in the year and the quantity that will be harvested will be in proportion to the quantity that have sprouted, in the case of each species of seed.

12. After the Moon has passed through the asterism of Rohiṇī, if there should be heard in every direction the sweet sound of birds and of animals, if the sky should be clear and the wind agreeable there will be prosperity in the land. We shall now proceed to state the effects of winds and clouds.

13. If, on the Rohiṇī yoga day, huge clouds, serpentlike in shape, should appear white-black in certain parts of the sky, white in certain parts and black in certain other parts with the

lightning for their tongues and if the clouds should be collected and appear twisted together;

14. If they should appear of the color of the nut of the lotus, if their neighbourhood should be illumined by the light of the Sun, if clouds of various hues should fill the sky or if they should appear of the color of the bee, of crimson or of the flower Kiṁśuka[8] ;

15. If the sky should be full of black clouds and if it be marked by lightning or beautiful rainbow thus presenting the appearance of a forest full of elephants, buffaloes and wild fire ;

16. If the clouds appear like black mountains or rocks or if their color should resemble that of the snow, pearls, conch, shells, and the Moon ;

17. Or if the clouds should be like elephants—with the lightning for the rope of gold, the flying cranes for the tips of their tusks, the rain for their juice (ichor), their sides moving like the sides of the elephants, with the rainbow for their flags of various hues, their dark color resembling that of the bark of the tamāla tree and the bee ;

18. If, immediately before sun-rise and after sun-set, the clouds should appear of the color of the blue lotus and, with the lightning, resemble the dark Viṣṇu dressed in cloth of gold ;

19. If there should be heard the sound of the peacock, of cātaka and of the frog, together with the roar of thunder clouds filling the whole of the visible sky ;

20. If the sky should be overcast by clouds as described above for 3 days or 2 days or a single day, there will be abundance of rain and mankind will be happy.

21. If, on the other hand, the clouds should be of disagreeable appearance, of small size, and dispersed by the wind or if they should be of the shape of the camel, the crow, dead bodies, the monkey and the like[9] and if they should at the same time remain mute, there will be no rain and mankind will not be happy.

22. If, on the Rohiṇī Yoga day, the sky should be clear and without clouds and the Sun exceedingly hot, there will be rain in the rainy season. If on the night of the Yoga day, the

sky with its glittering stars should resemble a tank with its lilies, there will also be rain.

23. If on the Rohiṇī Yoga day, clouds should first appear in the East, crops will thrive well. If they should appear in the South-east, destructive fires will afflict man-kind ; if in the South, the crops will suffer blight; if in the South-east, one half of the crops will suffer and if in the West, there will be good rain.

24. If the clouds should appear in the North-west there will be rain in some places and such rain will be attended by the wind ; if they should appear in the North, there will be good rain and if in the North-east, crops will thrive. The same effects are to be assigned to the winds blowing from the several quarters.

25. If on the Rohiṇī Yoga day there should be meteoric falls, lightning, thunder bolts, mock fires, and cometary and other unusual appearances, or if there should be earthquakes or if the sounds of birds and animals should be hoarse and disagreeable there will be no rain and mankind will not be happy.

26. If, on examining, the waters of the four pots from the north representing the four months from Śrāvaṇa should be found full there will be good rain in the several months ; if in any pot the water should have oozed out completely, there will be no rain in the month it represents and if incompletely, there will be a proportionate decrease in the quantity of the rainfall.

27. If it should be desired to ascertain the fate of any sovereign or country during the year, there should be placed fresh pots each to represent a sovereign or a country. If on examining, any of these pots should be found split or broken, the sovereign or the country represented will suffer miseries ; if the water should have disappeared, then also they will suffer and if full, they will be happy.

28. If the course of the Moon should lie to the South of the stars of the Rohiṇī group whether near or far,[10] mankind will be afflicted with miseries.

29. If the Moon should pass just touching the Northern most star of the group, there will be good rain, but there will also

be miseries ; if she should pass to the north of the group and not in contact with it there will be abundant rain and mankind will be happy.

30. If the Moon should enter the Rohiṇī group and pass through its centre, mankind will be rendered helpless and, troubled by the cries of children for food, they will travel to foreign lands, drinking the waters of muddy pools from their broken bowls.

31. If on the night of the Rohiṇī Yoga day the Moon, should rise first[11] and the group immediately next after it, there will be happiness in the land and women will become amorous and subject to the influence of men.

32. If on the other hand the Rohiṇī group should rise first and the Moon next after it,[12] men will become amorous and subject to the influence of women.

33. If on the night of the Yoga day the Moon at rising should be found to the South-east of the group, mankind will suffer miseries ; if she should be found to the South-west of the group, crops will suffer injuries in various ways ; if on the West and North-west the growth of the crops will be moderate ; and if in the North-east the crops will thrive.

34. If on the Yoga day, the Moon should pass in contact with the Yogatārā[13] (junction star) of the group, mankind will be tormented with various fears ; if the Yogatārā should be eclipsed by the Moon, the reigning sovereign will be assassinated by a woman.

35. If, towards nightfall, on the Rohiṇī Yoga day, when cattle, led out in the morning, re-enter the town, the first animal so entering should be either an ox or a goat, there will be abundant rain ; if it should be an animal black-white in color there will be moderate rain—if in the last case the black color should predominate the rainfall will be abundant and if the white color should predominate there will be no rain. If the animal that enters first should be of any other color there will be slight rain.[14]

36. If on the Rohiṇī Yoga day, the Moon should be rendered invisible by the intervention of thick clouds, mankind will suffer from severe diseases ; but there will be abundant rain and crops will thrive.

REFERENCES

1. Rohiṇī Yoga : This means the period of a day when the Moon passes through the asterism of Rohiṇī in the dark half of the lunar month of Āṣāḍha.
2. These prefatory remarks clearly show that what follow are important scientific truths in the eyes of Hindu astronomers : that the weather indications of one single day in a year should form the subject of so muco calculation with the Hindus in determining the future agricultural prospect of the land while to the inexperienced eye of a Western man of science, the day appears as indifferent or otherwise as any other day of the year argues that modern science is still far behind in her investigations of the laws of nature.
3. Fasting according to Garga.
4. By Gāyatrī homa according to the same authority.
5. According to Garga, the astronomer should observe these religious coremonies on the 8th lunar day of the dark half of Aṣāḍha.
6. The pots represent from the North the four months from Śrāvaṇa to Kārtika.
7. According to Garga the day alone, and not the night, should be divided into four equal parts to represent the four months of the rainy season and the observation should also be made during the day.
8. Kiṁśuka : the tree Butea Frondosa, a tree bearing beautiful red blossoms.
9. Like rats, dogs, etc., according to commentator.
10. This will unusually be the case astronomically, according to commentator.
11. That is, if the Moon's conjunction with Rohiṇī should take place immediately after rising.
12. That is, if the conjunction should have taken place immediately before rising.

13. Yogatārā : This is *generally* the brightest of the group.

14. These views accord with those of Garga, but Parāśara adds :

If an elephant, a horse or a chariot should enter the town first in the evening of the Rohiṇī Yoga day, there will be success in war; if a monkey, an ass, a camel, a mongoose, a cat or a dog should so enter there will be troubles. If a blindman should enter first, there will be fear from thunderbolts.

CHAPTER 25

On Swāti Yoga[1]

1. All that has been said with respect to Rohiṇī Yoga apply to both Swāti and Āṣāḍhī Yogas[2]; and but in the present chapter we shall only state certain special effects connected with Swāti Yoga.

2. Dividing both the day and night of the Swāti Yoga day each into three equal parts, if at night there should be a fall of rain during the first division, all the crops will flourish ; if during the second division, gingelly, kidney bean and black gram will thrive and if during the third division, the crops of Grīṣma will thrive and those Śarat will perish.

3. If there should be a fall of rain during the first division of the day, there will be abundant rain in winter ; the same remark applies to the second and third division ; but in these two cases worms and serpents will afflict mankind. If there should be a fall of rain throughout the day and night there will be uninterrupted rain for several days in winter.

4. To the due north of Citra[3] there is a star known as Apāṁvatsa. If the Moon should pass near it mankind will be happy.

5. If there should be a fall of snow on the dark night of seventh lunar day of the dark half of the month of Māgha—January and February, or if a strong wind should blow or if dripping clouds should roar uninterruptedly or if there should be constant lightning or if the Sun, Moon and Stars should be wholly concealed by the clouds, mankind will be happy and crops will thrive.

6. The same remarks apply to the Swāti Yogas occurring in the months of Phālguna (February and March) Caitra (March and April) and Vaisākha (April and May.) But of the Swāti Yogas, that occurring in the month of Āṣāḍha (June and July) is the most important.

REFERENCES

1. Swāti Yoga : This means the period of a day when the Moon passes through the asterism of Swāti in the month of Āṣāḍha.
2. Vide Chapter 26.
3. At a distance of about 5°.

CHAPTER 26

On Āsāḍhī Yoga[1]

1. On the day when the Moon passes through the asterism of U. Āṣāḍha in the lunar month of Āṣāḍha, the Jyotiṣaka shall weigh quantities of all seeds; if on weighing them again on the next day, any seeds should be found to weigh more, those crops will flourish ; is they should be found to weigh less, they will not grow at all. There are mantras to be addressed to the weighing machine while weighing.

2. Minerva, Goddess of Truth, thou art deserving of praise. Thou art now going to show that which is truth. O Truth, thou art ever truthful.

3. O Truth by whose might the Sun, the Moon, the planets and the stars rise in the East and set in the West, thou wilt show now.

4. That truth which is in all the Vedas, that truth which is spoken of by those that know Brahma and that truth which is to be found in the three worlds.

5. Thou art the daughter of Brahma ; thou art sung as Ādityā ; thy Gotra (family) name is Kaśyapa and thy simple name is Tulā (weighing machine.)

6. The Jyotiṣaka shall take two square pieces of white silk, the side being six inches long, and attach the four ends of each to the ends of four strings each ten inches long ; the length of the string attached to the middle of the beam shall be six inches.

7. He shall put gold weights in the Southern (right) scale and the several articles to be weighed in the Northern (left) scale ; waters to be weighed shall also be put into the northern scale ; if well water should be found to weigh more when weighed the next day, there will be no rain in winter ; if rain water should weigh more there will be moderate rain ; if

tank or lake water should weigh more there will be abundant rain.

8. The condition of elephants shall be determined by (weighing) their tusks; that of cows and horses by their hair; that of princes by gold, that of Brahmins and others by wax; that of countries, years, months and days shall also be determined by the wax, and that of other articles by the articles themselves.

9. Gold is the best material for making the beam of the balance; silver is of middle importance; if these two cannot be had, the beam may be of blackwood; it may also be of that arrow iron which was employed in killing a man. The length of the beam shall be twelve inches.[2]

10. That article which should be found to weigh less when weighed again will perish; that which weighs more will flourish; that which weighs neither more nor less will neither perish nor decay. These are the secret laws relating to the balance and these may also be followed on the occasion of the Rohiṇī Yoga day.[3]

11. In the Swāti, Āṣāḍhī and Rohiṇī Yogas, if the Moon should be accompanied by malefic planets, there will be misery in the land. If on account of the intervention of the intercalary lunar month, the Yoga day should occur twice, the observation shall be made on both the days and the effect, whether good or bad will be doubled.

12. If the observations of the three Yogas point to effects of the same character, the prediction may be made without hesitation; but if the effects are different, those of Rohiṇī Yoga should be adopted.

13. If on the Yoga day the wind should blow from the East, South-east, South, etc., there will be growth of crops, fear from destructive fires, slight rain, moderate rain, abundant rain, excessive rain attended by storms, good rain, and excellent rain respectively.

14. If there should be rain on the fourth lunar day of the dark half immediately following the Āṣāḍhī yoga day when the Moon is in the asterism of P. Āṣāḍha, the rainy season will be a prosperous one but not otherwise.

15. If on the Full-Moon Āṣāḍhī yoga day, the wind should blow from the North-east after sunset, crops will flourish.

REFERENCES

1. This means the period of a day when the Moon passes through the asterism of U. Āṣāḍha in the lunar month of Āṣāḍha—June-July.
2. An inch is the space covrdee over by 8 grains of barley placed side by side—or that of 3 grains of barley placed length-wise. It is also the breadth of the human finger.
3. Also on the Swāti Yoga day according to commentator.

CHAPTER 27

On the Winds

1. If, immediately after sunset, and on the Āṣāḍhī yoga day, there should blow the East wind, fresh from its contact with the waves of the east sea, warmed by the rays of the setting sun and cooled by the rays of the rising moon, the rainy season will be marked by dark dense clouds in all directions, and the crops of autumn and of spring will flourish.

2. If *then* there should blow the South-east wind from the Malaya hills there will be fear from destructive fires every where and the Earth will be covered with the ashes of objects consumed by such fires.

3. If *then* there should blow the South wind through forests in the branches of whose trees the monkeys swing as they are moved by the wind, the clouds, being forced by the winds, will yield as little rain as the elephant yields the juice of rut when struck with the driver's hook or a miser his wealth when well-beaten.

4. If, immediately after sunset on the Āṣāḍhī yoga day, there should blow the South-west wind, sweeping into the sea the cardamom and clove fruits, the Earth will be filled with the bones of those that die from want of food and drink and the appearance of the Earth will resemble that of a young lady just losing her husband.

5. If *then* the West wind should blow raising up dust clouds from the ground, crops will flourish; the chief rulers will engage in war and the Earth will be covered with the blood and flesh of those that are killed in battle.

6. If immediately after sunset on the Āṣāḍhī yoga day, the North-west wind should blow strong and fast, the Earth will put on a smiling and happy appearance from excellent rain, frogs will be heard croaking in all directions; there will

be one unbroken scene of green crops everywhere as far as the eye can reach and perfect prosperity will reign over the land.

7. If at the time when the Grīṣma season just comes to a close[1], the North wind should blow charged with the odour of the fragrant flowers of the Kadamba[2] tree, the Earth will be covered with water from clouds whose various hues will appear beautiful by the light of lightning, the Moon being invisible at the same time.

8. If the cool North-east wind should blow aloud, being felt agreeable by the Devas themselves, and charged with the odour of the flowers of Punnāga[3] of Agaru[4] and of Pārijāta[5] there will be good rain and crops will flourish; mankind will be under the protection of good rulers triumphant over their enemies.

REFERENCES

1. i.e. just after sunset on the full moon day of the lunar month of Āṣāḍha.
2. The tree Nauclea Kadamba, a tree with orange colored fragrant blossoms.
3. Punnaga : name of a tree, Rollievia Tinctoria (from the blossoms of which a yellowish dye is prepared).
4. Agaru : Agellochum, Amyris Agallocha (already explained).
5. Pārijāta : The coral tree.

CHAPTER 28

On Immediate Rain

1. If, in the rainy season when the astrologer is questioned about rain, the Moon should be in one of the watery signs[1] and if that sign should at the same time be either the rising sign or the fourth, the seventh or the tenth sign from it, it being then the light half of the month, there will be abundance of immediate rain; if it be the dark half of the month and the Moon in one of the watery signs and within sight of benefic planets, there will also be abundance of immediate rain; if, in the latter case, the Moon should be within sight of malefic planets, there will be slight rain. The same rules apply to Venus as to the Moon.

2. If the questioner, at the time should happen to touch a wet substance or any substance one of the meanings of whose name is water or if he should be at the time close to water or engaged in work connected with water or if at the time the word '*water*' should be heard from anybody, immediate rain may safely be predicted.

3. If, in the rainy season, the rising sun should appear dazzling or of the color of molten gold or glossy or bright as the cat's eye (gem) or if the mid-day Sun should be felt exceedingly hot, there will be rain that day before Sunset.

4. If, in the rainy season, the water should be without flavor or the sky of the color of the cow's eye or clear and without clouds or if salt should turn into water or if the color of the sky should be that of the crow's egg or if the atmosphere should be still and no wind should blow or if the fish should be found to jump from water on the bank or if the frog should be heard to croak incessantly, there will be immediate rain.

5. If the cat should be found to scratch the ground with

its claws, if metallic dross should be found to be of bad smell or if children should erect banks and bridges in the street with earth out of play, there will be immediate rain.

6. If mountains should appear black like collyrium, if the caves should be felt very warm or if the lunar halo should appear like the color of the eye of the cock, there will be immediate rain.

7. If the ant, when undisturbed and of its own accord, should leave its hole with its egg, if serpents should be found to copulate or to climb up trees, there will be immediate rain.

8. If the blood-sucker (lacerta cristata) should be found to stare at the sky from the tops of trees, or if cows should raise up their heads and look at the Sun there will be immediate rain.

9. If the sheep should be found reluctant to go out, if they should shake their ears or kick with their legs or if dogs should be found to do the same, there will be immediate rain.

10. If dogs should be found to get to the tops of houses, if they should look at the sky all round, or if during the day lightning should appear in the North-east, their will be immediate rain and the Earth will be covered with water.

11. If the Moon should be of the color of the eye of a parrot or a dove or of the color of honey or if the mock-moon should be green, there will be immediate rain.

12. If the sound of thunder should be heard at night, and lightning, red and straight like a rod, should appear during the day, or if the cool east wind should blow, there will be immediate rain.

13. If the tender leaves of plants and creepers should be found to grow with their heads pointed to the sky, if birds should be found to bathe in watery particles or if serpents should be found to rest on grass blades, there will be immediate rain.

14. If the clouds which appear at sun-rise or at sun-set should be of the color of the peacock, parrot, the blue jay or chātaka (arculus melanoleucus), if they should be as glossy as the China rose or the lotus or if they should be of the shape of undulating waves, of mountains, of crocodiles, of a tortoise, of

the boar or of the fish, and if they should float layer over layer, there will be immediate rain.

15. If, all round, the clouds should appear white like chalk or the moon and in the centre black like collyrium or the bee and glossy, if they should be of various shapes and dripping drops of rain and presenting the appearance of a flight of steps, if they should appear in the East and move towards the West or appear in the West and move towards the East there will be immediate rain.

16. If at the time of sun-rise or sun-set, there should be seen in the sky the rainbow, clouds-rod like in shape, the mock sun or parhelion or the appearance known as Rohita (straight rainbow), or lightning or halo, there will be abundance of immediate rain.

17. If at the time of sun-rise or sun-set the sky should be of the color of the wings of the partridge, or if there should be heard the sound of birds at play, there will be immediate rain and such rain will continue throughout the day and night.

18. If at the time of sun-set, the white straight rays of the sun should shoot out as if they formed so many out-stretched arms of the western ghauts and if clouds about the horizon should then begin to roar, there will be abundance of rain.

19. If, in winter, the Moon should be in the seventh house from Venus and within view of benefic planets, or if she should be in the 9th, 5th or 7th house from Saturn (also within view of benefic planets) there will be immediate rain.

20. Generally there will be rain at the periods of heliacal rising and setting of the planets, planetary conjunctions, of new and full moons, when the Sun is at the end of his ayans (course to the North or South) and when the Sun is in the asterism of Ārdrā.[2]

21. There will be rain if Mercury and Venus, or Mercury and Jupiter, or Venus and Jupiter should meet; if Saturn and Mars should meet and if they should not be accompanied by or within view of benefic planets there will be fear from storms and fire.

22. If the planets should be close to the Sun, either all to its east or all to its west the rain fall will be so great that the earth will be buried under one sea of water.

REFERENCES

1. Watery Signs : These are Kataka (cancer), Kumbha (Aquarius), Mīna (Pisces), the latter half of Kanyā (Virgo) and of Makara (Capricornus).
2. From about the 20th of June to the 3rd of July.

CHAPTER 29

On Flowers and Plants

1. Judging from the growth of the fruits and flowers of trees and plants we may determine beforehand what articles can be had cheap and in abundance and what crops will thrive.

2. If the Śāla tree should bear fruits and flowers, Kalama (white rice) will grow in abundance; if the red Aśoka should bear fruits and flowers red paddy will grow; if the Kṣīrikā should bear fruits and flowers white paddy will grow and if the black Aśoka should bear fruits and flowers black rice will grow.

3. The growth of the Nyagrodha (the Banyan tree) indicates the growth of Yava (barley); the growth of Tinduka indicates the growth of the Ṣaṣṭika rice; and the growth of the Aśwatha indicates the growth of all crops.

4. The growth of the Jambū (the rose apple) tree indicates the growth of the gingelly and black gram; the growth of Śiriṣa indicates the growth of the Kaṅgu; the growth of Madhūka indicates the growth of wheat and the growth of the Saptaparṇa indicates the growth of the barley.

5. The growth of Atimuktaka (mountain ebony) and that of Kunda (cassia) indicate the growth of Karpasa (cotton); the growth of Asana indicates the growth of Sarśapa mustard (plant); the growth of Badari (Jajube tree) indicates the growth of Kuluttha, and the growth of Ciribiha indicates the growth of the Mudga.

6. If the Atasī (common flax), Vetasa (the ratan) and Palāśa trees should bear blossoms, Kodrava will thrive; if Tilaka should bear blossoms, conch shells, pearls and silver can be had in abundance and if Iṅguda should bear blossoms, Sana (hemp) will thrive.

7. The growth of Hasti Karṅa (castor oil-tree) shows that

elephants will thrive; that of Aśwa Karṇa shows that horses will thrive that of Patala (trumpet flower) shows that cows will thrive and the growth of plantains shows that goats and sheep will thrive.

8. If the Campaka should bear blossoms, gold can be had in aboundance; if the Bandhujīvaka should bear blossoms corals can be had in abundance, if Kuravaka should bear blossoms, diamonds can be had in abundance and if Nandikavarta should bear blossoms, cat's-eye (gem) can be had in abundance.

9. The growth of the Sindhuvāra indicates that pearls can be had in abundance; that of Kusumbha (Safflower) indicates that Kumkuma can be had in abundance, that of the red lotus indicates that rulers will prosper and that of the blue lotus indicates that ministers will prosper.

10. If Suvarṇapuṣpa (the globe amaranth) should blossom, Merchants will prosper; if the lotus should blossom, the Brāhmaṇas will prosper, if the white water lily should blossom priests will prosper and if Sougandhika (the blue lotus) should blossom the Commanders of armies will prosper and if the Arka plant should blossom, gold will become cheap.

11. If the Mango should thrive well, there will be prosperity in the land; if Bhallātaka (marking nut plant) should thri ve, there will be fear in the land; if the Pīlu tree should thrive there will be health in the land; if Khadira and Sami should thrive, there will be famine in the land; and if the Arjuna tree should thrive there will be good rain.

12. If Picumanda (the nimb tree) and Naga should bear blossoms, there will be prosperity in the land; if Kapittha should bear blossoms, there will be storm; if Nicula (Hijjal) should bear blossoms there will be drought and if Kuṭaja should bear blossoms there will be disease in the land.

13. If Durva (bent grass) or the Kusa grass should blossom, sugar-cane will thrive; if Kov idāra should blossom there will be fear from destructive fires; and if Śy āmalatā should blossom, prostitutes will prosper.

14. There will be good rain in those countries where trees, shrubs and creepers grow luxuriantly with glossy leaves un-

injured by worms, but if the leaves should be otherwise there will be little rain.

GLOSSARY OF INDIAN BOTANICAL TERMS

Arjuna, The tree terminalia Arjuna.

Arka, The plant Calotropis Gigantea.

Asana, Pterocarpus Bilobus.

Asoka, Jonesia Asoka. It is a tree of moderate size belonging to the leguminous class with magnificent red flowers.

Aswakarna, Vatica Robusta.

Aswattha, The holy fig tree; ficus religiosa.

Atasi, Common flax.

Atimuktaka, Mountain ebony.

Badari, Jajube tree.

Bandhujeeva, Pentapetes Phaenicea.

Bhallata, Marking nut plant, Cashewnut plant.

Champaka, Michelia Champaka.

Chiribilva, A tree, Dalbergia Arborea.

Durva, Bent grass, panic grass Panicum Dactylon.

Hastikarna, Castor oil tree.

Inguda, Name of a medicinal tree—Terminalia Catappa.

Jambu, The rose apple tree, Eugenia Jambolana.

Kalama, White rice growing in deep waters; it is sown in May and June and ripens in December or January.

Kangu, A kind of panic seed; Panicum Italicum.

Kapittha, Feronia Elphantum.

Karpasa, Cotton.

Khadira, The tree Acacia Catechu, having hard wood.

Kodrava, A species of grain eaten by the poor, Paspalum Scrobiculatum.

Kovidara, A tree Baubinia Veriegata.

Ksheerika, The fig tree.

Kulutha, A kind of pulse, docichos eniflorus.

Kumkuma, The plant and the pollen of the flower-Crocus Sativus.

Kunda, Cassia.

Kuravaka, Crimson species of amaranth.

Kusa, Poa Cynosuroides.

Kusumbha, Safflower, Carthamus Tinctorius.

Kutaja, variety of Jasmine.

Madhuka, Bassia Latifolia.

Mudga, A sort of kidney-bean Phaceolus Radiatus or Phaceolus Mungo.

Naga, The small tree with fragrant blossoms, Mesua Roxburgha.

Nandikavarta, A species of plant, Nerium coronarium.

Nichula, The tree Barringtonia Acutangula commonly called hijjal.

Nyagrodha, The Indian fig tree.

Palasa, Butea Frondosa.

Panduka, A species of rice.

Parijata, A shrub Nictanthes Tristis.

Patala, The trumpet flower tree.

Peelu, A tree; Dillenia Speciosa.

Pichumanda, The nimb tree.

Punnaga, Rottleria Tinctoria from the blossoms of which a yellowish dye is prepared.

Sala, The Sal tree probably the Diospyros Ebenaster furnishing timber.

Sami, Acacia Suma possessing a tough hard wood supposed to contain fire.

Sana, hemp; Cannabis Sativa.

Saptaparna, The tree Alstonia or Echites Scholaris.

Sarshapa, Mustard seed.

Shashtika, A kind of rice of quick growth ripening in about 60 days.

Sindhuvara, The tree Vitex Negundo.

Sireesha, Acacia Sirisa.

Sougandhika, The blue lotus.

Sukara, A species of rice.

Suvarnapushpa, the globe amaranth.

Syamalata, A medicinal plant, Periploca Indica, country Sarsaparilla.

Tilaka, A species of tree with beautiful flowers.

Tinduka, The tree Diospyros, Embryopteres.

Vetasa, The Ratan; calamus Rotang.

Yava, Barley.

CHAPTER 30

On Twilight Hours

1. That period which precedes the moment when the Sun has just half risen and that which succeeds the moment when the Sun has just half set, during which the stars are invisible is known as Sandhyākāla or twilight period. From the peculiar indications of this period effects may be predicted as follows.

2. These indications are connected with animals, birds, the wind, the halo, the parhelion or mock sun, the Parigha,[1] the Abhravṛkṣa,[2] the rainbow, the Gandharvanagara, the Solar rays, the Daṇḍa[3] and dust clouds, their gloss and color.

3. If during the period of twilight animals should continue to howl fearfully, the village will perish; if these animals remaining to the South of an army should so howl with their faces turned to the Sun, such army will meet with rain.

4. If either animals should remain quiet or the winds should blow gently on the north side of an army there will be wars in the land; if this should take place on the south side of an army such army will be reinforced; if it should take place on both sides there will be rain.

5. If at day break, birds and animals should howl with their faces turned to the Sun, the country will perish; if they should so howl on the South side of a town such town will fall into the hands of enemies.

6. If immediately before sun rise or after sun set violent winds should blow breaking the tops of towers, trees and houses, carrying sand and pebbles along their course, howling fearfully and bringing down birds in flight there will be misery in the land.

7. If during the twilight hours either gentle winds or no winds should blow, or if birds and animals should either sound gently or remain quiet there will be prosperity in the land.

8. If during the twilight hours such appearances as the Daṇḍa, lightning, clouds fish like in shape, parhelion, halos, the rainbow and the appearance known as Airāvata (an imperfect rainbow) and solar rays should appear bright and glossy there will be immediate rain.

9. If the rays of the rising or setting sun should be broken, of unequal lengths, destroyed partly, altered in appearance, not straight, turning to the left, thin, small, short, blunt or ineffectual and dim there will be drought and wars in the land.

10. If, when the sky is clear, the rays should shoot into the sky and should be clear, straight, long and turning to the right, there will be happiness in the land.

11. If the rays of the rising, setting or mid-day sun should be white, glossy, unbroken and straight, the rays are known as Amogha (excellent) rays.

12. If the color of the rays of the rising or setting sun should be a mixture of white, black and yellow, or red-white or black-white, or variegated or red or green, or of the color of gold, and if the rays should extend throughout the sky, there will be rain and there will also be slight fear after seven days.

13. If the rays of the rising or setting sun should be of the color of copper, the commander-in-chief dies; if they should be yellow and red, he will suffer miseries; if green, animals and crops will perish, and if of the color of smoke cows will suffer.

14. If red, mankind will suffer from wars and destructive fires; if white-red, there will be rain attended with winds; if of the color of ash, there will be no rain; if the rays be variegated in color or if the color should be a mixture of black and other colors, there will be slight rain.

5. If the dust raised by the wind at sunrise or sun-set should be very red or very black, and if such dust should appear to move in the direction of the sun, mankind will suffer from various diseases; if the dust should be white, there will be happiness in the land.[4]

16. Daṇḍa is an appearance in the sky of the shape of a rod caused by the wind bringing together clouds and solar

rays; if this should appear in the south-east, south-west, north-west or north-east, rulers will suffer miseries, if it should appear in the east, south, west or north, the Brāhmaṇas will suffer.

17. If it should appear at sunrise or sunset or midday (in one of the corners), there will be wars in the land; if it should be white, red, yellow, or black, the Brāhmaṇas, the Kṣatriyas, the Vaiśyas or the Śūdras will suffer respectively; countries to which the Daṇḍa points will also suffer.

18. If the appearance known as Abhrataru (cloud tree) should be seen with its ends of the color of coagulated milk, the body being black, and if it should conceal from view the midday-sun, there will be abundant rain; also if the clouds should appear of beautiful yellow color and thick at the bottom, the rainfall will be abundant.

19. If the appearance of Abhravṛkṣa should for some time move regularly and then disappear, the king that marches out for fight will perish; if it should appear like a young tree, princes and ministers will perish.

20. If the twilight sky should be of the color of the blue lotus, of the cat's-eye gem, or of the nut of the lotus, and if the sun should have either begun to rise or should not have set, there will be immediate rain.

21. If during the rainy season the twilight hours should be marked by the appearance of clouds shaped malefically,[5] if the clouds should assume shapes known as Gandharva-nagara (Air Castles), and if the sky should be filled with snow, dust and smoke, there will be drought; if the same things should occur in any other season, there will be wars in the land.

22. If in the Śiśira (dewy) and other seasons of the year, the twilight sky should be naturally red, yellow white or variegated in color, or of the color of lotus or of Blood, there will be prosperity in the land during such seasons; but if the color be not a natural one, that is, brought on by dust storms and the like, mankind will suffer miseries.

23. If a cloud shaped like a man with a weapon in his hand should appear cut, and in this state move in the direction of the sun, there will be fear from enemies; if the sum should

appear to enter clouds of the shape of a white town, the ruler will get a new town and add it to his possessions.

24. If white thick cloulds shoud come forth from the south and conceal the sun, there will be rain; if clouds bush-like in shape and rising in quarters other than that in the direction of the sun and conceal the sun, there will also be rain.

25. If at sunrise the appearance known as Parigha should appear white, the reigning prince will suffer; if of blood color, his army will revolt; and if of the color of gold, the army will gain in strength.

26. If the appearance known as Parhelion (mocksun) should be seen on both sides of the sun and be large, there will be much rain; and if it should appear all round the sun, *not* a drop of rain will fall.

27. If at sunrise or sunset the clouds should appear of the shape of a flag or umbrella, a mountain, an elephant or a horse, the chief ruler will triumph in war; if they should be of blood color, there will be wars in the land.

28. If at sunrise or sunset clouds should resemble columns of smoke of burnt straw and be of agreeable appearance, the army will gain in strength.

29. If at sunrise or sunset clouds should appear to hang above the horizon and of the shape of trees and red and of disagreeable appearance, there will be prosperity in the land; if the clouds should assume the shape of towns, mankind will be happy.

30. If birds, the she-jackal and other animals should howl turning to the sun, if the twilight sky should de marked by dust and by the appearances, Daṇḍa and Parigha, and the sun should appear for several days of altered appearance, the chief ruler will die and there will be famine in the land.

31. Generally effects assigned to indications connected with the morning twilight hours will come to pass at once, and those of the evening twilight hours, either in the night or within 3 or 7 days; but effects assigned to halos, to dust storms and to Parigha, will either come to pass at once or take 3 or 7 days; those assigned to the solar rays, to the rainbow, lightning, to parhelion, to clouds and to winds will take effect

that same day; those assigned to birds will take 8 days, and those assigned to animals, 7 days.

32. The twilight sky is visible for a Yojana (5 miles); lightning for 6 Yojanas; the roaring of the clouds will be heard at a distance of 5 Yojanas; and there is no limit to the extent to which meteors might fall.[6]

REFERENCES

1. This is an appearance in the sky of the shape of an iron bar.
2. An appearance resembling a tree in shape assumed by the clouds.
3. An appearance in the sky resembling a club.
4. Parāśara says that if the rising or setting sun should be covered by dust resembling the white powder of conch, princes will triumph in war and mankind will be happy.
5. Like a crow, a vulture, an ass, and the like.
6. Accordingly, Devala says that effects assigned to meteoric falls are not confined to particular localities, but are felt throughout the land.

CHAPTER 31

Glow at the Horizon[1]

1. If the appearance of Digdāha should be of yellow color, rulers will suffer; if it should be of the color of fire, the country will suffer; if red and the wind should blow from right to left, crops will suffer.

2. If the appearance should be very bright and cast shadows, the rulers will suffer; if it be of blood color, there will be wars in the land.

3. If the appearance should be seen about the eastern horizon, rulers and Kṣatriyas will suffer; if it should be seen about the south-eastern horizon, painters, sculptors and children will suffer; if in the south, wicked men, the Vaiśyas, and messengers will suffer; if in the south-west, remarried virgin widows will suffer.

4. If the appearance should be seen about the western horizon, Śūdras and farmers will suffer; if in the north-western horizon, thieves and horses will suffer; if in the north, the Brāhmaṇas will suffer; and if in the north-east, heretics and merchants will suffer.

5. If when the sky is clear, the stars bright, and the wind blowing from left to right, the appearance of Digdāha should be of the color of gold, rulers as well as the country will prosper.

REFERENCE

1. Preternatural redness of the horizon as if on fire.

CHAPTER 32

On Earthquakes

1. Some say that earthquake is caused by huge water monsters and some that it is caused by the elephants supporting the Earth, resting for a time from their labor.

2. According to some earthquake is caused by the violent collision of winds and their striking the Earth in consequence, and according to others the cause is some invisible and unknown agency.

3. Once upon a time, in the days gone by, the Earth, being shaken by the rising and falling of winged mountains, addressed Brahma (the Creator) in the court of Indra, as follows, and with feelings of shame.

4. Lord, I was named by Thee as the Unmoving. This character has now suffered, and I am unable to bear the troubles caused by moving mountains.

5. Brahma, perceiving her broken speech, trembling lips, bent head and weeping eyes, spoke as follows :

6. "O Indra, relieve the Earth of her grief ; throw thy weapon—the Vajrayudha—to destroy the wings of mountains" Indra saying, "It is done," told the Earth not to fear and spoke to her as follows :

7. Vāyu (the wind), Agni (fire), Indra and Varuṇa (God of rain), will however henceforth shake thee respectively in the first, second, third and fourth, six hours of day and night, to indicate the future good or bad condition of the world.

8. The asterisms of U. Phalgunī, Hasta, Citrā, Svāti, Punarvasu, Mṛgaśirsa and Aśvini are known as the circle or division of Vāyu. The previous symptoms of an earthquake of Vāyu, occurring when the Moon is in any of these seven asterisms, will last for seven days.

9. These symptoms are : the sky will be filled with dust and

smoke, violent winds will shake the trees, and the rays of the sun will appear dim.

10. In a Vayavya earthquake the crops will perish; the Earth will become dry; forests will suffer; medicinal plants will be destroyed; and tradesmen will be afflicted with dropsy, asthma madness, fever and phlegmatic affections.

11. Prostitutes and men handling weapons, physicians, women, poets, musicians, merchants, painters and sculptors will suffer miseries, as well as the people of Surat, of Kuru, of Magada, of Dasarna and of Matsya.

12. The asterisms of Puṣya, Krittikā, Viśākha, Bharaṇī, Maghā, P. Bhādra and P. Phalgunī are known as the circle of Agni. The previous symptoms of an earthquake of Agni occurring when the Moon is in any of these seven asterisms, will last for seven days.

13. These symptoms are : the sky will be filled with the light of falling meteors, and the appearance of Digdāha will be seen about the horizon, and fire and wind will rage over the land.

14. In an, Agneya earthquake, the clouds will be destroyed; tanks and lakes will become dry; rulers will become hostile to one another, and mankind will suffer from ring-worms, cutaneous eruptions, fever, spreading itch and jaundice.

15. Also men of bright appearance, cruel men and the people of Asmaka, Aṅga, Bāhlīka, Tangana, Kaliṅga, Bengal and of Draviḍa, and numerous hill-men will suffer miseries.

16. The asterisms of Abhijit, Śravaṇa, Dhaniṣṭha, Rohiṇī, Jyeṣṭhā, U. Āṣāḍha and Anurādhā are known as the circle of Indra. The previous symptoms of an earthquake of Indra occurring when the Moon is in any of these seven asterisms, are as follows.

17. Clouds like so many moving mountains, roaring cloud, attended by lightning and black as the horn of a buffalo, as the bee and the black cobra, will yield abundance of rain.

18. In an Aindra earthquake, the Vedas, men of high caste and of high families, rulers and commanders of armies, will perish. Dysentery, inflammation or swelling of the neck, diseases of the face, and the vomiting disease will afflict mankind.

19. Varanasi, Yugandhara, Kirāta, Kīra, Abhisara, Hala, Madra, Arbuda and Malawa will suffer, and there will be rain to suit the wants of the people.

20. The asterisms of Revatī, P. Āṣāḍha, Ārdrā, Āśleṣa, Mūla, U. Āṣāḍha and Satabhiṣaj are known as the circle of Varuṇa. The previous symptoms of an earthquake of Varuṇa occurring when the Moon is in any of these seven asterisms are as follows.

21. Clouds of the color of the blue lotus, of the bee and of collyrium, sounding agreeably, in masses and attended by lightning, will yield sharp rain.

22. In a Varuṇa earthquake persons working at the sea or in rivers will perish; there will be excessive rain and rulers will cease to be hostile. The people of Gonardha, Cedi, Kukura, Kirāta and Videha will suffer miseries.

23. The effects assigned to earthquakes will occur within six months, these assigned to the other Utpatas will occur within two months: these occurrences are classified by some under the heads of the four circles above referred to.

24. Meteoric falls,[1] cloud castles, dust-storms, thunderbolts, earthquakes, fiery appearances about the horizon, violent winds, solar and lunar eclipses, changes in the appearance of stars.

25. Rainfall from a cloudless sky, the simultaneous occurrence of wind and rain, the appearance of smoke and sparks where there is no fire, the entry of wild animals into villages, the appearance of rainbow in the sky at night.

26. Any unusual appearance of the sky at sunrise or sunset, broken or imperfect halos, rivers running in opposite directions, there being heard the music of the drum in the sky, and the like unusual occurrences should be classified under the heads of the four circles of Vāyu, Agni, Varuṇa and Indra.[2]

27. As regards the effects of earthquakes classified with respect to time and Nakṣatra, whenever there is an inconsistency, the Aindra character with respect to time will take precedence over the Vayavya character with respect to Nakṣatra; and the Vayavya character with respect to time over the Aindra character with respect to Nakṣatra; and so in the case of the

Varuṇa and Agneya character of such earthquake, division with respect to time takes precedence over division with respect to Nakṣatra.[3]

28. If an earthquake should partake of the character of one of Agni and Vāyu, the chief ruler will perish, and mankind will suffer from hunger, fear, death and drought.

29. If an earthquake should partake of the character of one of Varuṇa and of Indra, there will be prosperity in the land good rain and gladness of heart, cows will yeild much milk, and rulers will cease to be hostile.

30. If an earthquake should partake of the character of one of Vāyu and Varuṇa, the people of Ujjain, of Puliṇḍa, of Videha, of Kashmir, of Draviḍa, of Vasanta, and those that live on the banks of the Sarayū, will suffer miseries.[4]

31. If an earthquake should partake of the character of one of Indra and of Agni, the people of Ikṣwaku, Asmarathya, Pata, Cara, Abhira; China and Marukacca, and prosperous rulers will suffer miseries.

32. In the the case of those Utpatas for the effects of which no period has been given, the rule is as follows : if the occurences belong to the circle of Vāyu, the period is four fortnights; if to the circle of Agni, three fortnights ; if of Indra, seven days; and if of Varuṇa, the effects will come to pass immediately.

33. In an earthquake of Vāyu, the shock will be felt at a distance of two hundred Yojanas (1000 miles) ; in one of Agni 110 Yojanas; in one of Varuṇa, 180 Yojanas, and in one of Indra 160 Yojanas.

34. If after the occurrence of an earthquake another should occur on the 3rd, 4th, 7th, 15th, 30th, or 45th day the chief ruler will perish.

REFERENCES

1. Stanzas 24 to 26 are taken from Varāhamihira's Samasa Saṁhitā.
2. Garga says; persons in whose Na kṣatras, earthquakes and

the like Utpatas occur will suffer miseries; they shall therefore perform expiatory ceremonies in honor of the particular Deva under whose influence the occurrences take place.

3. Garga says that if an earthquake is connected with two Nakṣatras, division with respect to time of day takes precedence.

4. Stanzas 30 and 31 are taken from Parāśara.

CHAPTER 33

On Meteors[1]

1. Meteors are appearances of those who, having enjoyed in the higher worlds the effects of their Punnyakarma (good-deeds), fall down to the Earth. These meteors are of 5 sorts known technically as 1. Dhiṣnya, 2. Ulkā, 3. Asani (thunder-bolt), 4. Vidyut (lightning), and 5. Tārā.[2]

2. Dhiṣnya produces its effects within a fortnight ; Ulkā takes also the same period ; Asani produces its effects within a month and a half ; Vidyut within 6 days and Tārā takes the same period.

3. Tārā produces only a fourth of the effects assigned to meteors in general. Dhiṣnya one half, and Vidyut, Ulkā and Asani produce their full effects.

4. Asani is a meteoric substance, circular in shape; it strikes with a loud report men, elephants, horses, deer, rocks, houses, trees and sheep, and passes into the Earth.

5. Vidyut is a large bent fiery substance and strikes, with a loud and feerful sound, living creat ures and collection of wood.

6. Dhiṣnya is a blazing fiery meteoric appearance, thin and with a small tail, and visible beyond a distance of 40 cubits. Its length is two cubits.

7. Tārā is a meteoric substance, a cubit in length, and of white or copper color, or of the color of the stem of the lotus; it will appear to move either horizontally or vertically down-wards or upwards as if dragged by some invisible force.

8. Ulkā (meteor) is an appearance with a large head, a very small tail and of the length of a man's body ; as it falls it in-creases in length. This appearance is of several kinds.

9. It assumes the shape of a dead body, a weapon, an ass, a camel, a crocodile, a monkey, a tusked animal, a plough, a deer, a lizard, a snake or smoke, and it sometimes appears double headed. It causes misery in the land.

10. If it should be of the shape of a flagstaff, of fish, an elephant, a hill, a lotus, the moon, a horse, melting silver, a swan, the Bilva tree, the vajrayudha (a weapon), or conch or a triangle, there will be prosperity in the land.

11. Numberless meteors fall from the sky ; these import misery to the reigning sovereign. Meteors that simply whirl round and round import misery to the world at large.

12. Those meteors which, when they fall, just appear to touch the solar or lunar disc, or to issue from it and which are at the same time accompained by earthquakes import a foreign rule, famine, drought and fears of various sorts.

13. If the meteors should appear to move from the right to the left of the sun and moon, houseless people will suffer miseries. If a meteor which appears to have issued from the sun should fall before one who marches out for fight, it imports good luck.

14. If the meteors should be white, red, yellow or black, the Brāhmaṇas, the Kṣatriyas, the Vaiśyas and the Śūdras will respectively suffer; the same effects will occur if the meteor falls with its head, breast, side or tail foremost.

15. If the meteor should be of fearful apearance and if it should fall in the north, east, south or west, the Brāhmaṇas, the Kṣatriyas, the Vaiśyas and Śūdras will suffer respectively.

If the meteor should appear straight, glossy and broken, and if in its fall it be visible to within a short distance from the Earth, the Brāhmaṇas and the others will prosper (according as the direction of the fall of the meteor is the north, east, south or West.)

16. If the color of the meteor should be white, black, red, blue, of blood color, of the color, of fire, or black, or of the color of ash, and if its appearance should be fearful, and if it should appear either immediately before sunrise or after sunset or during the day, or, if it should appear crooked or cut into halves, there will be fear of foreign invasion.

17. If the meteor should be seen to fall crossing the discs of stars and planets, the persons and objects represented by such stars and planets will suffer. If it should be seen to fall

crossing the discs of the sun or moon at rising or setting, houseless people will suffer.

18. If a meteor should be seen to fall crossing the discs of P. Phalgunī, Punarvasu, Dhaniṣṭha and Mūla, young women will suffer. If it should be seen to fall crossing the discs of Puṣya, Swāti and Śravaṇa, the Brāhmaṇas and the Kṣatriyas will suffer.

19. If it should be seen to fall crossing the discs of the pole star and benefic planets and stars, the chief rulers will suffer; if crossing the discs of malefic planets and stars, thieves will suffer, and if crossing the discs of ordinary stars, music and fine arts will suffer.

20. If the meteor should be seen to fall on the images of the Devas the rulers and their countries will suffer; if it should fall on the Sakra tree (Pentaptera Arjuna) kings will suffer, and if on houses, the owners thereof will suffer.

21. If it should be seen to fall crossing the discs of the direction planets,[3] the countries situated in the respective directions will suffer; if on threshing floor, farmers will suffer, and if on the sacred trees planted in public places virtuous men will suffer.

22. If it should fall at the entrance to towns, the towns will suffer; if on ornamental structures over buildings, the people will suffer; if in the middle of Brāhmaṇa habitations, the Brāhmaṇs will suffer; and if in cattle-fold, the owner of the herd will suffer.

23. If, while it falls, its noise should be like the roar of the lion, like the sound caused by striking against one's breast or like a combination of vocal and instrumental music the rulers with their countries will suffer.

24. If the meteoric appearance should be seen to hover in the sky for a long time, of the shape of a stick, or if it should be seen of the shape of Indra's banner suspended in the sky as if by threads, rulers will suffer.

25. If while it falls it should retrograde in its motion, merchants will suffer; if it should move horizontally, queens will suffer; if vertically downwards, rulers will suffer; and if vertically upwards, the Brāhmaṇas will suffer.

26. If the meteor should be of the color and shape of the

peacock's train, there will be misery in the land; if it should move like a serpent, women will suffer.

27. If it should appear circular in shape, towns will suffer; if of the shape of an umbrella, priests will suffer; and if of the shape of a clump of bamboos, the kingdom will be imperilled.

28. If it should be of the shape of a snake or a pig, or appear as if covered with sparks of fire, or cut or fall with noise, there will be misery in the land.

29. If it should appear of the shape of the rainbow, the kingdom will suffer; if it should disappear, in the sky, clouds will be destroyed; if it should move against the course of the wind or obliquely or retrograde in its motion, there will be misery in the land.

30. If it should fall on a town or an army, the ruler will suffer from such town or army; if it should appear to come blazing from a certain quarter, the prince that marches for fight in that direction will succeed in battle.

REFERENCES

1. This term has been made to include a number of unusual appearances—Vide text.
2. Garga says that weapons that have slipped from the hands of the Devas are known as Ulkās ("meteors.")
3. These are : the Sun—E.; Venus—S.E.; Mars—S.; Rāhu—S.W.; Saturn—W.; Moon—N.W.; Mercury—N.; and Jupiter—N.E.

CHAPTER 34

On Halos

1. When the sky is filled with thin light clouds, the solar or lunar rays, gathered together by the action of the wind, and made into circles of different sizes and colors, form what are known as Halos.

2. If the color of these halos should be red, their lord is Indra; if blue, Yama, if gray, Varuṇa, if of the color of the dove, Nirruti (a demon presiding over the S.W. point of the compass); if of the color of the clouds, Vāyu; if variegated in color, Eesanya (a deity presiding over the N.E. point of the compass); if green, Kubera (God of wealth); and if white, Agni.

3. Kubera also causes the halo to appear black, and the other gods to appear with the color belonging to each. If a halo should be seen to appear and disappear at brief intervals of time, it is caused by Vāyu, and it will not produce effects of a permanent nature.

4. If the halo should appear of the color of a peacock or fire or silver, or oil or milk, or water, and of the shape of a complete circle and glossy, there will be happiness in the land.

5. If the solar or lunar halos should continue from the rising to the setting of the luminaries, frequently changing in color, or if the halos should appear red or disagreeable or imperfect or oblongular or triangular in shape, or of the shape of a bow, there will be misery in the land.

6. If the halo should appear of the color of the neck of the peacock, there will be rain; if it should appear variegated in color, the chief ruler will be assassinated; if of the color of smoke, there will be fear in the land; if of the color of the rainbow or red like the flower of the Aśoka, there will be wars in the land.

7. If in the rainy season, the solar or lunar halo should

either appear of a single color, or glossy if of different colors, or occupied by clouds sword-like in shape, or if the sun, while surrounded by a halo, should appear very bright and yellow, there will be immediate rain.

8. If the solar or lunar halos should appear big at the eastern or western horizon or at the meridian, and if birds and animals should be found to howl with their faces turned to the Sun or Moon, and if the color of the halos should be dim, mankind will be tormented with various fears. If the halo should be crossed by meteors or lightning, the chief ruler will meet his death by a weapon.

9. If, daily,[1] the Sun and Moon should appear red, the chief ruler will die, if halos should be frequently seen round the Sun and Moon at rising or setting, or in the meridian, rulers will be killed.

10. If the halo should consist of two concentric circles, the commander-in-chief will be afflicted with fear, and there will also be wars but not of a fearful nature, if the halo should consist of three concentric circles, there will be wars; if of four circles, the first prince will suffer miseries; and if of five circles, the capital city will be seized by the enemy.

11. If the halo should include within it a planet the Moon and Stars, there will be either rain within three days or wars within a month. According to some that prince will suffer miseries the lord of the Lagna (rising sign) of whose nativity, the lord of the sign occupied by the Moon, and whose star should happen to be included within the circle of a lunar or solar halo.

12. If Saturn should be included within the circle of a lunar or solar halo, the minor crops will perish; there will be rain attended by storms and deaths among settled farmers.

13. If Mars should be so included, children and commanders of armies will suffer and there will be fear from wars and destructive fires. If Jupiter should be so included, priests, ministers and rulers will suffer.

14. If Mercury should be so included, ministers and permanent writers will be happy and there will be good rain. If Venus should be so included, princes that march out for fight will suffer and there will be good food in the land.

15. If Ketu should be so included, mankind will suffer miseries from hunger, fire, death, and from rulers. If Rāhu should be so included, pregnancy will miscarry, there will be disease in the land, and rulers will suffer.

16. If two planets should be included within a solar or lunar halo, there will be wars in the land; if three should be so included, mankind will suffer from hunger and drought.

17. If four planets should be included within a halo, rulers, ministers and priests will suffer; if five or six planets should be so included, the world will come to an end.

18. If while the comets do not appear, Mars and other planets should be separately eclipsed, or if the stars should be so eclipsed, rulers will perish.[2]

19. If the halo should appear on the first day of the dark or bright half of a lunar month, there will be deaths among the Brāhmaṇas; if on the second day, there will be deaths among the Kṣatriyas; if on the third day, there will be deaths among the Vaiśyas; and if on the fourth day, there will be deaths among the Śūdras; if the halo should appear on the fifth day, villages will suffer; if on the sixth day, towns will suffer; and if on the seventh day, treasuries and store-houses will suffer.

20. If the halo should appear on the eighth day of the dark or bright half of a lunar month, the first prince will suffer; if on the ninth, tenth or eleventh day, the king will suffer; if on the twelfth day, the chief town will be besieged by the enemy, and if on the thirteenth day, there will be confusion and dismay in the army.

21. If the halo should appear on the fourteenth day of the dark or bright half of a lunar month, the queen will suffer; and if on the fifteenth (new or full moon) day, rulers will suffer.

22. The inner circle of the halo represents citizens, the outer circle represents the army marching out for fight, and the central circle represents the army pursued by the enemy.

23. If any of these circles should appear of blood color or black or of fearful appearance, the persons it represents will suffer defeat. If any of these circle should appear glossy, white, and bright, the persons it represents will succeed in battle.

REFERENCES

1. According to Garga if the appearance should last for a single day, the chief ruler will die, and if for 7 days, the country will perish.
2. If comets appear at the time, the effects assigned to them will alone come to pass.

CHAPTER 35

On the Rainbow

1. The many colored rays of the Sun falling upon the clouds and being broken by the winds take the shape of the rainbow in the sky.

2. In the opinion of certain writers[1] the rainbow is formed of the expired breath of certain serpents of the divine order; princes that march out for fight in the direction of the rainbow will suffer defeat.

3. If two rainbows, similar to each other should appear perfect, unbroken, bent towards the Earth, bright, glossy, thick and variegated in color, there will be abundant rain.

4. Rainbows appearing in particular quarters of the sky will cause the death of the persons represented by such quarters.[2] and if the rainbow should be seen in places other than the sky, there will be deaths in the land; if it should appear white-red, mankind will suffer from weapons; if yellow, from fire; and if blue, from starvation.

5. If the rainbow should be seen in the middle of water, there will be drought; if on earth, crops will be injured; if on trees, there will be disease in the land; if on ant hills, there will be wars, and if seen at night, ministers will perish.

6. If the rainbow should appear when there is no rain; there will be rain, and if while it rains, the rain will cease if it should appear in the west, there will also be rain.

7. If at night the rainbow should be seen in the east, kings will suffer; if in the South, the commander-in-chief will die; if in the West, masters will suffer; and if in the north, ministers will suffer.

8. If, at night, the rainbow should appear white, red, yellow or black, the Brāhmaṇas, the Kṣatriyas, the Vaiśyas and the Śūdras will suffer respectively. If at night the rainbow should

appear in particular quarters of the sky, the rulers in those quarters of the Earth will perish.

REFERENCES

1. Kāśyapa and men of his school.
2. These are given in a subsequent chapter, viz. : the Chapter on Sakuna. They are : King—E; First prince—S.E.; Commander-in-chief—S.; Messengers—S.W.; Head-men—W.; Spies—N.W.; Brāhmaṇas—N.; the principal of a sacrificial fire—N.E.

CHAPTER 36

On Cloud Castles

1. If the appearance of Gandharvanagara should be seen in the north, priests will suffer; if in the east, rulers will suffer; if in the south, commanders of armies will suffer, and if in the west, the first prince will suffer. If the appearance should be white, the Brāhmaṇas will suffer; if red, the Kṣatriyas; if yellow, the Vaiśyas; and if black, the Śūdras will suffer.

2. If the appearance should be seen in the north citizens and rulers will suffer; if seen in the corners, the mixed races will suffer; and if seen in the direction opposite to the sun, rulers will triumph in war.

3. If the appearance should be seen in all directions and for a long time, princes and countries wlll suffer; if it should be of the color of smoke, fire, rainbow, thieves and forest-men will suffer.

4. If the appearance should be seen a little white, there will be suffering from thunderbolt and from storms; if in the direction of the sun, the chief rulers will perish; if seen on the left side, there will be fear from enemies, and if on the right side there will be success in war.

5. If it should appear of various hues and shapes or of the shape of a flag, banner or archway, such bloody wars will rage over the land that the Earth will drink large quantities of the blood of elephants, men and horses.

CHAPTER 37

On Parhelion

1. If the appearance of Pratisūrya or Parhelion should be of the color assigned to the Sun for the several seasons of the year and at the same time glossy, or if it should be of the color of the cat's-eye (gem) or clear and white, there will be prosperity in the land.

2. If the appearance should be yellow, there will be diseases in the land; if red, resembling the color of the Aśoka flower, there will be wars. If these appearances should together form a figure of the shape of a garland, there will be suffering from thieves and the chief ruler will perish.

3. If the appearance should be seen to the north of the Sun, there will be rain; if to the south of the Sun, there will be winds; if on both sides of the Sun there will be fear from floods; if seen above the Sun rulers will perish; and if below the Sun, there will be deaths in the land.

CHAPTER 38

On Dust Storms

1. If the dust storm should be so black and dense as to render mountains, towns and trees undistinguishable, the reigning prince will die.

2. If the dust storm should be of the color of smoke, there will be suffering in the countries in which the storm appears for the first time or disappears finally, within seven days from the occurrence of the event.

3. If the dust storm should resemble white clouds, ministers and people at large will suffer; there will be wars in the land and mankind will be afflicted with innumerable miseries.

4. If the dust storm should appear to hide the sky about sun-rise on one or two consecutive days, mankind will suffer from great fears.

5. If the storm should continue dense for a night, the chief ruler will perish; but other princes will prosper.

6. If in a particular country the storm should be found to remain for two days together, that country will be overrun by the army of the enemy.

7. If the dust storm should be found to continue for three or four days, there will be scarcity in the land, and juice will be injured; if it should continue for five days, contending armies will engage in fight.

8. If a malefic dust storm unaccompanied by the appearance of comets and the like abnormal phenomena should be seen in any Ṛtu (season) except Śiśira (from the middle of January to that of March), it will produce the full effects assigned to it.

CHAPTER 39

On Thunderbolts

1. When two winds come in collision, that which, being struck, falls on the Earth is known as thunderbolt; if at the time birds should begin to sound turning to the Sun there will be misery on Earth.

2. If there should occur a fall of thunderbolt at sunrise, officials, kings, rich men, soldiers, women, merchants and prostitutes will perish; if the fall should occur within three hours after sunrise, sheep, the Śūdras and citizens will suffer.

3. If the fall should occur before midday, the king's servants and Brāhmaṇas will suffer; if it should occur within three hours after midday, the Vaiśyas and clouds will suffer, and if before sunset thieves will suffer.

4. If the fall of thunderbolt should occur at sunset low-caste men will suffer; if it should occur in the first three hours after sunset, crops will suffer; and if before midnight, ghosts will suffer.

5. If the fall of the thunderbolt should occur within the three hours after midnight, horses and elephants will perish, and if before sunrise, travellers will suffer, and also those countries will suffer in the direction of which the roar of thunder appears to move.

CHAPTER 40

On Vegetable Horoscopy

1. We shall now proceed to state the laws or yogas (positions of the planets) as stated by Bādarāyaṇa (Vyāsa) (from which to determine the growth of the grīṣma or śarat crops) when the Sun just enters the sign of Vṛścika (Scorpio) or the sign Vṛṣabha (Taurus).

2. If at the time when the Sun enters the sign Scorpio, benefic planets should occupy the said sign, or the fourth, seventh or tenth houses from it, or if these four houses should be within sight of benefic planets, the grīṣma or summer crops will thrive.

3. If, when the Sun is in Scorpio, Jupiter should be in Aquarius and the Moon in Leo or *vice versa*, the summer crops will thrive.

4. If, when the Sun is in Scorpio, Venus or Mercury or both should occupy either the second house from the Sun, viz., Sagittarius or the twelfth house Libra, summer crops will thrive. If at the same time the sign of Sagittarius or Libra should be within sight of Jupiter, such crops will grow in great abundance.

5. If, when the Sun is in Scorpio, and between benefic planets, Jupiter and the Moon should be in the seventh house, Taurus, summer crops will thrive exceedingly well; and if, when he has just entered Scorpio, Jupiter should be in the second house, Sagittarius, the extent of the growth of such crops will be one half.

6. If, when the Sun is in Scorpio, Venus, the Moon and Mercury should respectively occupy the eleventh, fourth, and second houses (from Scorpio) and Jupiter the tenth house, summer crops will grow in abundance.

7. If, when the Sun has just entered Scorpio, Juptier should be in Aquarius, the Moon in Taurus, Mars and Saturn

in Capricornus, the summer crops will thrive well and there will also be fear of foreign invasion and diseases in the land.

8. If, when the Sun is in Scorpio, there should be malefic planets on both sides, crops will be injured; and if a malefic planet should occupy the seventh house, Taurus, crops will suffer blight.

9. If, when the Sun is in Scorpio, malefic planets should occupy the second house Sagittarius and if they are not within sight of benefic planets the first crops will suffer and the subsequent crops will thrive.

10. If, when the Sun is in Scorpio, two malefic planets should occupy the seventh house, Taurus, crops will be injured; but if such seventh house should be within sight of benefic planets at the same time, crops will grow here and there.

11. If, when the Sun is in Scorpio, two malefic planets should occupy the seventh and sixth houses, crops will thrive and the price of commodities will fall.

12. The growth of the autumnal crops should be determined from the position of the planets with reference to sign Taurus at the time when the Sun enters it just in the same way as the summer crops as stated above.

13. If while the Sun passes through the signs of Aries, Taurus and Gemini, he should be accompanied by or within sight of benefic planets, the summer crops will flourish, and the price of such produce will either be moderate or will rise.

14. If while the Sun passes through the signs of Sagittarius, Capricornus and Aquarius, he should either be accompanied by or within sight of benefic planets, the autumnal crops will flourish and the price of such produce will either be moderate or will rise; if at the time of harvest the sun should be either accompanied by or within sight of malefic planets, prices will either fluctuate or fall.

CHAPTER 41

On Commodities

1. I shall now proceed to state the Zodiacal division of commodities adopting the views of the sages of the past with a view to enable men to know before-hand what articles can be had in abundance and what will become rare.

2. Sign Mesha (Aries) represents cotton and woollen fabric, leathern oil jars, beans, wheat, raggy, barley, dry crops in general and gold.

3. Sign Vṛṣabha (Taurus) represents cloths in general, flowers, wheat; rice, barley, buffalo and cows; and sign Mithuna (Gemini) represents the autumnal crops, creepers, the root of the Lily and cotton.

4. Sign Karkataka (Cancer) represents Kodrava, plantains, bent grass, fruits, roots, leaves and bark; and sign Siṁha (Leo) represents food grains, juice, the skin of the Eon and the like animals and jaggery.

5. Sign Kanyā (Virgo) represents common flax, barley, horse gram, wheat, kidney-beans and nishpava (a kind of leguminous plaṇt—Dolichos tetraspermus); and sign Tulā (Libra) represents black gram, wheat, and mustard seed.

6. Sign Vṛścika (Scorpio) represents sugar-canes, wet grains, metals, and woollen fabric; and sign Dhanuṣ (Sagittarius) represents horses, salt, cloth, weapons, gingelly-seeds and roots.

7. Sign Makara (Capricornus) represents trees, bushes, wet grains, sugar-canes gold and black-lead; and sign Kumbha (Aquarius) represents waterfruits and flowers, gems and articles of various shapes.

8. Sign Mīna (Pisces) represents pearls and other shell-gems, diamonds, various oils and fishes.

9. If Jupiter should occupy the 4th, 10th, 2nd, 11th, 7th, 9th, or 5th house from any particular sign of the Zodiac or if

Mercury should occupy the 2nd, 11th, 10th, 5th, or 8th house from any particular sign.

10. Or if Venus should occupy the 6th or 7th house from a particular sign, the articles represented by that sign will perish; and if he occupies any of the other houses, the articles will flourish; if malefic planets should occupy the 2nd, 6th, 10th, or 11th house from a particular sign, the articles represented by that sign will flourish and the reverse will be the case if the planets occupy any of the other houses.

11. If powerful malefic planets should occupy any of the houses other than the 3rd, 6th, 10th, and 11th houses from a particular sign, the articles assigned for that sign will sell dear and become scarce.

12. Generally if benefic planets should be powerful in their several signs as stated above, articles will flourish and the prices will be moderate and the articles themselves can be had easily.

13. If at any time a particular sign should be within sight of benefic planets occupying malefic houses, the articles assigned for that sign will not be much injured, but if the planets should be powerful malefic planets the articles will perish.

CHAPTER 42

On the Price of Commodities

1. Judging from the phenomena of excessive rain, of meteoric falls, of the appearance of the Daṇḍa, of Halos, of eclipse and parhelion occurring on the New or Full Moon day of a particular month;

2. The astronomer shall determine that the price of commodities will rise; but if the phenomena should occur on any other days of the month, rulers will be at war.

3. If the phenomena referred to above should occur when the Sun is in the sign Meṣa (Aries), April—May, a tradesman shall purchase the produce of Śarat; and if the phenomena should occur when the Sun is in Vṛṣabha (Taurus), he shall store up wild roots and fruits; and if he should dispose of these articles in the fourth month after purchase, he will make much profit.

4. If the phenomena should occur when the Sun is in the sign Mithuna (Gemini), the tradesman shall store up juicy articles and grains, and if he should sell them in the sixth month he would make much profit.

5. If the phenomena should occur when the Sun is in the sign Karkataka, he shall store up honey, perfumes oil, ghee and sugar, and if he should dispose of them in the second month, they would fetch double their value; but if he should dispose of them before or after the second month, he would sustain loss.

6. If the phenomena should occur when the Sun is in the sign Siṁha (Leo) the tradesman shall store up gold, gems leather, armours, weapons, pearls and silver, and if he should dispose of these in the fifth month, there would be much profit; but if he should do so either before or after the fifth month, he would sustain loss.

7. If the phenomena should occur when the Sun is in the sign Kanyā (Virgo) the tradesman shall purchase Chamara (fan), asses, camels and horses; if he should dispose of them in the sixth month, he would get double their value.

8. If the phenomena should occur when the Sun is in the sign Tulā (Libra) the tradesman shall store up yarn goods, crystal wares, flowers of gold color and grains; if he should dispose of them in the sixth month, he would get double their price.

9. If the phenomena should occur when the Sun is in the sign Vṛścika (Scorpio) the tradesman shall store up fruits and roots of a lasting nature and various precious stones, and if he should dispose of them at the and of two years, they would fetch double their price.

10. If the phenomena should occur when the Sun in Dhanuṣ (Sagittarius) the tradesman shall store up conch shells, corals, articles of crystal and pearls; if he should dispose of them in the sixth month, they would fetch double their price.

11. If the phenomena should occur when the Sun is in the signs of Makara (Capricornus) and Kumbha (Aquarius) the tradesman shall store up iron and other metals, vessels and grains; if he should dispose of them at the end of a month they would fetch double their price.

12. If the phenomena should occur when the Sun is in Mīna (Pisces) the tradesman shall store up roots, fruits, vessels and precious stones; if he should dispose of them in the sixth month, they would fetch double their price.

13. If the Sun or Moon should happen to be in a single sign accompanied by an Atimitra (very friendly) planet, the tradesman may deal profitably in the articles assigned for that sign.

14. If the New or Full Moon should either be accompanied by or within view of benefic planets the price of commodities will rise. If the Sun should be either accompanied by or within view of malefic planets, the price will fall. Generally predictions are to be made on a full consideration of the strength or weakness of the Zodiacal signs.

CHAPTER 43

On Indra's Banner

1. The Devas addressed Brahma as follows:—"Lord, we are unable to defeat the Asuras in fight and we have therefore come to thee for help." Brahma spoke to the Devas as follows.

2. "The Supreme Viṣṇu of the sea of milk will give you a banner at the sight of which the Asuras, your enemies, will cease to oppose you in battle."

3. The Devas, including the great Indra, took leave of Brahma and, proceeding to the sea of milk, began to sing as follows the praises of Viṣṇu on whose breast shone brilliantly the Koustubha gem.

4. "Lord of Lakṣmī, the unthinkable, thou hast no equal; thou art omnipresent and thou existest invisibly diffused through the bodies of all corporeal creatures; thou art the Supreme Soul and thou hast neither beginning nor end."

5. God Nārāyaṇa, pleased with the praise of the Devas, gave them a Dhwaja (flag-staff) which at the same time served both as the Sun and the Moon respectively to the lotus-like face of the Deva and Asura females.

6. Indra was mightily pleased to accept the gift of the Dhwaja which had its origin in the Tejas (light) of Viṣṇu and which was set with precious stones and mounted on an eight-wheeled car shining brilliantly as the Summer Sun.

7. Planting erect the Dhwaja, which was adorned with a girdle of small bells, with garlands, with umbrellas and with a huge bell, Indra defeated his enemies in the field of battle.

8. Indra gave the Dhwaja, which was of bamboo wood, to Vasu, the ruler of the province of Cedi, who was gifted with

the power of flight into celestial regions, and Vasu them performed pūjā to the Dhwaja.

9. Indra, pleased with Vasu's pūjā spoke as follows:—those princes who might go through a similar ceremonial worship shall become as prosperous and successful rulers as Vasu, the ruler of Cedi.

10. The subjects of these rulers will also become happy and prosperous and be freed from fear and disease.

The Dhwaja itself shall indicate the course and nature of future events.

11. By command of Indra the ceremonial worship of the Dhwaja has been gone through by princes desirous of strength and victory. I shall now proceed to give a brief description of the same according to the Śāstras.

12. On an auspicious day in an auspicious hour and Nakṣatra, the astronomer shall leave for the forest accompanied by the carpenter.

13. He shall not cut any tree growing in flower gardens, in temples, on cremation grounds, on public roads on sacrificial fire-sites or trees of short growth, or dried trees or trees of stinted growth at the top, thorny trees or trees surrounded by creepers and over-grown with mistletoes.

14. He shall also reject trees with holes in which dwell numerous birds and trees injured by the wind or fire and he shall reject trees of feminine denomination, for all those trees are not fit for the staff of Indra's banner.

15. The five trees Arjuna,[1] Asvakarna,[1] Priyaka Dhava,[2] Udumbara,[3] are suited for the purpose. Either one of these or some other well known tree.

16. Or, some tree growing on yellow or black soil shall be selected by the astronomer who, alone and at night, approaching the same, shall touch it and address it as follows.

17. "May it be well with the demons that dwell in this tree, salutation to you all, accept these presents and be pleased to dwell in some other place.

18. "O excellent tree, the king wants thee for the construction of his Indra-Dhwaja. May it be well with thee. I entreat thee to accept of this honour."

19. The astronomer shall, facing either the East or North, cut the tree before sunrise ; if, while cutting, the axe should produce a rustling sound, it indicates evil. If the sound should be agreeable or loud, it indicates good.

20. If the tree should fall on the East or North side without breaking or bending or being caught by a neighbouring tree, the ruler will become triumphant in war. If it should fall otherwise, the tree shall be rejected.

21. He shall cut off four inches at the top and eight inches at the bottom, and shall then put the wood in water. He shall then remove it to the town gate either in a cart or on the shoulders of men.

22. If, while it is being carried in a cart, any of the spokes of the wheels should break, the king's army will revolt ; if the felly of the wheel should break, the army will suffer destruction. If the axle should break, the king's wealth will suffer ; if the pin or bolt (at the end of the pole) should break, the carpenter will die.

23. On the Aṣṭhami (8th lunar) day of the light half of Bhādrapada, the king, accompanied by the citizens, astronomers, astrologers, ministers and priests in their robes.

24. Shall cause the beam to be carried in procession round the town after covering it with a new cloth, and adorning it with flowers and perfumes, sweet music playing all the while.

25. The town shall be adorned with flags, festoons and garlands ; the citizens shall all be merry, the street shall be kept neat and clean and the party shall be accompanied by dancing women in their best attire.

26. The houses and shops shall be decorated; Vedic hymns shall be chanted aloud ; dancers, and dancing masters and singers shall dance and sing at every corner and at the junction of roads.

27. If the flags with which the town is adorned should happen to be white, there will be success in war ; if yellow, there will be disease ; if of mixed color, there will also be success in battle, and if red, there will be wars in the land.

28. If while the beam is carried, it should be struck down from its place by a frightened elephant or other animals the

king will be afflicted with various fears ; or if children should clap their hands or animals engage in fight there will be wars.

29. The carpenter shall again work the beam into a proper shape and plant it over the place prepared for the purpose. The King shall spend the Yekadasi (11th lunar) day by the side of the beam without sleep.

30. The priests, dressed in white robes and turbans shall perform homa (fire ceremony), chanting hymns in honor of Indra and Viṣṇu and the astrologer shall note the indications around and build his predictions thereon.

31. If the flame of the homa fire should assume the appearance of benefic objects, if it should emit good odour or appear bright and large, it indicates prosperity to the King and not otherwise. I have treated of this subject in my work entitled the Yoga Yātrā.[4]

32. If at the moment of the final *āhuti* (pouring of ghee into the fire) the flame should appear bright and fine and whirl to the right, the King will become the sole ruler of the entire tract of land watered by the Ganges and the Jamunā and surrounded by seas on both sides.

33. If the flame should be of the color of gold, of the flower of Aśoka, of Kuraṇṭa or lotus or of the color of Vyduria or the blue lotus, the King will become so prosperous and wealthy that the dark rooms of his palace will be illumined by the rays of light proceeding from abundance of splendid gems.

34. If the sound of the flame should resemble that of ruling chariots, the sea, the clouds and elephants or the sound of drum, the king will become so prosperous that numberless rutting elephants will be seen rubbing against one another in the direction of his march and forming one dark scene as far as the eye can reach.

35. If the flame should present the shape of a pot, a horse, an elephant, a banner, or a mountain, the King will become the sole ruler of the country to which the Eastern and Western Ghauts form as lips and the Himalaya and Vindhaya mountains form as breasts.

36. If the fire should smell like the juice of elephants in nut, like the earth, the lotus, parched grain or honey, the king will become so prosperous and powerful that the ground before his seat will be lit with the rays of the gems in the crowns of rulers bending in submission before him.

37. What has been said with respect to the homa fire on the occasion of the ceremony in connection with Indra Dhwaja applies as well to homa fires on occasions of nativity, sacrificial fire ceremonies, Graha santy (purification of houses), royal marches and of marriages.

38. After feeding the Brāhmaṇs with rich and sumptuous meals and presenting them with money, the prince either on the 12th lunar day, when the Moon is in the asterism of Śravaṇ or other stars, shall have Indra's banner duly planted in its place.

39. According to Manu, images known as Indra's daughters, and seven or five in number, shall be made under the direction of men learned in the Śāstras : of these a figure known as Nandā shall be attached to the beam at a point which is a quarter of its height from the ground ; another figure known as Upanandā shall be fixed at the middle point of the beam.

40. A third figure known as Jayā shall be placed at a point alone Nandā whose distance is one-sixteenth of the height of the beam ; a fourth figure known as Vijaya shall be fixed at a similar height above Upanandā. Two more figures, each known as Vasundharā, shall be fixed at the same height, the one above Jayā and the other above Vijayā. A seventh figure known as Sakragenitri (Indra's mother) shall be fixed in the intervening space, one-eighth of the banner in height, lying below the central point.

41. The King shall further cause to be made the several ornaments of various shapes which the Devas were pleased to present to Indra's banner.

42. The first ornament was presented by Viśvakarma. It was oblongular in shape and of the color of red Aśoka flower ; the second was presented by both Brahma and Śiva. It was a girdle of various hues.

43. The third was presented by Indra. It was octagonal in

shape and black red in color. The fourth ornament, known as Masūraka, was presented by Yama ; it was black and glossy.

44. The fifth ornament was presented by Varuṇa ; it was hexagonal in shape and looked like a line of waves ; it was white-red in color. The sixth ornament was presented by Vāyu ; it was made of the feathers of the peacock and looked like blue clouds ; it was a bracelet for the upper arm.

45. The seventh ornament was presented by Subramania ; it was his own bracelet of curious make. The eighth was presented by Agni ; it was of the color of fire.

46. The ninth was presented by the Moon ; it was made of a precious stone resembling the Vyduriya. The tenth was presented by Tvaṣṭā, the Sun ; it looked like the wheel of a chariot.

47. The eleventh was presented by Viśvadevas ; it was of the shape of the lotus and was an ear ornament. The twelfth was presented by the Sages ; it was of the color of the blue lotus ; this was also an ear ornament.

48. The thirteenth was presented by Jupiter and Venus ; it was a head ornament ; it was a little bent both at the top and bottom, but broad at the former end ; it was red and was of the color of shellac.

49. The several ornaments above enumerated have for their lords the several Devas by whom they were respectively presented.

50. The first ornament shall be placed at a distance from the foot equal to a third of the circumference of the beam; the second above the first at seven-eighths of the distance of the former from the foot of the beam ; the third above the second at seven-eighths of the distance between the first and second, and so on.

51. On the fourth day the ceremony shall be completed. The following mantras, quoted by Manu and found in the Śāstras, shall then be recited.

52—55. "As thou were at one time pleased to accept the gift of a variety of splended ornaments made by the Devas accompanied by Śiva, the Sun, Yama, Indra, the Moon, Kubera, Agni, Varuṇa, the Sages, the Apsaras, Sukra (Venus), Guru (Jupiter),

Subramania and others, so we request thee to be pleased to accept now of a similar gift from us. Thou art Viṣṇu, the deity that exists throughout eternity,—the all-pervading principle—who appeared in his Varaha Avatar. Though art Yama, Agni, Hiranyagarbha, Indra and Jupiter. I invoke the all knowing Agni, the protecting Indra, the lord of the Devas, who is knowing under the names of Sakkra and Vṛtra, that our heroes may be successful.

56. The above sacred texts are to be recited by the king fasting, on the occasion of the completion of the ceremony, of planting the pole, on it entry into town, and when it is bathed and adorned with flowers, and at the closing ceremony.

57. The pole shall be adorned with an umbrella, a flag, mirror, fruits, crescent-shaped jewels, garlands of flowers plantains, sugar canes, with the figure of the tiger and of the lion, with the various ornaments already mentioned, and with figures shaped like the window, together with the figures of the eight Dikpatis, placed around.

58. The rope shall be unbroken ; the peg, driven into the ground, shall be of strong wood ; the pole shall be secured at the bottom within a strong wooden framework, and the figures known as Indra's daughters shall also be of strong wood. All these having been secured the flag shall be hoisted up amidst the joyful noise of the people, the blessings and salutation of the priests, the loud sound of the kettle drum, of tabor, of conch shell and other musical instruments, the sound of Vedic texts chanted by the Brāhmaṇs and in the absence of any inauspicious sound.

59. The king should ralse the banner to the making of noise by people drowing the unauspicious sounds through the auspicious invocations and benedictions, the loud shouts of the peoples should include sounds of drums, conchs, kettle-drums etc., and the loud chanting of the Vedic hymns by the Brāhmaṇas.

60. The people shall offer with both their hands fruits, curdled milk, ghee, fried grain, honey and flowers. They shall also offer their salutations and praises and shall assist at the ceremony. The banner shall be so placed that its end might be

bent a little in the direction of the enemy's city that he might become powerless.

61. If the banner could be raised neither hurriedly nor too slowly but steadily, and so that the garlands and numerous ornaments might not be injured, it indicates prosperity to the king ; if otherwise it indicates evil which the priests shall take steps to avert by expiatory ceremonies.

62. If the hawk, the owl, pigeons, crows and vultures should settle on the pole, the king will get into dangers and difficulties. If the blue jay or king-fisher should sit at the top, the first prince will suffer. If a falcon should in its fight, strike the tip of the pole, the king will lose his sight.

63. If the umbrella should break and fall down, the king will die If bees should begin to deposit honey in a corner, thieves will increase ; if a meteoric fall should occur at the time, the king's chaplain will die ; if a thunderbolt should occur, the queen will die.

64. If the flag should accidentally fall to the ground, the queen will die ; if any of the ornaments should drop down, there will be drought in the land ; if the pole should break in the middle, the chief minister will suffer ; if it should break at the top ; the king will suffer ; and if at the bottom, the citizens will suffer.

65. If the pole should accidentally happen to be surrounded by smoke, there will be fear from destructive fires ; if it should be surrounded by darkness, the land will fall into some serious hallucination ; if the figure of the tiger should break and fall, ministers will suffer ; if the pole should break and fall towards the north, east, south and west, the Brāhmaṇas, the Kṣatriyas, the Vaiśyas, and the Śūdras will suffer respectively.

66. If the rope should break and fall, children will suffer ; if the figure known as Indra's mother should fall, the king's mother will die ; any indications, for good or for evil, occurring at the time and connected with children and travellers, will also come to pass.

67. After keeping the flag hoisted up for four days, on the 5th day the king shall, after due pooja to it, have the flag brought down and thus close the ceremony for the well-being of his subjects and his army.

68. That prince will have nothing to fear from his enemies who duly respects and performs the ceremony connected with Indra Dhwaja, which was duly performed first by Vasu, king of Cedi, who was gifted with the power of flight into celestial regions and after him by numerous other kings.

REFERENCES

1. Already explained.
2. Dhava—Acacia Leucophloca.
3. Udumbara—The tree Ficus Glomerata.
4. A manuscript copy of this work is with Dr. Kerne now in Leydon, Holland.

CHAPTER 44

On the Lustration of Arms[1]

1. Soon after Bhagavān Viṣṇu rises[2] (from bed) to whom the clouds form as eyebrows, the Sun and Moon as eyes, and whose naval pit is like the lotus, the king shall perform the ceremony of lustration of arms for the health and well-being of his horses, elephants and subjects.

2. The ceremony known as lustration of arms shall be performed on the 12th, or the 8th or full Moon day of the light half of the month of Kārtika or Āśvina.

3. On some pure spot in the north-eastern part of the town shall be constructed a structure of fine wood, 16 cubits high and 10 cubits square at the top.

4. A lustration room shall also be constructed of the timber of Sala and of Udumbara as main beams, and of the branches of the Kakuba for rafters and cross-sticks, and of a thick coating of grass with an arch-way, adorned with a *matsya dhwaja* constructed of bamboos.

5. *Bhallataka*, *rice*, *coshta* and *Siddharta* (the white mustard) shall together be tied to the neck of horses already taken to the lustration room, by means of a string for the health of these animals.

6. Seven days shall be spent in the worship of sacrifical fire by the recitation of Vedic hymns sacred to the Sun, to Varuṇa, to Viśvadeva, to Brahma, to Indra and to Viṣṇu for the benefit of these horses.

7. When the conch and other musical instruments are sounded the horses should not be allowed to get frightened, nor should any expressions of censure be directed towards them, nor should they be beaten.

8. On the 8th day, to the south of the wooden structure and east of the shed there shall be formed a platform (a fire

place) surrounded by Kuśa grass and the bark of trees, facing the north.

9. The king shall cause to be put into the pots sandal paste, *Koshta, samanga, haritata, manassila, priyangu, vacha, danti, amrita, anjana, rajani, suvarnapushpa, and agnimantha.*

10. Also the roots of *Sveta*, of *Purnakosa*, of *Katambhara*, of *Trayamana*, and of *Sahaderi;* also the planets *Nagakusuma, Swagupta, Sotavaree* and *Somarajee*.

11. And the king shall cause due honors to be paid to the pots, offering to them cakes and sweetmeats made of honey, milk, and flour.

12. The king that loves wealth shall also cause to be offered to the fire, Āhutis of the dried twigs of the trees Kadira, Palasa, Oodumbara, Kashmira, and Aswatha; and the ghee vessels shall be made of gold or silver.

13. The king shall sit on tiger skin near the fire facing the east with horses, physicians and astronomers by his side.

14. The laws relating to the fire place (Vedi), to priests and to fires in connection with the Lustration ceremony are the same as those stated in connection with Yatra, Gṛhayajña and Indra Dhwaja.

15. The king shall adorn with white new cloths, sandal paste, perfumes and garlands, both elephants and horses of good breed and priests who have bathed.

16. He shall, addressing king words to these and with the music of the conch-shell and other instruments take them gently to the platform near the wooden structure.

17. If the horse thus led by the king should stand with its left leg lifted from the gro und, the king would only triumph over his enemies.

18. If the horse should get frightened, the king would suffer miseries; the effects described for various other indications connected with elephants and horses in the work on Yoga Yātrā apply equally to the Lustration of arms.

19. The priests shall give to the horse to eat a rice ball, touching the same; if the horse should either smell or eat the ball, the king will triumph in fight and will suffer defeat if otherwise.

20. The priest shall dip a twig of the glomerous fig tree into the water jars and rub it over the bodies of the horses, chanting the Santika and Ponshtika mantras; he shall similarly rub the twig over the army, the elephants and the king himself.

21. Besides, for the prosperity of the country, the priest, after performing homa by means of the *abhichara* mantra, shall, with the spear, stab in the breast a fiigure of the enemy made of earth.

22. The priest shall then touch with his fingers the bit of the bridle and put it in the horse's mouth. The king, after purification by Lustration, shall get on the back of the horses and attended by his army, shall proceed towards the north and other directions for purposes of conquest.

23. The king cheered by gentle winds, rendered odorous by contact with the juice of rutting elephants; pleased with the music of the drum and conch-shell; bright as the rising summer sun, from the numerous sparkling gems of his crown.

24. Resembling Mount Meru with its swans from the moving chamara on both sides; with garlands and clothes moved to and fro by the chamara air made sweet by contact with sandal paste.

25. Beautiful as the rainbow from the various hues of the light issuing from diamonds and other gems of his crown, ear pendants, armlets and the like.

26. Attended by horses that appear to soar aloft in the sky, by elephants that with their tread seem to cleave the earth, and by soldiers resembling a host of the Devas after successful battle, and himself like Indra shall march on horseback for purposes of conquest.

27. Or, adorned with jewels set with diamonds and pearls, with white garlands, turban, sandal paste and clothes; with the white umbrella spread over his head and mounted on the back of a huge black elephant, thus resembling the bright Venus with the Moon near it and over the dark clouds, he shall march for conquest.

28. The king who marches for conquest attended by foot soldiers, cavalry, and elephants, all in high spirits and with numerous bright weapons of war and striking terror into the heart of the enemy, shall easily conquer the earth.

Notes : Stanza 9; Koshta: Costus Arabicus
Samanga : Bengal madder.
Haritala : Sulphuret of arsenic.
Manassila : Redarsenic.
Priyangu : Panic seed.
Vacha : Orris root.
Danti : The plant Crotose polyandrum.
Amrita : Piper longum.
Anjana : Salphuret of Antimony.
Rajani : Curcuma longa.
Suvarnapushpa : The Globe amaranth.
Agnimantha : Premna spinosa.

Notes : Stanza 10 : Sveta : Aconitum feron.
Purnakosa : Achyranthes aspera.
Katambhara : The plant Bignonia Indica.
Trayamana : a medicinal plant : Caesalpina pulcherima.
Sahadevi : Herbs used in certain rites of ablution at the consecration of an idol :
Nagakusuma : Rottlera tinctoria.
Swagupta : plant Mucuna pruitus.
Satavaree : Asparagus : racemosus.
Somarajee : a medicinal plant Serratula or Vernonia Anthelminties

Notes : Stanza 12 : Udumbara : fig tree Ficus glomerata.
Kasmira : Ficus elastica.
The other terms have already been explained—Vide pp. 145 to 147.

REFERENCES

1. A military and religious ceremony held by kings on the 19th of Āśvini before taking the field.
2. This is the 11th lunar day of the light half of Kṛttikā when Viṣṇu rises from sleep.

CHAPTER 45

On the Wagtail[1]

1. I shall here state the effects of the first appearance the bird known as Khañjana (wagtail) on the king's march as stated by Sages.

2. If the bird should be one of the species possessing a large body and a long and black neck, it is known as Bhadra; it forebodes good luck; if it be one of the species black up to the neck or face, it is known as Sampūrṇa; it forebodes success.

3. If it be one of the species with a dark spot in the neck and with white cheeks, it is known as Rikta; it forebodes evil. If it be yellow, it is known as Gopeeta; it also forebodes evil.

4. If it should be seen on trees of sweet fruits and fragrant flowers or close to sacred water, or on the heads of elephants, horses and serpants, on the tops of temples and on the king's palace, in flower gardens or on the mansions of the rich.

5. Near cows, cowpens, gatherings of sadhus or holymen sacrificial fire sites, festival places, kings, Brāhmaṇs, elephant-sheds, horse-sheds, an umbrella, a flag-staff, a chamara, and the like.

6. Near gold, white cloth, places adorned with the lotus and the water lily, in places, washed with cowdung, on vessels containing curdled milk, or on heaps of grain, it forebodes prosperity to the king.

7. If it should be seen near swampy places, the king would eat sumptuous meals; if on cowdung, he will get a good supply of milk and curd; if on green turf he would get good cloths, and if on chariots, he would leave his kingdom.

8. If it should be seen seated on the tops of houses, the king would lose his wealth; if on snares, he would be imprisoned; if on impure places, he would suffer from disease; and if on the back of the sheep, he would soon obtain his desired object.

9. If it should be seen seated on the back of a buffalo, a camel, an ass, on the bones of animals, on cremation grounds, in the corners of houses, on pebbles or gravels, or rocks, on the walls of towns, on ash and on hair, there would be deaths, diseases and fears in the land.

10. If it should be seen when it is shaking off its wings, there would be misery in the land; if when in the act of drinking water from the river, there would be prosperity; there would also be prosperity if seen about sunrise; and if about sun-set, there would be misery in the land.

11. If the king should march in the direction in which the wagtail should be seen to fly immediately after the Lustration ceremony is over, he would triumph over his enemies.

12. Where the wagtail should be seen to copulate, there would be treasure in the ground under; where it should be found to vomit, there would be crystal beads in the ground under it; where it passes stool, there would be found charcoal under ground; these may be found to be the case on actual examination.

13 If the wagtail should be found dead, the king would die, if of broken limbs, the king would suffer similarly; if covered with wounds, a similar fate will befall the king; if found to enter its nest, the king would get wealth and if perceived in its flight, his relatives will visit him.

14. If the king should chance to see in some pure spot a wagtail foreboding good, he shall then and there perform pūjā on the ground with sandal paste, flower, and perfumed smoke; he is then sure to prosper.

15. If he should chance to see a wagtail foreboding evil, he shall perform pūjā to Brāhmaṇas, preceptors, yogis and the Devas; he will escape the evil effects. He shall abstain from meat for 7 days.

16. The effects of the first sight of the wagtail will come to pass within a year; if during this peroid the wagtail should be seen again, the effects of such second sight will come to pass that same day before sunset; in making predictions from the wagtail the astrologer shall take into account the direction of its flight, its place, bady, the rising Zodiacal sign at the time,

the Nakṣatra or the Moon's place at the time, and whether the bird is seen with its face turned to the sun or away from the sun.

REFERENCE

1. The bird is known as Khañjana in Sanskrit. It is a species of wagtail. Mounta alla, Alba.

CHAPTER 46

On Portents

A

Portents connected with idols or statues of the Devas in the Temples.

1. I shall now proceed to state the Laws relating to portents which Bhagavān Garga taught to Atri; what follows is a summary of the same.

2. Mankind, because of their sins, suffer misfortunes, and the approach of these is indicated by portents, stellar, atmospheric and terrestrial;

3. Mankind, by their misdeeds, offend the Devas, and the Devas send down portents to indicate their displeasure; the king shall perform expiatory rites for the redress of the miseries which otherwise are sure to befall mankind.

4. Unusual phenomena connected with the planets and stars are known as stellar portents. Meteors, thunderbolts, tempests, halos, cloud castles, rainbows and the like are known as atmospheric portents.

5. Any unusual phenomena connected with both movable and immovable terrestrial objects are known in terrestrial portents. The effects of these can be avoided by means of expiatory rites, whereas the effects of atmospheric portents can only be *softened* by such ceremonies, and in the opinion of some the effects of stellar portents cannot be avoided of softened by any means.

6. Our own opinion is that even stellar portents can be assuaged in the rigour of their effects by large gifts of gold, food, cows and lands, and by drawing down the milk of cows on the temple floor and by a crore of *āhutis* in the sacred fire.

7. The king, in consequence of his sins in his former birth,

will be afflicted in his own person, in his children, treasury, vehicles, citizens, wives, priests and subjects at large.

8. If the Liṅga and the Idols of the Devas in the temple should for no apparent cause break, move, perspire, shed tears, fall down, speak or do the like, the king's country would suffer miseries.

9. If on festive occasions the car, the axle, the wheel, the yoke, or the flag should break or fall, or if any of them should be found to have been removed from its place and another put in its stead, or if the tie should break and the parts get loose or if the car should stick into the ground and refuse to move, the king will suffer with his country.

10. Portents connected with the idols or statues of the Sages, of Yama, the Pitridevas and of Brahma will affect the Brāhmaṇas, the Kṣatriyas and the Vaiśyas. Those connected with the statues of Rudra and the Dik Palakas will affect the lower animals.

11. Portents connected mith the statues of Jupiter, Venus and Saturn will affect the family priest. Those connected with the statue of Viṣṇu, will affect mankind at huge. Portents connected with the statues of Skanda and Taska will affect the provincial rulers.

12. Portents connected with the statue of Vedavyāsa will effect the minsiters; those connected with the statue of Vināyaka will affect the commanders of armies; those connected with the statues of Dhātā and Vidhātā indicate the instruction of the world.

13. Portents connected with the statues of the sons, doughters, wives and servants of the Devas will affect the king's sons, daughters, wives and servants.

14. Portents connected with the statues of the demons, the goblins, the Yakṣas and the Nāgas will affect in before the king's sons, daughters, wives and servants. The above will all take effect within eight months.

15. When any unusual phenomena portentous in their nature occur in connection with the statues of Devas in temples, the priests shall bathe and fast for 3 days, and with a pious mind also bathe the statues in water and adorn them with flowers, sandal paste, cloth and the like.

16. He shall satisfy the Devas by the offer of Madhunparka,[1] sweetmeats and cooked rice, and he shall throw *āhutis* of boiled rice into the fire, chanting mantras appropriate to the several Devas.

17. That king who for seven days shall perform homa, feed Brāhmaṇas and worship the Devas accompanied by music and dance, and who shall present large sums of money to the Brāhmaṇas, shall be freed from the effects of all his sins.

B

Portents connected with Fire

18. That prince will suffer with his kingdom in whose province a fire breaks out where there is no fire or fire ceases to burn even when fed with fuel.

19. If either water or flesh or any wet substance should catch fire and burn, the king will suffer miseries; if weapons of war should catch fire and burn, there would be war in the land.

20. If temples and palaces of kings or the mansions of the rich, archways or gates, flag staff and the like should catch fire and burn, or if these should do so being struck by lightning, there would surely be a foreign invasion of the land 6 months after occurrence.

21. If smoke should appear in a place where there is no fire, or if a dust storm or darkness should cover the land during day time, or if the stars should be invisible at night when the sky is cloudless, or if the stars should be visible during the day time, mankind will be subject to various fears.

22. If fire should break out for no apparent cause, towns, quadrupeds, birds and men will suffer. If beds, clothes or the hair on one's head should be seen to smoke or with sparks of fire, there would be deaths in the land.

23. If weapons of war should be seen to catch fire, or become like snakes, or should sound or come out of their case or quiver, there will be fearful wars in the land.

24. When portents connected with fire occur the king shall satisfy god Agni by homa ceremonies, throwing, into the fire *āhutis* of the twigs of milky trees, of mustard seed and of ghee, and he shall present gold to the Brāhmaṇas.

C

Portents connected with Trees

25. If the branches of trees should break and fall down for no apparent cause, there would be wars in the land; if the trees should be heard to laugh, the king would quit his dominions; if they should be heard to weep, diseases would increase.

26. If the trees should bear fruits or flowers in the wrong season, the country will be attacked by the enemy; if young trees should blossom, children will perish; if the juice of trees should ooze out, all articles will suffer.

27. If toddy should ooze out from trees, the king's vehicles will suffer injuries; if blood should ooze out, there will be wars in the land; if honey, mankind will suffer from diseases; if oil, there will be famine, and if water, there will be great fears.

28. If a dead tree should sprout and grow, or if aliving tree should suddenly die, there will be decrease of strength and food in the land; if a tree which has fallen should rise of itself, there will be fear from diseases.

29. If the superior trees should bear blossoms or fruits in the wrong season, or if such trees should catch fire or smoke, kings will be killed.

30. If trees should grow like serpents or talk, mankind will suffer death. In the case of portents connected with trees, the effects will begin to be felt after ten months.

31. For the expiation of the evils the priests shall honor the tree with flowers, sandal paste, perfumed smoke, cloths, and the like, and hold an umbrella over it, and placing a Śivaliṅga at its foot shall perform Rudrajapa and offer to the fire six *āhutis* in honor of Rudra.

32. The king shall feed Brāhmaṇas with rice cooked in milk, with honey and with ghee. In the case of portents connected with trees, the Sages have directed that the king shall make gifts of land to the Brāhmaṇas.

D

Portents connected with Crops

33. If the stem or stock of the lotus, barley and the like should be found to divide into branches, or if crops should bear

double fruits or double flowers, the owner or proprietor of the land will die.

34. If crops should grow over-luxuriantly, or if a single tree should bear a variety of fruits or flowers, the country will be invaded by the enemy.

35. If the gingelly should yield double the usual quantity of oil, or if such seed should contain no oil, or if rice should be found without flavor, mankind will suffer from great fears.

36. Flowers or fruits portentous in their nature should be removed beyond the limits of the village or town. In such cases, the priests shall satisfy God Soma by the offer of rice *āhutis* to the fire or by animal sacrifices.

37. In the case of any portents connected with crops, both the crops and the land should be presented to the Brāhmaṇas. In the middle of the very land the king shall satisfy the earth by the offer to the fire of rice āhuti : the evils will then disappear.

E

Portents connected with Rainfall

38. Drought forebodes famine; excessive rain forebodes suffering from hunger and foreign invasion; rainfall in the wrong season forebodes disease, and rainfall from a cloudless sky forebodes the king's assassination.

39. When the seasons are otherwise good the presence of heat in the place of cold or that of cold in the place of heat, or the absence of either, forebodes that 6 months after and through supernatural interference the kingdom will be in danger and mankind will suffer from diseases.

40. If there should be continued rain for 7 days in a wrong season, the chief minister and the sovereign will die; if there should fall a shower of blood, armed men will engage in fight; if there should fall a shower of flesh, bones, or marrow, mankind will suffer from pox or plague.

41. If there should fall a shower of grain, gold, skin, fruits, flowers or the like, mankind will suffer from various fears, and if there should fall a shower of charcoal or dust, the town will perish.

42. If when the sky is cloudless, there should fall a shower of stones or of creatures of unusual appearance, or if there should be either a drought or excessive rain, the crops will suffer injuries known as Eetibadha.[2]

43. If there should fall a shower of milk, ghee, honey, cardled milk, blood or warm water, the country will meet with rain; in the case of a shower of blood, the king will be at war.

44. If when the sun shines bright and when he is not hid by clouds or the like, objects should be found to cast no shadows at all, or if the shadows should be of wrong shapes, the country will suffer from various fears.

45. If when the sky is without clouds, the rainbow should appear at day or night in the east or west, there will be a great famine in the land.

46. In the case of portents connected with showers, the priest shall perform homa in honour of the Sun and of the deities presiding over the clouds and the winds; and the king shall also give to the Brāhmaṇas grain, rice, cows and gold.

F

Portents connected with Water

47. If rivers should, in course of time, recede from towns, or if deep lakes in the neighbourhood should become dry, such towns would be deserted by the inhabitants.

48. If rivers should be seen to run carrying oil, blood or flesh, or if the water should be found very muddy, or if they should be seen to run in opposite directions, there would be foreign invasion of the country after six months.

49. If wells should be found to blaze, to smoke, to boil, to weep, to call, to sing or to spring mankind would suffer from plague or pox.

50. If water should be found to spring from places undug, or if its smell or flavor should suffer change, there would be great fears in the land; if any unusual phenomena should occur near pieces of water, there would also be great fears. The king shall perform expiatory rites in the very places as prescribed below.

51. In the case of portents connected with water, the priest shall perform homa in honor of Varuṇa, reciting the mantras sacred to him.

G

Portents connected with Births

52. If two, three, four or more children should be born to a woman at a time, or if the offspring should be of defective organs, or if it should be born with extra organs, the country would suffer miseries as well as the family.

53. If a mare, a she camel, a buffaloe or a cow should bear twins, these animals would perish after six months; in the case of portents connected with births, Garga has prescribed, in two stanzas, certain expiatory rites.

54. He (the husband) who desires prosperity should banish the woman to foreign lands and should satisfy Brāhmaṇas by the gift of what they are fond of, and shall also perform expiatory homa ceremonies.

55. In the case of quadrupeds, they too shall be separated from the herd and expelled to foreign lands; if not, the ruler of the towns as well as the herd of cattle would perish.

H

Portents connected with Quadrupeds

56. Among quadrupeds if an animal of one species should copulate with one of another and procreate issues, cows and birds would suffer; if either bulls or cows or dogs should suck each other.

57. There would be foreign invasion of the country after three months. Garga has prescribed, in two stanzas, certain expiatory rites :

58. The animals shall either be rejected or expelled to foreign lands or given away to others. The Brāhmaṇas shall also be satisfied with presents. Japa and Homa ceremonies shall also be performed.

59. The priest shall satisfy God Dhātā by the offer to fire

of rice and by animal sacrifice by means of the Prajāpati mantras; Brāhmaṇas shall also be fed largely and given money.

I

Portents connected with the Wind

60. If vehicles should move when not drawn by horses or other animals, or if they should refuse to move when so drawn, the country would suffer from various fears, and the army would perish.

61. If, when unstruck, instruments of music should be heard to sound, or if they should not sound when struck or produce wrong sounds, there would be foreign invasion or the reigning sovereign would perish.

62. If vocal or instrumental music or the sound of the drum or any other mysterious noise should be heard in the sky, or if moving objects should refuse to move and immovable objects begin to move, or if a drum should be found to be mute when struck, the ruler would suffer death, disease or defeat in battle.

63. If monkey-apes should be seen to copulate, or if ladles, winnowing baskets or other utensils should be heard to sound in an unusual manner, or if a jackal should be heard to howl, there would be wars in which armed men would engage in fight, according to the sages.

64. In the case of portents connected with the wind the king shall worship a representation of God Vāyu made of the flour of barley, and shall have the five mantras beginning with "Avayo" recited by Brāhmaṇas.

65. He shall satisfy the Brāhmaṇas by feeding them with rice cooked in milk and by the gift of money to them, and by rice homa ceremonies shall also be performed and the officiating Brāhmaṇas shall be paid liberally.

J

Portents connected with Animals and Birds

66. If country birds should begin to dwell in woods, or if wild birds should begin to dwell in towns, or if day birds should

be found to move about at night, or if night birds should be found to move about during the day.

67. If either animals or birds should be found to move in circles either immediately before sunrise or after sunset, or if they should be herd together and howl in the direction of the sun, the country would suffer miseries.

68. If dogs should be found to cry at the gates of houses in a weeping tone, or if jackals should be found to howl facing the sun, or if a dove or owl should enter the palace of the king.

69. If the cock should be heard to cry soon after sunset, or if the cuckoo should be heard to cry in the hemanta (cold) season, or if the hawk and the like birds should be found to move in circles from right to left, there would be misery in the land.

70. If birds should swarm about houses, places of worship, towers or gates, or if honey-combs or ant-hills or lotus should be found to be formed or to grow in such places, there would be misery in the land.

71. If dogs should bring within human dwellings bones or limbs of dead bodies, there would be plague in the land. If animals and weapons should be found to speak, the king would die; and the Sages of old say as follows.

72. In the case of portents connected with birds and animals homa (fire) ceremonies shall be performed, and the officiating Brāhmaṇas shall well be paid. Five Brāhmaṇas shall be appointed to recite the mantra beginning with "Devaḥ Kapotaḥ."

73. A large number of cows shall be presented to Brāhmaṇas, each gift being made by the recitation of the mantra beginning with "Sudeva." The Brāhmaṇas shall also be made to recite Śakūnisūktam as well as the Upaniṣads and the Śivasankalpa mantras.

K

Miscellaneous portents

74. If Indra's banner, bolts, pillars or gates should break

or fall down, or if doors, towers, flag-staffs should break or fall down, the king would die.

75. If both the morning and evening sky should appear to be burning, or if there should be smoke in a forest where there is no fire, or if ditches should appear in places where there were none before, or if earthquakes should occur, there would be misery in the land.

76. That country would suffer miseries whose ruler respects heretics or atheists, or who refuses to follow the rules of life observed by the great and holy men of the land, or who is of an irascible temper, or who is jealous or fearful and who is inclined to quarrel with his subjects.

77. That country will also suffer in which children are found with weapons, pieces of wood or sticks in their hands beating (animals) and uttering such expressions as beat, kill, cut, break and the like.

78. That house will meet with ruin in whose walls figures of dead men or of the master of the house is drawn with charcol or red chalk.

79. That house will also suffer miseries in which is seen the spider's web or which is not swept clean and adorned with flowers both morning and evening, or in which there is constant quarrel between persons, or where the lady of the house is for ever dirty.

80. If Rākṣasas are seen, there will be plague in the land. Garga has prescribed ceremonies for the expiation of the evils of all miscellaneous portents.

81. The eighteen Mahāśānti ceremonies (great ceremonies of expiation) prescribed in the Adharvana Veda must be performed. Bali (food) shall also be offered in honor of Indra and Indrani (Indra's queen) who shall also be worshipped in every month.

L

Phenomena which are not portents

82. If after the occurrence of a portentous phenomenon, either the king should die or the country should suffer miseries,

or if a comet should appear, or a solar or lunar eclipse should occur, or if the phenomenon is one due to the particular season, the evils described for such phenomenon would not come to pass.

83. What phenomena are not portents but are due to the particular seasons are briefly stated by the sons of Sages (in the following 12 stanzas).

84. If in the Vasanta Ṛtu (April—May) there should occur a thunderbolt or an earthquake, or if the roar of thunder should be heard immediately before sun-rise and after sun-set, or if the appearance of a halo, dust-storm or smoke should be seen, or if the sun should appear very red both at rising and setting.

85. Or if trees should yield fool, juice, oil, honey, flowers or fruits, and if cows and birds should appear lustful, there would be prosperity in the land.

86. If in the Grīṣma Ṛtu (summer) shooting stars and meteors should fall, and the discs of the sun and moon should appear brown, or if things should appear to burn or smoke or covered with sparks, in the absence of fire, or if the sky should be full of dust or disturbed by the wind.

87. Or if the red sky of the morning and evening should appear disturbed and agitated as the sea, or if rivers should fall or become dry, there would be prosperity in the land.

88. If in the winter season such appearance as the rainbow, halos and lightning should mark the sky, or if a dead tree should sprout and grow, or earthquakes occur, or elevated grounds should become hollow or hollow grounds should become elevated, or if mysterious noise should be heard from below the earth, or if ditches should be formed on the surface of the earth.

89. Or if tanks, rivers, ponds and the like should be flooded with water, or if such water should overflow the banks, or if landslips occur or houses should break and fall, there would be no cause for fear.

90. If in the Śarat Ṛtu (October and November) the wives of the Devas, or the Demons, the Gandharvas or the vehicles of the Devas should appear in the sky, or if during the day the

planets, the constellations, or any of the stars should become visible.

91. Or if music, vocal or instrumental, should be heard in forests or on hills, or if crops should thrive or water decrease in quantity, there would be no cause for fear.

92. If in the Hemanta Ṛtu (December and January) cold winds should blow or snow should fall, or if animals and birds should be heard to cry, or if Rākṣasas and Yakṣas should be seen or voice should be heard in the sky.

93. Or if the horizon, the sky, the forests and mountains should appear dark as if covered with smoke, or if the sun should be invisible both at rising and setting, there would be prosperity double in the land.

94. If in the Śiśira Ṛtu (February and March) snow should fall or portents connected with air should occur, or any unusual or wonderful appearances should be seen, or if the sky should appear black as collyrium, or if shooting stars or meteors should fall;

95. If women should give birth to children of unnatural form, or if cows, sheep, horses, deer or birds should do the same, or if leaves, sprouts or creepers should be of unnatural appearanee, there would be prosperity in the land.

96. If unusual phenomena, due to particular seasons, occur in such seasons, there would be prosperity in the land, and if they occur in other seasons, there would be misery in the land.

97. The utterances of mad men, of children and of women will never fail to come to pass.

98. Words of truth are to be found in the Devas, from them they come to men; human words are therefore prompted by the Devas and are therefore true.

99. Even though ignorant of astronomy and astrology, if a person should be well learned in the laws of portents, he would become famous and would be liked by the king. I have thus stated the secret views of the Sages by a thorough study of which one acquires a knowledge of the past, of the present and of the future.

REFERENCES

1. Madhuparka : a mixture of honey and clarified butter.
2. Eetibadha : plague, distress, drought, excessive rain, swarm of rats and foreign invasion.

CHAPTER 47

Motley Miscellany

1. I have stated the effects of a number of stellar, atmospheric and terrestrial phenomena, and of the motions, conjunctions, courses and the like of the planets to some extent.

2. An attempt at recapitulation of the above will be deemed a fault in Varahamihira, who is so well known for his brevity in composition. It is no doubt improper to estate what have been once stated, but Jyotiṣakas will set deem it fault on the present occasion. For it is a well known fact that every work on Saṁhita must have a chapter of this nature, technically known as Mayūrachitraka.

3. Mayūrachitraka is a repetition of what has been once said. If I should omit this Chapter, even then, I should be open to the fault of an omission of what ought to find a place in a work on Saṁhita.

4. If the five planets should be of brilliant appearance and should pass through the northern path, there would be prosperity and plenty in the land; if they should be of dim appearance and pass through the southern path, there would be famine and deaths in the land and mankind would suffer from robbers.

5. If Venus should pass through the asterism of Maghā while Jupiter passes through that of Puṣya, rulers would cease to be hostile with one another, and would become happy and the people would be freed from diseases and would become happy.

6. If the moon and the five planets should oppress[1] any of the asterisms of Kṛttikā, Maghā, Rohiṇī, Śravaṇa, and Jyeṣṭhā, iniquity would prevail in the western countries.[2]

7. If, in the evening, the planets should appear of the shape of a flagstaff in the eastern sky, the eastern rulers would

be at war with one another; if the planets should be seen of the same shape but of disagreeable appearance and in mid-heaven, the people of Madhyadesha would suffer miseries. But if the appearance should be agreeable, there would be no suffering.

8. If the planets should so appear in the southern sky, there would be drought in the southern countries; and if the planets should appear of small ugly discs, the rulers would be at war with one another; but if the discs should be large and bright, there would be prosperity in the land.

9. If the planets should be seen of bright appearance in the northern sky, the northern rulers will be freed from evils; but if the discs of the planets should be small and of ashy color, the ruler will suffer with their countries.

10. If the constellations, the stars and the planets, should appear to smoke, to burn or to be covered with sparks of fire, or to lose their light for no apparent cause, the rulers and the world would perish.

11. If two moons should be seen in the sky, the Brāhmaṇas would prosper; if two suns should be seen, the Kṣatriyas would be at war; if three or four suns should be seen in the sky, the world would come to an end.

12. If a comet should be seen to pass through or be in contact with the constellation of Ursa Major (the Saptarṣtis), the Abhijit, the Pole star and the constellation of Jyeṣṭha, the clouds would be destroyed; there would be good deeds in the land, and men would suffer from grief. If the comet should appear in contact with Āśleṣa, there would be drought in the land; and the people with hungry children would quit their countries and travelling to foreign lands would their perish. This is certain.

13. When Saturn is seen to retrograde through any of the seven asterisms from Kṛttika, there will be famine in the land and mankind will suffer from great fears; friends will become hostile to one another, and there will also be drought in the land.

14. When the course of Saturn or of Mars or of a comet should lie through the circle (Sakata) of the constellation of

Rohiṇī, the whole world would sink in the deep as of misery and perish; and how can I adequately describe the condition of suffering humanity then!

15. If a comet should continue visible for a long time, or if it should pass through all the constellations, all the creatures together with all the movable and immovable objects would suffer miseries in accordance with their previous karma.

16. If the moon should appear like a bow, be of disagreeable aspect and of blood color, mankind would suffer from hunger. People living in the direction of the bow string would become powerful and successful in fight. If the moon's horn should point downwards, cows and crops would suffer; if it should appear to blaze or smoke, rulers would perish.

17. If the moon should appear bright, glossy and of large disc, and if both her horns should be alike, broad and elevated, and if the course of the moon should lie through the north of the Nāga Vīdhi and she should be within sight of benefic planets and free from the influence of malefic ones, mankind would be happy.

18. If the course of the moon should lie to the south of the asterism of Magha, Anurādhā, Jyeṣṭhā, Viśākhā or Citrā, there would be misery in the land; but if her course should lie through the middle or to the north of the same asterisms, there would be prosperity in the land.

19. The line of clouds across the sun's disc at rising or setting is known as Parigha; Paridhi is also known as Pratisūrya or Parhelion, and Daṇḍa is an appearance of the shape of a straight rainbow.

20. The long rays of the rising or setting sun as known as Amogha rays and Airāvata is an appearance resembling a long straight broken rainbow.

21. Sandhyā is the period of time when the stars continue invisible both before sun-rise and after sun-set.

22. If the appearances of Parigha and the like should be seen during the period of Sandhyā (twilight), there would be prosperity in the land, and if the appearances should be glossy, there would be immediate rain; and if of disagreeable appearance, there would be wars and the like in the land.

23. If the appearance known as Parigha should be perfect and unbroken, if the sky should be clear, the solar rays blue and glossy, the rainbow white, and if lightning should be seen in the north-eastern sky, and if the appearance known as Abra-vṛkṣa (cloud-tree) should be glossy and covered by the rays of the sun, and if the evening sun should be hid by clouds, there would be immediate rain.

24. There would be anarchy in that country in which the sun should appear broken or if irregular shape, or black or small, or with spots of the shape of the crow and of disagreeable aspect.

25. If a swarm or carnivorous birds should follow an army marching out for fight, such army would suffer defeat in battle, but if the birds should fly before the army, there would be success in battle.

26. If at the hour of sunrise or sunset the army resembling cloud castles should hide the solar disc, the king would be entangled in a fearful war.

27. If birds and animals should cry aloud in the direction opposite to the sun, and if the twilight sky should be of bright appearance and rendered agreeable by gentle winds, there would be prosperity in the land. If, on the other hand, such twilight sky should be covered with dust or of the color of the blood or of disagreeable appearance, the country would suffer miseries.

28. Of the many truths stated by Sages in their Chapter entitled Mayūracitraka, I have rejected those which were mere repetitions and stated the rest. Even after hearing the musical note of the cuckoo the crow is not mute; and when it caws, it is not with a view to imitate or excel the cuckoo.

Note—It may be well to add here certain notes relating to the phenomena of nature called from other Śāstras.

There will be famine as long as the course of Jupiter and that of Saturn lie through the end of the signs Aries and Scorpio and through the middle of Taurus and Leo.

During the period when Jupiter and Saturn occupy a single sign of the Zodiac, there would be pestilence, cholera and death among the people.

As long as Jupiter and Venus continue together in a state of disappearance, mankind will suffer from devils, diseases, thieves and enemies.

If the course of Saturn or the retrogade motion of Mars should lie through the signs of Sagittarius, Aries, Taurus, Pisces or Leo, there would be such deaths among men and animals that only a third of mankind, of elephants, horses, cows and other animals, of birds and of creatures of water would survive.

If the motion of Mars should be an accelerated one, there would be fear from destructive fires; if he should retrograde and enter another sign, the people would suffer from heat and many families would suffer, and if his course should lie through a sign longer than the calculated period, there would be drought in the land and rulers will be at war.

If Jupiter should retrograde or if his motion should be an accelerated one, and if in this state he should enter another sign, the rivers would not be full; the kings would lose their glory and suffer from diseases.

If Saturn should, after a long direct course, begin to retrograde or have an accelerated motion, and in this state enter another sign, there would be diseases, famine and drought in the land and vehicles will suffer destruction.

If, when Jupiter should enter another sign when in his accelerated motion, Saturn should be in his slow motion, Venus should have disappeared, and Mercury should have reappeared, the country would perish.

If Saturn, Mars and Jupiter should be within sight of each other, men with their children would suffer from hunger and from weapons.

If, while the course of the sun lies through the end of the signs Taurus, Gemini, Scorpio and Leo, Jupiter and Mars should be in conjunction with it, mankind would suffer from famine, and the deaths would be so many that in the cremation grounds of villages and towns, Piśācas might be seen with hundreds of dead bodies in their mouths.

If two or three or four planets should meet together, people would suffer from death and famine. If five planets should meet, there would also be famine ; if six, the chief ruler would run away from his kingdom, and if seven, humanity would come to an end.

If the course of Mars and Saturn, through the signs of Cancer, Leo and Pisces should be retrograde or re-retrograde, there would be much suffering on earth. There would also be a scarcity of water and wars in the land ; grains would be destroyed and mankind would suffer from robbers.

If Saturn and Rāhu should meet, crops would be injured ; commodity would become scarce ; husbands and wives would be at strife, there would be drought and famine in the land ; cows would suffer death and men would become exceedingly lazy.

If the course of the sun and moon, both of brilliant discs, should lie through the seven asterisms from Kṛttikā, Madhyadesa would suffer miseries.

If the course of the Sun, the Moon, Mars and Venus should lie through the seven asterisms from Maghā, there would be grief and disease among men, and the God of death would be busy in his wide work of destruction in the southern countries.

If the course of Jupiter, the Moon and Mercury, all of brilliant discs, should lie through the seven asterisms from Anurādhā, the western countries, as far as the sea, as well as the western sea itself with its creatures, would suffer miseries.

If the course of the Sun, Venus and Mars should lie through the seven asterisms from Śraviṣṭha, the northern countries would suffer miseries. If the benefic plants should appear of the color of gold, the Brāhmaṇas, the Kṣatriyas, the Vaiśyas and the Śūdras would all attend to their respective duties and would become happy.

This brings us to the end of Saṁhitā Proper or the first half of Saṁhitā. In this part over one thousand phenomena of nature have been treated, each of which must have taken the ancient Hindus years of observation and tabulation. As these affect the well-being of humanity, a study of same must be calculated to add to human happiness ; most of the phenomena might appear improbable of occurrence, but it would be wrong, judging from our limited experience of Nature's ways to say that she will never be caught playing this trick or that, or guilty of this freak or that. The solar spots is now an admitted fact. This was soon followed by a green sun. The mysterious noise heard recently in parts of Southern India is another instance of the kind. A few years ago it was reported in certain newspapers that in the District of Cornwall, England, there occurred a shower of flesh—vast fields being found literally covered with flesh several inches deep, more instances of the kind may be quoted. Indeed mysterious are the ways of nature, and there is no saying what she may or she may not be capable of. The present volume therefore becomes exceedingly interesting, as it embodies in a small compass a vast body of useful and curious information regarding the phenomena of Nature together with their effects and the means for removing the evils thereof.

The second part would be more interesting to the general public. A variety of interesting subjects are treated of in it. It would be well to state here briefly a few of such subjects :—

The Chapter on Puṣyāsnana treats of a particular bath for the king. This might as well be used by any body else—the ingredients to be put into water containing evidently certain magnetic properties.

The Chapter on the Royal Sword contains certain methods for tempering cutting instruments.

The Chapter on Aṅga Vidyā relates to the interpretation of accidental gestures, movements, utterances and the like of man especially. It rests on the basis that an all-pervading universal intelligence speaks in a thousand ways, and that it is for man to interpret such language and benefit himself by it. Scoffers will be least benefited by this chapter. Earnest enquirers after truth, studying this branch of the science will be enabled to make pretty correct predictions.

The Chapter on Under Currents is also an interesting one. The author proposes to discover the position, depth and course of under-currents from the appearance of the ground above. The subject requires investigation. If there should be truth in the author's statements, many of the ṭube wells and boring instruments may be very well dispensed with.

Equally interesting is the chapter relating to the plantation and growth of trees. According to the author, all seed trees can be made to grow like creepers by preparing the seeds in a particular way.

The subject of house building, and with it that of the preparation of strong cements, known as Vajralepana are also treated.

The auther then treats of the features and other qualities of superior elephants, horses, dogs and the like. In this connection the subject of Samudrika, which relates to the determination of the fortunes of man from the marks and lines of his body and of which palmistry is a branch, is also treated.

The subject of the kind treatment of women is then taken up. Rules are also laid down for the preparation of scents and perfumes. A few lines are devoted to the subject of sexual love and of beds and cots.

The author then examines the qualities of superior diamonds, rubies, pearls and the like.

The subject of omens and prognostications is also treated.

The above is by no means an exhaustive list. While part I is instructive, Part II is interesting.

REFERENCES

1. Oppress : This means cutting through, retrograde motion, conjunctions and the like.
2. Western countries : also there would be famine, the crops would fail and rivers would become dry.

CHAPTER 48

Royal Bath

1. The king forms the root of the tree of Society. As the Society prospers or suffers according as the king is in a healthy or unhealthy condition of mind or body, he becomes an important subject for consideration.

2. That ceremony of purification dictated by Brahma to Bṛhaspati for the benefit of Indra and learning which Vṛddha Garga taught to Bhāguri, hear now from me.

3. The priest and the astrologer shall advise and help the king to have the bath known as Puṣya Sṇāna. There is no bath as effective as this in freeing the king from all evils.

4. The site for the bath shall be free from the trees Sleshmataka[1] and Aksha[2], and from thorny trees and trees of pungent and bitter flavor as well as trees of bad odour; and the place shall also be free from owls, vultures and the like birds.

5. It may be a beautiful forest full of luxuriant trees, shrubs, creepers, thin tendrils, thick foliage, and of tender leaves.

6. Or it may be some pure building near a forest rendered beautiful by the presence of the cock, the pheasant, the parrot, the peacock, the woodpecker, the king-fisher, the haritala pigeons, the krikava (a kind of partridge), the cuckoo, the francoline partridge, the chataka, the manjula the turtle dove and the like.

7. And by bees intoxicated by sucking the honey from flowers, and by the cuckoo and the like ;

8. Or it may be the beautiful and agreeable beds of rivers with lines made by birds at play.

9. Or it may be by the side of a tank with the blue lotus for its eyes, the jumping swan for its umbrella, and with the music of the duck, the osprey, and the crane, thus resembling Indra.

10. Or it may be by the side of a tank of lotus whose stem resembles a girl with the full blown flower for her eyes, the music of the swan for her voice, and the big buds for her bosom.

11. Or it may be a cow pen rendered agreeable by the falling foam from the mouth of the cows, by their dung, their foot-prints, and by the skipping of the new born calf.

12. Or it may be some spot on the sea beach near a harbour full of tall ships, that have made successful voyages and rendered pleasant by birds living in the hijjal trees.

13. Or it may be the sacred hermitage of some sages in which the lion is not feared by the doe, and in which a promise of protection is given to helpless birds and to the young deer.

14. Or it may be some human dwelling rendered happy by the presence of a beautiful young woman whose gait is impeded by the weight of her girdle, her anklet and her heavy hips, whose eyes are soft as those of the deer, and whose voice is sweet as the musical note of the cuckoo.

15. Or it may be some pure and holy place of worship on the banks of sacred rivers or flower gardens, or some beautiful ground or the banks of rivers flowing from west to east or from south to north, or some spot where the river moves in a curve from left to right.

16. It must be a spot free from ash, charcoal, bones, saline soil, hair, ditch, crab holes, hog holes, rat holes and ant hills.

17. The site may be firm, of good scent, of agreeable appearance and of sweet soil and even, or the ground may be one which at one time was occupied by an army, if such ground were of the description given above. If the king performs his Puṣya Snāna in any of these places he will triumph in war.

18. The astrologer, the minister and the priest shall leave the town by night and march towards the north or north-east.

19. There the priest shall perform pooja to the Devas with fried grain, colored rice, curdled milk and flowers; the mantras for the invocation of the Devas have also been stated by the Sages.

20. I invite the presence here of all the Devas whom this pooja might please and in whose honor this pooja is performed—the Dik Devas, the Nāga Devas and the Brāhmaṇa Devas.

21. On inviting the Devas as prescribed above, the priest shall address them as follows : you shall all receive pooja again tomorrow, and after blessing the king may depart.

22. After offering pooja to the Devas invited, the party shall spend the night at the spot, and the interpretation of the good or bad dreams that may be dreamt is given in my work on Yoga Yātrā.

23. The party shall rise early next morning, and proceeding to the forest shall procure the several articles required for Puṣya Snāna, and there are ślokās of Ṛṣis on this point.

24. On the ground intended for the bath, the priest shall draw a circle, cover it with gems and mark in it places for the several Devas.

25. The priest shall than represent in the circle the figures of the Nāgas, the Yakṣas, the Devas, the Pitra, the Gandharvas, the Upsarasas, the Ṛṣis and the Siddhas.

26. He shall also represent the figures of the planets, the constellations, the Rudras, the Saptamātās (seven mothers), Subbramania, Viṣṇu, Viśākhas, the Lokapālas and the wives of the Devas.

27. The figures shall be made of various agreeable and scented colors, and the priest shall perform pooja to them as prescribed in the Śāstras with saudal paste, wreathes of flowers and the like.

28. He shall satisfy the Devas by the offer of sweet, meats, various preparations of rice, fruits, roots, meat, sweet and agreeable drinks, liquor, milk and alcohol.

29. I shall now proceed to state the Pūjā rules contained in the Śāstras; as regards Pūjā to the planets the rules of Gṛha Yagnam should be followed.

30. The Piśācas, the Asuras and the Rakṣasas shall be gratified by the offer of meat, rice, toddy and the like. The Pitris shall be gratified by the pouring out of oil over the figures representing them, by eye salve, and by the offer of gingelly, meat, rice and the like.

31. The Ṛṣis shall be honored by the recitation of the Sāma mantras, Yajur mantras, Ṛk mantras, and with sandal paste, scented smoke and flower wreathes. The Nāga Devas shall be honored by the recitation of the Aśleṣaka Varṇas, and

by the offer of sugar, honey and ghee.

32. The Devas shall be satisfied by the offer of scented smoke, ahutis of ghee, flower wreathes, gems, praises and prostration. The Gandharvas and Upsarasas shall be gratified by the offer of sandal paste, flower wreathes and scented smoke.

33. The other Devas shall be gratified by the offer of various kinds of food eaten by all castes of men. All the Devas shall be adorned with cord amulets, banners, ornaments and sacred threads.

34. The priest shall then form a fire on the western or southern side of the circle on ground prepared for the purpose, and shall procure a quantity of the long Kuśa grass containing no inner blades and other requisites for the fire ceremonies.

35. He shall procure fried grain, oil, colored rice, cardled milk, honey, mustard seed, sandal paste, flowers, scented smoke, yellow pigment (Gorocanā) collyrium, gingelly seed, and the several sweet fruits of the season.

36. He shall also procure ghee and rice cooked in milk—all in earthen plates, and with all the above shall perform Pūjā on the western side of the alter (prepared ground) which alter shall also be used for the bath.

37. On the four corners of the alter shall be placed strong pots with white threads tied round their neck and with their mouths covered with leaves of milky trees and fruits.

38. There shall be placed pots filled with water for Puṣya Snāna, into which shall be thrown gems and the several substances for the bath. Garga has given a list of the substances required for the purpose.

39. The seeds or roots to be thrown into the pots are Jyotiṣmatī,[3] Trāyamāṇā,[4] Abhayā,[5] Aparājitā,[6] Jīva,[7] Viśveśvarī Pāṭhā[8], Samaṅga Vijayā.[9]

40. Sahā,[10] Sahadevī,[11] Pūṇakośā,[12] Śatāvarī,[13] Ariṣṭikā,[14] Śivā,[15] Bhadrā.[16]

41. Brāhmī,[17] Kṣemā,[18] Ajā[19] and all seeds as well as gold and all plants and juices of good properties.

42. He shall also put into the pots gems, various fragrant substances, the leaves of Bilva, and the root of long pepper

and creepers bearing good names, as well as silver and other good substances.

43. This over, the skin of a full grown fine bull shall be spread on the ground with the head towards the east.

44. Over it shall be spread the skin of the Yodha, over it again, the skin of the lion, and over it the skin of the tiger.

45&46. On spreading these skins one over the other on the alter in an auspicious hour while the moon is in the asterism of Puṣya, the king's throne (seat) made purely of gold or silver or copper, or of the wood of milky trees, shall be placed over the skins.

47. The height of the seat may be either a cubit or a cubit and a quarter or a cubit and a half; if the seat be of the height mentioned above, the king will triumph over his enemies, will be the ruler of vast tracts of land, and will be happy and prosperous.

48. Gold shall be placed in the middle of the seat and the king shall sit over it with a happy and peaceful mind surrounded by ministers, friends, priests, astronomers, aged citizens, and persons bearing agreeable names.

49. The heralds shall sing aloud the praises of the king and the Brāhmaṇas shall chant hymns from the Vedas, and with those shall be sounded the drum and the conch shall driving away all evils from the king.

50. The king shall be dressed in new white silk clothes, and the priest shall spread over him a woollen shawl, and pour over him several pots of ghee after dedicating the same to the Devas.

51. The number of the ghee vessels shall be eight, twenty-eight or one hundred and eight. If this number is increased, there will be an increase of prosperity. There are mantras for the ghee bath stated by Ṛṣis.

52. Ghee is stated to be light; it washes off sins; it is the food of the Devas, and the world continues to exist by it.

53. May all the sins committed by thee in your incarnations on the Earth, in Svarga and in the middle region be washed off by contact with ghee.

54. The priest shall then remove the shawl from the king's person and shall bathe the king in the holy waters of Puṣya

Snāna, strewn over with fruits and flowers, chanting the following mantras.

55. May the ancient Siddlia Devas, Brahma, Viṣṇu and Rudra, the Sādhya Devas and the Marut Devas bathe thee in the holy waters of Puṣya Snāna.

56. May the twelve Adityas (suns), the eight Vasus, the eleven Rudras, the two Aswani Devas (celestial physicians), Aditi (the mother of the Devas), Swaha (the wife of Agni), Siddhi, and Saraswati bathe thee in the holy waters of Puṣya Snāna.

57. May Keerti, Lakshmi, Dhriti, Sree, Sinivalee, Kuhu, Danu (the mother of Asuras), Surasa (the mother of the Rākṣasas), Vinatā (the mother of Garuḍa), Kadru (the mother of the serpents), bathe thee in the holy waters of Puṣya Snāna.

58. May the other wives and mothers of the Devas not mentioned above and all the Apsarāsas bathe thee in the holy waters of Puṣya Snāna.

59. May the deities presiding over the Nakṣatras, over the Muhūrtas, the Pakṣas (fortnights), the Ahorātras (day and night), the Sandhis (periods of interval), the Saṁvatsarās (years), the Vāras (weeks), the Kalās, the Kāṣṭhas, the Kṣanas and the Lavās bathe thee in the holy water of Puṣya Snāna.

60. May all the Devas presiding over various other divisions of time, may the Devas moving in their celestial vehicles, may the Manus and the Sāgaras bathe thee in the holy waters of Puṣya Snāna.

61. May the Seven Seers with their wives, the Devas residing in the Palar regions, may Marīchī, Atri, Pulaha, Pulastya, Kratu and Aṅgirasa.

62. May Bhṛgu, Sanat Kumāra, Sanaka, Sanandans, Sanātana, Dakṣa, Jaigiṣavya, Bhagandara.

63. May Ekata, Dvita, Trika, Jābalī, Kaśyapa, Durvāsa (above control), Kaṇva and Kātyāyana.

64. May Mārkaṇḍeya of great devotion, Sunaśyepa, Vidūratha, Ūrva, Saṁvartaka, Cyavana, Atri and Parāśara.

65. Dvaīpāyana (Vyāsa), Yavakrīta, Devarāja, his younger brother and other Ṛṣis learned in the Vedas and who act up to them.

66. With their disciples and their wives bathe thee in the

holy waters of Puṣya Snāna, as well as the deities presiding over mountains, trees, creepers, sacred places of devotion or worship.

67. May the Devas presiding over large rivers, the Nagas, the Kimpuruṣas, the renowned Vyghanasas (a sect of Vānaprasthas) and the birds of the air.

68. May Prajāpati, Diti, the all useful cows, the vehicles of the Devas and the spirit presiding over the whole Universe and over movable and immovable objects.

69. May also the Agnis (fires), the Pitṛ a Devas, the Stars and the Spirits presiding over the clouds, the sky, the several directions or points of the compass and other Devas of fame.

70. Bathe thee in the holy waters of Puṣya Snāna and thereby free thee from all evils; may they bless thee with long life, health and happiness.

71. There shall then be recited the Rudragaṇa mantras, the Kuṣmāṇḍa, mantras, the Mahāruhiṇa mantras, and mantras sacred to Kubera, all referred to in Adharva Kalpa.

72. Also the three mantras beginning with Āpohiṣṭhā and the four mantras beginning with Hiraṇyavarṇa, shall be recited. After the bath the king shall wear a couple of cotton clothes.

73. The king shall then perform the Ācamanya ceremony and pooja to Deva, to his Guru and to the Brāhmaṇās, and he shall pay due honors to his umbrella, to his banner and weapons—sweet music playing all the while.

74. "Āyuṣyam Varcasyaṁ" and "Rāyaspoṣa" and other Ṛks shall then be recited, and the king shall then dress himself in military attire.

75. The king shall then proceed to the second Alter and take his seat on skins which shall be laid one over the other as follows.

76. The bull skin shall be laid next to the ground; over it shall be laid the skin of the cat; over it again the skin of the Ruru (a kind of deer); over it the skin of the spotted antelope; over it again the skin of the lion, and over it the skin of the tiger.

77. The priest shall perform the homa (fire) ceremony offering to the fire dried twigs, gingelly seeds, ghee and the

XX 224

like, reciting ṛks sacred to Rudra, India, Bṛhaspati, Viṣṇu and Vāyu.

78. The astrologer shall note the several indications connected with the Homa fire and make the predictions as stated in the Chapter on Indra Dhvaja, and the priest, after completing what might remain of the ceremony, shall with clasped hands, speak out as follows :

79. May the Devas on receiving due pooja from the king bestow blessings on him and depart.

80. The king shall please the astrologer and the priest by the gift of large sums of money, and he shall also present money to the other Brāhmaṇas learned in the Vedas according to their merit.

81. The king shall then give his subjects assurances of good government, and shall release from jail all prisoners, excepting those who may have been just then punished for offences.

82. If the Puṣya Snāna be repeated every month when the Moon passes through the asterism of Puṣya, the king will enjoy increase of wealth, health and fame. If the Puṣya Homa ceremony be performed when the Moon passes through any other asterism, the king will only enjoy one half of the good effects prescribed for it.

83. On the occurrence of portents, of eclipses and of planetary conjunctions, the king shall have the bath known as Pṣhya Snāna.

84. There are no portents whose evil effects are irremediable by Puṣya Snāna and there are no ceremonies calculated to do a king as much good as the ceremony of Puṣya Homa.

85. The king that desires an increase of power and the king that desires sons will be benefited by Puṣya Snāna.

86. Thus have been stated by Bṛhaspati to Indra the rules relating to the ceremony of Puṣya Snāna—for the increase of his family and of his wealth.

87. That king who bathes in the waters of Puṣya Snāna his elephants and horses will have these animals freed from all evils and become prosperous.

REFERENCES

1. The tree Cordia mixa.
2. Eleocarpus Ganitrus.
3. Jyotiṣmatī, Trigonella foenum Graecum.
4. Being already explained.
5. Abhayā, Plant Terminalia scritrina.
6. Aparājitā, Plant Clitoria ternatea.
7. Jīva, probably Jīvanta, kind of pot herb.
8. Pāṭhā : a climbing plant possessing various medicinal properties. Chypea Hernandifolia.
9. Vijayā : Orris root.
10. Sahā : the Alce plant.
11. Already explained.
12. -do-
13. -do-
14. Ariṣṭikā : The Soap berry tree.
15. Śivā : Cicca disticha.
16. Bhadrā : a fragrant grass, Cyperus rotundus.
17. Brāhmī : plant Elerodeudrum siphonanthus.
18. Kṣemā : a kind of perfume.
19. Ajā : a plant whose bulb resembles the udder of a goat.

CHAPTER 49

On Crown Plate[1]

1. Able writers have fully treated of the subject of Crown. I shall here give a summary of their statements, not omitting however the important points.

2. That it may do good, the king's crown shall be 8 inches broad in the middle, the queen's shall be 7 inches broad, and the prince's shall be 6 inches broad.

3. The general's shall be 4 inches broad in the middle. The *Prasādapaṭṭā* (which is worn by a person as a token of royal favor) shall be 2 inches broad. Thus crown are five in number.

4. If the crown were made of pure gold, and twice as long, with its sides half as broad as the dimension at the middle, it would make the wearer happy.

5. The king's crown shall have five points or crests; the queen's and the prince's shall have three crests; the general's shall have a single crest and the *Prasādapaṭṭā* shall have no crest.

6. If gold plate while being beaten out for the crown should extend easily, the king would enjoy an increase of prosperity and success and his subjects too would be happy.

7. If, while being beaten out, the plate should be wounded in the middle, the king's life and power would suffer destruction. If it should break either at the middle or at the sides, there would be misery and the plate should be rejected.

8. If, while the crown is being made, evil omens should occur, the learned astrologer shall prescribe expiatory ceremonies for the benefit of the king. If good omens should occur at the time there would be an increase of territory.

REFERENCE

1. A frontlot or fillet worn round the head.

CHAPTER 50

On the Sword

1. A sword 50 inches long is a good one and one 25 inches long is a bad one ; the measurement is to be made by means of the inch scale. Marks at the odd inches would produce evil.

2. Marks along the back of the sword of the shape of the Bilva tree, a platter, an umbrella, a sivalinga, pendants, a lotus, a banner and a weapon of war, are indicative of prosperity.

3. Marks of the shape of a lizard, a crow, a heron, a hawk, a headless trunk and a scorpion are indicative of eivil.

4. A sword that is broken, or short, or blunt, or split at the back, or ill-formed or without sound, is indicative of evil; if otherwise it indicates good luck.

5. If the sword should sound like lyre, the king would die; if it should come out of the scabbard of itself, the king would be defeated in battle; if it should move forward of itself, there would be wars in the land; and if it should appear to shine brilliantly, there would be success in battle.

6. The sword shall not be taken out for no purpose; nor shall it be rubbed against a substance, nor shall its edge be looked at, nor its price stated, nor the place of its manufacture mentioned, nor shall it be compared to anything, nor shall it be touched by a person who is impure.

7. That is a good sword which resembles the tongue of the cow, or the petal of the blue lotus or the leaf of the bamboo or assafoetida, or one whose end is pointed like the end of a spear or round.

8. After making a sword of the prescribed dimensions, it shall be rubbed against a whetstone that it may not be broken. If it should break about the hilt, the master would die, and if about the end, his mother would die.

9. If there be a mark in the handle of the sword, there will also be a mark in the sword itself just as a spot on the face of a woman indicates the presence of a spot on her privity.

10. If a querent wearing a sword appear before an astrologer, the latter shall determine the marks of the sword from the particular parts of his body which the querent may happen to touch.

11. If the part of the body touched should be the head, there would be a mark in the first inch of the sword; if it be the forehead, there would be a mark in the 2nd inch; if the eyebrows, there would be a mark in the 3rd inch; and if it should be the eye, there would be a mark in 4th inch.

12. If the part touched should be the nose, the lips the cheek, the chin, the ears, the neck, the shoulders, the breast, or the armpit, then there would be marks on the sword in the 5th, 6th, 7th, 8th, 9th, 10th, 11th, 12th, or 13th inch respectively.

13. If the part touched should be the nipple, the heart, the belly, the abdomen, the navel, its root the lower belly, the hips, or the privity, then there would be marks on the sword in the 14th, 15th, 16th, 17th, 18th, 19th, 20th, or 21st inch respectively.

14. If the part touched should be the two thighs, their middle parts, the knees, or the shanks, there would be marks on the sword in the 22nd, 23rd, 24th or 25th inch respectively.

15. If the part touched should be the middle of the shanks, the ankle, the heels, the feet, or the toes, there would be marks on the sword in the 26th, 27th, 28th, 29th or 30th inch respectively. The above are the views of Garga.

16. The marks in the several inches of the sword from the first to the 5th indicate respectively the death of the son, acquisition of wealth, loss of wealth, prosperity and confinement.

17. The marks in the several inches from the 6th to the 13th indicate respectively the birth of a son, dissensions, the getting of an elephant, the death of a son, the acquisition of wealth, the loss of wealth, the getting of a wife, and mental pain or grief.

18. The marks in the several inches from the 14th to the 21st indicate respectively gain, loss, gain of a wife, torture, increase, death, joy and loss of wealth.

19. The marks in the several inches from the 22nd to the 30th indicate respectively the acquisition of wealth, of health, acquisition of wealth again, death, wealth, poverty, wealth again, death again, and sovereign power.

20. Marks beyond the first 30 inches do not signify much. Generally marks on the odd inches indicate evil and marks in the even inches indicate good. According to same, marks beyond the first 30 inches do not signify anything at all.

21. If the sword should smell like the leaf of the plant Assafoetida, the blue lotus, the juice of the rutting elephant, ghee, saffron, the white water-lily, or the champaka, it indicates prosperity; but if it should smell like the cow's urine, mire, or marrow, it indicates evil.

22. If the sword should smell like the tortoise, serum, blood, or salt, it indicates fear and grief. If the sword should appear bright as viduriya, gold or lightning, it indicates increased success and health.

23. The following methods of tempering swords and cutting instruments are taken from the works of Sukra : He who desires bright prosperity shall temper the weapon in blood ; he who desires an excellent son shall temper the weapon in ghee; and he who desires great wealth shall temper it in water.

24. If the weapon be tempered in the blood of the mare, a she camel or a she elephant, there will be acquisition of wealth by wicked deeds; if it be tempered in the fit of the fish, or in the milk of the deer, or of the horse, or of the goat, or in the juice of the palm fruit, the weapon will become so strong that the trunk of the elephant can be cut with it.

25. After smearing oil over the weapon there shall be smeared over it again a preparation or mixture of the black powder of the burnt horn of the ram, the excrement of the turtle dove and of the rat, and the milk or juice of the plant Calotropis gigantea, the weapon shall then be tempered in any of the ways described. It will not break at all when rubbed against the whetstone.

26. Salt shall be dissolved in the juice of the plantain and the juice shall be kept so for a day; if the weapon be tempered in it the next day, it will not break when rubbed against the whetstone, and no other metal can injure it in any way.

CHAPTER 51

On Limbs

1. It shall be the duty of an astrologer to examine and note indications connected with the direction, place, and anything carried, as well as the motion connected with the body of the querent or of any other person, and *time*. For the All-knowing Universal Intelligence pervading all movable and immovable objects indicates coming events by motions and casual words to devout souls who have faith in Him.

2. That place is known as *Soma Sthāna* which is shaded over by trees overgrown with fruits and flowers, inhabited by birds of fine glossy plumage, unapproached by evil birds and bearing good names. Dwelling places of the Devas, the Ṛṣis, the Brāhmaṇas, the Sādhus and the Siddhas, places rendered agreeable by fragrant flowers and crops, and places covered over with green turf, and from its purity and waters calculated to exhilirate one's spirit, are also good places.

3. That is not a good place in which are found trees cut or split eaten through by worms or covered with thorns, or burnt or of ugly appearance, or crooked or indebited by evil birds, or of bad names or with most of their leaves or their bark dry or fallen.

4. That is not a good place which is either a cremation ground or a deserted place of Tapas (psychical training) or any uneven ground, or ground with barren or saline soil, or ground with excrement, charcoal, pot-shred, ash, or dried grass.

5. That is not a good place in which is found a person who has abandoned all worldly cares, or a mute person, or a barber, or an enemy, or which may be a place of detention or custody, or in which may be found butchers, chandalas, gamblers, ascetics or diseased persons, or which may be a place where weapons or liquor may be sold.

6. The East, North and North-east indicate good luck to

the querent; the North-west, West, South-west, South and South-east do not indicate good luck. Fore-noon indicates good luck, night, twilight hours and the afternoon do not indicate good luck.

7. The various good and bad indications described in my work on Yātrā are also applicable here. Judgment on queries shall be pronounced on examining the things before the astrologer, the things that may be brought before him or that the querent may have in his hands or about his clothes.

8. The organs that point to a male are the thighs, lips, nipples, testicles, feet, teeth, arms, hands, cheek, hair, throat, nails, thumb, arm-pit, shoulders, ears, anus and the genital organ.

9. The organs that point to a female are the brows, the nose, the buttocks, folds of the belly, the hip and fingers with good lines.

Also the tongue, the neck, the calves of the leg, the heels, the ankles, the navel, the sides, the heart, the chin, the eyes, the penis, the breast, or the lower part of the spine.

10. The organs that point to a hermaphrodite are the head and forehead. Face and other parts of the body point to delay in effect. Parts of body that point to a hermaphrodite as well as parts of disagreeable appearance or that may be wounded or broken, do not point to success in undertaking.

11. If the big toe is either touched or shaken it indicates sore eyes ; if any other toe is touched or shaken there will be grief on account of one's daughter. If the head is struck, there will be fear from the rulers.

12. If the breast is accidentally struck, husbands and wives will part from each other. If any torn or dirty clothes over a person be pulled, there will be poverty ; if while putting the query, the querent should have his clothes stuck to his feet, the querent will gain his desired object.

13. If lines be drawn on the ground with the big toe, the matter quesited relates to fields ; if the feet be scratched by the hand, the matter relates to a maid servant.

14. If palm, bark-dress or clothes be seen, the matter quesited relates to a cloth remaining in a place where hair, husk, bones, or ash is deposited ; if a rope or net be seen, there will

be disease, and if bark-dress be seen, the matter relates to one's kinsmen.

15. If long pepper, pepper, dried ginger, varida,[1] rodra, kushta, cloth, water, cumin seed, gandha-mamsi,[2] oil, or tagara be seen, the matter quesited relates respectively to what follows.

16. A woman, a man, an offender, an afflicted person, goods, son, wealth, grain, son, a biped creature, a quadruped and the earth.

17. If the fruits of the Nyagrodha, Madhuka, Tinduka, Jambū, Plakṣa, the Mango, be seen in the hand, the matter relates respectively to the acquisition of wealth, as gold, man, metal, cloth, silver or copper.

18. If a vessel full of grain or water be seen, there will be an increase of family. If the excrement of an elephant, a cow or a dog be seen, the matter relates respectively to stolen property, or girl or friends.

19. If a cow, an elephant, a buffaloe, a lotus, silver or tiger be seen, there will be a large acquisition of sheep, wealth, dwelling house, sandalwood, white silk or jewels.

20. If at the time of query, there be seen an old man, a *Baudha*, ascetic, the matter quesited relates to a friend, to gambling, to wealth, to a prostitute, to a king or to a woman just delivered.

21. If a Baudha, a preceptor, an arhat, a naked Sanyasi, any omen, a scientific work, or a fisherman be seen, the matter relates to a thief, a general, a merchant, a maid servant, a soldier, an article for sale, or a person to be killed.

22. If a hermit be seen, the matter relates to a person who has gone abroad to travel ; if a dealer in liquor be seen, the matter relates to the protection of animals; if a person be seen gathering grains in market places, the matter relates to some danger or difficulty.

23. If the querent be heard to say, "I like to question," the matter relates to a wish to enjoy a woman ; if he begins by stating "say," the matter relates to a family ; if the expression be "I want to see," the matter relates to gain ; if the expression be "requests that orders may be made," the matter relates to wealth.

24. If the expression be "may the information be given," the matter relates to success ; if the expression be "examine soon and discover my thoughts," the matter relates to something connected with roads ; if the expression be "what is in the midst of all people should be soon examined," the matter relates to kinsmen who have been abducted away.

25. If the motion refers to the inner organs, the matter relates to one's own people ; if to the outer organs, then, to other people ; if to the toes or fingers, then, to man or a maid servant ; if to the knees, then, to one's servant ; if to the navel, then, to one's younger sister ; and if to the heart, then, to one's wife ; and to the toes or other fingers, then, to a son or daughter.

26. If the cheshta refers to the belly, the query relates to one's mother ; if to the head, then, to one's preceptor ; if to the right or left arm, then, respectively, to one's brother or brother's wife.

27. If, after leaving the inner organs, the outer organs be touched, or if at the time of query, the querent drops down any thing in his hand while ejecting phlegm or passing urine or excrement, the matter quesited relates to theft.

28. If any part of the body be greatly bent and then concealed, or if any person be seen to possess an empty vessel, the matter relates to thieves ; if at the time of query, such expressions as "carried away," "fallen," "wounded," "forgotten," "lost," "broken," "gone" "stolen," "dead," and the like be heard, then, the stolen property cannot be recovered.

29. If the husk of grain, bones or poison be seen, or if moaning and sneezing be heard, the sick man will die ; if the wind should blow on one's body and then carry away some heavy substance from within a room, judgment shall be pronounced that a person after eating to excess and being over-satiated has died.

30. If the forehead be touched or barley be seen, then Salya rice is indicated ; if the breast be touched, then the Shashtika rice is indicated ; if the neck be touched, barley rice is indicated.

31. If the abdomen, nipples, belly or knees be touched, the matter relates respectively to black-gram, milk, gingelly, or

barley ; if one is seen to swallow or lick the lip, sweet flavor is indicated.

32. If the tongue be struck against the pallet, the matter refers to an object of desire ; if one is seen to make a wry face, sour substance is indicated ; if one is seen to hiccuh, then the substance indicated is either pungent, bitter or astringent ; if one is seen to sputter, salt substance is indicated.

33. If one is seen to spit phlegm, a small dry bitter substance is indicated ; if the brow, the cheek, or the lip be touched, the flesh of the vulture has been eaten.

34. If the head, neck, hair, chin, throat, ears, the shanks, the knees or the lower belly be touched, judgment shall be pronounced that the meals eaten contained respectively the flesh of the elephant, buffalo, sheep, pig, cow, hare or deer.

35. If bad omens be seen or heard, the meals eaten contained the flesh of the iguana and the fish ; questions connected with pregnancy shall be determined as follows :

36&37. If the organs or parts of body representing the male, female or hermaphrodite sex be seen, thought over or touched a child of that sex will be born ; if any drink, rice or flower be seen, prosperity is indicated ; if the point between the brows or if fingers be touched by the thumb, the matter relates to pregnancy ; if honey, ghee, gold, gems, corals and the like be touched or seen, or if the mother or the nurse or the son should be hear, pregnancy is indicated.

38. If the hand is seen on the belly, the matter relates to pregnancy ; if bad omen should occur, the matter does not relate to pregnancy ; if the belly be pulled or the seat be disturbed, or if the hands be seen one over the other, the matter does not relate to pregnancy.

39. If the right nostril be touched, the delivery will occur after a month ; if the left nostril be touched, after two months; not so if the ears be touched; but after two months; if the right ear be touched, and after four months, if the left ear be touched ; also after four months if the right nipple be touched, and after eight months if the left nipple be touched.

40. The root of the plaited hair indicates 3 sons, the ears indicate 2 daughters, the hands 5 sons, the tip of the thumb 3 sons, the tip of the big toe 5 sons, the two heels a daughter.

41. If the right or left thigh be touched, a son or a daughter is indicated ; if the centre or end of the forehead be touched, 4 or 3 sons will respectively be born.

42. The head, the forehead, the brows, the ears, the cheek, the jaw, the teeth, the neck, the right shoulder, the left shoulder, the hand, the chin, the wind pipe.

43. The breast, the right nipple, the left nipple, the heart, the sides, the belly, the hip, the buttocks, the anus, the genital organs, the two thighs, the knees, the ankles and the feet are respectively parts of the body represented by the twenty-seven asterisms from Kṛttikā.

44. Thus have I described the several matters connected with Aṅgavidyā on a full examination of the treatises relating to the subject ; that person who, possessed of a broad intellect and of a generous disposition masters this branch of the science, will be respected by the king and people.

REFERENCES

1. Varida, a kind of perfume or fragrant grass, Andropogon Scheenanthus.
2. Gandha-mamsi : a kind of Indian spikenard.

CHAPTER 52

On Pimples

1. Pimples breaking out in the Brāhmaṇas, the Kṣtriyas, the Vaiśyas and the Śudras should respectively be white, red, yellow and black, in order that they may produce the effects described below.

2. If glossy and clear pimples break out in the head, there will be acquisition of wealth ; if in the crown of the head, there will be good fortune ; if in the two eye-brows, there will be bad luck and the meeting of friends ; if between the eye-brows, there will be loss of character ; if on the eye-lids, there will be sorrow and the gaining of the desired object : if in the temples, the person will turn out a hermit ; and if on both sides of the nose where the tears fall, there will be great anxiety.

3. If the pimple breaks out in the nose, the person will get new cloth ; if in the cheek, he will get a son ; if in the lips or just below them, he will get good food ; if in the fore-head or in the corners of the mouth, there will be acquisition of wealth : if in the throat, the person will acquire ornaments, food and drink ; if in the ears, he will acquire a collection of ornament and a knowledge of Ātmā.

4. If the pimple breaks out in the joint of the head, the neck, the heart, the two nipples, the two sides, or in the breast, the person will get respectively a blow with an iron rod, a blow, a son, a son again, any gain, grief, and any object of desire ; if it breaks out in the two shoulders, there will be much wandering for alms and destruction ; and if the two arm-pits, the person will acquire wealth and comfort.

5. If the pimple breaks out in the back there will be grief and ruin ; if in the two upper arms, the enemy will perish ; if in the two wrists, there will be imprisonment ; if in the two lower arms, there will be an acquisition of ornaments.

6. If the pimple breaks out in the hands, fingers or belly, there will respectively be an acquisition of wealth, good luck or grief; if it breaks out in the navel, the person will get good food and drink ; if just under the navel, there will be theft of property by robbers ; if in a man's genital organs, he will get a young woman and good sons ; if in the anus : he will aquire wealth, and if in the testicles, there will be good fortune.

7. If the pimple breaks out in the thighs, the person will get a carriage and a woman ; if in the knees, there will be injury from enemies ; if in the shanks, there will be wound from weapons ; and if in the ankles, there will be trouble from a journey on foot and from imprisonment.

8. If the pimple breaks out in the buttocks, heels or soles of the feet, there will respectively be loss of wealth, adultery or the troubles of a journey on foot ; if in the toes, there will be imprisonment ; and if in the big toe there will be presents from kinsmen.

9. Any extraordinary eruptions, boils and pimples breaking out on the right side, and hurts, occurring on the left side of males, indicate the acquisition of wealth ; the reverse is the case with females.

10. Thus have I stated the effects of pimples breaking out in the several parts of the body from head to foot, the same effects apply to wounds, dark spots, pustules, small bunches of hair of crowded growth and to a whirling growth of hair.

CHAPTER 53

On House-Building

1. We shall now proceed to treat of the science of house-building, which has come down to us from the Ṛṣis who obtained it from Brahmā, for the pleasure of learned astrologer.

2. At one time, a monster appeared with a body so vast as to conceal the Earth and the sky. The Devas then caught hold of parts of his body and forcibly laid him down with his face towards the ground.

3. The several Devas now preside over the several parts of the body held by them. The monster therefore, known as Vāstupuruṣa, represents in his body all the Devas by order of Brahmā.

4. The king's house shall be one of five sorts. The breadth of the superior house shall be 108 cubits, and that of each of the four inferior houses shall be 8 cubits less than the next preceding one. The length of each house shall be one-quarter as much more as its breadth.

5. The general's house shall be one of five sorts. The breadth of the superior house shall be 64 cubits, and that of each of the four inferior houses shall be 6 cubits less than the next preceding one. The length of each house shall be one-sixth as much more as its breadth.

6. The prime-minister's house shall also be one of five sorts. The breadth of the superior house shall be 60 cubits, and that of each of the four inferior houses shall be four cubits less than the next preceding one. The length of each house shall be one-eighth as much more as its breadth.

The dimensions of the houses of the queens shall be one-half of the dimensions of the houses of the prime-minister.

7. The first prince's house shall also be one of five sorts. The breadth of the superior house shall be 80 cubits, and that

of the each of the four inferior houses shall be six cubits less than the next preceding one. The length of each house shall be one-third as much more as its breadth.

The dimensions of the houses of the younger princes shall be one-half of the dimensions of the houses of the first prince.

8. The houses of the tributary princes, of worthy persons and of the king's officers, shall be of the difference of the dimensions of the houses of the king and prime minister. The houses of the chamberlain and of the king's concubines and artists shall be of the difference of the dimensions of the houses of the king and the first prince.

9. The houses of the superintendent of the king's household and of the comptroller of public accounts shall be of the dimensions of the king's treasury and bed-rooms. The houses of the peons of the superintendents shall be of the difference of the dimensions of the houses of the first prince and the prime minister.

10. The houses of the Court astrologers, priests and physicians, shall be one of five sorts—the superior one being 40 cubits broad and the breadth of the four inferior ones shall be severally 4 cubits less by turns ; the length shall be one-sixth as much more as the breadth.

11. If the houses in all the cases can be made as high as they are broad, they will conduce to prosperity. In cases where a house has an inner verandah, the length of the house shall be twice its breadth.

12. The houses of the four castes from the Brāhmaṇas downwards are also of five sorts—the breadths of the houses being 32, 28, 24, 20 and 16 cubits. A house less than 16 cubits broad shall be for the use of the men of low class.

13. The length of the houses of Brāhmaṇās shall be one-tenth as much more as the breadth, that of the houses of Kṣatriyas shall be one-eighth as much more ; that of the houses of the Vaiśyas shall be one-sixth as much more ; and that of the houses of the Śudras shall be one-fourth as much more.

14. The dimensions of the treasury and bed rooms shall be the difference of the dimensions of the houses of the king and the general. The dimensions of the houses of those honored by

the king shall be of the difference of the dimensions of the houses of the general and the several castes from the Brāhmaṇas downwards.

15. The dimensions of the houses of the Pāraśavas and the like shall be one half of the sum of the dimensions of the houses prescribed to their class. If the houses described above for all classes be of greater or smaller demensions than what we have stated, they will produce evil.

16. No dimensions are prescribed for the houses of the cows, the ascetics, for granaries, for the arsena, for fire and for sexual enjoyment. However men learned in house-building are opposed to the breadth of these exceeding 100 cubits.

17. Add 70 to the breadth (in cubits) of the house of the king or the general and divide the sum by 14 and the same sum again by 35. The quotients will give the breadths of the inner veranda and of the outer veranda in front of the house door of the house of the king or the general.

18. In the case of the five sorts of houses of the four castes from the Brāhmaṇas downwards, the breadth of the inner verandas shall respectively be 4 cubits 7 inches, 4 cubits 10 inches, 3 cubits 3 inches, 3 cubits 15 inches, and 3 cubits 13 inches.

19. The breadth of the outer veranda in front of the house door in the case of these five houses shall respectively be 3 cubits 19 inches, 3 cubits 8 inches, 2 cubits 20 inches, 2 cubits 18 inches, and 2 cubits 3 inches.

20. The breadth of the Vīdhi around the house shall be one-third of the breadth of the inner veranda. If the Vīdhi be in front of the house, such house is known as *soṣṇīṣa*.

21. If the Vīdhi be found behind the house, it is known as *Sāyāśrayam*, and if the Vīdhi be found on a side of the house, such house is known as *Sāvaṣṭambham*, and if the Vīdhi be found all round the house, the house is known as *Susthitam*. Men learned in house-building speak favorably of every one of these Vīdhis.

22. The height of the floor shall be one-sixteenth of the breadth of the house plus 4 cubits. Generally, the height of the floor of a house may be one-twelfth less according to the nature of the ground.

23. The thickness of the walls shall be one-sixteenth of the

breadth of the house. The wall may be built of burnt bricks or of wood.

24. In the cases of the house of the king and general, add to the breadth of the house (in cubits) its eleventh part and add 70 to the sum, the height of the entrance shall be so many inches. The breadth of the entrance shall be one-half of the height.

25. In the case of the houses of the four castes from the Brāhmaṇas downwards, add one-fifth of the breadth of the house to 18 inches ; nine-eighths of this sum is the breadth of the entrance. Double the breadth of the entrance is its height.

26. The breadth of the two vertical frames shall be as many inches as the number of cubits in the height of the entrance. The breadth of the bottom and top frames shall be half as much more as the breadth of the side frames.

27. Multiply the height by 7 ; one eightieth of the product shall be the thickness of each frame. Multiply the height of the house by 9 ; one eightieth of the product shall be the diameter of the pillar at the bottom. Nine-tenths of this shall be the diameter of the pillar at the top.

28. A four-sided pillar or column is known as *Rucaka*. An eight sided pillar is known as *Vajra*. An eighteen sided pillar is known as *Dvivajra*. and a thirty-two sided one is known as *Pralīnaka*. A pillar that is round in the middle is known as *Vṛtta*.

29. Divide the height of the pillar into equal parts. The parts are known as *Vahana*, *Ghaṭa*, *Padma*, *Uttaroṣṭha*, and so on, the names returning again.

30. The thickness of the heavy beams of the sloping roof shall be that of the pillars. The other beams higher up the roof shall be each three-fourths as thick as the beam next below it.

31. The house of the King or Deva which is surrounded by outer verandas on all the four sides, and with an entrance on each side, is known as *Sarvatobhadra*.

32. The house which is surrounded by four distinct outer verandas and with an entrance on each side except on the west, is known as *Nandyāvarta*.

33. The house which has two outer verandas commencing at the entrance with an external veranda on the southern side

and one on the western side and with an entrance on the southern side, is known as *Vardhamāna*.

34. The house which has an outer veranda on the eastern side, two parallel outer verandas on the southern side, and ending in the east with a separate one on the northern side and with an entrance on the eastern side, is known as *Swastika*.

35. The house which has distinct outer verandas on each side with an entrance on each side except the northern side, is known as *Rucaka*.

36. The Nandyāvarata and Vardhamāna houses are the best ; the Swastika and Rucaka houses are of middle importance, and the remaining house known as Sarvatobhadra, is best fitted for kings to live in.

37. The house which has inner verandas on all excepting the northen side, is known as *Hiraṇyanābha*. It brings on wealth. The house which has inner verandas on all excepting the eastern side, is known as *Sukṣetra*. It brings on prosperity.

38. The house which has inner verandas on all excepting the southern side, is known as *Cullī*. It destroys wealth. The house which has inner verandas on all excepting the western side, is known as *Pakṣaghna*. It brings on the death of the sons and produces enmity.

39. The house which has inner verandas on the western and southern sides is known as *Siddhārtha*, and the house which has inner verandas on the western and northern sides is known as *Yamasūrya* ; that which has inner verandas on the eastern and northern sides is known as *Daṇḍa*, and that which has such verandas on the eastern and southern sides, is known as *Vāta*.

40. The house which has inner verandas on the eastern and western sides is known as *Gṛhacullī*, and that which has such verandas on the northern and southern sides is known as *Kāca*. The Siddārtha house will bring on wealth and the Yamasūrya house will bring on the death of the master.

41. The Daṇḍa house will bring on death by a daṇḍa or a club ; the Vāta house will bring on fears and disturbance ; the cullī house will destroy wealth, and the Kāca house will bring on the enmity of kinsmen.

42. Divide the house ground into 81 squares by 10 lines drawn from east to west and 10 lines drawn from north to

south. 32 Devas occupy the 32 exterior squares and 13 Devas occupy the inner squares (as follows) :

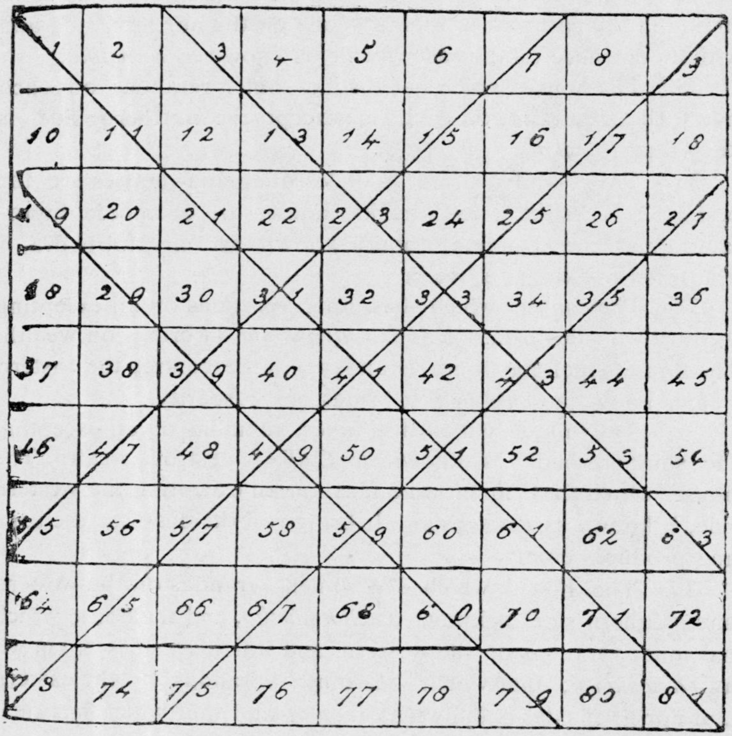

43, 44&45. The eight southern squares, 9, 18, 27, 36, 45, 54, 63 and 72 are respectively occupied by Vāyu, Pūṣā, Vitatha, Bṛhatkṣata, Yama, Gandharva, Bhṛṅgarāja and Mṛga. The eight western squares, 81, 80, 79, 78, 77, 76, 75 and 74 are respectively occupied by Pitṛ Danvārika, Sugrīva, Kusumadanta, Varuṇa, Asura, Śoṣa and Pāpayakṣma, and the 8 northern squares, 73, 64, 55, 46, 37, 23, 19 and 10 are respectively occupied by the Devas Roga, Ahi, Mukhya, Bhallāṭa, Soma, Bhujaga, Aditi, and Diti.

46 & 47. The nine central squares 31, 32, 33, 40, 41, 42, 49, 50 and 51 are occupied by Brahma. The square 23, due east of Brahma is occupied by Aryama. From Aryama, the alternate squares all round Brahma from left to right, viz , 25, 43, 61, 59, 57, 39 and 21 are respectively occupied by Savītṛa, Vivasvan, Indra, Mitra, Rājayakṣma, Pṛthvīdhara and Āpavatsa.

48. The inner north-eastern square 11, is occupied by Āpa ; the inner south-eastern square 17 is occupied by Sāvītra ; the inner south-western square, 71, is occupied by Jaya, and the inner north-western square, 65, is occupied by Rudra.

49. The group of five Devas occupying the north-eastern portion of the house-ground, (squares 1, 2, 10, 11, and 21), viz., Agni, Parjanya, Diti, Āpa and Āpavatsa and similar groups, each of five Devas, occupying the south-eastern, south-western and north-western portions of the house-ground, are known as Padikas.

50. The remaining 20 Devas occupying the other squares known as Dwipadas. The Devas occupying the due eastern, southern, western and northern squares—23, 43, 59, 33—viz., Aryam, Vivasvan, Mitra and Prithvīdhara are known as Tripadas.

51. The Vastupuruṣa (house demon) lies with his face turned towards the ground and head in the north-east. Agni holds his head, Āpa his face, Aryama his right nipple and Āpavatsa his breast.

52. The Devas from Parjanya to Sūrya occupying the outer squares hold respectively the right eye, ear, breast, and shoulder ; the five Devas from Satya hold the right arm ; Savītṛa and Sāvītra hold the right hand ; Vitatha and Bṛhatkṣata hold the right side.

53. Vivaswan holds the belly ; the four Devas from Yama hold the right thigh, knee, shank and buttock.

54. These Devas hold the right limbs of the Vastupuruṣa. Similarly the other devas hold the left limbs. Indra and Jaya hold his penis ; Brahma his heart and the Pitṛ Devas his feet.

55 & 56. Or, divide the house ground into sixty-four equal squares ; draw the main diagonal lines. The four central squares marked 28, 29, 36, 37, are occupied by Brahma. The four squares occupying the inner corners, viz., 19, 22, 46, and 43, as

well as the four squares occupying the outer corners, viz., 1, 8, 64 and 57, are divided each into two halves. The other squares, all round Brahma, viz , 20, 21, 30, 38, 45, 44, 35 and 27, and the other outer squares, viz., 2 to 7, 16 to 56, 63 to 58 and 49 to 9, are twenty-four. The number thus mon-

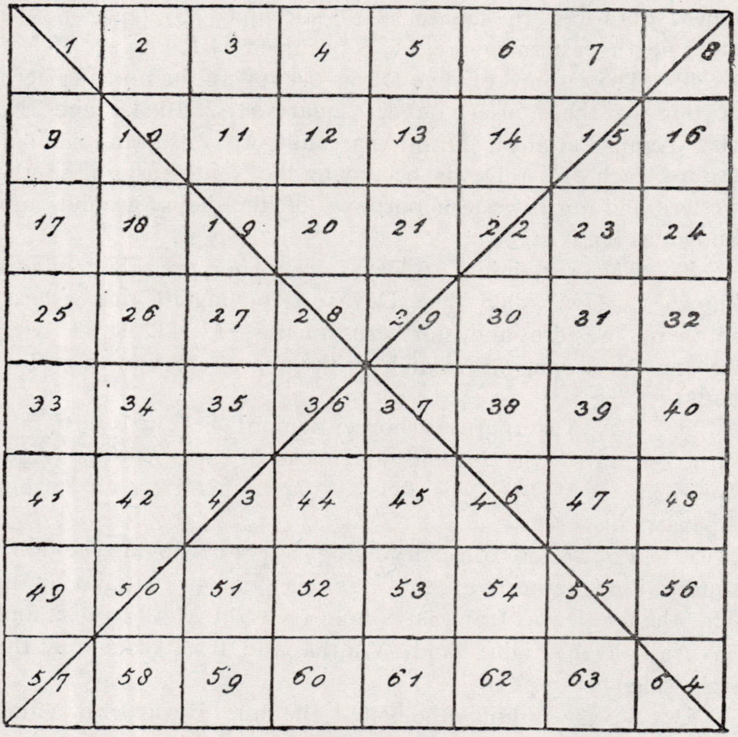

tioned is 44, and the remain-*Marmasthalas*—vital parts. These parts shall not be molested by the erection of pillars over them or in any other way.

57&58. If these vital parts are defiled or molested by impure substances, pot-shreds, pegs or pillars and by Salyas (substance lying underground), the master of the house will suffer in those parts of his body which correspond to the parts thus tormented.

59. That portion of the house ground contains Salya which corresponds to the part of body scratched by the master of the house (at the time of his first entry) or where bad omens or portents connected with fire occur at the time of the homa ceremony.

60. If the Salya be wood, there will be destruction of wealth ; if bones, animals will suffer, and there will be much suffering from diseases ; if metals, there will be injury from weapons ; and if skulls or hair, there will be death.

61. If the Salya be charcoal, there will be fear of robbery ; if ashes, there will always be fear from destructive fires ; if it be any substance other than gold or silver lying buried at the Marmasthala, there will be great fears.

62. If the Salya be the husk of paddy lying either at the Marmasthala or at other places, there will be acquisition of wealth ; if it be the teeth of snake lying at the Marmasthala, there will be misery.

63. The diagonal line, from the Roga Deva (73) to Vayu Deva (9) is known as a *Vaṁśa.* The diagonal line from Pitṛ Deva (81) to Agni Deva (1) is another *Vaṁśa.* A line drawn from Vitath Deva (27) to Śoṣa Deva (75) is also a *Vaṁśa,* and that drawn from Mukkya Deva (55) to Bhrisa Deva (7) is another *Vaṁśa.* A line drawn from Jayanta Deva (3) to Bhṛṅga Rāja (63) is also a *Vaṁśa,* and a line drawn from Aditi (19) to Sugrīva (79) is another *Vaṁśa.*

64. The six lines cut one another in nine points. These points are known as Atimarma places. The area of a Marmasthala is equal to one-eighth of the area of a square.

65. The breadth of a *Vaṁśa* line is as many inches as the length of a side of a square is in yards, and the length of a Sira is one and a half times the breadth of the *Vaṁśa* line.

66. If the master of the house desire prosperity, he shall take particular care of the portion of the house which is the seat of Brahma. If this portion be defiled by impurities, the master of the house will suffer miseries.

67. If the right arm of the Vāstupuruṣa be wanting, there will be loss of wealth and women will lose their character ; if the left arm be wanting, there will be loss of wealth and grain ; if the head be wanting, every virtue will quit the house hold.

68. If any of the senses of the Vāstupuruṣa should suffer injuries, women will lose their character, sons will perish, and the master of the house will became a slave under another. If the Vāstupuruṣa does not suffer in any way, the dwellers of the house will get honor, wealth and comfort.

69. The Devas occupy their several places as above enumerated not only in houses but in towns and villages. The Brāhmaṇas and other castes shall live in places appropriate to them.

70. The Brāhmaṇas and other castes shall dwell respectively on the northern, eastern, southern and western sides.

71. Either in the division of the house ground into 81 squares or in that into 64 squares, the effects of having the main-entrance in spots occupied by Agni and the other Devas are as follow.

72. If the entrance is opened in any of the 8 eastern squares beginning from the north-eastern corner, the effects will respectively be injury from 'fire, birth of daughters, gain of immense wealth, the friendship of the king, increase of anger, the vice of lie, that of cruelty and that of theft.

73. If the entrance is opened in any of the 8 southern squares beginning from the south-eastern corner, the effects will respectively be few sons, servitude, becoming a chandala, excessive eating and drinking with an increase of sons anger, ingratitude, poverty and the loss of sons and of valor.

74. If the gate is opened in any of the 8 western squares beginning from the south-western corner, the effects will respectively be suffering of sons, the increase of the enemy, the want of wealth and sons, the increase of sons, of wealth and of strength, opulence, fear from kings, loss of wealth, and disease.

75. If the gate is opened in any of the 8 northern squares beginning from the north-western corner, the effects will respectively be increase of cruelty and kinsmen, increase of the enemy, gain of wealth and sons, the possession of all virtues,

the acquisition of sons and wealth, hatred of sons, the loss of character of women and the loss of wealth

76. There will be misery if, opposite to the gate, there be roads, trees, street corners, wells, pillars or gutters. If these should be beyond a distance of double the height of the house, they will produce no harm.

77. If the obstruction be a car running street, the master of the house will die ; if it be a tree, the son will suffer ; if it be a permanent mire, there will be grief ; if it be any gutter or passage for water, there will be waste.

78. If the obstruction be a well, there will be an attack of epilepsy ; if it be the image of some Deva, there will be death ; if it be a pillar, women will lose their chastity ; if the gate be opposite to the squares of Brahma, the family will perish.

79. If the door should open of itself, there would be as attack of madness; if it should close of itself, the family would perish; if the gate should exceed its stated dimensions, there would be fear from kings and robbers; and if the gate be in a low ground, there will be grief.

80. Gate over a gate and a gate which it is difficult to enter will not conduce to prosperity; an entrance which is not closed will produce suffering from hunger; an entrance which is either very short or bent will bring about the ruin of the family.

81. A troublesome entrance will bring on troubles. One that is bent inside will bring on destruction; one that is bent outside, will bring on travels to foreign land, and one that is not in the proper spot, will bring on theft by robbers.

82. The front entrance shall not be of the size of the inner entrance; such front entrance shall be constructed after due ceremonies with water-pots, fruits, flowers and with curdled milk.

83. The four corners of the house beginning from the north-eastern point, are occupied respectively by four Deva women known as *Charaki, Vidāri, Pūtanā and Rāksasī.*

84. Those that live in the corners of houses, villages and towns will suffer miseries. Persons subsisting on the flesh of dogs and the chandalas, will become prosperous by living in such corners.

85. The Laksha[1] the Banyan, the Udumbara[2] and the Aswattha will bring on miseries if situated on the south, west, north and east sides of the house, and they will bring on prosperity if they be respectively situated in the north, east, south, and west side of the house.

86. If thorny trees grow near houses, there will be fear from enemies; if milky trees, there will be waste of wealth; if fruit trees, the children will die. The wood of these trees shall also be rejected.

87. If it be felt inconvenient to remove the several trees mentioned above, a number of superior trees shall be grown between them. These are Punnaga[3], Asoka[4], Arishta[5], Vakula[6] Panasa[7], Sami[8], and Sala.[9]

88. Any spot where the ground is smooth and without holes, where the earth is sweet, fragrant and of bright appearance and where there grow superior crops, trees and creepers is calculated to afford comfort to the weary traveller, and if a house is permanently built in such a spot how happy should the dwellers feel.

89. If the house of the minister be near, there would be loss of wealth. If the house of a cheat be near, sons will die; if a temple be near, there will be various fears, and if four roads meet in the neighbourhood, the house will bear an evil reputation.

90. If a Boudha temple should be near, there would be fear from evil spirits; if ant-hills with numerous holes be near, there will be danger; if any low ground or ditch be near, there will be suffering from thirst; and if a tortoise dwell near there will be loss of wealth.

91. If the northern, eastern, southern or western side be low, the Brāhmaṇas, the Kṣatryas, the Vaisyas or the Śudras will suffer respectively. The Brāhmaṇas may live in all places; but the other castes shall live in their appropriate places.

92. In the centre of the house-site dig a pit a cubit deep, (broad and long) and fill it with the earth taken from it; if the earth is found too little, there will be misery; if it be found just enough, the site is one of middle importance, and if it be found too much, there will be increase of wealth.

93. Or fill the pit with water and walk 100 feet from it.

If, on returning, the water be found not to have fallen, there will be an increase of wealth; or if the quantity be and adhaka of 64 phalas, there will be an increase of wealth.

94. Or place an unburnt earthen vessel in the pit; and in it burn a wick. The ground will be fit for the use of that class of men in whose direction the flame is seen to be inclined.

95. The ground will also be fit for the use of that class of men the flower of whose appropriate color is found neither to fade nor lose its hue when thrown in a pit in the ground. Generally a ground is fit to live in, if a person has a special liking for it.

96. If the ground be white, red, yellow or black, or if it be found to smell like ghee, blood, cooked rice or liquor, the Brāhmaṇas, the Kṣatryas, the Vaisyas or the Śudras will respectively prosper.

97. If the ground be over-grown with kuśa grass, sara or wild reeds, the durva grass, or reeds, or if its flavor be found to be sweet, astringent, sour or pungent, the Brāhmaṇas, the Kṣatryas, the Vaiśyas or the Śudras will respectively prosper.

98. The house ground shall first be either ploughed or grown with the sprouts of seed grains or dwelt by cows or by Brāhmaṇas. The person who desires to build a house in it shall in an auspicious hour, as ascertained by an Astrologer, enter it and commence building work.

99. He shall then perform pūjā to the Devas with various cakes, curdled milk, colored rice, sandal paste, flowers and perfumed smoke; and shall also shew due honor to Brāhmaṇās and to the builders and shall satisfy them with presents.

100. The Brāhmaṇas, the Kṣatrias, the Vaiśyas and the Śudras shall respectively touch their foreheads, breasts, thighs and feet and draw lines marking the site of the house to be built.

101. The person (the master of the house) taking in his hand gold, gems, silver, pearls, curdled milk, fruits, flowers or colored rice, shall draw the line with his thumb, the middle finger or the fore-finger.

102. If the line be drawn with a weapon, there will be death by weapons. If it be drawn with a piece of metal there will be imprisonment. If with ashes, there will be fear from

destructive fires; if with a piece of straw, there will be fear from robbers; and if with a piece of wood, there will be fear from kings.

103. If the line be drawn with the foot or be indistinct and not straight there, will be fear from weapons and from grief. If it be drawn with a piece of leather, with charcoal, bone or tooth, the master of the house will suffer miseries.

104. If the line be drawn from right to left, there will be enmity; and if from left to right, there will be prosperity. If at the time of drawing the line, cruel words are heard, or if anybody be seen to spit or to sneeze, there will be misery.

105. The builder shall enter the house either half built or wholly built, and shall carefully observe where the master of the house stands and what parts of his body he touches.

106. If at the time birds be seen to sound disagreeably, facing the Sun, there will be bone corresponding to that of the part of body touched, lying buried at the spot, where the master of the house stands.

107. Or if, at the time, an elephant, a horse, a dog or the like be heard to sound, then the bones of these animals corresponding to that of the part of body touched by the master of the house, will be found buried at the spot.

108. If, when the rope is tied up, the ass is heard to cry, bone lies buried; and the same thing may be declared in case the rope is crossed over by a dog or a jackal.

109. If birds are seen to sing melodiously, facing the quarter opposite to the Sun, there is treasure under ground either at the spot where the master of the house stands or in that part of Vāstu-puruṣa's body, which corresponds to the part of body, touched by the master of the house.

110. If the rope should break there would be death; if the peg should come out or be found turned upside down, there would be severe disease; and if the master of the house or the builders should forget to take with them any necessary substance or article, there would also be death.

111. If the water pot should slip down the shoulder, there would be head-ache. If the water should run out, the family would suffer; if the pot should be broken, the servants would

die; and if it slip down from the hand, the master of the house would die.

112. After finishing the pooja, the first foundation stone shall be laid on the north-eastern corner, and then, all round from left to right, the other stones shall be laid. The pillars shall also be erected, in the same order.

113. The ceremony of erecting the tall pillars of the entrance shall be performed carefully with umbrellas, flower wreaths, cloth, perfumed smoke and sandal.

114. The same good effects shall be predicted from the entry of birds into holes, the shaking of their wings, their fall and flight as in the case of the Indra Dhwaja.

115. If the north-eastern corner be of a higher level than the rest; there will be loss of wealth and sons; if the ground emit bad smell, sons will die; if the ground be of irregular shape, kinsmen will die; if the sides are irregular, there will be no pregnancy.

116. He that desires prosperity shall raise the houseground equally on all sides. If any portion of the ground be of a higher level than the rest, there will be misery. If unavoidable, the eastern or northern side may be of a slightly higher level.

117. If the eastern side be of a higher level, there will be hatred of friends; if the southern side, there will be deaths in the family; if the western side, there will loss of wealth; and if the northern side, there will be grief.

118. The apartment for the Devas shall be built in the north-east; the kitchen in the south-east; the room for the household utensils shall be erected in the south-west; and the treasury and the granary rooms shall be erected in the north-west.

119. If there be any piece of water in the east, south-east, south, south-west, west, north-west, north and north-east, there will respectively be the death of sons, injury from fire, troubles from enemies, quarrels among women, unchastity among women, poverty, increase of wealth and increase of sons.

120. For the purpose of house-building other trees shall be cut down than those in which birds reside, or that are broken or have dried or are burnt, or in which the Devas live or which

grow on cremation grounds, as well as milky trees, the *dhava*, the *vibhītaka*, the *margosa* and the *aranes*.

121. Cooked rice shall be offered and puja performed to the tree at night, and it shall be cut down from left to right next day. If it falls on the north or east side, there will be increase of wealth, and if it falls on any other side, it shall be rejected.

122. If the cut be not irregular, the tree will bring on prosperity ; if the portion cut be of yellow color, there will be an iguana inside the tree.

123. If the color be bright-red, there will be a frog within ; if black, a cobra ; if red, a blood-sucker ; if of the color of kidney bean, there will be a stone within ; if brown, there will be a rat, and if of the color of the sword, there will be water within.

124. He that desires prosperity shall not sleep on a higher level than that of grain, cows, preceptor, fire, and the Devas ; nor shall he sleep under a beam, nor with his head towards the north or west, nor naked nor with wet feet.

125. After due puja to the Devas with perfumed smoke, sandal paste and various articles of food, the house shall be entered with a large quantity of flowers, with festoons and water pots, the Brahmins chanting vedic hymns.

REFERENCES

1. Laksha : Ficus virens.
2. Udumbara : Indian Fig tree.
3. This term is explained in pages 145 to 147 of Part I.
4. -do-
5. Arishta : The soap-berry tree.
6. Vakula : The tree Mimusops Elengi.
7. Panasa : The Jack tree.
8. This term is explained in pages 145 to 147 of Part I.
9. -do-

CHAPTER 54

On Under-Currents

1. We shall now proceed to treat of the science of under-currents by which man may get at water and observe the duties of life and be happy. Just in the same way as there are arteries for the circulation of blood in human bodies, there are water courses running in all directions above and below within the Earth.

2. Water that falls from the clouds is of one color and one flavor ; after contact with the Earth, both the color and the flavor vary with those of the ground through which it flows. This will be found to be the case on actual examination.

3. The lords of the eight quarters of the horizon beginning from the east and going round from left to right are Indra, Agni, Yama, Nirṛti, Varuṇa, Vāyu, Soma and Śiva.

4. There are eight currents bearing the same names, as those of the eight Dik-patis (lords) above enumerated, and there is a big current in the centre known as Mahasirs. Besides these there are hundreds of well-known minor currents bearing distinct names.

5. There are four currents issuing from the centre of the Earth and reaching the east, south, west and north. These are good currents. There are four other currents running towards the north-east, south-east, south-west and north-west. These produce evil. We shall now proceed to state the several indications leading to the discovery of Under-currents.

6. At a distance of 3 cubits to the west of the Vetasa[1] growing on dry lands and at the depth of a man and a half, there runs a current westwards.

7. In the course of digging will be found a white frog at the depth of half a man ; below it there will be yellow-earth, below it again there will be a piece of stone blocking up the current, and under it there is good water.

8. At a distance of 3 cubits to the north of the Jambu and at the depth of two men runs a current eastwards. While digging, the earth will be found to be white and of the color of metal and there will be a frog at the depth of a man.

9. If there be an ant-hill to the east of the Jambu and near it, there runs a current to the south of the ant-hill at the depth of two men. The water will be very sweet.

10. In digging, there will be a fish at the depth of half a man ; as far below it, there will be a stone of the color of the dove ; below it again there will be black soil ; and below it there will be water which will last for years.

11. At the distance of 3 cubits to the west of the Udumbara and at the depth of two men and a half there runs a current of good water. In digging, there will be found a white snake at the depth of a man ; below it there will be a piece of stone black as collyrium.

12. If there be an ant-hill to the north of the Arjuna tree, there will be a current at the distance of 3 cubits to the west of the hill and at the depth of 3 men and a half.

13. In digging there will be found a white iguana at the depth of half a man ; below it, at the depth of a man, will be found loose black earth ; below it will be found soil yellow-white in color and of good odor, and below it there will be much water.

14. If the plant known as Nirguṇḍī be seen to grow on an ant-hill, there will be a current at a distance of 3 cubits to the south of the hill and at a depth of two men and a quarter. The water will last for ever and will be sweet.

15. At intervals of the depth of half a man there will be found a red fish, yellow earth, white soil, earth mixed with pebbles and finally water.

16. If there be an ant hill to the east of the Badari, then, to the west of it there will be water at the depth of 3 men. In digging there will be found a white house lizard at the depth of half a man.

17. If both the Pālāśa and the Badari be seen to grow together, there will be water on the west side at a depth of three men and a quarter. In digging there will be found a frog at the depth of a man.

18. If the Bilva and the Udumbara be seen to grow together, there will be a current at a distance of 3 cubits to the south and at a depth of 3 men. In digging there will be found a black frog at the depth of half a man.

19. If an ant-hill be seen at the foot of the Kakodumbari, there will be a current at the spot at a depth of 3 men and a half running westward.

20. In digging, at the depth of half a man, the soil will be found yellow white ; below it there will be a stone of the color of milk ; and below it there will be found a rat of the color of the Kumudā.

21. If, on dry lands, the tree Kampillaka be seen to grow, there will be a current at the depth of 3 cubits to the east of the tree and the current will run southwards.

22. In digging, at the depth of a cubit the soil will be of the color of the blue lotus, or of the dove. Below it there will be seen a fish of the smell of the goat and below it there will be a small quantity of salt water.

23. On the north-western side of the tree Śoṇāka, at a distance of 2 cubits and at a depth of 3 men, there runs a current known as Kumudā.

24. If an ant-hill be seen on the southern side of the Vibhītaka and near it, there will be a current at the depth of a man and a half to the east of the ant-hills

25. If an ant-hill be seen at the distance of a cubit to the west of the Vibhītaka, there will be a current at the depth of four men and a half running north wards.

26. In digging, there will be found a white Viśwambhara, at the depth of a man ; below it there will be a crimson colored stone. The current that runs on the western side will dry up in three years.

27. If an ant-hill overgrown with the Kuśa grass be seen on the north-eastern side of the Kovidāra, there will be a current at the depth of four men and a half between the tree and the ant-hill and the water supply will be inexhaustible.

28.In digging, there will be a snake of the color of the inside of the lotus and at the depth of a man ; below it the soil will be red ; below it, will be found a precious stone known as Kurvinda.

29. If an ant-hill be seen surrounding the foot of the Saptaparṇa, there will be a current to the north of the tree at the depth of five men and the indications are given below.

30. In digging, there will be seen a green frog at the depth of half a man ; below it the soil will be of the color of yellow orpiment ; below it there will be found a stone of the color of the clouds, and below it there will be a current of good water running northwards.

31. Generally, if a frog be seen below a tree, there will be a current at the distance of a cubit from the tree and at the depth of four men and a half.

32. In digging there will be found a mongoose at the depth of a man ; below it there will be black soil ; below it there will be yellow soil ; below it there will be white soil ; and below it will be found a stone resembling the skin of the frog.

33. If a snake hole be seen to the south of the Karaṇja, there will be a current at the distance of 2 cubits to the south of the hole and at the depth of three man and a half.

34. In digging, there will be found a tortoise at the depth of half a man ; below it there will be a current flowing eastward and another of sweet water flowing northwards ; below it there will be a green stone and below it there will be water.

35. If a snake hole be seen to the north of the Madhūka, there will be a current at the distance of 5 cubits to the west of the hole and at a depth of seven men and a half.

36. In digging, at the depth of a man there will be found a cobra; below it the soil will be red-black; below it there will be a stone of the color of horse-gram; below it there will be a current flowing eastwards—an ever-running stream covered with foam.

37. If there be a fine ant-hill overgrown with the kuśa grass and the dūrvā grass to the south of the Tilaka tree, there will be a current to the west of the hill at the depth of five men running eastward.

38. If a snake hole be found to the west of the Kadamba, there will be a current at the distance of 3 cubits to the south of the hole and at a depth of five men and three quarters of a man.

39. The current runs in a northerly course; the supply of

mineral water is inexhaustible; in digging there will be yellow soil at the depth of a man; below it there will be frog of the color of gold.

40. If either the Palm or the Cocoa be surrounded by an ant-hill at its foot, there will be a current at the distance of 6 cubits to the west of the tree and at a depth of four men.

41. If there be a snake hole to the south of the Kapittah, there will be a current at a distance of 7 cubits to the north of the hole and at a depth of five men.

42. In digging, there will be a snake of many colors at the depth of a man; below it there will be black soil; below it there will be a stone blocking up the current; to the west of the stone there will be white soil and below it runs a current northwards.

43. If to the north of the Aśmantaka there be seen either the Badari or a snake hole, then, at the distance of 6 cubits to the south of such tree or hole, there will be a current at the depth of three men and a half.

44. In digging, at the depth of a man, there will be a tortoise; at an equal depth below it there will be a stone covered with dust; below it again, the soil will be a mixture of sand and mud; and below it there will be seen first a current flowing southwards; and to the north of this there will be another current running eastwards.

45. If to the north of the Haridra there be seen an ant-hill, there will be a current at the distance of 3 cubits to the east of the hill and at a depth of five men, and three-quarters of a man.

46 In digging, at the depth of a man, there will be a black snake; below it there will be a stone green as emerald; below it there will be black soil; below it there will be a current flowing westwards, and to the south of this current there will be another current.

47. If in the middle of an arid tract of land there be seen to grow plants or tree which generally grow in wet places, or if Vīraṇa and the Dūrvā grass be seen to grow luxuriantly, there will be a current at the spot at the depth of a man.

48. There will also be a current at the distance of two cubits to the south of the Bharangi, Trivṛta, Dantī, Sūkarapādī,

Lakṣmaṇā and Navamālikā, and at a depth of three men.

49. Where trees are seen to grow luxuriantly with low branches and short twigs, there will be under-currents in the neighbourhood; but where trees are seen with holes and stiff leaves and of disagreeable appearance, there will be no water near.

50 & 51. If the trees Tilaka, Āmrātaka, Varuṇa, Bhallātaka, Bilva, Tinduka, Aṅkolla, Piṇḍāra, Śirīṣa, Añjana, Parūṣaka, Vañjula and Atibalā, be seen to grow luxuriantly and surrounded by ant-hills, there will be a current at the distance of three cubits to the north of the trees and at a depth of four men and a half.

52. If there should appear a spot covered with grass where there is usually no grass or a spot devoid of grass while there is grass all round, there will respectively be under such spot a current or a treasure.

53. If a thorny tree or plant should grow without thorns, or if thorns should appear on trees or plants that are without them, there will respectively be a current or a treasure at the distance of three cubits to the west of the spot and at a depth of three men and three quarters of a man.

54. Where the ground when struck with the foot produces a loud sound, there will be a current at the spot flowing northwards at a depth of three men and a half.

55. If a branch of a tree should either be low or white, there will be a current directly under it at the depth of three men.

56. If the fruits or flowers of a tree should be of extraordinary growth or luxuriance, there would be a current at the distance of three cubits to the east of the tree and at a depth of four men. Under the current there are stones and yellow soil.

57. If the Kaṇṭakāri should be seen to grow without thorns or with white blossoms, there will be a current at the spot at a depth of three men and a half.

58. If the Kharjuri should be seen to grow with only two branches in the middle of an arid tract, there will be a current to the west of the tree at a depth of three men.

59. If the Karṇikara or Palāśa be seen with white blossoms,

there will be a current at a distance of two cubits to the north of the tree and at a depth of three men.

60. Where there is heat or smoke, there will be a current at the spot at a depth of two men. The current will be one of great dimensions carrying a large body of water.

61. Where the crops are found to die out or appear over-luxuriant or very white, there will be a large current at the spot at the depth of two men.

62. We shall now proceed to describe the under-currents in arid tracts of land. The currents are generally of the shape of the ass's neck.

63. If an ant-hill be seen to the north-east of the Pīlu tree, there will be a current to the west of such ant-hill running northwards at a depth of five men.

64. In digging, the soil will be found to be of the color of a mixture of green and yellow at the depth of a man; then at equal depths there will be, one below the other, green earth, then a stone, and then water.

65. If an ant-hill be seen to the east of the Pīlu tree, there will be a current at the distance of four and a half cubits to the south of it and at a depth of seven men.

66. In digging, at the depth of a man, there will be a snake spotted black and white and of the length of a cubit; to the south of it there will be a large current of salt water.

67. If a snake hole be seen to the north of the Karīra then to the south of it there will be a current of sweet water at a depth of ten men; in digging there will be seen an yellow frog at the depth of a man.

68. If snake hole be seen to the west of the Rohītaka there will be a current at a distance of three cubits to the south of the hole and at a depth of twelve men running westwards.

69. If an ant-hill be seen to the east of the Indratara, there will be a current at the distance of a cubit to the west of the hill and at a depth of fourteen men; in digging there will be seen an iguana of brown color at the depth of a man.

70. If a snake hole be seen to the north of the Suvarṇa tree, there will be a current at the distance of two cubits to the south of the hole and at a depth of fifteen men.

71. The water in the above spot will be saltish; in digging, there will be a mongoose at the depth of half a man; below it there will be a copper colored stone, below it there will be red soil, and below it there will be water running southwards.

72. If the Badari and the Rohita be seen to grow together, though there may be no ant-hill in the neighbourhood, there will be a current at the distance of three cubits to the west of the trees and at a depth of sixteen men.

73. In digging, there wīll be seen a scorpion at the depth of a man; below it there will be white soil; below it there will be a stone resembling a ball of flour, and below it runs a current of sweet water flowing southwards; to the north of this current there will be another current.

74. If the Badari and the Karīra be seen to grow together, there will be a large current at a distance of three cubits to the west of the trees and at a depth of eighteen men flowing in a north-easterly direction.

75. If the Pīlu and the Badari be seen to grow together, there will be a current containing an abundant supply of salt water at a distance of three cubits to the east of the trees and at a depth of twenty men.

76. If the Kakubha be seen to grow with either the bamboo or the Bilva, there will be a current at the distance of two cubits to the west of the trees and at a depth of twenty-five men.

77. If either the Dūrvā or the Kuśa grass be seen to grow white on ant-hills, a well may be sunk at the spot and the current run at the depth of twenty-one men.

78. Where the Kadamba is seen to grow or ant-hills are found overgrown with Dūrvā grass, there will be a current at the distance of three cubits to the west of such tree or hills and at a depth of twenty-five men.

79. If the Rohitaka tree be seen to grow in the middle of three ant-hills with three other trees, there will be an undercurrent at the spot.

80. In digging, there will be a stone at a distance of four cubits and sixteen inches to the north of the central spot and at a depth of forty men.

81. If the Śamī is found covered with knots and an ant-hill be seen to the north of it, there will be a current at the distance of five cubits to the west of the hill and at a depth of fifty men.

82. If of several ant-hills in a spot, the central one be white, there will be a current at the spot at the depth of fifty-five men.

83. If the Palāśa tree be seen to grow with the Sāmī trees, there will be a current to the west of the trees at the depth of sixty men. In digging, there will be seen a snake at the depth of half a man and below it there will be yellow soil mixed with sand.

84. If the white Rohitaka tree be seen surrounded by ant-hills, there will be a current at the distance of a cubit to the west of the tree and at the depth of seventy men.

85. If the Śamī be seen white and full of thorns, there will be a current to the south of the tree at a depth of seventy-five men. In digging there will be found a snake at the depth of half a man.

86. It would be wrong to proceed to judge of under-currents in dry but fertile lands from the several indications given for arid lands. As regards the Jambū and the Vetasa, the depths of under-currents given for these trees shall be doubled if the trees are seen to grow in arid lands.

87 & 88. If the trees Jambū, Trivṛt, Maurvī, Śiśumārī, Sariba, Śivā, Śyāmā, Vīrudhi Vārāhī, Jyotiṣmatī, Garuḍa-vegā, Sūkarikā, Māṣaparṇī, Vyāghrapadā are seen to grow by the side of snake holes, there will be an under-current to the north of the holes at the distance of three cubits and at a depth of three men and a half.

89. The above apply to purely wet lands. But if the trees are seen to grow in dry but fertile lands, the depth of under-currents will be five men and in arid lands the depth will be seven men.

90. In the case of lands in which neither tree nor plants are seen to grow, in which no ant-hills are found to grow, and which present a smooth and even appearance, there will be under-currents in those spots where the appearance of the soil is of an unusual nature.

91. For instance, if the spot appears wet or hollow or sandy, or if it be found to resound to the tread of foot, there will be a current at the depth of four and a half or five men.

92. There are under-currents containing an abundant supply of water to the south of trees of luxuriant growth and at the depth of four men. In places full of trees, if the ground should present any unusual appearance, the existence of the current may be determined as stated above.

93. In dry but fertile lands as well as in wet lands, if the ground be found to sink under the foot, there will be a current at the depth of a man and a half; and if while there are no houses in the neighbourhood, worms are seen in large quantities, there will be an under-current at the spot.

94. If the ground be felt both hot and cold, there will be hot and cold currents at the spot at a depth of three men and a half; and if a rainbow, a fish or an ant-hill be seen at the spot there will be a current at the distance of four cubits from them and at a depth of three men and a half.

95. If, of a number of ant-hills about a spot, one be seen above the rest, there will be a current under it, and there will also be currents in places where crops do not grow.

96. If the Banyan, the Palāśa and the Udumbara trees be seen to grow together, there will be a current under them. If the Banyan and the Pippala trees be seen to grow together, there will be a current to the north of the trees.

97. If a well be situated to the south-east of a village or a town, there will be much suffering from various fears and from thirst.

98. If the well be situated in the south-western quarter, children will perish. If in the north-west, women will suffer. Wells situated in the north-east will conduce to prosperity.

99. I have thus stated in the Āryā metre the views of the Sage Sāraswata on the subject of Under-currents. I shall now proceed to state the views of Manu on the same subject.

100. Wherever trees, shrubs and creepers are seen to grow luxuriantly, with glossy and uninjured leaves, there are under-currents; and there are also under-currents in places where the Padma, Kṣura, Uśīra, Kula, Guṇdra, Kāśa, Kuśa, and Nalikā are seen to grow.

101 & 102. There are under-currents in places where the Kharjura, Jambū, Arjuna and the Vetasa trees are seen to grow, or where there grow milky trees, shrubs and creepers, or where the Chatra, Ibha, Nāga, Satapatra, Nīpa, Sinduvāra and Naktamala trees are seen to grow. Again, where the tree Vibhītaka or Madayantikā is seen to grow, there will be a current at the spot at a depth of three men. If rocks are found one over the other, there will be under-currents at a depth of three men at their foot.

103. Where the earth is found overgrown with the Muñjā grass, with reeds and with the Kuśa grass, the soil black and mixed with pebbles, as well as in places where the soil is black or red, there will be under-currents containing a large supply of sweet water.

104. If the soil be red and mixed with pebbles, the water will be astringent in its flavor; if it be brown, the water will be saline; if white, it will be saltish; and if black it will be sweet.

105. Wherever the trees Śāka, Aśvakarṇa, Arjuna, Bilva, Sarja, Śrīparni, Ariṣṭā, Dhava, and Śiṁśapa are found to grow, or where the leaves of trees, bushes and creepers are found perforated with holes, or where such trees, bushes and creepers put on a forbidding appearance, there will be no water in the neighbourhood.

106. If the ground be seen of the color of the sun, fire, ashes, camel or ass, there will be no water in the locality. But if the bambu be seen to shoot out, of a red color, or if the soil be found red, there will be under-currents lying immediately under stones.

107. Where there are found stones of the color of Vaidurya, kidney-bean or of the clouds or of the color of the fruit of the fig tree when about to ripen, or of the color of the bee or collyrium or of brown color, there will be water in the neighbourhood.

108. If the stone be of the color of the pigeon, of honey, of ghee, or of white silk, or of the color of the Soma plant, there will be an abundant supply of water in the neighbourhood.

109. But if the stone be red or with spots of various colors, or of the color of the white ashes or the camel, the ass or the

bee, or of the color of the Aṅguṣṭhikā flower or of the color of the sun or fire, there will be no water in the neighbourhood.

110. Where stones are found of the color of the moonlight or crystal or pearl or gold, or of the color of vermillion or collyrium, or of the color of the rising sun, or of the color of haritala, that is, sulphuret of arsenic, there would be prosperity. Thus have we stated the views of Manu on the subject of Under-currents.

111. Stones which cannot be broken and which conduce to prosperity, are dwelt in by the Yakṣas and the Nāgas at all times. Countries in which such stones are found will never suffer from drought.

112. If stones that cannot be broken be heated in the fire fed by the dry leaves and the wood of the Tinduka tree and then drenched in lime water, they can be easily broken.

113. Or mix the ashes of the Mokṣaka with water heat the mixture, add to it the juice of reeds and drench the stones seven times with the preparation, then heat the stone it will become brittle.

114. Or mix together butter-milk, boiled rice water and arrack, and throw into the mixture a quantity of horse-gram and the fruit of the Badari, keep the mixture for seven days and then drench the stone with it and heat it, it will become brittle.

115. Soak in the urine of the cow the leaves of the margosa as well as the sesamum plant, and the plants. Apāmārga, Tinduka and Guduchi and obtain a decoction. After drenching the stone with it six times heat the stones, it will become brittle.

116. Form a mixture of the juice of the plant Calotropis gigantea, the black powder of the burnt horn of the ram, the excrement of the turtle dove and of the rat, rub this over the stone cutter's chistle, stir it in oil and then temper the instrument. It will neither break nor become blunt when worked in stone.

117. Or mix together the juice of the plantain or butter milk. Allow the mixture to remain so for a day and then temper in it any cutting instrument which shall afterwards be

rubbed against the wetstone. The instrument will never break when worked in stone or metals.

118. There will be an abundant supply of water under the bank at the foot of a mountain, if the bank runs from east to west and not if it runs from north to south. Where there may be streams running along the bank, the bank breaks generally when the waves strike against it. In the absence of such streams water shall be collected by the side of the bank by means of dykes constructed of stones or wood. The water shall then be stirred up by horses, elephants and other animals, the waves dashing against the bank will break it.

119. Along the margin of a pond or other piece of water shall be grown the Kakubha, the Banyan, the Mango, the Platcha, the Kadamba, the Niccūla, the Jambu, the Vetasa, the Nīpa, the Kuravaka, the Tala, the Aśoka, the Madhuka, and the Vakula.

120. In the case of tanks a sluice or an outlet for water shall be erected of stones in one spot. It should be capable of being closed by means of thick beam shutters or planks thrust between stones, and when closed the other side shall be covered with earth to prevent the escape of water.

121. The fragrant plants of Anjana, Musta and Uśīra together with the powder of Rājakośataka and Amalaka and with the fruit of the Kataka, shall be thrown into wells.

122. If the well water be muddy, bitter, brackish, without flavor or of bad smell, it will become clear, sweet, fragrant and possessed of other good properties.

123. The work of sinking wells shall be commenced when the Moon passes through one of the asterisms of Maghā, Anurādhā, Puṣya, Dhaṇiṣṭā, U. Phalguni, U. Ashadha, U. Proshtapada, Rohiṇī and Sataya.

124. Worship shall be performed to God Varuṇa, and a pike of the Banyan or Vetasa shall be driven into the ground at the spot directly over the current after due puja to it with flowers, sandal paste and perfumed smoke.

125. I have already treated of the subject of rains, adopting the views of Baladeva, and now by the grace of the Munis, I have well treated of the subject of Under-currents.

REFERENCE

1. The names of over 100 trees are given in this chapter. They are explained in the glossary printed at the end of Chapter 55.

CHAPTER 55

On Gardening

1. The sides of rivers and lakes and other water banks will not be pleasant and agreeable if devoid of shady trees. It is therefore necessary to form gardens on the banks of waters.

2. Soft soil is congenial to the growth of all trees. Such a soil should be selected for the garden, and the Sesamum plant should first be grown in it. As soon as the plant begins to bear blossoms, it must be cut and removed from the spot.

3. The trees Ariṣṭa[1] Aśoka, Punnāga and Sīriṣa shall be grown either in gardens or in houses by their seeds and they will conduce to prosperity.

4 & 5. The trees Panasa, Asoka, Plantain, Jambu, Lakucha, Dadima, Draksha, Pālivata, Bījapūra and Atimuktaka shall be grown by planting either their roots after clipping them or their branches, smearing cow-dung over the parts cut.

6. Trees that grow without branches shall be grown in the Śiśira season, and in the Hemanta shall be grown trees that grow with branches; in the winter season shall be grown trees possessing good trunk. The trees may be planted in any quarter of the garden.

7. The growing of trees by smearing over them from the root to the branches a mixture of ghee, of Uṣira, of Sesamum seeds, of honey, of Viḍaṇga, of milk and of cowdung, is known as Sankramaṇa growth.

8. The person planting the tree shall do so after bathing and after washing it with water and adorning it with sandal. The trees will then bear the leaves of their parent trees.

9. In the dry season the trees shall be watered both in the morning and evening; in the cold season they shall be watered at mid-day, and in the rainy season whenever the ground is found dry.

10 & 11. The Jambu, the Vetasa, the Vānīra, the Kadamba, the Udumbara, the Arjuna, the Beejapuraka, the Mridvika, the Lakucha, the Daḍina, the Vañjula, the Nakta-māla, the Tilka, the Panasa, the Timira and the Āmrātaka shall be grown on wet soil.

12. An interval of twenty cubits between trees is the best; one of sixteen is passable; and one of twelve is injurious.

13. The trees that are planted very near each other get their branches interwoven as well as their roots and such trees get choked and do not grow well.

14. Cold winds and hot sun produce diseases in trees, and the trees turn white and do not put forth new leaves; the branches become dry and the juice oozes out.

15. To cure the tree of these diseases, first scrape off or otherwise remove the parts dead from the tree with a knife; rub over the parts a mixture of Viḍaṅga, ghee and mire and pour at the roots water mixed with milk.

16. If the fruits are seen to die out, then heat a mixture of horse gram, black gram and (kidney bean), sesamum seeds and barley; after the mixture has fully cooled pour it at the roots. Then the trees will yield an increase of flowers and fruits.

17 & 18. Get two adhakas[2] of the excrement of the goat and the ram, an āḍhaka of Sesamum seed, half an āḍhaka of saktu[3], an āḍhaka of water and a tula[4] of cow's flesh. Form a mixture of these, keep it untouched for seven days, and if at the end of the time spreading creepers, plants and trees be watered with mixture, flowers and fruits will grow in abundance.

19 & 20. Keep the seeds soaked in milk for ten days; then rubbing ghee over the hands the seed shall be taken up in the hands and passed from hand to hand till it is covered with ghee. It shall then be rubbed over several times with cow-dung and exposed to the smoke of the flesh of the hog and the deer. It shall then be mixed with the serum or marrow (of the flesh) of the fish and the pig, and when dry it shall be sown in a well prepared soil and watered with a mixture of milk and water. When it grows, it will grow with flowers.

21. Mix together the flour of rice, of black gram and of Sesamum seeds with the flour of barley (fried before ground)

with the dead or decayed flesh, and with a small quantity of water, soak the seed of the tamarind in the mixture and expose it to the smoke of the root of the turmeric. The seed when sown will grow as a creeper.

22 & 23. Put into the milk of the cow the roots of Asphota, Dhatri, Dhava, Vāśika, Palasini, Vetasa, Suryavalli, Śyāmā and Atimukta and heat the milk on fire; after it has cooled, put into it the seed of the Kapittha and allow it to soak for 100 ghatikas[5] and dry the seed in the sun for 30 days. If the seed be then sown in the soil it will grow as a creeper.

24, 25 & 26. Dig a pit in the ground a cubit square and two cubits deep, and fill it with water prepared with a mixture of the flesh of the fish. Allow the pit to dry up completely; dry it further by means of fire; rub the sides and bottom with a mixture of honey, ghee and ashes, fill the pit now with the flour of black gram, of Sesamum seeds and of barley mixed with earth; pour over the pit water prepared with the flesh of the fish and pound the mixture well till it becomes hard. Sow any seed at a depth of four inches and water of the fish. The seed will grow as a fine creeper with tender leaves over terraces and the roof of houses in a most wonderful manner.

27 & 28. Soak any seed one hundred times either in the Kalka (decoction) or in the oil of Aṅkola, or in the fruit of the Śleṣmātaka. The moment the seed is put into the ground it grows with branches laden with fruits. What wonder !

29 & 30. Soak any seed in the fruit of the Śleṣmātaka after removing its seeds, and then soak it in the water gymn of the ripe fruit of Aṅkola and dry it in shade; repeat the operation seven times; rub the seed over with the dung of the buffalo, and keep it buried in the same dung for some time; then sow it in the soil drenched with the waters of the cocoanut. The seed will grow and bear fruits in a day.

31. When the Moon passes through any of the fixed[6] asterisms or the soft[7] asterisms, or through the asterisms of Mūla, Viśākha, Puṣya, Śravaṇa, Aśvinī and Hasta, trees shall be planted or seeds sown according to the views of Sages possessed of the inner eye of knowledge.

Notes—The following have been extracted from a work known as *Bṛhat Sarngadhara*.

1. Mix with earth a variety of fragrant flowers; use the mixture as manure to a tree of scentless, flowers; pour at the roots the juice of Dhava and Khadira; smear over the tree sandal paste, and expose the tree to the smoke of ghee; its scentless flowers will become fragrant.

2. Use as manure to the roots of the cotton the leaves of barley, Sesamum and of turmeric, and pour at the roots water prepared with a mixture of these leaves. The plant will yield cotton throughout the year bright and red as fire.

3. Mix with water the juice of the sugarcane and the root of the Vidari; heat the mixture and rub it over the roots of any flowering tree, and pour at the roots the juice of the sugarcane. The trees will yield flowers at unusual seasons.

4. Make cakes of a mixture of Madhuyaṣti, sugar, koṣta and Madhupuṣpa, and cover with the cakes the roots of fruit trees and throw earth over the parts. The fruits will grow without bones.

5. Kill a goat and immediately tie its shoulder skin over the branches of fruit trees. The fruites will ever remain unripe.

6. Pound in a stone mortar the bone of the monkey mixed with the juice of the elephant in rut ; rub the preparation over the roots of fruit trees. The fruits will remain unripe for a year.

7. Tie over the branches of fruit trees the skin of an animal and grass ; rub over the branches a mixture of Vidanga, honey and milk ; pour at the roots a mixture of milk and water. The ripe fruits will stick to the tree for a very long time.

8. Mix with milk the serum or marrow (of flesh) of the fish and the hag as well as the flesh of the two creatures. Soak any seed in the mixture ; dry it and expose it to the smoke of ghee. The seed when sown will grow in an unusual and wonderful manner.

9. If the seed of the pomegranate be soaked in the blood of the cock 21 times dried and each time, it will, the moment it is put into the ground, grow and bear fruits in a most wonderful manner.

10. Thrust into the root of the Kumuda (the esculent white

water lily) a variety of colors, soak the root in urine, rub over it ghee and honey, and then sow it in the soil, it will grow and bear flowers of the several colors originally put into the root.

11. Mix together the buffalo's dung and urine, rub the mixture over the seed of the fruit of the Kumuda for seven days drying the seed each time. If the seed be then sown into the ground, it will grow as a Karavira plant.

12. Soak the seed of the pumpkin or of the brinjal, or of the serpent cucumber and the like in the serum or marrow (of flesh) of the fish or hog and dry the seed. If the seed be then sown in good soil and watered it will bear fruits of very large size and without bones.

13. Soak the seed of the Castor oil plant in the blood and serum (of flesh) of the hog and dry it ; soak it again in the oil of the Aṅkola and dry it. If the seed be now sown in the soil, it will grow and bear the fruits of Karavalli.

14. Use as manure to the root of the plantain the excrement of the ass and the horse ; burn dry twigs over the root ; the plantain will then yield fruits as big as the trunk of the elephant, and the fruits will appear as if to tear out the tree.

15. If the root of the plantain be drenched with the blood or serum (of flesh) of the hog or with the decoction of the fruit of the Ankola, it will bear pomegranate fruits.

16. If the Rambha (plantain) be watered with a liquid mixture consisting of the flesh, serum and blood of man and the powdered tooth of the elephant and water, the tree will yield mango fruits.

17. Mix together the shining decoction of the fruits of Aṅkola, human flesh, the milk of the goat and oil cakes. Use the mixture as manure to the seed of the mango put into the soil. The seed will grow out as a spreading creeper like the vine and will bear fruits at all times.

18. Form a mixture of Krimiripu, of barley, of Madhuyashti and of jaggery ; rub it over any tree yielding bitter fruit, after slightly grazing out the bark with a knife, pour at the root a mixture of milk and water ; the tree will thenceforth yield sweet fruits.

19. Soak any seed many times in human flesh and in the oil of the Aṅkola, drying the seed each time. Take a quantity of

earth in the hand, bury the seed in it and pour water over it ; the seed will grow that instant.

20. Dig a pit, burn in it the bones and the dung of the cow and the hog ; remove the ashes ; fill the pit with earth. Plant in it the root of the Mūlaka, the root will grow to the size of the pit.

REFERENCES

1. Ariṣṭa, &c. For an explanation, vide glossary at the end of this chapter.
2. Āḍhaka is two Madras measures.
3. Saktu, the flour of barley or rice fried.
4. Tula. One hundred Palas.
5. Aghatika is 24 minutes.
6. The fixed asterisms are Rohini, U. Phalguni, U. Ashada and U. Proshtapada.
7. The soft asterisms are Mrigasīrṣa, Chitra, Anurādhā and Revati.

Glossary of Botanical terms occurring in the last two Chapters, arranged alphabetically.

A

Āmalaka—The fruit of the Emblic myrobalan.

Āmra—The Mango.

Amraṭaka—Hog-plum. Spondias mangifera. Adivie mamadie, Amatum ; Beng. Amna.

Añjana—probably Kalanjana—a small shrub used as a purgative.

Aṅkola—Alangium hexapetalum. Tel. Woodooga ; Hind. Akola. The roots are aromatic ; the fruit is edible.

Apamārga—Name of a plant. Achyranthes aspera employed often in incantations, in medicine, in washing linen and in sacrifices.

Ariṣṭa – The soap berry tree ; Sapindus detergens ; Azadirachta Indica.

Arjuna—The tree Terminalia Arjuna.

Arka – Name of the plant Calotropis gigantea.

Aśmantaka – Name of a plant from the fibres of which a Brahmin's girdle may be made ; probably Indian hemp.

Aśoka—Name of the tree Jonesia Aśoka.

Aspota—Calatropis gigantea.

Aśvakarṇa—The tree Vatica robusta.

Atibala—Name of a Medicinal plant, Sidonia cordifolia and Rhombifolia or Annona squarmosa. Custard apple.

Atimukta—Name of a tree Dalbergia Ougeinensis.

B

Badarī—The Jujube tree. Zyzyphus jujuba. Tel. Regoo ; Beng. Kool. Flowers greenish, yellow and fruit eatable. It is sweet and mealy.

Bījapura—A variety of citron.

Bhallata—Markingnut plant.

Bharngi—

Bilva—Aegle marmelos, the Bell tree or the Wood-apple. Its leaves are employed in the ceremonial of the worship of Śiva. Tel. Maredoo; Beng. Bell.

C

Chatra—Name of a kind of grass. Name of a plant, Anithum sowa. Tel. Sompa.

D

Dāḍima—Pomegranate.

Dantī—The plant Croton polyandrum. Tel. Konda, Amadum ; Beng. Duntī ; Hind. Hakoose. The seeds are used a purgative.

Dhātrī—Emblica officinalis.

Dhava—The plant Grislea tomentosa. Tel. Sirinjie ; Beng Dhaee-phool.

Drākṣa—Vine.

G

Garudavega—Name of a plant.

Guduchi—The shrub Cooculus cordifolius. Tel. Tippatingay ; Beng. Guluncha. This is a twining shrub.

Gundra—A kind of grass. Saccharum Sara, pen-reed grass. Beng. Shur or Saro.

H

Haridra—Turmeric.

I

Ibha—Probably Ibhakesara. The tree Mesua Roxburghii or Ibhakana. The plant Scindapsus officinalis.

Indrataru—The tree Pinus Devataru.

J

Jambu—Syzygium Jambol Janum. Tel. Nareddoo. Hind. Jāmoon. The fruit is eatable. Flowers small white.

Jyotiṣmatī—Heart pea. Cardispermum helicacabum.

K

Kadamba—The tree Nauclea Kadamba. Flowers small orange colored and fragrant. Tel. Rudrakshakamba ; Beng. Kudum ; Hind. Cuddum.

Kakodumbarika—Opposite leaved fig tree Ficus oppositifolia.

Kakubha—The tree Terminalio Arjuna.

Kampilla—Crinum amaryllacea.

Kantakarika—Solanum Jacquini. Tel. Vankula ; Hind. Kootaya.

Kapittha—The Elephantor Wood apple. Feronia elephantum. Tel. Velaga ; Hind. Khoet. The fruit is eaten.

Karañja—Pongamia glabra. Tel. Kanooyoo ; Hind. Kurung ; Beng. Kurunjee. Leaves unequally pinnated.

Karavalli—Momordica charantia. Beng. Kurula.

Karavira—The Plant Assafoetida.

Karira—A cluster of shooting bamboos.

Karnikara—The tree Pterospermum acerifolium. Also Cassia fistula.

Kasa—A species of grass. Saccharum spontaneum. Beng. Kash ; Hind. Kagara ; Tel. Relloogaddy.

Kataka—The clearing nut plant. Strychnos potatorum.

Khadira--The tree Acacia catechu. Having very hard wood. Tamil. Wothalay ; Tel. Podeelmaun ; Beng. Khuera.

Kharjuri—The Wild Datura tree.

Kovidara—Bauhinia variegata. Hind. Sona. The buds are eaten as vegetables.

Krimiripu—An anthelmintic plant. Vidanga, a shrub used in medicine as a vermifuge.

Kshura—Tribulus Lanuginosus. Tel. Palleroo ; Beng. Gokhoor.

Kula—Name of several plants ; a kind of ebony. Disopyros tomentosa. Hind. Tumal

Kuranka—A Crimson species of Amaranth.

Kuśa—Sacred grass used at certain religious ceremonies, Poa Synosuroides. A grass with long stalks and numerous pointed leaves.

L

Lakshumana—Name of various pl ants. Oshadi, Prinsiparul and c.

Likucha—A kind of bread fruit tree. Arithocarpus Lacucha.

M

Madayantika—Arabian jasmine.

Madhuka—Bassia longifolia or latifolia. Tel. Ippa ; Hind. Mohe. Its oil is used by the poorer classes.

Madhupuṣpa—Mahwah 'tree. Bassia latifolia. Tel. Ipie ; Beng. Mahwah or Muhova.

Madhuyaṣṭi—Sugarcane.

Mashaparna—A and of leguminous shrub. Glycine debilis.

Mokshaka—A species of tree.

Mounjaka—A blade of Munja grass, Saccharum munja.

Mridvika—A vine, a bunch of grapes.

Mulaka—An esculent root ; a radish.

Mārvā—Sanseviera Roxburghiana. A sort of creeper from the fibres of which bow strings and the girdle of the Kṣatryas are made.

Mustā—A species of grass. Cyperus rotundus.

N

Naga—Rottera tinctoria. Tel. Vasuntagunda ; Hind. Camul.
Naktamala—The tree Pongamia glabra or Dalbergia arborea.
Nala—A kind of fragrant substance ; a perfume ; red arsenic.
Navamalika—Arabian Jasmine. Jasminum sambal. Tel. Boondoo Mall ; Beng. Butmoo grah
Nīpa—The tree Nauclea cadamba. Tel. Rudrakshakamba.
Nachula—The tree Barringtonia acutangula.
Nimba—Azadirachta Indica.
Nirgundi—Vitex negundo. Tel. Wagala ; Hind. Nisinda.
Nyagrodha—The Indian fig tree. Ficus Indica.

O

Oosira—The fragrant root of the plant Andropogon muricatus.

P

Padma—A species of fragrant plant. Tel. Yerratamaray.
Palasa—The tree Butea frondosa. Tel. Moduga ; Hind. Palas ; Eng. Bastard teak. Blossoms rich scarlet color.
Palasini—A species of climbing plant.
Palivata—Name of a tree.
Panasa—The jack tree. Artocarpus integrifolia.
Parushaka—Xylocarpus granatum. Beng. Parusha.
Peelu—Salvadora Persica. Tel. Ghoonia
Pindara—A species of tree. Flacourtia sapida. Tamil, Sottacla ; Tel. Conrew.
Plaksha—The holy fig tree. Ficus religiosa.
Punnaga—Rottleria tinctoria, from the blossoms of which a yellowish dye is prepared.

R

Rajakosataka—A kind of fruit.
Rambha—A plantain, Musa sapientum.

S

Saka—Pot herb. Sirisha tree.
Sami—Acacia suma, possessing a very tough and hard wood supposed to contain fire.

Saptaparna—The tree Alstonia or Echites scholaris. Do feet. Flowers greenish white. Planks used as school boards.

Sariba—Sarsaparilla.

Sarja—The sal tree. Shorea robusta.

Satapatra—Lotus. Nelumbium speciosum.

Simsapa—The tree Dalbergia Sisu.

Sinduvara—The small tree or shrub Negundo.

Sirisha—Sirissa tree. Acacia speciosa. Flowers small, white and fragrant. Tel. Dirisana; Beng. Sirissa.

Sisumari—The plant Nauclea cordifolia.

Śiva—The Sami tree. Yellow Myrobolan.

Somalata—The moon plant. Sarcostema viminalis.

Sonaka—Bignonia or Calosanthes Indica A handsome looking tree. The timber is soft and spongy. Young leaves are used in the treatment of ulcers. Tel Pampena; Hind. Shyona.

Śrīparṇī—A lotus or the tree Premna spinosa. The wood of which produces fire by attrition. Tel. Tagoomooda.

Śukarapadī—Sakara is a sort of moss. [Lycopodium imbricatum.

Sukarika—A sort of moss. Do.

Suriavalli—Cleome pentaphyllas, which, according to Jaffrey, is Gynandropsis.

Suvarna—The tree Cassia fistula. The thorn apple.

Śyāmā—Ichnocarpus frutescens, used as a substitute for Sarsaparilla.

T

Tala—The palmyra or fan palm. Borassus nabelliformis. Tel. Tady; Hind. Talgachh. Liquor called toddy is extracted from the tree.

Tilak—The red wood tree. Adenanthera Pavonina. Tel. Bandigooroo vindza: Hind. Koochunduna.

Timira—A sort of aquatic plant.

Tinduka—Dyospyros embryopteris or Dyospyros glutinosa.

Trivṛtā—A creeping medicinal plant; a substitute for jalap.

U

Udumbara—Ficus racemosa. Tel. Maydi; Hind. Gooler. Red wooded fig tree or country fig tree. The fruit is edible.

Uśīra—The fragrant root of the plant Andropogon maricatus. Tel. Cassavoo; Beng. Khuskus.

V

Vakula—A kind of tree. Mimusop elengi.

Vanira—A sort of cane or ratang. Calamus rotang.

Vañjula—Jonesia Asoka.

Varahi— A particular kind of bulbous plant said to be an esculent root or yam.

Varuna—Evasia longifolia.

Vasika—Adhatoda vasika.

Vaṭa—The banyan or Indian fig tree. Ficus Indica.

Vīrana—A fragrant grass. Cuscus grass. Tel. Cooroovayroo or Kussavoo; Beng. Khuskus; Hind. Useer. The root is fragrant.

Vetasa—Calamus rotang. Rattan cane. Tel. Bettam; Hind. Beta. Sometimes the growth is to the length of 500 or 600 feet.

Vibhitaka—The tree Terminalia Belerica. Tel. Taondee or Tady; Beng. Bahura. Length 100 feet. A medicinal tree.

Viḍaṅga—Erycibe paniculata. A medicinal substance considered of great efficacy as a vermifuge.

Viḍārī—The plant Hedysarum gangeticum. The climbing plant Ipomoea paniculata.

Virudhi—A spreading creeper.

Vyaghrapada—The plant Flacourtia sapida.

CHAPTER 56

On the Building of Temples

1. After procuring an abundant supply of water, and forming gardens round it, there shall be erected on the spot temples for Devas for the increase of one's fame and virtue.

2. The person who desires to go to worlds to which go persons who perform sacrificial fire ceremonies and dig water tanks, shall erect temples for the Devas. He prospers both in this world and in the world above.

3. Places where there are waters and gardens, whether natural or artificial, are dwelt by the Devas.

4. The Devas are ever at play in tanks made shady by the leaves of the lotus and white by the water-lilies moved to and fro by the wings of the swan.

5. In tanks rendered agreeable by the music of the swan, the duck, the curlew and the ruddy-goose and be the water animals, resting in the shade of the hijjal growing on the banks.

6. In places where there are rivers adorned by lines of curlew birds serving as a girdle with beads, full of the sweet music of the teal with the watery sheet for robes and with the ilisha fish for belts.

7. In places where there are rivers with blossomed trees on their banks for their head ornaments, with the junction of the streams as their loins, the sandbanks as their breasts and with the sounding swans as their ankle beads.

8. And in gardens, streams, hills, places through which pass mountain currents and in the canals of flower gardens.

9, Places which have been described as suitable for the erection of houses for the Brāhmaṇas and others are also suitable for the erection of temples.

10. In the case of temples the site shall always be divided into 64 squares and the entrance shall be in the middle of the

wall and the walls shall be due east and west and due north and south.

11. The height of the temple shall be twice its breadth and its *kati* shall be a third of its height.

12. The Garbhagraha or the inner apartment shall be half as the breadth of the temple and walls shall be raised all round. The breadth of the entrance to the Garbhagraha shall be a fourth of the breadth of the room and its height shall be twice the breadth.

13. The breadth of the two vertical side frames as well as of the two horizontal frames above and below shall be a fourth of the height of the entrance, and the thickness of the vertical frames shall be a fourth of the breadth of the entrance.

14. The number of vertical frames of the door of the entrance may be 3, 5, 7, or 9, and two small openings shall be made at one-fourth of the height of the door from below.

15. The other parts shall be adorned with the figures of birds, trees and pots, and with male and female figures as well as those of leaves, creepers and of the fiends attending on Śiva.

16. The height of the image of the Deva with its pedestal shall be $\frac{7}{8}$ths of the height of the entrance. The image shall be double the height of the pedestal.

17 & 18. Twenty different sorts of temples are referred to by writers. These are Meru, Mandara, Kailāsa, Vimānachhanda, Nandana, Samudga, Padma, Garuḍa, Nandivardhana, Kuñjara, Guharāja, Vṛṣa, Haṁsa, Sarvatobhadra, Ghaṭa, Siṁha, Vṛtta, Catuṣkona, Ṣoḍaśāśi and Aṣṭaśri.

19. I shall now proceed to describe each of the twenty sorts of temples.

20. The building known as Meru consists of six sides, twelve stories with numerous caves and with four entrances and shall be thirty-two cubits long.

21. The building known as Mandara is thirty cubits broad and consists of ten stories with pinnacles. The building known as Kailāsa is twenty cubits long and consists of eight stories with pinnacles.

22. Vimāna is twenty-one cubits long with windows and air holes. Nandana has six stories, is thirty-two cubits long

and has sixteen Andas (domes).

23. Samudga is round; Padma is of the shape of a lotus, 8 cubits long with a single story and pinnacle.

24. Garuḍa is of the shape of the Brahmany kite; Nandivardhana is 24 cubits broad with seven stories and twenty Andas.

25. Kuñjara is of the shape of the back of the elephant with four sides, each 16 cubits broad. Guharāja is 16 cubits long and has 3 stories with verandas.

26. Vṛṣa is 12 cubits broad, round on all sides with a single story and pinnacle. Haṁsa is of the shape of the swan. Ghaṭa is 8 cubits broad and is of the shape of a pot.

27. Sarvatobhadra has four entrances with numerous and with apartments in upper stories; ıt consists of 5 stories and is 26 cubits broad.

28. Siṁha is twelve-sided and 8 cubits broad containing the figure of the lion. The four remaining structures are of black color; of these four, Caturaṣra has 5 Andas.

29. The height of a story shall be 108 inches and $3\frac{1}{2}$ cubits according to what was stated by Viśwakarma to Māyā.

30. In the opinion of persons learned in the science of temple building, a temple furnished with pigeon holes is deemed perfect though it might contain defects.

31. In this Chapter, I have briefly described all that has been stated by Garga, and my attempt has also been to summarize the wide accounts given by Manu and other Sages on the subject of Temple Building.

CHAPTER 57

On Durable Cements

1 & 2. Put into a droṇa of water the raw leaves of the Tinduka and of the Kapittha, the flowers of the Salmali, the seeds of the Śallakī[1], the bark of the Dhanvana[2], and a small quantity of Vacā; heat the water on fire till it is reduced to one-eighth of its original quantity. Remove the jar from fire.

3. Put into the kalka thus prepaced Gulgulu[3] and the juice of the Sreevasaka[4] and of Sarja and Bhallāta, Kundurūka[5] and the fruit of the Atasi and of Bilva. The cement thus formed is known as Vajralepa.

4. In the construction of temples and of the palaces of kings, of turrets, and in fixing the Liṅga or the image in the temple, in the construction of walls and wells, if the vegetable cement above referred to, be m elted and used, the structures will last for a crore of years.

5 & 6. Form a mixture of shel-la c, the resin of the plant Boswellia thurifera, Bdellium, soot in the ceilings of houses, the fleshy part of the fruit of Kapitha and of Bilva, the fruit of the Nāgabala[6], Madhuka and Mañjīṣṭtā, the juice of the Sarja as well as vinegar made from fruit, and put it in a jar of water, heat it till it is reduced to an eighth of its bulk; the resulting kalka is also known as Vajralepa and is an excellent one and can be used for the several purposes already mentioned.

7. Form a mixture of the horns of the cow, the buffalo, and the goat reduced to powder, the hair of the ass, the skin of the buffalo, the milk of the cow and the juice of the Nimba and the Kapittha trees : throw the mixture in a jar of water and heat it, the resulting kalka is also an excellent animal cement.

8. Melt together eight parts of lead, two parts of bronze,

and one part of brass; the result will be a strong metallic cement. This is according to Maya.

REFERENCES

1. Śallakī : The Gum olibanum tree, Boswellia Thurifera. Beng. Salai, Hind. Luban.
2. Dhanvana : The plant Alhagi Maurorum. Eng. Hebrew Manna, Hind. Juwasa.
3. Gulgulu : Bdellium.
4. The juice of the Śrīvasaka : turpentine.
5. Kundururuka : The resin of the plant Boswellia Thurifera.
6. Nāgabala : The plant Uraria Lagopodioides.

CHAPTER 58

On Temple Images

1. The fine particles moving in the rays of the sun coming into a room through the window opening are known as atoms. Is not the atom the first of all measurements ?

2. Eight atoms make an hair's end; eight hair's ends make a nit; eight nits make a louse; eight lice make a barley seed; eight barley seeds make an inch, which is known as a unit of measure.

3. The height of the pedestal of an image shall be one-third of seven-eighths of the height of the entrance. The height of the image shall be twice the height of the pedestal.

4. The breadth and length of the face of the image shall each be 12 inches. The sage Nagnagit says that in the Drāviḍa country the face of the image is 14 inches long.

5. The nose, the forehead, the chin, the neck, and the ear of the image shall each be 4 inches; the mouth shall be 2 inches the breadth of the chin shall also be 2 inches.

6. The forehead shall be 8 inches long; 2 inches from it are the frontal bones which shall be 4 inches, and the ear shall be 2 inches broad.

7. The space between the ear and the eyebrows shall be four inches and a half and the lobes of the ear shall be well formed.

8. According to Vasiṣṭha the interval between the end of the eye and the ear shall be 4 inches; the lower lip shall be an inch broad and the upper one shall be one-half the size of the lower.

9. The Goccha shall be half an inch; the mouth shall be 4 inches long; the breadth of the mouth when open shall be 3 inches, and the opening shall be an inch and a half.

10. The nose shall be two inches broad; the sense of smell is at the tip of the nose; the nose shall be two inches high; the

interval between the eye and the tip of the nose shall be four inches.

11. The eye-lid shall be two inches broad; the eye-ball also be two inches broad; the breadth of the pupil of the eye shall be two-thirds of an inch. The eye-lids shall be open with a space of half an inch. The centre of the pupil of the eye where the sense of sight remains shall be one-fifth of two-thirds of an inch.

12. From one end of an eyebrow to the other end of the other eyebrow shall be ten inches. The breadth of the eye-brow shall be half an inch. The interval between the eyebrows shall be two inches; and the length of each eyebrow shall be four inches.

13. The breadth of the hair of the eyebrows shall be half an inch throughout; at the end of the eye shall be formed the figure of the Karavira flower about an inch in dimensions.

14. The breadth of the head shall be 32 inches; the same when measured across shall be 14 inches. In painting 12 out of the 32 inches shall be visible and the rest shall be invisible.

15. The face with the hair growing about it shall be 16 inches according to Nagnajit; the neck shall be 10 inches broad the same when measured around shall be 21 inches.

16. The heart shall be 12 inches below the neck; the navel shall be 12 inches below the heart, and the genital organ shall be 12 inches below the centre of the navel.

17. The thighs shall be 24 inches long; the shanks shall also be 24 inches; the knee-shell shall be 4 inches, and the feet shall be 4 inches high.

18. The length of the feet shall be 12 inches and the breadth shall be 6 inches; the length of big toe shall be 3 inches; the same when measured around shall be 5 inches; the next toe shall also be 3 inches.

19. The other three toes shall each be one-eighth less than the length of the toe before it. The height of the big toe shall be an inch and a quarter.

20. The learned say that the nail of the big toe shall be three-fourths of an inch broad and that the toe-nails shall each be half an inch or less.

21. The shanks when measured around at the end shall be 14 inches. The breadth at the place shall be 5 inches. The breadth of the shanks at the middle shall be 7 inches; the shanks when measured around at the middle shall be 27 inches.

22. The knee shall be 8 inches broad at the middle; the knee when measured around at the middle shall be 24 inches. The breadth of the thigh at the middle shall be 14 inches; the same when measured around at the middle shall be 28 inches.

23. The hip shall be 18 inches broad; the same when measured around shall be 44 inches. The navel shall be an inch deep.

24. The measure of the body round the middle of the navel shall be 42 inches. The interval between the two nipples of the breast shall be 16 inches and the armpit shall be at a distance of 6 inches from the nipple.

25. The shoulders shall be 8 inches long; the upper arm shall be 12 inches long; the lower arm shall be 6 inches and the wrist shall be 4 inches.

26. The upper arm when measured around at its root shall be 16 inches and the lower arm when measured around at the wrist shall be 12 inches. The breadth of the palm shall be 6 inches and its length shall be 7 inches.

27. The middle finger shall be 5 inches long; the forefore-finger shall be shorter than the middle finger by one half of the length of its middle-joint; the length of the ring finger shall be the same as that of the fore-finger, and the little finger shall be shorter than the middle finger by its last joint.

28. The thumb shall consist of two joints, and the others fingers of three joints each. The breadth of the nails shall be one-half of the length of the joints on which they grow.

29. The images shall be shaped and adorned according to the fashion of the country. By placing images in temples a person becomes prosperous.

30. The images of Rāma, the son of Daśaratha and of Bali, the son of Virocana, shall each be 120 inches high. The Devas of middle importance shall be 108 inches high and the inferior Devas shall be 96 inches high.

31. The image of Bhagavan Viṣṇu shall have either 8 hands or 4 hands or 2 hands; there shall be a mole at the breast known as Sreevatsa; and the figure shall be represented to wear at the breast the gem known as Koustubha.

32. The body shall be of the color of the Atasi flower; the cloth shall be of yellow color; the countenance cheerful, and the image shall be made to wear pendants and crowns. The neck, the breast, the shoulders and the arm shall be large.

33. Three of the right hands shall hold a sword, a stick and an arrow, and the fourth hand shall appear stretched and held vertically.[1] The four left hands shall hold the bow, the target, the discus and the conch shell.

34. If the image of Viṣṇu be made with only four hands, one of the two right hands shall hold the stick and the other shall be raised as an abhaya-hasta. Of the two left hands one shall hold the conch-shell and the other the discus.

35. If the image be made with only two hands, the right hand shall be raised up as an abhaya-hasta and the left shall hold the conch-shell. He who desires prosperity shall make an image of Viṣṇu as stated above.

36. The image of Bala-deva shall be made with plough in one hand, with eyes dim through pride, with a pendant and a body white like conch-shell, moon and the stem of the lotus.

37. Between the images of Bala-deva and Kṛṣṇa (Viṣṇu) shall be placed the image of a beautiful woman with her left hand in her middle and with a lotus in her right hand.

38. If the figure be made with four hands, the two left hands shall hold the lotus and a book and one of the right hands shall be shaped as a *Varada-hasta*[2] and the other hand shall hold a rosary of crystal beads.

39. If the figure be made with eight hands, the four left hands shall hold the water bowl, the bow, the lotus, and a book; and of the four right hands, one shall be made into a Varada-hasta and the other three shall hold the arrow, the mirror and crystal heads.

40. The image of Śāmta (son of Balarāma) shall be made with a stick in one hand; and that of Pradyumna (son of Kṛṣṇa) with a bow in his hand; the images of the wives of these shall be made each with a sword in one hand, a target in the other,

41. The image of Brahmā shall be made as seated in a lotus with a water jar in one hand and with four faces. The image of Subbramania shall be made to appear young with the weapon known as Śakti in his hand, and as mounted on a peacock.

42. The image of Indra shall be mounted on a white elephant with four tusks and with the weapon known as Vajrayadha in his hand; there shall be a third eye in the forehead of the figure.

43. The image of Śiva shall be made with the figure of the Moon in his head as it appears in the third lunar day after the New-moon, as mounted on a bull with a third eye in his forehead, with the trident in one hand and a bow known as Pināka in the other. The left half of the image may be made of half the body of Pārvatī, Śiva's wife.

44. The image of Buddha shall be made as seated in a lotus with the hands and feet marked with the figure of the lotus, with a cheerful countenance and with short hair.

45. The image of the God of the Arhats shall be made with hands hanging down to the knees with the mole known as Śrivatsa in his breast, with a placid look and as naked, young and beautiful.

46. In the image of the Sun, the nose, the forehead, the shanks, the thighs, the cheeks and the breast shall be large. In adorning the image, the method followed in the northern countries shall be followed. From breast to the feet shall appear covered.

47. The Sun shall be represented as holding a lotus in each hand, as wearing a crown and pendants, with garlands hanging from his neck and as surrounded by Devas.

48. The face shall be bright as the lotus. The body shall be covered with stitched coats; the countenance shall be cheerful and the lustre of the gems shall add beauty to the image. He who fixes in a temple an image of the Sun of the above description will enjoy prosperity.

49. An image only a cubit high is good; one 2 cubits long will bring on wealth; and if the height be 3 or 4 cubits there will be plenty and prosperity.

50. If the image has an extra organ the master will suffer

from kings; if it be one of defective organs, the master will suffer from diseases; if the belly be depressed, there will be suffering from hunger, and if the figure appear thin there will be loss of wealth.

51. If the image be wounded, the master will die by weapons; if the left side of the image be bent, the master's wife will suffer, and if the right side be bent, the master will meet with early death.

52. If the eyes of the image look upwards, the master will become blind, and if the eyes look downwards, the master will suffer from anxieties of mind. These remarks apply as well to the images of the other Devas as to that of the Sun.

53. The height of the Liṅga shall be equal to the length of the circumference; the lower one-third of the Liṅga shall be four-sided, the central third shall be eight-sided, and the upper third shall be round.

54. The lower part of the Liṅga shall be planted into the ground, the middle part shall be made to fit the hole in the pedestal. The breadth of the pedestal all round the hole shall be of the length of the portion of the Liṅga above.

55. If the Liṅga be thin and tall, the country will perish; if a side be defective, towns will perish; and there will be suffering if there be any wound in the head of the Liṅga.

56. The images of the mother deities shall also be made after the manner of the country and agreeably to their names. The image of Revanta (son of Surya) shall be represented as mounted on a horse and as surrounded by a party of hunters.

57. The image of Yama (God of death) shall be mounted on a buffalo and as holding a club in his hand. The image of Varuṇa shall hold a rope in his hand and be mounted on a swan. The image of Kubera shall be reprepresented as being borne by men, with a large belly and wearing a beautiful crown.

The image of Gaṇeśa shall be represented with the face of the elephant, with a hanging belly, with an axe in his hand, with a single tusk, and with the root of the Mulaka with its black leaves.

REFERENCES

1. This position of the hand is known as abhaya-hasta—telling men not to fear.
2. Varada-hasta : as if granting the worshippers their wishes—the hand is made to hang down with the palm towards the worshipper and the fingers slightly bent up.

CHAPTER 59

On Entry into the Forest[1]

1. On an auspicious day selected by the astrologer and suited to the master, when the several indications referred to in my work on Yātrā are all good, the party shall leave for the forest.

2. They shall not cut trees that grow on cremation ground, in roads, in temples, ant-hills, flower gardens, the abodes of religious devotees, places of worship, junctions of rivers as well as trees grown by human labour.

3. They shall not cut trees that are bent, that are covered with creepers or struck down by lightning or broken by the wind, or that have fallen of themselves or that are broken by elephants or that have dried or have been burnt or that contain the bee-hive.

4. The trees that are of glossy leaves, flowers and fruits, are fit for the purpose; the tree selected shall be adorned with flowers and duly honored.

5. If the master is a Brāhmaṇa, the trees Devadaru, Sandel, Śamī and Madhūka are fit for the purpose. If the master is a Kṣatriya, the trees Margosa, Aśvattha, Khadira; and Bilva are fit for the purpose.

6. If the master is a Vaiśya, the trees Jīvaka, Khadira, Sindhuka and Syandana should be selected for the purpose; and if the master is a Śūdra, the trees Tinduka, Kesara, Sarja and Arjuna should be selected.

7. In the formation of the Liṅga or an image, the sides of the trees as it grew shall be preserved; for this purpose the sides as well as the bottom and the top shall be marked before cutting.

8. The tree to be cut shall first be worshipped with rice cooked in milk, sweet-meat balls, rice, curdled milk, and sweet-meats made of ground Sesamum and sugar and the like, liquor,

flowers, scented smoke and sandal paste.

9. Then shall be worshipped at night the Devas, the Pitṛs, the Piśācās, the Rākṣasas, the Nāgas, the Asuras, the Ganadevas, Vināyaka and others. The tree shall be touched by the hand and the following mantras shall be pronounced.

10. O tree, thou hast been selected for the image of such and such a Deva. Salutation to thee. I request thee to accept the puja duly performed by me.

11. The Bhutas that might dwell in this tree are requested to accept the presents offered and depart and dwell in some other place. Kindly bear the troubles we subject you to. Salutation to you.

12. Early next morning water shall be poured over the root of the tree; the axe shall be rubbed over with honey and ghee, and the tree shall first be cut on the north-eastern side, and the other parts shall be cut round from left to right.

13. If the tree falls on the eastern, north-eastern or the northern side, it indicates prosperity. But if it falls on the remaining five sides—the south-east, the south, south-west, &c, there will respectively be fear from fire, suffering from hunger, disease, disease again, and the death of the horses.

14. Matters connected with the fall of the tree, the cutting of it, and with what might be inside the tree have been treated of by me in the Chapter on Indra-Dhwaja and on House-holding. They apply here also.

REFERENCE

1. For the purpose of cutting wood for the images of the Devas.

CHAPTER 60

On the Fixing of the Images in Temples

1. Either on the northern or eastern part of the temples, the person learned in the matter shall erect a shed with openings on all sides and adorn it with plantains and festoons.

2 & 3. The eastern part of the shed shall be adorned with garlands of flowers and with flags of various colors. The south-eastern side shall be adorned with garlards and flags of red color. The southern and south-western sides shall be adorned with those of black color. Garlands and flags on the western side shall be white; those on the north-western side shall be white-red; those on the northern side shall be of bright color, and those on the north-eastern side shall be of yellow color.

4. Images made from wood or earth will give the master long life, wealth, strength and success. Images made of gems or precious stones will do good to the world at large. Images made of gold will give the master good health.

5. Images of silver will increase the master's fame. Images of copper will increase his family. Images of stone or the Liṅga will bring him much lands.

6. If a pike is seen driven into an image, the master will perish with his family; if there be holes in images, the master will suffer from diseases and never ending troubles.

7. The platform in the centre of the shed shall be washed with cow-dung; it shall then be covered with sand, and over it shall be spread the Kuśa grass; and the image shall be placed in it in the Bhadrāsana posture—with a leg resting on the ground and the other bent up horizontally at the knee.

8. The image shall be bathed with the milk of the Plakṣa, Aśvattha, Udumbara, Śiriṣa, and Vaṭa, and with water mixed with the Kuśa grass and the like sacred plants.

9. It shall also be rubbed with earth taken from place-trodden over by elephants and bulls, from the neighbourhood of mountains, from ant-hills, from the junction of rivers and lotus tanks. It shall also be bathed with sacred waters and with Pancāgavya[1].

10. It shall be bathed in fragrant waters in jars in which shall be thrown gold and gems attended with various music and with the chanting of Vedic hymns; while bathing, the image shall be placed to face the east.

11. While the image is being bathed, the Brāhmaṇas shall chant the mantras sacred to Indra on the eastern side; and on the south-eastern side shall be chanted mantras sacred to Agni. The master shall pay the Brāhmaṇas well and show them due honors.

12. The Brāhmaṇas shall throw Āhūtīs into the fire, chanting hymns sacred to the particular Deva whose image is before them. The indications, together with their interpretations, connected with the homa-fire have already been stated by me in the Chapter on Indra-Dhwaja.

13. If the flame should be attended with smokes and sparks, and if it should whirl from right to left, it indicates evil. If the officiating priest should be of forgetful memory or begin to quote a wrong portion of the Vedict text, it indicates evil.

14. After bathing the image, it shall be dressed in new cloth and adorned with flowers and sandal and shall be laid by the master on a well-spread bed.

15. The night shall be spent by the side of the image in music and dance by persons that do not sleep, and the fixing ceremony shall be done at the hour mentioned by the astrologer.

16. The next day the image shall again be adorned with flowers, cloth, and sandal and shall be taken round the temple attended with the music of the conch-shell and other instruments.

17. A large quantity of cooked rice shall be presented to the image; learned Brāhmaṇas shall be duly honoured and pieces of gold shall be thrown into the central pit of the pedestal.

18. Special honours shall be paid to the officiating priest,

the astrologer, the Brāhmaṇas, learned men and artists. The master will enjoy prosperity in this world as well as in the next.

19. The Bhāgavatas are the worshippers of Viṣṇu the Magas are the worshippers of the Sun; Brāhmaṇas wearing ashes are the worshippers of Śiva. Persons possessed of a knowledge of the Devas attendant on the Mātri Devas are the worshippers of the Mātri Devas. The Brāhmaṇas generally are the worshippers of Brahmā. The Śākyas are the worshippers of the God of the Arhats. The Buddhists are the worshippers of Buddha. The ceremony of fixing the images and the like ceremonies shall be performed by the respective worshippers of the several images.

20 & 21. The ceremony of fixing the image shall be performed in the Uttarāyaṇa—when the Sun's course is towards the north—in the light half of a month, when the Moon occupies the house, the Navāṁsā, the Triṁśāṁśa, the Drekkāṇa or the Dvādasāṁsā of Jupiter; when the rising sign and the rising Navāṁśa are fixed, when benefic planets occupy the Kendra or the Trikoṇa houses, and the malefic planets occupy the 3rd, 6th and 11th houses, when the Moon passes either through any of the fixed asterisms or the soft asterisms, or through the asterism of Śravaṇa, Puṣya or Svātī, on any week day excepting Tuesday, and on a day suited to the master's star.

22. Thus have I treated briefly of the subject of fixing the Images in Temples, for the benefit of the people at large. Surya has, in his work, treated at full length of matters connected with Adhivasana (watching the image at night with music and dance) and with fixing the image in its pedestal.

REFERENCE

1. Pancāgavya : a mixture of the cow's milk, coagulated or sour milk, ghee, urine and dung.

CHAPTER 61

On the Features of Cows and Oxen

1. All that Parāśara told Bṛhadratha about cows and oxen I shall here briefly state. I shall however treat scientifically of the animals possessing good features.

2. Cows whose eyes are dim and with tears and disagreeable to look at and whose eyes resemble those of the mouse, will bring on misery. Cows whose horns are moving and flat, whose bodies are rough and whose color resembles that of the ass, will also bring on evil.

3. Cows having ten, seven or four teeth and those whose heads are hanging and hairless, whose backs are bent or depressed, necks short and thick, hip resembling a grain of barley in shape, whose hoofs are broken.

4. As well as those with long, red, black tongues with small ankles, with a large hump on the back, with thin slender bodies and with either defective or excessive organs, will bring on evil.

5. The ox whose testicle is large and hangs down, whose breast is covered with muscles, whose check is large and marked with sinews, and whose penis is thick in three places, will bring on evil.

6. The ox, whose eyes resemble those of the cat, whose color is brown, whose body is rough, whose lips, jaws and tongue are black, whose breathing is like snoring, and which causes annoyance to the herd of cows, is not fit for the Brāhmaṇas.

7. The ox that passes excrement in large lumps, whose horns do not grow, whose belly is white, whose body is of the color of the deer and which causes annoyance to the herd of cows, is to be rejected though it may be a home-bred one.

8. The ox which is black, of ashy color, or of the color of

the Sun, and whose eyes resemble those of the cat, is not fit for Brāhmaṇas.

9. The ox, which, while at work lifts up its leg as if from a mire, whose neck is thin and eyes fearful, is an animal of inferior kind. Such animals cannot carry heavy burdens.

10. The ox whose lips are soft, close and red, whose ears are small, short and raised up, whose belly is fine, whose ankles are prominent.

11. Whose hoofs are red and close, whose breast is strong, the hump on whose back is large, whose skin and hair are fine, whose horns are red and small.

12. Whose tails is thin and long, whose eyes are red at the ends, whose breathing is loud, whose shoulders are like those of the lion, whose dew-lap is soft and small and whose gait is beautiful, is of an excellent kind.

13. The ox, the curl of hair or ringlet on whose left side is from right to left and the one on the right side is from left to right, and whose ankles resemble those of the deer, is an excellent one.

14. The ox whose eyes are like Vaidurga or the jasmine or the water bubble, whose eye-lids are thick and whose hoofs are close, is also excellent and will carry heavy burdens.

15. The ox with a wrinkle at the end of its nose, whose face is like that of the cat, whose right side is white, whose colar is that of the white or blue lotus or red cotton, whose tail is fine and whose speed is like that of the horse.

16. Whose testicle is hanging, whose belly is like that of the goat and whose buttocks and breast are contracted, will bring on prosperity, carry heavy burdens and go great distances.

17. The ox which is white, whose eyes are of brown color, whose horns are red and whose face is large, is known as *Haṁsa*. It brings on prosperity and an increase of the herd.

18. The ox whose tail hangs to the ground, whose buttocks and eyes are red, and the hump on whose back is fine, and whose body is variously colored, will make his master the lord of wealth at once.

19. The ox, one of whose legs is white, is also a good one, whatever may be his color. If oxen of excellent sort cannot be had, those of middle importance may be procured and used.

CHAPTER 62

On the Features of the Dog

1. The dog which has five nails in each of its hind legs, three in the left front leg, and six in the right front leg, whose lips and the tip of whose nose are red, whose gait is like that of the lion, which walks smelling the ground, and whose tail is hairy, eyes like stars, ears hanging and soft, will before long make his master exceedingly wealthy.

2. The bitch which has five nails in each of the hind legs, six in the left front leg and five in the right front leg, whose eyes are like jasmine, whose tail is curled up and whose body is of brown color and ears hanging, will protect the kingdom of her master.

CHAPTER 63

On the Features of the Cock

1. The cock whose wings and fingers are straight, whose mouth, nail and comb are red, whose body is white, and which crows melodiously early in the morning, will bring on prosperity to the king, his kingdom and his horse.

2. The cock whose neck is of the shape of the barley, whose body is of the color of the fruit Badari, and one whose head is large and body of different colors, are excellent in fight. The cock of the color of honey or the bee will bring on success; one that is of thin body and of a weak throat and lame legs is not a good one.

3. The hen which crows softly and melodiously, whose body is fine and glossy, and whose face and eyes are beautiful, will bring to a king wealth, fame, success, health and strength.

CHAPTER 64

On the Features of the Turtle

1. The turtle which is of the color of the crystal or silver, adorned with black lines, whose body is of the shape of the pot, and whose back-bone is beautiful, and the turtle whose body is of the color of the Sun and covered with numerous small spots, will make a person as prosperous as a prince if they dwell in his house.

2. The turtle which is black as the bee or collyrium with beautiful spots over his body, which has no defective organs, whose head is like that of the serpent and whose neck is large, will increase the territories of the king.

3. The turtle of the color of Vaidurya, whose neck is large, whose body is smooth and of triangular shape, and whose back-bone is beautiful, is of excellent kind. It shall be put in pleasure tanks and water pots by kings for the increase of their prosperity.

CHAPTER 65

On the Features of the Goat

1. We shall now proceed to describe the bad and good features of the goat. A goat which has 8, 9 or 10 teeth will bring wealth to a person if it dwells in his house. One that has 7 teeth shall be rejected.

2. A white goat which has a black ringlet on the right side brings on prosperity. A goat that resembles the antelope whose color his black-red and which has a white ringlet, conduces to prosperity.

3. The fleshy excrescence which hangs from the neck of a goat is known as *Maṇi.* A goat with a single maṇi brings on prosperity ; one that has two or three maṇis brings on wealth.

4. A goat that has no wool on it will make the owner prosperous, and one that is either wholly white or wholly black, or half white and half black, or half brown and half black, will bring on wealth.

5. The goat which passes as the foremost of the herd or which first gets into water, will do good as well as one with a white head or with a tikkika in the head.

6. A goat which has a ringlet in the neck or head, or, one which is of the color of the Sesamum flour, or with red eyes or of white body and black legs, or of black body and white legs, will bring on prosperity.

7. A goat whose body is white, whose testicles are black, and which has a strip of cast off skin round the waist as well as the goat that walks gently and with noise will bring on prosperity.

8. A goat whose horns and legs resemble those of the antelope, as well as the one whose front part is white and the hind part black, will bring on prosperity. The following is Garga's stanza on the subject of the goat.

9. The four species of goats known as *Kuṭṭak, Kuṭila, Jaṭila* and *Vāmana* are the children of Lakṣmi, the Goddess of wealth. These will never be found to live under the roof of poor people.

10. A goat that bleats like the ass, whose tail is bright, nails disfigured, body of bad color, ears cut our clipped, head resembling that of the elephant, and mouth corners and the tongue black, will not conduce to prosperity.

11. A goat which is of excellent color, with a fine mane and with no wool on its body, and whose eyes are red, will bring to his master health, fame and wealth.

CHAPTER 66

On the Features of the Horse

1. The horse whose neck and eyes are long, breast and mane broad ; lips, tongue and the corners of mouth red ; skin hair and tail thin ; hoof, gait and face beautiful ; cars, lips and tails short ; shanks, knees and thighs round ; teeth even and white and limbs symmetrical, fine, smooth and clean, will ease the death of the enemies of the king.

2. The horse which has a ringlet under the eyes, in the chin, cheek, heart, neck, the part between the nostrils, temples, the buttocks, part below the nostrils, knees, testicles, navel, hump on the back, anus, right belly and feet, will bring on evil.

3. The horse which has ringlets, in the upper-lip, neck, ears, back, loins, eyes, lips, thighs, front legs, belly, sides and fore-head, will bring on prosperity.

4. Of these benefic curls and ringlets, there shall be only one in the upper lip, one named *Dhruva* in the fore-head and mane and two in the *Randhara* and *Uparandhra* parts of its head and in the breast.

5. A colt has six white teeth. If the teeth be of brown color, the animal is 2 years old ; if the central and corner teeth in both lines have fallen and sprouted again, the animal is from 3 to 5 years old, according as the number of such teeth is 3, 4 or 5 ; if the lines known as *Kālikā*, *Apeta* (a yellow line), *Sukta* (black line), *Kaca* (white line), *Makika* (of the color of the bee) or *Śaṅkha* (of the color of the conch shell) appear in the teeth, the age of the animal will respectively be from 6 to 8, 9 to 11, 12 to 14, 15 to 17, 18 to 20 or 21 to 23. If depressions appear in the teeth or if the teeth have begun to shake, or if they have fallen, the age varies from 24 to 60.

CHAPTER 67

On the Features of the Elephant

1. The elephant whose tusks are of the color of honey, whose limbs are well defined, whose body is neither large, nor small, and which is capable of bearing heavy burdens, whose limbs are symmetrical, whose back bones are like bows and whose buttocks resemble those of the pig, is known as *Bhadra*.

2. The elephant whose breast, arm-pits and folds of skin are loose, whose belly is hanging, whose skin and neck are thick, whose abdomen resembles that of the crow, and whose eyes are like those of the lion, is known as *Manda*.

3. The elephant whose lips, tail and genital organ are short, whose legs, neck, tusks, trunk and the ears are small and whose eyes are large, is known as *Mṛga*. The elephant which posses-ses the three sets of features above referred to is known as *Saṅkīrṇa*.

4. The Mṛga class of elephants are 5 cubits high, 7 cubits long and 8 cubits broad. The Manda and Bhadra classes are larger by one and two cubits respectively in each respect. No fixed measurement is prescribed for the Saṅkīrṇa class of elephants.

5. The Bhadra is of green color and is a rutting elephant. The Manda is of yellow color. The Mṛga his of black color and is also a rutting elephant. The Saṅkīrṇa is of mixed color and a rutting elephant.

6 & 7. The elephant whose lips and mouth are red, whose eyes resemble those of the sparrow, whose tusks are shining, rising and with sharp end, whose face is large and long, whose back bones are like bows, long and invisible, whose *mastakas* (round protuberances on the temples) are covered with hair and resemble the turtle, whose ears, mouth corners, navel, fore-head and genital organs are large, whose body resembles the turtle, whose nails are 18 or 20, whose trunk has three lines and is

round, whose tail is beautiful, and whose juice (when in rut) is felt to be of good smell when the animal blows through its trunk, will bring on wealth.

8. The elephant whose tail is long, trunk red, roar like that of the clouds, and neck large, long and round, will bring wealth to a king.

9 & 10. Non-rutting elephants, those which possess extra or defective organs, those which are lame or short or whose tusks resemble the horns of the sheep, whose testicles are visible those which possess little or no trunk, whose mouth corners are brown, blue, black or of different colors, those which possess very little hair about the face, those which have no tusks, those which have no virility female elephants possessing the features of a male elephant, and pregnant elephants must be sent away to foreign lands. They produce misery.

CHAPTER 68

On the Features of Man

1. A learned person shall examine a man's (1) Kṣhetra (body), (2) Mṛjā (complexion), (3) Svara (voice), (4) Śara (strength), (5) Saṁhati (joints), (6) Sneha (gloss) (7) Varṇa (color), (8) Anuka (shape of the face), (9) Unmāna (height), (10) Māna (weight), (11) Prakṛti (disposition) and (12) Gati (gait) and then predict his fortune.

I.—*Kṣetra* (*Physical Features*)

2. If the *feet* be dry, with soft soles, of the color of the lotus, with close toes, beautiful red nails, beautiful heels, always warm without visible sinews, with invisible and raised like the person will be a king.

3. If the *feet* be like winnows, crooked or bent, covered with sinews, dry, with toes not close and with nail white and not glossy, the person will be poor. If the feet be large, he will walk much ; if of brown color, his family will perish ; if the soles be of the color of burnt clay, he will murder a Brāhmaṇa ; and if the color be yellow, he will have sexual intercourse with women under prohibition.

4. If the *shanks* be covered with hair, thin and scattered, and if they be round, if the *thighs* be like the trunk of the elephant, and if the *knees* be large and both alike, the person will be a king. But if the shanks resemble those of a dog or a jackal, the person will be poor.

5. If a single *hair* grow from each cell over the body, the person will be a king ; if two hairs grow from it, the person will be learned and will scrupulously observe the duties of life as prescribed in the Vedas ; if three or more, the person will be poor and afflicted with grief. The same remarks apply to the hairs of the head.

6. If there be no flesh in the *knees*, the person will die in

his travels ; if the knees be small, he will become popular ; if broad, he will become poor ; if sunk, he will be subject to women ; if covered with flesh, he will become a king, and if large, he will live long.

7. If the *penis* be small, the person will be rich ; if large he will have no sons ; if it be inclined on the left side, he will be poor ; if not straight, he will be without sons and without money ; if straight, he will have sons ; if pointing to the ground, he will be poor ; if covered with muscles, he will have very few sons; if the nut of the penis be large, he will live in comfort, and if the penis be soft, he will die of urinary and the like diseases.

8. If the nut be invisible, he will be a king ; if the penis be long and fallen, he will be poor ; and if either straight and round or small and with sinews, he will be rich.

9. A person with a single *testicle* will suffer death by drowning ; if the testicles be not alike, he will be found of Sexual intercourse; if both be alike, he will be a king ; if they be raised up, the person will not live long ; and if they hang down he will live to the age of 100 years.

10. If the nut of the penis be red, the person will be rich ; if it be either white or of dim color, he will be poor ; if the urine fall with noise, the porson will live in comfort ; and if without noise, he will be poor.

11. If the *urine* fall in two, three or four lines and twisting from left to right, the person will be a king ; and if it fall broken and scattered, he will be poor.

12. If the urine fall in a line and twisted, the person will get a very beautiful son. If the glans penis be glossy, raised and even, the person, will enjoy wealth, women gems.

13. If the *glans penis* be depressed in the middle, the person will get daughters and will be poor ; if raised in the middle, he will possess many cows ; if it be not very large or very much raised, he will be rich.

14. If the urinary orifice be dry, the person will be poor and ugly ; if the semen smell like a flower, the person will be a king.

15. If the *semen* should smell like honey, the person will be very rich : if it smell like fish, he will have many children ; if it be thin, he will get daughters, and if of the smell of flesh, he

will live in great comfort.

16. If it be of the smell of alcohol, the person will perform sacrificial fire ceremonies ; if of the smell of salt, he will be poor. A person whose sexual intercourse lasts for a short time, will live long ; if otherwise, he will die early.

17. A person whose *rump* is large, will be poor If the rump be full of flesh, the person will live in comfort ; if it be half the average size, he will be sickly ; and if it resemble that of a frog, he will be king.

18. If the *loins* resemble those of the lion, the person will be a king ; if they resemble those of the monkey or the camel, he will be poor ; if the *abdomen* be even, the person will live in comfort ; if it be like a pot, he will be poor.

19. If the *sides* be not defective, the person will be rich; if they be depressed and bent, he will have no enjoyment; if the belly be even, the person will live well; if it be depressed, he will have no enjoyment.

20. If the *belly* be high, the person will be a king; if it be uneven, he will be a man of perverted understanding if it be like that of the serpent, he will be poor and gluttonous.

21. If the *navel* be broad and high all round, the person will live in comfort; if it be small and if the pit be not visible, the person will be afflicted with miseries.

22. If the *navel* be in the middle of a fold of the skin or if it be depressed, the person will suffer from belly-ache and will be poor; if the navel turn from right to left, the person will be a cheat; if it turn from left to right, he will be a man of good perception and strong memory.

23. If the navel extend on both sides horizontally, the person will live long; if it extend vertically upwards, he will be rich; if vertically downwards, he will have cows; and if it be like the color of the lotus, the person will be a king.

24. If there be one, two, three or four *folds of skin* in the belly, the person will die wounded by a weapon, will enjoy women, will become a teacher and will be vastly learned respectively. If there be no folds, the person will be a king.

25. If the folds be not straight, the person will be wicked and will have sexual intercourse with women under prohibition;

if they be straight, he will live in comfort and will never covet the wives of other men.

26. If the sides be fleshy and soft and if the ringlets of hair over them turn from left to right, the person will be a king. If otherwise, he will be poor and wretched and will serve under others.

27. If the *nipple* of the breast be not high, the person will be popular; if the two nipples be long and not alike, he will be poor; if they be large, whether high or sunk, the person will be a king and will live in comfort.

28. If the *bosom* be high, broad, fleshy and firm, the person will be a king; if otherwise and covered with stiff hair and muscles, the person will be the meanest of mankind.

29. If the bosom be even, the person will be rich; if large, he will be a hero; if small, poor; if uneven, he will be poor and die by a weapon.

30. If the *collar bones* be not alike, the person will be wicked; if the joints of the bones be large, he will be poor; if they be high, he will live well; if depressed, he will be poor; and if large, he will be rich.

31. If the *neck* be flat or dry or covered with muscles, the person will become poor; if it be like that of the buffalo, he will be a valiant soldier; and if it be like that of the ox, he will die by a weapon.

32. If the neck be like the conch shell, the person will be a king; if it be hanging, the person will be a glutton; if the *back* be even and without hairs, the person will be rich, otherwise, he will be poor.

33. If the *armpits* be dry, large, high, of good smell, both alike and with much hair, the person will be rich; if otherwise, he will be poor.

34. If the *shoulders* be without flesh, covered with hair, sunk and small, the person will be poor; but if broad, high and close, he will live in comfort and be powerful.

35. If the two *arms* be round, like the trunk of the elephant, large, both alike, and hanging down to the knees, the person will be a king; but if they be short and covered with hair, he will be the meanest of mankind.

36. If the *fingers* of the hand be long, the person will live

in comfort; if they be without skin folds, he will be popular; if small, he will be intelligent; and if flat, he will serve under others.

37. If the fingers of the hand be large, the person will be poor, and if bent upwards, he will die by weapons. If the *hands* be like those of the monkey, the person will be rich, and if like those of the tiger, he will be wicked.

38. If the *wrists* be invisible, firm and close, the person will be a king; if otherwise and if the joints be loose, the hands will suffer sword-cut; and if they should crack, he will be poor.

39. If the *palm* of the hand be hollow, the person will not inherit his father's property; if it be round and hollow, he will be rich; and if high, he will be generous.

40. If the palms of both hands be alike, the person will be poor and wicked; if red, he will be rich; if yellow, he will cohabit with women under prohibition; and if dry, he will be poor.

41. If the *nail* resemble the husk of paddy, the person will be a hermaphrodite; if flat and split, he will be poor; if of bad color, he will be of wrong views; and if red, he will be a king.

42. If, in the middle of the *thumb*, there be lines of the shape of a barley, the person will be rich; if the same be found at the root of the thumb, he will have sons. If the joints of the fingers be long, the person will be popular and will live long.

43. If the lines in the palm of the hand be glossy and deep, the man will be rich; if otherwise, he will be poor, if the fingers be not close, the person will be poor; and if close, he will earn much money.

44. If the three lines issuing from the wrist reach the middle of the palm, the person will be a king, and if there be two marks of the shape of the fish in the middle of the palm, the person will daily feed many people.

45. If the lines in the palm be of the shape of vajrayudha, the person will be rich; if they be of the shape of the tail of the fish, he will be learned; if of the shape of a conch shell, an umbrella, a palankin, an elephant, a horse or a lotus, the person will be a king.

46. If the lines in the palm of the hand be of the shape of a pot, the stem of a lotus, a flag or the hook of the elephant driver, the person will be a guardian of treasure. If the lines appear twisted like a rope, or if the lines be triangular in shape, the person will be rich.

47. If the lines in the palm of the hand be of the shape of the discus, the sword, the axe, the club, the spear or the bow, the person will be a commander of armies; if the lines be of the shape of a mortar, the person will perform sacrificial fire ceremonies.

48. If the lines in the palm of the hand be of the shape of a crocodile, a flag, or a cow-shed, the person will be very rich; if the lines at the root of the thumb be of the shape of a *Vedi* (sacrificial altar), the person will perform sacrificial rites.

49. If the lines in the palm of the hand be of the shape of a tank, a temple and the like, or if they be triangular in shape, the person will do acts of charity. The big lines below the thumb indicate sons and the small lines daughters.

50. Lines reaching the root of the forefinger indicate the age of the person to be 100; if the line be of shorter length, the age shall be ascertained by proportion. If the lines be broken the person will fall from a tree; if there be either many lines or no lines, the person will be poor.

51. If the *chin* be very small and long, the person will be poor; if covered with flesh, he will be rich; if the lower lip be red and straight, the person will be a king; and if small he will be poor.

52. If the *lips* be split or appear cut or of bad color or dry, the person will be poor. If the *teeth* be glossy, close, sharp and regular, the person will be happy.

53. If the *tongue* be red, long, smooth and even, the person will live in comfort; but if it be white or black and dry, he will be poor; the same remarks apply to the corners of the mouth.

54. If the *face* be beautiful, slightly open-mouthed clear, smooth and even the person will be a king; and if otherwise, he will be afflicted with grief; if the face be large, the person will be happy.

55. If the face be like that of a woman, the person will

have no sons; if it be round, he will be a cheat; if long, poor; and if timid, wicked.

56. If the face be oblongular in shape, the person will be a cheat; if depressed or sunk, he will have no sons; if very small, a miser; and if full and beautiful, happy.

57. If the hair about the face be not split at the ends be soft, and bent, the person will be happy; and if it be red, not glossy and small in quantity, the person will be a hief.

58. If the *ears* be without flesh, the person will die an unnatural death; if like a cup, he will live in comfort; if small, he will be a miser; and if they taper in a point like a cone, the person will be a king.

59. If the ears be covered with hair, the person will live long; if they be broad, he will be rich; if covered with muscles, he will be wicked; and if they hang and be fleshy, he will live well.

60. If the *cheek* be not sunk, the person will live in comfort, if it be fleshy, he will become a minister. If the *nose* be like that of the parrot, the person will live in comfort; and if it be dry, he will live long.

61. If the nose appear as if cut, the person will cohabit with women under prohibition; if it be long, he will be wealthy; if bent, he will be a thief; and if flat, he will be killed by a woman.

62. If the end of the nose be bent, the person will be rich; if it be bent on the right side, he will be wicked and gluttonous; and if it be straight, with small holes and appear beautiful, the person will be wealthy.

63. If the *sneeze* occur twice or thrice at a time and the sound be not disagreeable, the person will be rich; and if it be long and of the same sound throughout, he will live long.

64. If the *eyes* be like the petals of the lotus, the person will be rich; and if the corners be red, he will be wealthy and prosperous; if of the color of honey, he will be exceedingly rich; and if they resemble the eyes of the cat, the person will be wicked.

65. If the eyes be like those of the deer or round or squint, the person will be a thief; if they see obliquely, he will be

wicked; and if they be like the eyes of the elephant, the person will be a king.

66. If the eyes indicate courage, the person will be rich; if they be of the color of the blue lotus, he will be learned; and if the eyes be exceedingly black, the person will become blind.

67. If the eyes be large, the person will be a minister; if red-black, he will be wealthy; if they appear to be meek and imploring, the person will be poor; and if glossy, be will be very rich and will live in comfort.

68. If the *brows* be high and not broad, the person will die early; if high and broad, he will live in comfort; if both brows be not alike, the person will be poor; and if they be bent like the young moon he will be rich.

69. If the brows be long and do not meet, the person will be rich; if they appear broken, he will be poor; and if they be bent in the middle, he will cohabit with women under prohibition.

70. If the *temples* be high and broad, the person will be rich; and if sunk, he will have neither sons nor money. If the *fore-head* be not even, the person will be poor; and if it be like the half moon, he will be rich.

71. If the fore-head be like the pearl oyster and broad, the person will be a preceptor; if covered with muscles, he will be wicked; and if the muscles be high and triangular in shape, he will be rich.

72. If the fore-head be low, the person will be assassinated or put in prison and will be addicted to cruel deeds; if it be high, he will be a king; and if narrow, he will be poor.

73. If the *weeping* be without tears, agreeable to the ear and not of an imploring nature, the person will be happy; if otherwise, he will be miserable.

74. If the *laughter* be unattended by the motion of the body, the person will be happy; if it be attended by the closing of the eyes, he will be wicked; if it be of frequent occurrence, he will be happy; and if it be repeated at the end, he will become mad.

75. If there be three long lines in the forehead, the person

will live for 100 years; if four lines, he will be a king and will live for 95 years.

76. If the lines be broken, the person will cohabit with a woman under prohibition; if there be no lines in the forehead, he will live for 90 years; and if the lines be near the hair of the head, he will live for 80 years.

77. If there be five lines in the forehead, his age will be 70; if the lines be of the same length, his age will be sixty; if there be many lines, the age will be 50; and if the lines be bent, it will be 40.

78. If the lines in the forehead be in contact with the brows, the age will be 30; if they be bent on the left side, it will be 20; if short, the person will meet with early death. If the lines be imperfect, the age shall be ascertained by proportion.

79. If the *head* be round, the person will possess many cows; if it be broad and round like an umbrella, he will be a king; if flat, he will lose his parent when young; and if long, he will live long.

80. If the head be like a pot, the person will be fond of meditation; if it appear as if two heads were joined together, he he will be poor and wicked; if sunk, he will be a great man; and if exceedingly sunk, he will meet with ruin.

81. If the hair of the head grow singly, be glossy, black, curling, with no split ends, soft, and not too much in quantity, the person will live in great comfort or will be a king.

82. If the hairs grow several together and if they be not of the same length or be of brown color or thick, split at the ends, not glossy, short, curling too much and too much in quantity, the person will be poor.

83. If the limbs be of disagreeable appearance without flesh and covered over with muscles, the person will be unhappy; and if otherwise, happy.

84 To be a king three places must be broad, three things must be deep or high, six places high, four small seven red, five long and five soft, as follows.

85. The breast, the forehead and the face must be broad, the navel, the voice and strength must be deep or high.

86. The breast, arm-pit, nails, nose, face and the nape of

the neck must be high ; the penis, the back, the neck and the shanks must be short.

87. The corners of the eyes, soles of feet, palm of the hand, the corners of the mouth, the lower lip, the upper lip and the tongue must be red. Teeth, fingers, hair of the head, the skin and nails must be soft or smooth.

88. The mouth, the eyes, the arms, the nose and the part between the nipples must be long

II.—*Complexion*

89. Complexion in man, animals and birds is detected by persons learned in the matter and indicate both good and evil and is like a lamp placed within a crystal vessel throwing its light on the objects around.

90. The complexion discernible in shining teeth, skin, nails and hairs of the body and of the head will be attended with good smell if it be caused by the element of earth. It will make the person happy, rich, prosperous and virtuous.

91. The complexion which is glossy, white, clear green and agreeable to look at is caused by the element of water ; it will make all creatures possessing it happy and successful in all their attempts and will produce wealth, comfort, luxury and prosperity.

92. The complexion which indicates fear and is unbearable and of the color of the lotus, gold or fire, and which also indicates strength, power, and valor, is caused by the element of fire.

93. The complexion which is dirty, not glossy, black and of bad odour is caused by the element of air. It will cause to the person death or imprisonment, disease, ruin and loss of wealth. The complexion which is of the color of the crystal, noble, clear and indicating wealth and generosity, is caused by the element of ether (Akas). It will give a person all that he desires.

94. Thus has been described the complexion caused by the elements of earth, water, fire, air, and akas—five in number. Some writers treat of five more complexions caused by the Sun, Viṣṇu, Indra, Yama and the Moon, and they have described in detail the properties of each.

Notes

Physical man is composed of the five elementary principles —earth, water, fire, air and akas. The lords of these are respectively Mercury (earth), Venus and the Moon (water), Mars and the Sun (fire), Saturn (air), and Jupiter (akas). Human life is divided, into a number of Dāsa periods presided over by the several planets (vide Chapter VIII of Bṛhat Jātaka). In the period of a particular planet will predominate the elementary principle belonging to him, and therefore the complexion due to such principle will become discernible in such Dāsa period. Suppose the Dāsa period to be that of Mars, his element is fire ; the complexion caused by the elementary principle of fire is described in stanza 93. This complexion will become discernible in the Dāsa period of Mars; and so for the other planets.

Again, in stanza 21 of Ch. VIII of his Bṛhat Jātaka' Vārāhamihira states that the complexion will be accompanied by certain other qualities due to the five elementary principles and discernible by their respective organs of sense. The main property of earth is smell, a quality discernible by the nose ; that of water is taste, a quality discernible by the tongue ; that of fire or light is shape or appearance, discernible by the eye ; that of the air is touch, discernible by the body ; and that of akas is sound, discernible by the ear. Now suppose the Dāsa period to be that of Venus. His element is water ; the quality belonging to water is taste, discernible by the tongue ; therefore in the Dāsa period of Venus, the person will eat juicy meals according to his desire. Again, suppose the Dāsa period to be that of Jupiter, his elementary principle is Akas ; its property is sound, discernible by the ear ; the person's speech will be sweet and agreeable to the ear. In the Dāsa period of Mercury (earth, smell) the person's body will be with an agreeable odour ; in the period of Mars (fire, sight), he will be of agreeable appearance, and in that of Saturn (air, touch), he will be of soft body. From these the particular Dāsa period of a person may be ascertained.

III.—*Voice*

95. If the voice be like the sound of the elephant, the bull,

the chariot, the drum, the lion or the clouds, the person will be a king ; but if it be hoarse and rough like the braying of the ass, the person will be poor and unhappy.

IV.—*Strength*

96. Strength consists in seven things—in the serum of flesh, the marrow of bones, the skin, bones, semen, blood and flesh. We shall now describe the properties of each.

97. If the mouth, lips, gum of teeth tongue, corners of eyes, the anus, the hands and feet be red, the person is strong in blood ; he will live in comfort and will be married wealth and with sons.

98. If the skin be glossy, the person will be rich ; if oft, he will be happy and prosperous ; and if thin, intelligent. Such a person will be strong in marrow. He will possess a fair body. Persons strong in the serum of flesh will be rich and will have sons.

99. If the bones be large, the person will be strong in bones. He will be strong, learned and beautiful. If the serum be thick and much in quantity, he will be happy, prosperous, learned and beautiful.

100. A person of full growth will be learned, rich and beautiful. He will be strong in flesh.

V.—*Joints*

If the joints be close and well fitted, the person will live in comfort and ease.

VI.—*Gloss*

101. If the five parts—mouth, tongue, teeth, eyes and nails be glossy, the person will have sons and will be rich, happy and prosperous ; if they be otherwise, he will be poor.

VII.—*Color*

102. If the color be very bright and glossy, the person will be a king ; if moderately so, he will be wealthy and will have sons ; if the color be disagreeable to the eye, he will be poor ; if of a single color, he will be happy ; and if mixed, miserable.

VIII.—*Peculiarity of Character*

103. The peculiar character of a person must be ascertained from his face; if the face be like that of the cow, the ox, the tiger, the lion or the Brahmini kite, he will defeat his enemies, be successful in fight, and will become a king.

104. If the face be like that of the monkey, the buffalo, the hog or the goat, he will have sons, will be rich and will live in comfort; and if the face be like that of the ass or the camel, the person will be poor and unhappy.

IX.—*Height*

105. If the height of the person be 108, 96, or 84 of his own inches (breadth of finger), he is respectively a superior, an average and an inferior man.

X.—*Weight*

106. If the weight of the body be half a *bhāra* or 80 lbs., the person will live in comfort; if less, he will be afflicted with grief; if the weight be a bhāra (160 lbs), he will be rich; and if it be a bhāra and a half (240 lbs), he will be an emperor.

107. The measurement of both height and weight is to be taken at the age of 20 in the case of women and 25 in the case of men, or it may be done in the last quarter of life.

XI.—*Innate Disposition*

108. Man is of the nature of the earth, water, fire, wind, akas (ether), the Devas, the Naras, or the animals and birds. We shall describe each.

109. A person of the nature of earth will be of the odour of good flowers, will indulge in sexual intercourse, and will be of good breeding and of firm mind. A person of the nature of water, will drink much water, will be fond of women and will eat juicy meals.

110. A person of the nature of fire will be hasty and thoughtless, wicked and cruel, angry, hungry and gluttonous. A person of the nature of the wind will be fickleminded, thin and of irascible temper.

111. A person of the nature of Akas will be able, open-mouthed, skilled in a knowledge of sound and with holes in his

limbs. A person of the nature of the Devas, will be liberal in gifts, slightly angry and attached to friends.

112. A person of human nature will be fond of music and jewels and inclined to share what he has with others.

113. A person of the nature of a Rākṣasa will be exceedingly angry, wicked and sinful. A person of the nature of a Piśāca (devil) will be hasty, thoughtless, dirty and talkative and of a large body.

114. A person of the nature of animals and birds will be timid, hungry and gluttonous. Thus the learned have described the Satwa quality of a man and this quality is also known as Prakriti—nature.

XII.—*Gait*

115. If the gait be like that of the tiger, the swan, the elephant in rut, the bull or the peacock, the person will be a king. If the gait be noiseless and slow, the person will be rich ; and if it be fast and skipping, he well be poor.

116. Generally, a person who has opportunities of walking out when suffering from ennui, of drinking when thirsty, and of protection when in fear, is considered by those learned in the lore as exceedingly happy.

117. Thus have I described briefly the features and qualities of man on examining the views of Sages. He who studies this will be liked universally and will be honored by the king.

CHAPTER 69

On the Five Great Men

1. Five Mahapuruṣas or eminent men will be born when the five planets from Mars to Saturn are powerful and occupy their houses, exaltation signs or the Kendra houses. I shall now describe them.

2. If the powerful planet be Jupiter, the person born is known as *Haṁsa* ; if Saturn be powerful, the person born is known as *Śaśa* ; if Mars, he is known as *Rucaka* ; if Mercury, he is known as *Bhadra* ; and if Venus, he is known as *Mālavya*.

3. If the Sun be powerful, the body will be strong ; and if the Moon be powerful, the mind will be strong. The Mahapuruṣas will be of the nature of the houses occupied by the powerful Sun or the Moon.

4. They will be of the nature of the houses occoupied by the powerful Sun or Moon in point of gloss, color, shape, strength and the like ; is the Sun or the Moon be not powerful at the time of birth, the peson is known as *Saṅkīrṇapuruṣa*.

5 If at the time of birth, Mars be powerful, the person will be very strong ; if Mercury be powerful, he will be very heavy ; if Jupiter, he will possess a good voice ; if Venus, he will be of glossy appearance ; and if Saturn be powerful, the person will be of good color. If none of the planets be powerful, he will possess very little of the qualities described above.

6. The Saṅkīrṇapuruṣas will not become kings, but will enjoy ease and comfort in the Dāśa period of the most powerful planet. Saṅkīrṇapuruṣas are of five sorts according as the most powerful planet occupies an inimical sign, a depression sign, a position beyond the exaltation sign or is aspected by a benefic or a malefic planet.

7. The Haṁsapuruṣa is 96 inches high or of the height of the length of the two arms stretched horizontally, and the

remaining 4 persons—the Śaśa, the Rucaka, the Bhadra and the Mālavya puruṣas—are each successively three inches taller than the one above him.

8. If the Sattvaguṇa (good temper) predominate is a person he will be merciful, firm-minded, strong, sincere and with a due regard for Brāhmaṇas. If the Rajo-guṇa or passionate temper predominate in a person, he will be a poet, learned in the various arts, will perform sacrificial rites, will be found of women and will be bold and courageous.

9. If the Tamo-guṇa or dark temper predominate in a person, he will be deceitful, ignorant, idle, angry and sleepy. If the three guṇas be variously mixed in a person, there will be four more distinctions—or seven distinct characters in all.

10. A Malavya puruṣa will have arms resembling the trunk of the elephant with fleshy joints, a smooth and beautiful body, narrow loins, face 13 inches long, the space between the root of the nose to the centre of the ear holes 10 inches long, bright beautiful cheek, white even teeth and the two lips without much flesh.

11. He will rule over Malwa, Baroach, Surat, Laṭa, Sindh and countries extending to the Pāriyātra mountains and will be master of much self-earned wealth.

12. He will live to the age of 70 years and will die in water. Thus have I described fully the character of the Mālavya puruṣa, and I shall now proceed to describe the character of the four other puruṣas.

13. The Bhadra puruṣa and large, round, equal and hanging arms, is of the height of the two arms stretched and has cheeks covered with thin, soft and close hairs.

14. The Bhadra puruṣa will be strong in skin and semen; his breast will be broad and large; the Sattvaguṇa will predominate in him; he will have the face of the tiger and will be firm-minded, patient, charitable, grateful, with the gait of an elephant and vastly learned.

15. He will be a man of great intelligence, of fine body, forehead, frontal bones, belly and nose; will be learned in the arts, courageous, with the hands and feet of the color of the inside of the lotus, will live in ease and comfort and will have brows close and alike.

16. The hairs of his head will be of the smell of the earth just made wet, of fragrant leaves, of saffron, of the juice of the elephant in rut and of the fragrant tree of Agaru[1]; they will be found to grow singly and in curls; his genital organ will be hid from view like that of the horse or elephant.

17. In his hands and feet will be found lines of the shape of the plough, the pestle, the club, the conch-shell, the discus, the elephant, the shark, a lotus or a chariot. His wealth is open to the enjoyment of all classes of people; but he will not help his own kinsmen and will over be inclined to follow his own independent views.

18. He will be 84 inches high and will be 160 lbs. in weight, and will rule over Madhyadeśa, If three planets, be powerful at the time of his birth, he will rule over all countries.

19. After ruling over countries acquired by himself, the Bhadra puruṣa will die at the age of 80 in water and will reach Swarga.

20. The Śaśa puruṣa will have a slightly uneven head, small teeth and nails, projecting eyes, a swift gait, will be skilled in metallurgy and in trade, will have large cheeks, will be deceitful, will be a commander of armies, will be fond of sexual union, and will covet the wives of other men, will ever be moving, will be valiant and dutiful to his mother, and will be fond of forests, mountains, rivers and places unfrequented by man.

21. He will be 92 inches high; will do deeds with fear and suspicion; will know the tricks of other men; will be strong in marrow; will be of a retiring nature and will not be very heavy.

22. In his hands and feet will be found lines of the shape of the target, sword, lyre, cot, garland, drum, trident as well as vertical lines.

23. He will either rule over the Mlechas or will be a provincial governor. He will die at the age of 70 after suffering from dysentery, belly-ache, and personal disgrace.

24. The Haṁsa puruṣa's cheek will be large and red; his nose will be high and face of the color of gold; his head will be round; his eyes will be of brown color; the nails red; the lines in the hands and feet of the shape of a garland, a string,

the elephant driver's hook the conch-shell, two fish, the Yupa,[2] a pot or a lotus flower, the nails will be perfect, the feet beautiful and organs of sense bright and full.

25. He will indulge in water-sports, will be strong in semen, will be 1,6C0 Palas (128 lbs) in weight and 96 inches in height.

26. He will rule over the countries of Khasa, Surasena and Candahar and the regions between the Jumna and the Ganges, and will die in forest at the age of 90.

27. Rucaka puraṣa will have beautiful brows, and hairs on his head and will be red-black; his neck will be like the conch-shell and his head will be long; he will be valiant and cruel; will be an excellent minister or the chief of thieves and will be a good gymnast.

28. His loins will be as broad as his face is long; his body will be bright; he will be strong in flesh, will destroy his enemies and do deeds in a determined manner.

29. The lines in his hand and feet will be of the shape of a club, a lyre, a bull, a bow, a vajrayudha, a spear, the moon or the trident; he will respect the Brāhmaṇas and the Davas; will be 100 inches high and 1,000 Palas (80 lbs) in weight.

30. He will be skilled in black magic; his shanks and ankles will be thin; he will rule over the countries bordering on the Vindhya and Sahya mountains and over Ujjain, and will die at the age of 70 by weapons or by fire.

31. The Saṅkirṇa puruṣas are of five classes known as the *Vāmanaka*, the *Jaghanya*, the *Kubja*, the *Maṇḍalaka* and the *Sācin;* they will serve severally under the fire Maha puruṣas. I will now proceed to describe them.

32. The Vāmanaka puruṣa, will have perfect limbs; his back will be bent; his lips, armpits and body will be large; he will be a man of renown; he will be generous and a worshipper of Viṣṇu, and he will serve under the Bhadra puruṣa.

33. The Jaghanya puruṣa will serve under the Mālavya puruṣa; his ears will be semi-circular in shape; his joints will be strong; he will be strong in semen; and will be a tale-bearer, a poet of disagreeable appearance and of large fingers.

34. He will be rich, cruel and of dull intellect; he will ridicule other men; the lines in his land, feet and breast will

be of the shape of a sword, a spear, a string or an axe.

35. The Kubja puruṣa will serve under the Haṁsa puruṣa; he will be a pure man; the parts below his lotus will be thin; the front part of his body will be bent forward; he will be an atheist; he will be rich, learned and with craft; will carry tales and will be grateful.

36. He will be learned in the various arts and fond of fight; he will have numerous servants and will be subject to female influence; he will give up his connection with eminent men for no apparent cause and will be of active habits.

37. The Maṇḍalaka puruṣa will serve under the Rucaka puruṣa and will be skilled in black magic, witchcraft and spirt-lore both practically and theoretically.

38. He will appear like an old man with the hair on his head stiff and not glossy; he will destory his enemies and be subject to the influence of women; he will respect the Brāhmaṇas, the Devas, sacrificial fire ceremonies and the practice of yoga and he will also be intelligent.

39. The Sācin puruṣa will serve under the Śaśa puruṣa and will be of the character of his master; his appearance and color will be disagreeable; he will be generous and will successfully execute every great deed commenced by him.

REFERENCES

1. Amyris Agallocha.
2. Yupa : an eight-sided post in sacrificial rites to which the animal to be sacrificed is tied.

CHAPTER 70

On the Features of Women

1. He who wishes to rule over countries shall marry a woman the nails of whose toes are glossy, high, thin and red, whose ankles are large, beautiful and both alike, whose toes are close and the soles of whose feet are of the color of the lotus.

2. If the lines in the feet be of the shape of the fish, the elephant driver's hook, the lotus, barley-grain, the plough or the sword, or if the feet be dry and soft, if the shanks be round and without hair and visible muscles, and if the knees be fleshy and both alike, the woman will be happy.

3. If the thighs be like the trunk of the elephant, without hair and firm, the genital organ be broad and triangular in shape, the part just above it be large and high and like the shell of the turtle, if the glans penis be hid from views, the woman will be wealthy and happy.

4. If the buttocks be large, broad and fleshy, the woman will wear a girdle; if the navel be broad, deep and turning from left to right, she will be happy.

5. If the abdomen be without hair, with three skin fold, and if the bosoms be round, firm, large and both alike, the breast above it be without hair and soft and the neck be like the conch-shell, the woman will be wealthy and happy.

6. If the lower lip be red like the China rose, fleshy, beautiful and red like the cherry fruit, if the teeth be even and like the buds of jasmine, the woman will enjoy the pleasures of married life and will be happy.

7. If the voice be sweet, simple and not meek and like the sound of the cuckoo or the swan, if the nose be smooth and beautiful and the holes alike, and if the eyes be of the color of the leaves of the blue lotus, the woman will be happy.

8. If the brows do not meet and be not very broad, if they

do not hang, if they be bent like the young moon, if the forehead be like the half moon, without hair and even, the woman will be happy.

9. If the two cars be not very long, be fleshy, soft and both alike, and if the hairs on the head be glossy, black, soft, bent and grow singly, and if the head be even, the woman will be happy.

10. If the lines in the hands[1] and froth be of the shape of a pitcher, a seat, a horse, an elephant, a chariot, the bilva tree, an eight sided post, an arrow, a flower wreath, a pendant, a chamara, an elephant driver's hook, a barley grain, a mountain, flag-staff, an arch-way, a fish, a cross, a sacrificial altar, a fan, a conch-shell, an umbrella or a lotus flower, the woman will become a queen.

11. If the wrists be invisible, the hands be like the lotus flower and soft, and if the finger joints be long, the woman will become a queen; if the palm of the hand be neither deep, nor high, if it be covered with benefic lines, the woman will live long, leading a married life and will have sons; she will live in comfort, be wealthy and in the enjoyment of sexual pleasures.

12. If there be found a line issuing from the wrist and reaching the middle finger, or if vertical lines be found in the palm of the hand, either the woman will become a queen or her husband will become a king.

13. If there be found a line issuing from below the little finger and reaching a place between the forefinger and the middle finger, the woman will live long; if short, her age will be proportionately short.

14. The big lines below the root of the thumb indicate sons, and the small lines daughters. If the lines be perfect, the children will live long, and if broken or short they will die early.

15. Thus have been described the good features of women; the bad features are the reverse of these. We shall however proceed to state briefly the more remarkable ones.

16. If either the little toe or the one next to it do not touch the ground, or if the toe next to the big toe be longer than the big toe, the woman will become unchaste and will commit deeds of wickedness.

17. If the calves of the leg be found to grow larger as they approach the knees, or if the shanks be covered with muscles, without flesh or with too much flesh or covered with hair, if the genital organ be sunk, small, with the hair growing from right to left, if the belly be like a pot, she will suffer grief.

18. If the neck be short, the woman will be poor; if very long, her family will perish; and if large she will be of angry temper.

19. If the eyes be wild and disturbed and of yellow color, or if they be brown and of wandering look, or if dimples appear in the cheeks while laughing, the woman will become unchaste.

20. If the forehead be low, the brother of the woman's husband will die; if the belly be found to hang, her father-in-law will die; if the buttocks be found to hang, her husband will die; if the upperlip be covered with hair or if the woman be taller than her her husband, she will suffer miseries.

21. If the bosoms be covered with hair, or if they be not of bright appearance, or if they be too large, or if the ears be not both alike, the woman will suffer grief. If the teeth be large, uneven and of disagreeable appearance, if the gum be black, she will suffer miseries and be addicted to thieving.

22. If the lines in the hands be of the shape of a hawk, a wolf, a crow, a heron, a serpent, an owl, or if the hands appear dried up, covered with muscles and both not alive, the woman will be poor and miserable.

23. If the upper-lip be high, if the front look be of disagreeable appearance, the woman will be quarrelsome; Generally vice follows deformity and virtue follows beauty.

24. The (1) feet and ankles, (2) the shanks and knees, (3) the thighs and genital organ, (4) the loins and the navel, (5) the belly, (6) the breast and the bosoms, (7) the shoulders, (8) the neck and the lips, (9) the eyes and the brows, and (10) the forehead and the head represent the tea dasa periods beginning from birth; so that if a particular organ be defective, a person will suffer miseries in the dasa period represented by it. If the organ be perfect and beautiful, he will be happy during such period.

Notes—120 Years is the maximum length of life and each

dasa period consists of 12 years. If, for instance, there be defects in the thighs, the person will suffer miseries between the ages of 24 and 26.

REFERENCE

1. In the case of a woman, the left hand and in the case of a man, the right hand, shall be examined.

CHAPTER 71

On Injuries to Garments

1. Divide the garment into nine rectangles by Naras joining the opposite points of trisection of the sides. The Devas occupy the four rectangles at the corners. The Naras (men) occupy the two middle squares at the two codes and the Asuras occupy the three remaining central squares. The same remarks apply to seats and shoes.

2. If the inner garment be new, and if it be disfigured with ink, dung, mud and the like, or if it be cut, burnt or torn, the effects whether good or bad will fully come to pass; if the injured garment be one that has been used, the effects will be slightly felt; if the garment be a decayed one, the effects will be very slightly felt. If the outer garment be injured, the effects will be greatly felt.

3. If the injury occur to an Asura part, the person will either suffer from diseases or will die; if it occur to a human part, there will be birth of sons and an improved appearance of the body; if it occur to a Divine part, there will be an increase of comfort. Generally, if the injury occur about the edges, there will be misery.

4. If the cut appearing in the divine parts of a garment be of the shape of a heron, a duck, an owl, a dove, a crow, a hawk, a jackal, an ass, a camel, or a snake, there will be danger to the life of the person.

5. If the cut in the Asura part of the garment be of the shape of an umbrella, a banner, a cross, a platter, a bilva tree, a pot, a lotus flower, a flower wreath, and the like, the person will soon become wealthy and prosperous.

6. If a new garment be worn when the Moon is in the asterism of Aśvanī, the person will get more garments; if it be worn when the Moon is in the asterism of Bharani, he will be

robbed of property; if when the Moon is in the asterism of Kṛttika there will be fear from destructive fires; if when in the asterism of Rohiṇī, there will be acquisition of wealth.

7. If a new garment be worn when the Moon is in the Mṛgaśirṣa, there will be suffering from rats; of Ardra, the person will die; of Punarvasu, there will be prosperity; if in that of Puṣya there will be acquisition of wealth.

8. If a new garment be worn when the Moon is in the asterism of Asleśa, there will be loss; of Magha, there will be death; of Pūrvaphalguni, there will be fear from the king; of U-Phalguni, there will be acquisition of wealth.

9. If a new garment be worn when the Moon is in the asterism of Hasta, there will be success in works undertaken; of Chittra, there will be prosperity ; of Swaty, there will be prosperity and good meals; of Visākha, there will be popularity.

10. If a new garment be worn when the Moon is in the asterism of Anuradha, there will be acquisition of friends; of Jaiṣṭha, the person will get more garments; of Moola, there will be death by drowning or seavoyage; of P-Āṣāḍa, there will be disease.

11. If a new garment be worn when the Moon is in the asterism of U-Āṣāḍa, the person will get good meals; of Śrāvaṇa, there will be eye disease; of Sravishtha, there will be acquisition of grain; of Satabhishak, there will be much fear from poison.

12. If a new garment be worn when the Moon is in the asterism of P. Proshtapada, there will be fear of death by drowning; of U. Proshtapada, the person will get man, of Revati, there will be acquisition of grain.

13 & 14. A new garment presented by Brahmins with their benedictions or by the king for marit or on occasions of marriage, may be worn irrespective of the position of the Moon in the lunar Zodiac and the effects will always be good.

Notes—If the injured garments be very valuable silks and the like, the effects described will occur after three or six year; in the case of woollen shawls, after three years; and in the case of ordinary garments after six months. According to Garga whether the injury occur to valuable or ordinary garments, there shall be a recitation of Vedic hymns by the Brahmins; in the case of torn garments, the evils are not be escaped by the sale of the garments; they should be given away to Brāmaṇas gold, in which case, a person becomes freed from evils.

CHAPTER 72

On Chamara[1]

1. Expressly for the use made of their tail the Chamari deer (Bos Grunniens) appears to have been created in the caves of the Himālayās, the hair growing at the end of their tail is either white or black or yellow.

2. If the hair be glossy, much in quantity, soft, pure, white, and with a small bone at the root, the Chamara is one of a superior kind; but if the hair be knotty, split, broken or small in quantity, the Chamara will not conduce to prosperity.

3. The length of the handle shall be either a cubit and a half or a cubit or four inches less than a cubit. It shall be made of wood and covered with gold or silver not with gems and precious stones. Such a Chamara will conduce to the prosperity of the king.

4. The beam or the shaft or the handle, as the case may be, of the lute, the umbrella, the elephant driver's hook, the cane, the bow, the canopy, shall be yellow, red, of the color of the honey, and black in the case of the Brāhmaṇas, Kṣatriyas Vaiṣyas and Śūdras respectively.

5. If the handle contain two, four, six, eight, ten or twelve joints, the effects will respectively be the death of a person's mother, loss of lands, of wealth and of family, disease or death.

6. If the handle contain three, five, seven, nine, eleven, or thirteen joints, the effects will respectively be success in the object of a journey, ruin of the enemy, much gain, acquisition of lands, increase of cows or the gain of a desired object.

REFERENCE

1. The bushy tail of the Bos Grunniens used as a fan and as one of the insignia of royalty.

CHAPTER 73

On Umbrellas

1 & 2. The king's umbrella shall be made of the feathers of the swan, the gallineous fowl; the peacock and the crane, covered with a new white silk and hung with lines of pearls all round; the handle shall be set with crystal; the shaft shall be 6 cubits long, made of gold, and shall contain seven or nine joints.

3. The length of the radius of the umbrella shall be half the length of the shaft; the several joints shall be firm and the umbrella shall be raised at the centre; such an umbrella will bring to the king success and prosperity.

4. The umbrellas of the first prince, the queen, the commander-in-chief, and the magistrate, shall have shafts 6½ cubits long, and shall be 2½ cubits broad.

5. The umbrellas to be used by the king's favourites shall be made of the feathers of the peacock with its top adorned with the prasada patta and shall be hung with lines of pearls all round. The other umbrellas shall consist of four sides, and the shaft of the umbrella of the Brahmins shall be round.

CHAPTER 74

On the Praise of Women

1. In a country acquired by a king by conquest the town is the most important place; in towns, houses are important places; in houses, the bed room is an important place; in it, the cot and the bed are important, and on it a woman bedecked with jewels forms the essence of the pleasures of royalty.

2. Gems derive beauty from women; women derive no beauty from gems; for women, when without gems, are lovely and provoke men's desires, and not so gems when alone.

3. To kings struggling to conceal their desires when in public, anxious to conquer their enemies, meditating on a hundred schemes of administration either half executed or not attempted at all, obliged to follow the advice of their ministers, ever suspecting fear and failure in every attempt and buried in a sea of cares and anxieties, the embrace of an excellent woman is the only bit of pleasure falling to their lot.

4. In no world has Brahmā created a gem superior to women, whose speech, sight, touch, thought, provoke pleasurable sensations Such a gem in the shape of a woman is the fruit of a person's good deeds, and from such a gem a person obtains both sons and pleasure. A woman therefore resembles the goddess of wealth in a family, and must be treated with respect, and all her wants must be satisfied.

5. It appears to me that those are bad men who, out of a dislike for all things, speak ill of women, and these men are never found to speak of the virtues of women.

6. Is there any vice with which women are not charged by men ? Speak the truth. Those that reject women do so out of a stupid firmness of mind. According to Manu, women possess more virtues than men.

7. Soma-deva has blessed women with personal purity;[1] the Gandharvas have given them pure speech; Agni-deva has allowed to them the privilege of eating any kind of food without restrictions. Women are therefore without faults.

8. The Brāhmaṇas, are pure in their feet[1], the cows, in their buttocks; the sheep and the horse, in their face, and women all over their body.

9. Women are exceedingly pure and are without faults. These,[2] if any, leave them with their menses.

10. Those houses will meet with ruin as if by witchcraft, which are cursed by women who are not treated with respect.

11. The Śāstras say that a woman is both a man's wife and mother[3], and men owe their birth to women. Those that speak ill of women therefore are ungrateful persons. How can you people be happy ?

12. In the eye of the Śāstras, adultery in man or woman is equally condemned. Man leglects this condemnation, while women respect it. Hence the superiority women over men.

13. According to the Śāstras a man that commits adultery shall dress himself in the skin of the ass with the hairy side without, and beg his meals for six months for his purification.

14. Though one might indulge in sexual pleasures for 100 years, the appetite for the same is not satiated. Whenever men refrain from sexual pleasure after the death of their wives, they do so, because of their inability; while women after the death of their husbands boldly preserve their chastity continuing in a state of widowhood.

15. A man who blames a faultless woman is not unlike a thief who, suspecting an innocent person to be a thief, sets up a hue and cry.

16. A man when alone with his wife speaks to her sweet language and no more thinks of her after her death; while a woman often enters the funeral pile along with her diceased husband out of her love for him.

17. A person who is fortunate enough to have an excellent wife, though he might be poor, appears to me as happy as a king. The main pleasures of a king are women and good meals. These serve as sticks to increase the fire of his desires.

18. That a pleasure like that of embracing a woman who

has just attained womanhood, whose speech is short, soft, sweet and broken, whose bosoms are high and large and who herself is full of sexual passion, is not to be found in the house of Brahmā, the Creator is my opinion.

19. In the Brahmā loka, the Munis, the Siddhās, the Celestial mucisians may pay due honors to persons deserving them. What pleasures can there be in receiving such honors? These persons cannot be as happy as those who enjoy excellent women.

20. From Brahmā down to worms, we fined pairs indulging in sexual love. What is there to be ashamed of in the matter—one for which the Supreme Śiva assumed four faces.[4]

REFERENCES

1. The idea is one somewhat foreign to foreigners. A pure part is one the touch of which does not pollute a person though the part may suffer pollution.
2. The Commentator interprets "these" to mean faults of the mind. As regards faults of the body, expiatory ceremonies are prescribed in the Shastras.
3. The idea is that a person is born over again in the shape of his own son.
4. The allusion is to a visit paid to Śiva by Tilottama, a dancing woman, attached to the Court of Indra. As she went round Śiva by way of worship, he was so much attracted by her beauty that he kept looking at her with four faces which he assumed, while his one face was directed towards his consort Parvati whom he did not wish to offend.

CHAPTER 75

On Amiability

1. A man of agreeable manners enjoys sexual pleasures fully and not so one of a morose nature; for he cannot secure the love of women. A woman, though at a distance, conceives a child of the shape of the person she loves ardently and thinks of at the time.

2. Just in the same way as a tree that grows is not different from the parent tree, whether we plant a branch or sow a seed, so the main features of the child partake of the features of its father, though there might be slight changes due to the soil.

3. The subtle soul co-operates with the *manas* (the mind); the mind, co-operates with the senses; the senses, perceive objects; all this takes place in little or no time. The above is the connection between the soul and the objects around us. What is there which the mind cannot comprehend ? Therefore, wherever the mind enters, the soul follows it.

4. The soul being subtle whenever it enters another soul, it requires some time and an effort of the mind to know the latter. The soul, which intensely meditates on an object, assumes the shape of that object, and therefore young women's thoughts are always directed towards amiable persons.

5. Real love makes one beloved of other, and hatred makes person unpopular. There is great sin attaching to attempts at winning the favor of a person by the practice of magic or the use of drugs or by stratagems, and no pleasure can come out of it.

6. A person who is not selfish becomes popular and selfishness makes a man unpopular. A selfish person executes his work with much difficulty, and an unselfish man through his sweet manners and speech finds it easy to do his work, being helped by others.

7. It is not manly in a person thoughtlessly to attempt to do a thing or to utter falsehood with a view to please others. A person who, even while successfully executing a business, does not feel proud nor indulge in selfish praise is truly noble.

8. A person who desires to become a general favorite shall speak of the merits of other men in terms of praise, and a person who speaks of the demerits of other men becomes wicked himself.

9. All men wish to help a person who aims at the good of the people. The renown which a person will derive from an act of assistance to his enemy when in difficulties is a fortune resulting from numerous good deeds.

10. Where there are real merits, the attempt to suppress them only increases their splendour just like an attempt to suppress flaming fire by means of dry grass. A person who out of envy aims at ruining the reputation of other men is hated by all.

CHAPTER 76

On Spermatic Drugs and Medicines

1. If the blood should exceed, the issue will be a female child; if the semen virile should exceed, the issue will be a male child; if both be equal, the issue will be a hermaphrodite. It is therefore necessary to take medicines for the increase of the semen virile.

2. The tops of storied houses, moon-light, sweet liquor, beautiful women with the passion of love, the music of the lute, love speech, solitude, and flower wreaths, are things whose union provokes sexual passion.

3. Prepare a mixture of *Mākṣika Dhātu*,[1] honey, pārada (quick-silver), iron-dust, *Patthya*, bitumen, *vidanga* and ghee. Take this for 21 days. Though 80 years old and weak with age, you will indulge in sexual union with the energy of a youg man.

Note.—With the exception of honey and ghee, the other drugs shall be powdered and mixed in equal parts and firmed into a paste with honey and milk.

4. Put into the milk of the cow, the root of the *kapikacchu* and heat the milk and then drink it; or roast a quantity of broken black-gram in the ghee obtained by churning pure uncurdled milk. Eat 6 handfuls of the seed and then drink milk. You will engage in sexual union with great energy.

5. Soak in the juice of the pumpkin its powdered root and dry it; repeat the operation 7 times. Put the powder into milk heated with sugar, and drink it. You will require many women.

6. Soak in the juice of the fruit of the Emblic Myrobolam its dried fruit powdered and dry it. Repeat the operation 7 times; mix it with honey, sugar and ghee, and lick it and drink milk. You will require many women.

7. Put into the milk of the cow the testicle of the goat, heat the milk, soak in it a considerable quantity of sesamum seeds, and dry it; repeat the operation 7 times; eat the seeds. You will outbeat the sparrow in sexual union.

8. Mix with the cooked Ṣaṣṭika rice the cooked broken seeds of black gram; eat the rice and then drink milk; you will go to bed with much sexual passion.

9. Mix together equal quantities of the powder or the flour of sesamum seeds, of the root of the Aśvagandhā, of Kapikacchu, the pumpkin and of the Ṣaṣṭika rice. Form the mixture into a paste by adding the milk of the goat and make cakes of it, roast them in heated ghee and eat the cakes.

10. Or, put into the milk of the cow the root of either of Gokṣura or the pumpkin; heat the milk, and drink it; though old you will indulge in sexual union with the energy of a young man. We will now prescribe remedies for dyspepsia.

11. Mix together equal quantities of the powder of sison, rock-salt, Harītaki, ginger, and long pepper, and put the mixture either in liquor or in butter-milk or water, slightly heated and drink it. You will begin to have a keen appetite for food.

12. If while taking the cordials described above you eat with your rice much of vegetable preparations which are exceedingly sour, bitter, saltish or pungent you will, though young, lose your sexual energy and like an old person state false excuses before women.

Notes :—The following is extracted from a medical work named Ratnakośa.

1. Soak in the water of the cocoanut the broken seeds of black-gram and dry the seeds, repeat the operation 7 times; make the seeds into a paste by grinding, make cakes of it and roast them in heated ghee and eat the cakes and then drink milk; you will require a hundred women.

The following are taken from a work named Prayoga Sara :—

2. Mix together in an iron vessel filled with ghee equal quantities of grapes, Māṣikadhātu, Śilājit, quick-silver, the

excrement of the turtle dove, Vidanga and Harītakī powdered; take a dose of the mixture every morning; you will become strong and healthy and will be freed from poison and from jaundice, and will have an increase of semen virile.

3. Mix together the power of Triphala with either jaggery or sugar, eat the mixture and drink milk heated with the root of Kapikacchu mixed with it; you will have an increase of semen virile.

4. Mix together the milk of the cow with the juice of the bark of the silk-cotton tree; heat the mixture till it is reduced and to one-half of its bulk. Mix with it one-third part of honey. A woman who takes a karśa (one-fourth pala) of this milk will have an increase of blood.

5. There will also be an increase of blood if a woman will take dried grapes ground with honey on a stone and then mixed with either milk or gruel.

6. There will also be an increase of blood if the juice of the bark of the mango be drawn into the nose.

The following are from Suśruta :—

7. Form into a paste either a mixture of the powder of sesamum seeds, black-gram, and the root of the pumpkin, or the flour of the Sali rice, by grinding if on a stone with the juice of the sugarcane and mix with it rock salt and the serum of flesh of the hog; form cakes of it; roast them in heated ghee, and eat the cakes; you will require a hundred women.

8. Put into milk the testicle of the goat; heat the milk; drench in it sesamum seeds 7 times, drying them each time; mix with them the serum of flesh of the gangetic porpoise; make cakes of the mixture and roast them in ghee and eat the cakes; you will require a hundred women.

9 Mix together long pepper, rock salt, and the testicle of the goat; form the mixture into cakes and roast them in ghee obtained from uncurdled milk; eat the cakes. You will require a hundred women.

10. Form a mixture of the powder of equal quantities of either long pepper, black-gram and Sali rice, or of barley and wheat; form the mixture into cakes, roast them in ghee; eat the cakes and then drink milk mixed with sugar and heated. You will require ten women.

11. Drench in the juice of the pumpkin its powdered root 7 times, drying the powder each time; add to it ghee, and honey and eat it; you will require 10 women.

12. Drench 7 times in the juice of the fruit of emblic myrobolan the powder of its dried fruit, drying the powder each time; mix with it ghee, honey, and sugar and eat it and then drink milk. Though you may be 80 years old you will begin to possess the energy of a young man.

13. Mix together long pepper, rock salt, and the testicle of the goat; put the mixture in ghee, heat it and eat it. You will have an increase of semen virile. The testicles of the Gangetic porpoise, the crab, the turtle, or the crocodile may be similarly mixed with the other ingredients. The effect will be the same.

14. Drink the semen virile of the buffalo, the ox, or the sheep.

15. Or put into milk the fruit, root, bark and the calyx of the young buds of Asvattha (the holy fig tree); heat the milk, add to it honey and sugar; drink the milk. You will outbeat the sparrow.

16. Mix well with honey and ghee a pala of the flour of black-gram and eat the mixture.

17. Put into milk the root of the Kapikacchu and the flour of wheat; heat the milk; as soon as it cools add to it ghee, and drink it, and then drink ordinary milk.

18. Put into ghee the testicle of the crocodile or the rat or the frog or the sparrow; heat the ghee and rub it on the soles of the feet. You will enjoy as many women as you please as long as you do not set your foot on the ground.

19. Mix with sugar the powder of the seeds of the Kapikacchu and Ikshuraka. Put the mixture into milk; heat it and drink it while it is hot.

20. Put into milk the powder of Ucchata, heat the milk and drink it.

21. Put into milk the roots of Ucchata and Satavari; heat the milk and drink it.

22. Put into milk the seeds of Kanikacchu and the broken seeds of black-gram; heat the milk and drink it.

23. Put into milk the seeds of Kapikacchu, Gokshuraka and Ucchata; heat the milk; add to it sugar and drink it.

24. Put into milk black-gram, the root of the pumpkin and of Ucchata; heat the milk, add to it ghee and honey and put sugar in it and drink it.

25. Drink the milk of a sow having a grown up pig or the milk of a cow subsisting on the leaves of the black-gram plant. In all these cases there will be an increase of semen virile.

REFERENCE

1. Vide glossary at the end of Chapter 77 for an explanation of the various medical and botanical terms occurring in this and in the next chapter.

CHAPTER 77

On Perfume Mixtures

1. To a person whose hairs are white, flower wreaths, sandal paste, perfumed smoke, clothes and jewels can give no beauty. It is therefore necessary to blacken and embellish the hair. The same attention shall be paid to it as to collyrium and jewels.

2. Put into an iron vessel vinegar or the like sour liquor; put in it a quantity of the Kodrava[1] grain after removing the husk and iron dust; heat the mixture; grind it well on a stone; rub it over the hairs of the head freed from oil; tie over the hairs the moist leaves of the Aragvadha and the like trees; remain so for six hours.

3. Then remove the mixture from the hairs, and rub over them the paste of the fruit of the Amalaka (Emblic myrobolam); cover them with moist leaves as before and remain so for another six hours; bathe as prescribed below; the hairs will become black.

N. B.—The Commentator advises the application of the mixture to shaven heads.

4. Then bathe in waters prepared for the purpose; rub over the hairs fragrant oil, thus removing the disagreeable scent of the mixture; the pleasures of royalty may then be enjoyed by a king by means of various kinds of perfumes.

5. Mix together equal quantities of cinnamon, Kuṣṭha, Reṇu, Nalikā, Spṛkkā, Myrrha, Vālaka, Tagara, Kesara and Patra and grind them on a stone forming them into a paste; rub it over the head and then bathe; such a bath is suited to kings.

6. Mix together in oil the powder of Mañjiṣṭhā Vyāghra-nakha, Sukti, cinnamon, Kuṣṭha and myrrha; heat the mixture in the sun. It is known as campaka gandhi oil.

7. Grind together equal quantities of Patra, Turuṣka, Vāla and Tagara and you will get a perfume provoking sexual passion. Add to this perfume Prianguka and expose the mixture to the smoke of Kaṭukarohini and Hiṅgulika. You will get a perfume which is known as Vakulagandha. To this add Kuṣṭha and you will get a perfume known as Utpalagandha. Add to this sandal, you will get again the perfume known as Campakagandha. Add to this nutmeg, cinnamon and Kustumbari; you will get a perfume known as Atimuktagandha.

8. Mix together one-fourth parts of Śatapuṣpā and Kunduruka, half parts of Nakha and Turuṣka, and one part of Sandal and Priyaṅgu; grind them well and expose the mixture to the smoke of Guda and Nakha. You will then get an excellent perfume.

9. Grind together equal quantites of Jaṭāmāṁsī, Valuka, Thurushka, Nakha and Sandal and form a paste; expose it to the smoke of Bdellium, Valuka, lac, Musta, Nakha and Sarkara.

10. One part of Harītakī, 2 parts of Śaṇkha, 3 parts of Kshudramusta, 4 parts of Drava, 5 parts of Ambu, 6 parts of Guda, 7 parts of Utpala, 8 parts of Sylaka and 9 parts of Musta give you a perfume. Numerous kinds of perfumes may be similarly prepared by mixing together different parts of each substance.

Notes

The text gives an instance of the proportion in which the ingredients are to be mixed. Similarly, of the 9 substances we can take from 1 to 9 parts of each, and no mixture ought to contain the same number of parts of any two substances. The question is to find the number of different varieties of mixtures. Suppose the nine substances to be represented by the nine letters from A to I, the proportion of the parts being from 1 to 9. As each substance may be taken from 1 to 9 parts and as no two substances shall be taken the same number of parts the number of mixtures required is the number of ways in which the figures from 1 to 9 may be written under the letters from A to I. This is the number of permutations of 9 things taken altogether, which is equal to $1 \times 2 \times 3 \times 4 \times 5 \times 6 \times 7 \times 8 \times 9 = 362880$. The Stanza gives us therefore 362880 different varieties of perfumes.

11. Mix together 4 parts each of Sita, Śaila, and Murta 2 parts each of Śrī and Sarja, and one part each of Nakha and Bdellium, grind them all on a stone with honey; add to the mixture, Camphor. You will then get a porfume known as Kopachada (destroyer of anger) fit only for kings.

12. Mix together Cinnamon, Uśīra, and Patra one part each, and Śukṣmaila half a part; powder them well; add to the mixture equal parts of Musk and Camphor. You will get an excellent perfume.

13 & 14. Of the 16 substances Ghana, Valaka, Syleyaka, Karpura, Uśīra, Nāgapuṣpa, Vyāghranakha, Spṛkkā Agaru, Madanaka, Nakha, Tagara, Dhānya, Takkola, Cora and Sandal, any four mixed in the proportion of 1, 2, 3, and 4 parts will form a perfume. As the number of four substances out of 16 is large and as each of the four substances may be mixed from 1 to 4 parts the number of mixtures will be very large. The process is known as Gandhārṇava—ocean of perfumes.

15. Dhānya and Karpūra being substances of strong scent, a part of the former and a little less than a part of the latter shall be added—these two substances shall never be mixed in 2, 3, or 4 parts.

16. The mixtures shall be exposed first to the smoke of Sreevatsa, secondly, to that of Sarjara, thirdly, to that of Guḍa, and lastly to that of Nakha. Add to the mixture both Camphor and musk.

17. The process gives us 174720[2] different varieties of perfumes.

18. One part of a substance can be mixed with 2, 3 or 4 parts of three other substances in 6 ways. Similarly 2, 3 or 4 parts of the same substance can be mixed respectively with 1, 3, 4,—1, 2, 4,—1, 2, 3 parts of the 3 other substances each in 6 ways.

19. Thus beginning with a single substance we get 24 varieties of perfumes; beginning with each of the 3 other substances we shall get 72 varieties;[3] or 96 varieties in all.

20. The number of four substance out of the 16 substances is 1820.

21. Every set of four substances gives us 96 varieties; by multiplying 1820 by 96 we shall obtain the number already stated, viz. 174720.

Notes.—The above number has been obtained on the supposition that the two substances Dhanya and Karpūra enter into the mixtures in 2, 3 and 4 parts also, which however is not the case. The actual number will therefore be less than the number stated above. We shall first explain how the number was arrived at by the author, pointing out an error committed by him which has permanently crept into the text and then find out the actual number of mixtures under the conditions given.

In the Chapter on combinations in Algebra, we learn that the number of combinations of n things taken r at a time.

$$= \frac{n\,(n-1)\,(n-2)\,(n-3)\ \ldots\ (n-r+1)}{1\ .\ 2\ .\ 3\ \ldots\ldots\ r}.$$

∴ the number of combinations 16 things taken 4 at a time

$$= \frac{16\times15\times14\times13}{1\times2\times3\times4} = 1820$$

Again take one of these sets of 4 substances. Call, the substances by the letters A, B, C, D; each of these enters into the mixture in 1, 2, 3 and 4 parts; but no two substances enter in the same number of parts. The question now is to find out the number of mixtures that can be formed of each set of four substances. The number required is the number of ways in which the figures 1, 2, 3 and 4 may be written under the letters A, B, C, D. This is the number of permutations of four things taken all together, which is equal to $1\times2\times3\times4=24$. The author is therefore wrong when he says that the number of such mixtures is 96.

We shall show his error by actually putting down the proportions of the various Mixtures.

A.	B.	C.	D.
1	2	3	4
,,	2	4	3
,,	3	2	4
,,	3	4	2
,,	4	2	3
,,	4	3	2

Total 6

A.	B.	C.	D.
2	1	3	4
,,	1	4	3
,,	3	1	4
,,	3	4	1
,,	4	1	3
,,	4	3	1

Total 6

A.	B.	C.	D.
3	1	2	4
,,	1	4	2
,,	2	1	4
,,	2	4	1
,,	4	1	2
,,	4	2	1

Total 6

A.	B.	C.	D.
4	1	2	3
,,	1	3	2
,,	2	3	1
,,	2	1	3
,,	3	1	2
,,	3	2	1

Total 6

In all 24 varieties for each set.

Now the author says that we shall get another 24 varieties beginning with the several parts of B and 24 beginning with the several parts of C and 24 beginning with the several parts of D, thus 96 varieties in all. It is clear that Varahamihira must have 'dozed a little' when he wrote stanza 19; for the number of varieties in reality is only 24 and not 96. For the 24 varieties we have given above include and are identical with the 72 more varieties of the author. We will begin for instance with the several parts of B. These are

B.	A.	C.	D.
1	2	3	4
,,	2	4	3
,,	3	2	4
,,	3	4	2
,,	4	2	3
,,	4	3	2

Total 6

B.	A.	C.	D.
2	1	3	4
,,	1	4	3
,,	3	1	4
,,	3	4	1
,,	4	1	3
,,	4	3	1

Total 6

B.	A.	C.	D.
3	1	2	4
,,	1	4	2
,,	2	1	4
,,	2	4	1
,,	4	1	2
,,	4	2	1

Total 6

B.	A.	C.	D.
4	1	2	3
,,	1	3	2
,,	2	1	3
,,	2	3	1
,,	3	1	2
,,	3	2	1

Total 6

In all 24 varieties beginning with the several parts of B. Now comparing these with the 24 varieties already given, it will be found that two lists are identically the same. So that 4 substances mixed in the proportion of 1, 2, 3, 4 parts each, give us only 24 mixtures, and not 96. Therefore, the total number of mixtures is $24 \times 1820 = 43680$ and not 96×1820 or 174720 as stated by the author. It is strange that Utpala, the commentator, has not noticed the error.

As two of the 16 substances do not enter into the mixtures in 2, 3 and 4 parts, we will find the actual number of varieties under the conditions given——a point which the author has omitted. Keeping aside the two substances. the number of sets of four substances out of 14 is the number of combination of 14 things taken 4 at a time.

This is equal to $\frac{14 \times 13 \times 12 \times 11}{1 \times 2 \times 3 \times 4} = 1001$. As before each set will give us 24 mixtures. The total number on mixtures therefore is $1001 \times 24 = 24024$——(I).

Again the number of 3 substances out of $14 = \frac{14 \times 13 \times 12}{1 \times 2 \times 3}$ $= 364$. We will now find out the number of varieties of mixtures, which each set of 3 substances will give us, taking them in 2, 3 and 4 parts. Let the letters A, B, C, denote the 3 substances and the figures 2, 3, 4 denote the parts. The number required is the number of ways in which the figures 2, 3, 4 can be written under the letters A, B, C. This is the number of permutations of 3 things taken all together $= 1 \times 2 \times 3 = 6$. Therefore the total number of mixtures of 3 substances out of $14 = 364 \times 6 = 2184$. Adding to each of these mixtures one part of

Dhānya we get 2184 mixtures of 4 substances.— —(II).

Adding to the same a little less them a part of Karpura we get 2184 mixtures of 4 substances———(III).

Now as under the conditions of the case no two substances shall enter into a mixture in the same number of parts, and as the two substances Dhānya and Kārpūra are only to be added in one part each; it is evident that these two do not enter into a mixture together——otherwise we shall have to find out the number of sets of 2 substances out of 14 and the number of mixtures of each set, each substance being taken from 2 to 4 parts and to each mixture thus obtained add a mixture of one part of Dhanya and a little less than a part of Karpūra. Such however does not appear to be the object of the author. He evidently wants that each mixture shall contain 10 parts.

The total number of mixtures under the conditions given is 24024+2184+2184=28392.

22. Beginning from unity form several series of numbers by adding together each figure with the next and the sum with the next and so on omitting only the last. The last of the series will represent the number of combinations required.

Notes :—In this stanza, the author lays down a rule for finding the number of combinations of n things taken r together when n and r are known. For instance, required the number of combinations of 7 things taken 4 together. Write in a line the figures from 1 to 7 and call it the first series: thus 1, 2, 3, 4, 5. 6, 7 ... ... (1).

Form the second series from the 1st as follows: 1+2=3; 3+3=6; 6+4=10; 10+5=15; 15+6=21. So that the 2nd series is 1, 3, 6, 10, 15, 21. ... ... (2).

Form the 3rd series from the 2nd as follows: 1+3=4; 4+6=10; 10+10=20; 20+15=35. So that the 3rd series is, 1, 4, 10, 20, 35 ... ... (3).

Form the 4th series form the 3rd thus : 1+4=5; 5+10=15; 15+20=35; so that the 5th series, is 1, 5, 15, 35...(4) and so on. The number of combinations, therefore, of 7 things taken 4 together is the last number of the 4th series, viz., 35.

The above may appear to be a somewhat clumsy process. Bhaskarachariar in his Lilavati (Arithmetic) gives the indentical rule now found in Western works on Algebra, He says: Form fractions with the figures, say, from 7 to 1 for numerators, and from 1 to 7 for denominators thus :

$$\frac{7}{1}, \frac{6}{2}, \frac{5}{3}, \frac{4}{4}, \frac{3}{5}, \frac{2}{6}, \frac{1}{7}.$$

The number of combinations of 7 things taken 2 together is the product of the first two fractions=21. The number taken 3 together is the product of the first three fractions=35. The number taken 4 together is the product of the first 4 fractions= 35 and so on. This process is also mentioned in the Aphorisms of Pingala known as Chandas Sutra, a very ancient work.

23. Agaru, Patra, Turuṣka and Śaileya shall be mixed in two, three, five and eight parts and Priyaṇgu, Mustā. Rasā and Keśa shall be mixed in five, eight, two, and three parts.

24. Spṛkkā, Cinnamon, Tagara and Māṁsī shall be mixed in four, one, seven and six parts; and Sandal, Nakha, Śaika, and Kunduruka shall be mixed in seven, six, four, and one parts.

25. Each set of four substances may be mixed in all possible ways in the parts mentioned—the number of parts being always eighteen in the case of each mixture. The mixtures form perfumes, ointment, and the like.

Note—As before, each set of four substances will give 24 varieties of mixtures.

26. To the mixtures mentioned above, add equal parts of Nakha, Tagara, Turuṣka, Nutmeg, Camphor and musk and expose them to the smoke of Guda and Nakha. You will get what are known as *Sarvatobhadra* perfumes.

27. If, to the same mixtures, you add equal parts of nutmeg, musk and camphor, and drench the resulting mixtures in Sahakara and honey you will again get what are known as *Sarvatobhadra* perfumes.

28. Whenever the substances Sarjarasa and Śrīvasaka are mentioned with other substances for giving perfumed smoke remove the two and use in their stead Vālaka and cinnamon. The resulting mixture will serve for bath.

29 & 30. Mix together any three out of the nine substances, Lodhra, Uśīra, Nata, Agaru, Musta, Malaya, priyaṅgu, Dhana and Pattya. Add to the mixture one part of Sandal, one part of Turushka, half a part of Nakha and a quarter part of

Satapuṣpa; expose the mixture to the smoke of Katuka, Hiṅgula and Guda; we thus get 84 different varieties of mixtures.

Notes : The number of combinations of nine substances taken 3 at a time is equal to $\frac{9}{1}\times\frac{8}{2}\times\frac{7}{3}=84$.

31. Allow the tooth-brush[4] to soak in the urine of the cow mixed with the powder of Harītakī for 7 days. Then put it in fragrant water prepared as described below.

32. Fragrant water shall be prepared with cardamom, cinnamon, Patra, Añjana, honey, Maricha, Nāgapuṣpa and Kuṣta and allow the tooth-brush to remain in the water till it becomes fragrant.

33. Mix together the powder of 4 parts of nutmeg, 2 parts of Patra, and one part of cardamom and camphor; smear it over the tooth-brush and dry it in the sun.

34. Tooth-brush prepared as stated above shall be used by the Brāhmaṇas, the Kṣtriyas, and the Vaiśaya only. By its use the appearance of a person will become bright, his countenance will, become agreeable, his mouth pure and of good smell and his voice sweet.

35. The chewing of Tamboola[5] excites sexual passion, brightens personal appearance, promotes prosperity, causes the mouth to smell sweet, increases strength, removes phlegmatic affections and produces many other benefits.

36. A due admixture of lime reddens the lips. If the nut exceed its measure it will bring down the color; if the lime exceed its measure, the mouth will smell ill and if the leaves exceed their measure the mouth will be of good smell.

37. If the leaves exceed their measure at night or the nut exceed its measure by day the effect will be good; if the case be otherwise, the Tamboola will not be found sweet. If the Tamboola contain as its ingredients Takola, Arecanut, Lavalīphala and Pārijāta, it will exhilirate the spirit and excite sexual passion.

REFERENCE

1. For an explanation of the various botantical terms occurring in this Chapter the reader is referred to the Glossary at the end.

2. Wrong. Vide notes which follow.

3. Wrong. Vide notes which follow.

4. This is a piece of stick or small twig of particular trees (vide Chap. 85) used as tooth-brush.

5. This consists of Arecanut and betel mixed with lime.

——

Glossary of Medical and Botanical terms Occurring in Chapters 76 and 77.

A

Agaru, Amyris Agallocha.
Ambu, the plant Andropogon Schoenanthus.
Anjana, Antimony.
Arag-vadha, the tree Cathartocarpus Fistula.
Aswagandha, the plant Physalis Flexuosa.

C

Chora, a kind of perfume. The plant Chrysopogon Aciculatus.

D

Damanaka, Artemisia Indica.
Dhana, the plant Alhagi Maurorum.
Dhanyaka, Coriander seeds.
Drava, Myrrh.

G

Ghana, the bulbous root of the plant Syperus Hexastychus Communis.
Gokshuraka, the plant Asteracantha Longifolia.
Guda, a kind of bdellium.

H

Haritaki, the fruit of the Terminalia Chebula. Hinguka; the prickly night Shade; Solanum Jacquini.

I

Ikshuraka, Asteracantha Longifolia.

J

Jatamamsi, the plant Nardostachis Jatamamsi.

K

Kapikacchu, the plant Mucuna Pruritus.

Katuka, a fragrant grass, Trichosanthes Dioeca.

Kesa, the plant Andrapogon Schoenanthus.

Kesara, Mimusops Elengi.

Kodrava, a species of gram eaten by the poor. Paspalum Scrobiculatum.

Kunduruka, the resin of the plant Boswellia Thurifera.

Kushtha, a medicinal plant Costus Speciosus or Arabicus.

Kustumburi, Coriander seeds.

L

Lavaliphala, the fruit of the Averrhoa Acida.

Lodhra, the tree, Symplocos Racemosa, the bark of which is used in dyeing.

M

Makshika-dhatu, a kind of pyrites,—a kind of honey like mineral substance.

Malaya, Sandal-wood.

Manjishtha, Bengal madder.

Mriga, Musk.

Mudra, Cyperus Rotundus.

Musta, a species of gross. Cyperus Rotundus.

N

Nagapushpa, Mesua Roxburghi

Nakha, a vegetable perfume.

Nalika, a fragrant substance.

Nata, the seed of the Cassia Tora.

P

Parijata, nutmeg.

Pathya, citron. Terminalia Chebula.

Patra, the leaf of the Cassia.

Priyangu, a medicinal plant and perfume.

R

Renu, a drug or medicinal substance fragrant but bitter and slightly pungenti taste and of a greyish color.

S

Sahakara, a sort of fragrant Mango tree.

Sailaka, bitumen.

Sarja, the resinous exudation of the Sal tree.

Sarkara, grit.

Satapushpa, a sort of dill or fennel. Anethum Sowa.

Satavari, Asparagus Racemosus.

Sita, grit.

Sprikka, the plant Trigonella Corniculta.

Sree, Turpentine.

Sukshmaila, small cardamoms.

Sukti, a sort of perfume in appearance like the dried Shell fish.

T

Tagara, the seed of Cassia Tora.

Takkola, the tree Pimenta Acris.

Triphala, the three myrobalans, the fruits of Terminalia Chebula, Terminalia Bellerica, Phyllanthus Emblica.

Turushka, a species of Kunduruka Olibanum, Indian incense: the resin of Boswellia Serrata.

U

Ucchata, the root of Cyperus Juncifol.

Usira, the fragrant root of the plant Andropogon Muricatus.

Utpala, the plant Costus Speciosus.

V

Vala, a fragrant grass, Andropogon Shoemanthus.

Valuka, a species of Cucumber.

Vidanga, Erycibe Paniculata.

Yyaghranakha, a kind of medicinal herb with a fragrant root.

CHAPTER 78

On Sexual Union

1. King Vidūratha was killed by his queen who concealed a weapon in her plaited hair; and the king of kāśī was killed by his queen, who disliked him, with poison which she carried in her anklets.

2. Thus wives who do not love their husbands have killed them. Of what use is it to quote more instances. Husbands shall therefore ascertain in various ways whether they have secured the affection of their wives.

3. A loving wife shows her love in various ways. She will, in the presence of her lord, show, as if by accident, her navel, arms, and ornaments and will adjust her garments; will allow the hairs of her head to fall loose as if by accident, will raise her eyebrows, will tremble, and will cast a side-look at her husband.

4. She will spit aloud; laugh openly; get first into the bed; crack her joints; yawn; beg for the gift of trifles; embrace a child and kiss it; will for a time look at her friend; look at her husband when his look is turned from her scratch her ears; and will speak in his praise in his absence.

5. A loving wife will, besides, speak affectionately to her husband, assist him with her money, will give up her anger at the sight of her lord and will be filled with pleasurable sensations; will meet any calumnious attacks on him by recounting his virtues.

6. She will show due respect to the friends of her lord and hate his enemies; she will feel grateful to him for his helps: will feel distressed during his absence.

7. An unloving wife will contract her eye-brows; turn her look away from her lord; will be wanting in gratitude; will not move from her place at the sight of her husband; will never feel

cheerful ; her lips will be dull and motionless ; she will be-friend the enemies of her lord and will be harsh in her speech.

8. She will shake with fear at the sight or touch of her lord ; will feel haughty ; will not attempt to pacify her lord when he leaves her company in anger ; she will wipe off her face after sexual enjoyment ; will go to bed before her lord and rise after him.

9 & 10. Begging women, female devotees, maid servants, the nurse, girls, the laundress, the flower-woman, the harlot, a friend, the barbar woman, these generally serve as messengers or go-betweens for women and bring disgrace and ruin or respectable families ; it is therefore necessary to protect family women from the intrigues of these persons and to maintain the honour, fame, and respectability of the family.

11. To go out at night, to keep awake on the pretence of a religious observance, to excuse herself on the false plea of illness, to be found for ever in the houses of other persons, to attend plays and the like, to consult astrologers, to frequent mourning houses or festivals are acts from which women should be kept back.

12. A modest wife is one who out of shame does not first exhibit an inclination to sexual embrance ; who throughout is nevertheless subject to sexual passion.

13. The virtues of a woman are young age, beauty, decoration with ornaments, being agreeable to her lord, being learned in matters which will make married life happy and being of a playful nature. A lady possessing these virtues is known as a female gem. A woman not possessing these virtues is loathed by man of taste as a disease.

Notes.—Vyasa says : A woman who is chaste and innocent, who eats pure meals, who is of sweet speech and who is fondly attached to her husband is known as (goddess of wealth).

Again, a woman who has ugly eyes, who is dirty, quarrelsome, talkative, is known as a Fury.

14. A woman shall not indulge in low language ; nor shall she wear bad colored clothes ; nor be of a dirty body.

15. A good wife is one who breathes unlike men ; who extends her arms to her lord to serve as a pillow for his head ; the hair of whose head is of good smell, who is fondly attached

to her hasband ; who sleeps after him and rises before him.

16. A woman of a wicked nature and one of weak health shall be rejected. A woman whose Sonita (blood) is black, green yellow, or of copper color shall also be rejected.

17. A person shall not join in sexual union a woman who sleeps too much, whose blood discharges are excessive, who is of an over bilious, phlegmatic or windy temperament, who perspires often, who is of defective or extra organs and whose hair is short or grey.

18. Whose calves are exceedingly fleshy, whose belly is large, who is noisy and who is possessed of other vices described in the Chapter on the features of women.

19. That blood is faultless which resembles the blood of the hare or the juice of red-cotton and which when well rubbed disappears.

20. If the blood flow out without pain and noise, and stops after three days, there will be conception at the next sexual union.

21. For the three days from the day of appearance of the menses a woman shall not bathe, wear flowers, or sandal, and on the fourth day she shall bathe as prescribed as the Smṛts.

22. After this, the vegetable ingredients prescribed for Puṣya Snāna shall be brought and put in water and the several *mantras* therein mentioned shall be pronounced ever the vessel and the woman shall bathe in the water.

23. On the even nights (from the day of appearance of the menses) a woman conceives a male child and on the add nights, a female child. If the conception occur early the issue will be a beautiful child of long and happy life.

24. If the foetus be on the right side the issue will be a male child, if on the left side ; it will be a female child ; if on both sides there will be a birth of twins and if in the middle of the abdomen the issue will be a hermaphrodite.

25. A person shall join a woman in sexual love when the benefic planets occupy the angles or the triangular signs ; when they occuy the rising sign and the sign occupied by the Moon ; when malefic planets occupy the third, sixth and eleventh houses ; and in male planetary yogas.[1]

26. At the time of union a person shall not wound a

woman with his nails and teeth ; there shall be no union beyond the first sixteen days from the day of appearance of the menses or in any of the first three days.

Notes.—Add to these restrictions the number of malefic planetary yogas described in chapter IV of Bṛhat Jātaka.

Again, according to the Śāstras a person shall cease cohabit with a woman after the birth of a son—the object of marriage being thereby secured.

Again, the Smṛtis refer to a number of days in which cohabitation is prohibited, such as the new-moon and full-moon days, the eleventh lunar day and the like. The Sages of old appear to have strictly followed all these rules. If the whole world could be equally firm minded, there would probably be no occasion for so many curious, eloborate and sometimes even frightful solutions of the problem to check the growth of population. You allow the evil to grow and then seek a remedy ; but the Śāstras aim at nipping the evil in the bud. Of course when the demand exceeds supply and a disturbance of the social equilibrium occurs, nature restores it by applying her own remedy—by carrying away, every now and then, thousands by wars, by the plague and the like epidemics.

On the first appearance of the menses : The four asterisms from Kṛttika are known as inner asterisms and the four from Punarvasu are known as the outer asterisms. Again the four from Magha are known as inner asterisms, and the four from Chitra are known as outer asterisms, and so on, till we come to the end of the lunar Zodiac. For a list of the 23 asterisms *vide* page 86, Part I. If the first appearance of the menses occur when the Moon passes through one of the inner asterisms, there will be prosperity, increase of family and the like. If the first appearance of the menses occur when the Moon passes through one of the outer asterisms, there will be misery, widowhood, death of sons, sorrow and the like.

Again, divide the 27 asterisms (omitting Abhijit) into seven groups of 3, 3, 3, 3, 5, 7 and 3 asterisms beginning from U. Ashadha. If the first appearance of the menses occur in any of these, the effects will respectively be gain of wealth, gain of sons, servitude, sweet speech, ruin, attachment to husband and widowhood.

Again, if the first appearance occur when the rising sign is Aries, the woman will become unchaste ; when it is Taurus, she will annoy others ; if Gemini, she will become rich and happy ; if Cancer, she will cohabit with an out-caste ; if Leo, she will get a son ; if Virgo, she will become rich ; if Libra, she will become deformed ; if Scorpio, she will become unchaste. If the first half of Sagittari, she will become wicked ; if the second half, she will be chaste ; if Capricorn, she will become shameless ; if Acquar ius, she will become poor and barren ; and if Pisces, she will become beautiful.

Also, if the first appearance of the menses occur on a Sunday, the woman will be afflicted with diseases ; if on a Monday, she will become chaste ; if Tuesday, she will suffer grief ; if Wednesday, she will get sons ; if Thursday, she will live in plenty ; if Friday, she will prosper well ; and if on a Saturday, she will meet with early death.

Also, if the first appearance of the menses occur in the forenoon, the woman will be happy ; if in the afternoon, she will suffer miseries ; if at noon, she will be neither happy nor miserable.

Again, if the first appearance of the menses occur within 12 Ghatikas at night, the woman will be happy. To prevent the death of the child in the womb Sounaka has prescribed the following ceremony : Perform Ajya Homa (pouring ghee into the fire) reciting the *mantra* commencing.

"Brahmanag samvidanah" rub over the woman a portion of the ghee remaining in the vessel and cause her to bathe and then drink the remaining ghee.

To prevent the death of children soon after birth, Sounaka has prescribed an elaborate ceremony. The reader is referred to Sounka's Santi Kalpa.

REFERENCE

1. Vide Stanzas 11 and 12 of Chapter IV of the Bṛhat Jātaka.

CHAPTER 79

On Cots and Seats

1. As Cots and Seats are useful to all people at all times and especially so to Kings, I begin to treat of them here.

2. The wood of the following trees is suited for the construction of Cots and Seats—Asana,[1] Spandana,[2] Candana, Haridra, Suradāru,[3] Tindukī, Śāla (palm), Kāśmari,[4] Añjana, Padmaka, Śāka, and Śiṁśapā.

3. The trees described below shall be rejected: tree that have fallen owing to an attack of lightning, flood, winds or elephant, those containing bee-hives or in which birds dwell, those that grow in places of worship, in cremation grounds or in roads, those whose barks have dried up or which are covered with twining creepers.

4. Trees which are covered with thorns or which grow at the junction of great rivers or in temples or which when cut fall on the western or southern side shall also be rejected.

5. If Cots and Seats be made of such trees, the family will suffer miseries and there will be diseases, fear, loss, quarrels, and the like.

6. If there be the wood of any trees already cut down available for the purpose it shall first be examined: if a child gets on it, a person will get cows and children by its use.

7. If white flowers, a rutting elephant, curdled milk, colored rice, water pots, gems and the like benefic objects be observed at the time, there will be prosperity.

8. The length of 8 grains of barley rice placed close and parallel to one another, is known as the Carpenter's inch; the length of the king's cot shall be 100 such inches.

9. The Cots of the first Prince, the Minister, the Commander in Chief and the Priest shall respectively be 90, 84, 78 and 72 inches long.

10. The breadth of the Cot shall be $\frac{7}{18}$ths of the length, according to Viśvakarma; and the height of the legs shall be a third of the length.

11. If the Cots be wholly made of the wood of Śrīparṇi, or Tinduka there will be acquisition of wealth, and if made of Asana, there will be health.

12. If the Cot be wholly made of the wood of Śiṁśapā, there will be prosperity in various ways; if of Sandal, a person will be freed from troubles from his enemies, and will, live long, leading a life of virtue and renown.

13. If the Cot be wholly made of the wood of Padmaka, there will be long life, prosperity, wealth and skill in the use of weapons; if of the wood of Saka or Sala there will be happiness.

14. A king who uses a Cot made wholly of Sandal wood and covered with gold set with various gems will be honored even by Devas.

15. If the wood of the Tinduki, Śiṁśapā, Śrīparṇi, Devadaru or Asana be coupled with other wood it will not conduce to prosperity.

16. The wood of Śāka and Śāla may be used either separately or jointly. The same remark applies to the wood of Haridra and Kadamba.

17. A Cot made wholly of the wood of Spandana will not conduce to prosperity; one made wholly of the wood of Amba will bring on death and one made of the wood of Asana coupled with other wood will bring on numerous miseries.

18. If the legs be made of the wood of Spandana, Amba or Candana, they will conduce to prosperity. Cots and seats made wholly of the wood of fruit trees will also conduce to prosperity.

19. Cots made of wood and set with ivory are excellent; various ornamental works shall be done in ivory.

20. In cutting ivory a length equal to double the circumference at the root of the tusks shall be left; if the elephant be one dwelling on water banks a larger portion shall be left and if it be one dwelling in the mountains a smaller portion may be left.

21. If, in the cut, there be lines of the shape of the cross or a dish, an umbrella, a flag-staff, or a Cāmara there will

respectively be health, success, wealth, prosperity and comfort.

22. If the lines be of the shape of a weapon there will be success; if quadrangular in shape the king will recover a lost country. And if of the shape of a clod, he will recover a country obtained and lost.

23. If the lines be of the shape of a woman there will be loss of wealth; if of the shape of a golden pitcher, the king will get sons; if of shape of a pot, he will get hidden treasure, and if of the shape of a club his intended journey will be stopped.

24. If the lines be of the shape of a bloodsucker, a monkey, or a snake there will be dearth and disease, and the king will fall into the bands of his enemies, and if the lines be of the shape of a vulture, an owl, a crow, a hawk, the king's subjects will suffer from plague.

25. If the lines be of the shape of a rope or a headless trunk the king will die or his subjects will suffer miseries respectively; if blood comes out, or if the cut be black ar red-black or of disagreeable appearance or of bad smell there will be misery.

26. If the cut be white, even, glossy and of good smell there will be prosperity. The effects ascribed to the cutting of ivory apply also to the cutting of wood for cots and the like.

27. In joining the beams of a bed-stead the ends shall be made to come round from left to right;[5] if the reverse be the case or if the ends do not point to all the four quarters there will be an attack of evil spirits.

28. If a single leg should have its end pointing to the ground; the person will suffer injuries to his leg; if two legs should be so, he will suffer from indigestion; and if three or four, he will suffer from grief or be killed or imprisoned.

29. If the knot at the top of the leg be found with a hole or of a bad color there will be suffering from disease, and if there be a knot at the centre of the leg there will be suffering from belly-ache.

30. If there be a knot just below the centre the master will suffer injuries to his shanks; if the knot be a little lower down he will suffer loss of wealth.

31. If there be a knot at the foot of the leg hoofed animals will suffer; if there be three knots in the frames there will be much suffering.

32. The holes in the four frames of a bedstead are of 6 sorts, known as Niṣkuṭa, Kolākṣa, Sūkaranayana, Vatsanābha, Kālaka, and Dhundhuka.

33. A hole which is large within and with a small mouth thus resembling a pot is known as Niṣkuṭa; a black hole of the size of a grain of black gram is known as kolakṣa.

34. An irregular hole which is of one of the main colors and whose length is that of a finger joint and a half is known as Sukaranayana and one which turns from right to left, which is split and of the length of a finger joint is known as Vatsanabha.

35. A black hole is known as kalaka and one which is split is known as Dhundhuka. Generally if the holes be of the color of the wood, they do not point to evil.

36. A Niṣkuṭa hole will bring loss of wealth, a Kolakṣa hole will bring the ruin of the family; a Sukara hole will bring fear and injury from weapons, and a Vatsanabha hole will bring suffering from disease.

37. Kalaka and Dhundhunka holes as well as a hole caused by worms will not conduce to prosperity; if the holes be in knotty parts, the wood is fit for no purpose.

38. If the Cot, Seat, and the like be made of one wood of fruit trees, there will be gain of wealth; if of two sorts of wood there will be great gain of wealth, if of three, sons will increase, and if of four, the person will become wealthy and famous.

39. If the Cot be made of five different sorts of wood of fruit trees the person sleeping on it will meet with death; and if it be made of six, seven or eight different sorts of wood, his, family will suffer ruin.

REFERENCES

1. Asana, the tree Terminalia *Tomentosa.*
2. Spandana : the tree Dalbergia Ougeinensis.

3. Suradāru : the Devadāru; pine; Pinus Deodera.
4. Kāśmari : the tree Gmelina Arborea. The other terms have already been explained.
5. The end of the northern frame shall point to the east, that of the eastern one shall point to the south and so on.

CHAPTER 80

On Diamonds

1. A good gem brings prosperity to the king and a bad one brings misery. It is therefore necessary to examine the properties of gems with the help of persons learned in the science; for a person's fortune depends upon the gems he possesses.

2. Elephants, horses and women possessed of excellent virtues are also known as gems; but diamonds and the like gems to be treated of in this Chapter are stones and the like possessed of many excellent qualities.

3. According to some, gems are the bones of Balāsura and according to others they are the bones of the sage Dadhichi. In the opinion of some, gems are various sorts of stones which naturally exist in the earth.

4. Twenty-two different sorts of gems are mentioned: These are the diamonds, sapphire, emerald, karketana, ruby, Blood Stone, vydurya, pulaka, vimalaka rājamaṇī crystal or quartz, moon-stone.

5. Saugandhika, gomedaka, conch-shell, mahānīla, topaz, brahma-maṇī, jyotirasa, opal, pearls and corals.

6. Diamonds found on the banks of the river Veṇā are white; those found in the province of Kosala are somewhat yellow; diamonds found in Surat are somewhat of the color of copper and those of Supa are black.

7. The Himālayan diamonds are somewhat of the color of copper and those found in the Mataṅga mountains are somewhat yellow. Ganjam diamonds are also yellow. Bengal and Bihar diamonds are green.

8. A diamond which is white and has six sides is sacred to Indra; one that is black and of the shape of the mouth of

the serpent is sacred to Yama; one that is green and of various shapes is sacred to Viṣṇu.

9. A diamond which is of the shape of a female's genital organ and of the color of the flower of Karṇikāra (Pterospermum Acerifolium) is sacred to Varuṇa; one that is of the shape of the fruit of Śṛṅgāṭaka (Trapa Bispinosa) and of the color of the eyes of the tiger is sacred to Agni.

10. A diamond which is of the shape of a grain of barley and of the color of the flower of the Aśoka is sacred to Vāyu[1]. Diamonds are generally found in rivers, lakes, deep or marshy places.

11. The Kṣatriyas shall wear red or yellow diamonds; the Brāhmaṇas shall wear white diamonds; the Vaiśyas shall wear diamonds which are slighty yellow and the Śūdras shall wear those which are black.

12 & 13. Eight mustard seeds (white) make a Tanḍula. The price of a diamond weighing 20 Tanḍulas is 200,000 Kārṣāpaṇas [2]; and the price of diamonds weighing two tanḍulas less and less are respectively three fourths two-thirds, one-half, one-third, one-fifth, one-sixteenth, one twenty-fifth, one-hundredth and one-thousandth parts of 200,000 Kārṣāpaṇas.

Notes : The following table shows the price of diamonds :—

Weight in Tanḍulas	Price in Kāraṣāpaṇas	Weight in Tanḍulas	Price in Kāraṣāpaṇas
20	200,000	10	40,000
18	150,000	8	12,500
16	133,333	6	8,000
14	100,000	4	2,000
12	66,666	2	200

For intermediate weight, the price shall be determined by proportion.

14. A superior diamond is one which cannot be broken with any other substance, which is light and dazzling, which is of the color of lightning, fire or rainbow and which floats in water. It always brings prosperity.

15. The faults of the diamond are, lines of the shape of the foot of the crow, a fly or a hare or being mixed with other minerals, or covered with holes like gravel, being with split

ends, appearing soiled or with dark spots and being of unsteady light or split or broken. Such diamonds are not fit for use.

16. Diamonds with bubbles or split ends or flat and king shall be priced one-eighth less than the price assigned.

17. Persons learned in the science say that a woman desirous of sons shall wear diamonds. According to some diamonds are not to be worn at all; diamonds of the shape of the fruit of Śṛṅgāṭa, of the pulse, of the coriander seed, and of the hip-bone shall be worn by women desirous of sons.

18. A person wearing bad diamonds, will lose his people, wealth and life. Good diamonds worn by kings will free them from the attacks of lightning, poison, and enemies and will bring great prosperity.

REFERENCES

1. The *mantras* sacred to particular devas shall first be pronounced and the diamonds shall then be worn.
2. A Kārṣāpaṇa is 20 Rs. as it obtains among merchants. It is a gold coin whose weight is 16 Mashas equal to one-fourth pala.

CHAPTER 81

On Pearls

1. Pearls are produced in elephants, serpents, oyster-shells, fish, clouds, bamboos, whales, and boars. Of these, pearls of the oyster-fish are produced in abundance and are beautiful.

2. Ceylon, the island of Paraloka, Surat, the Tāmraparṇī river, Persia, the isle of Kubera, the country of Pāṇḍyavāṭa and the Himālayas, are places in which pearls are largely found.

3. The pearls of Ceylon are of various shapes, glossy, of the color of the swan and large. The pearls found in the mouths of the Tāmraparṇī are white or slightly copper colored and pure.

4. The pearls of the isle of Paraloka are black, white or yellow, mixed with minerals and rough; the pearls of Surat are neither very large nor very small and of the color of butter.

5. Persian pearls are bright, white, heavy, and of excellent qualities. The Himalayan pearls are light, brittle, of the color of curdled milk, large, and of various shapes.

6. The pearls of the isle of Kubera are rough, black, white, light, large and bright; and those of Pāṇḍya Vaṭaka are of the color of the fruit of the margosa, resembling a pulse or the coriander seed.

7. Pearls which are blue are sacred to Viṣṇu and those which are white like the Moon are sacred to Indra; those which are yellow are sacred to Varuṇa and those which are black are sacred to Yama.

8. Pearls which are red like the ripe fruits of the pomegranate or the cocoon of the silk worm or the gunja seeds (Abrus Precatorius) are sacred to Vāyu and those which are of the color of the flame of fire or of the lotus flower are sacred to Agni.

9. The price of a superior pearl weighing four Mashas[1] is 5,300 kārṣāpaṇas.

10. The prices of pearls weighing half a masha less and less are respectively 3200, 2000, 1200, 800, and 353 kārṣāpaṇas.

11. The price of a single pearl which is a masha in weight is 135 Kārṣāpaṇas and the price of a pearl which is 4 gunjas in weight is 90 kārṣāpaṇas, and that of one which is 3½ gunjas in weight is 70 kārṣāpaṇas.

12. The price of a pearl which is 3 gunjas in weight is 50 kārṣāpaṇas, and the price of a pearl which is 2½ gunjas in weight is 35 kārṣāpaṇas.

13. One-tenth of a pala is known as a Dharaṇa. The price of a collection or string of 13 good pearls weighing a Dharaṇa is 325 kārṣāpaṇas.

14. The price of a string of 16 pearls weighing a Dharaṇa is 200 kārṣāpaṇas; of 20 pearls of the same weight is 170 kārṣāpaṇas; of 25 pearls of the same weight is 130 kārṣapaṇas.

15. The price of a string of 30 superior pearls weighing a Dharaṇa is 70 kārsāpaṇas. One of 40 pearls of the same weight is 50 karṣāpaṇas and one of 55 pearls of the same weight is 40 kārṣāpaṇas.

16. The price of a string of 80 pearls weighing a Dharaṇa is 30 kārṣāpaṇas; that of a string of 100 pearls of the same weight is 25 kārṣāpaṇas; of 200 pearls of the same weight is 12 kārṣāpaṇas; of 300 pearls, 6 kārṣāpaṇas; of 400, 5 kārṣāpaṇas, and of 500, 3 kārṣāpaṇas.

17. A collection or string of 13 pearls weighing a Dharaṇa is known as Pikkā; one of 16 pearls of the same weight is known as Pikkā; one of 16 pearls of the same weight is known as Piccā; one of 20 pearls is known as Ardhā; one of 25 is known as Arghā, one of 30 as Ravaka; one of 40 as Sikta; one of 55 as Nigra; one of from 80 to 500 pearls is known as Cūrṇa.

Notes : According to Buddha Bhaṭa the price of a superior pearl weighing 5 mashas is double the price of one weighing 4 mashas, and the price of a pearl weighing 6 mashas is double the price of one of 5 mashas, and so on, doubling the price for each additional weight of a masha.

18. Thus have I described the price of various collections of superior pearls weighing a Dharaṇa. The prices of collections of pearls of intermediate numbers shall be ascertained by proportion. If the pearls be not of superior quality, the price shall be reduced.

19. If these superior pearls be black or white or slightly rough the price shall be reduced by a third; if they be only very rough the price shall be reduced by a sixth; and if yellow by one-half.

20. An elephant of the Iravata family born when the Moon passes through the asterism of Puṣya or Śrāvaṇa, on a Sunday or Monday in the Uttarāyaṇa (*i.e.* when the Sun passes from sign Capricorn to sign Cancer) and at the solar or lunar eclipse is known as Bhadra.

21. Pearls which are bright, of various shapes and large are produced in large quantities in the tusks, testicles and crests of the Bhadra elephant.

22. These pearls cannot be valued and cannot be bored through. They are exceedingly bright and will bring to the wearer success, health and sons, and make him pure. They are fit to be worn by kings.

23. Pearls of superior qualities and of the color of the moon are produced at the roots of the hog's teeth and pearls of good qualities and which are large, pure, and of the shape of the eye of the fish are found in whales.

24. Pearls of the shape of the hail and which fall from the seventh region of the atmosphere and resembling the lightning are produced in clouds; they are carried away by the Devas.

25. Pearls are also produced in the heads of serpents of the family of Takṣaka and Vāsuki; they are black and glossy.

26. When the rain-fall occurs out of season, pearls which fall from the sky into vessels of silver placed on pure spots are known as Nāga pearls.

Notes—According to Buddha Bhaṭa rain may be produced in the dry season as follows : the priest shall, after bathing, and in an auspicious hour get to the tops of storied buildings whose floor reflects the sky above and shall recite aloud mantras accompanied by the music of the Dundubhi. Heavy rain will fall.

27. The Nāga pearls worn by kings bring to them success, renown, the ruin of the enemy and freedom from misery.

28. Pearls produced in bamboos are of the color of camphor or crystal, and are flat and rough. Those produced in conch-shell are of the color of the Moon and round, bright and beautiful.

29. Pearls produced in conch-shells, whales, bamboos, elephants, hogs, serpents and clouds are not to be bored through. As they are of very superior qualities, the Śāstras have not stated their value.

30. All these are pearls of superior qualities, and they make the wearer wise, wealthy, happy and renowned, free him from diseases and grief and secure for kings the object of their desire.

31. A collection of pearls consisting of 1,008 strings, each 4 cubits long is known as Indra Chhanda. This must be used as ornaments for the Devas only. A collection of pearls consisting of 504 strings each 2 cubits long is known as Vijaya Chhanda.

32. A collection of pearls consisting of 108 strings each 2 cubits long is known as a Hāra; one of 81 strings of the same length is known as Deva Chhanda; one of 64 strings is known as Ardha-hāra; and one of 54 is known as Raśmi Kalapa.

33. A collection of pearls consisting of 32 strings each 2 cubits long is known as Guccha; one of 20 strings is known as Ardha-Guccha; one of 16 as Manavaka; and one of 12 as Ardhamanavaka.

34. A collection of pearls consisting of 8 strings each two cubits long is known as Mandāra, and one of 5 strings is known as Hāraphalaka and a necklace, a cubit in length, consisting of a string of 27 pearls is known as a Nakṣatra Māla.

35. A Nakṣtra Māla with gems or gold beads between the pearls is known as Maṇisopāna. A Maṇisopāna with a central gem is known as Chatakara.

36. A necklace, a cubit in length and consisting of an indefinite number of pearls is known as Ekāvalī. An Ekāvalī with a central gem is known as Yaṣṭi among Jewel-merchants.

REFERENCE

1. A masha is equal to 5 gunja seeds.

CHAPTER 82

On Rubies

1. Rubies are formed from Saugandhika, from Kuruvinda, and from crystals. The Saugandhika rubies are of the color of the bee, collyrium, clouds or the fruit of the rose-apple, and are glossy.

2. The Kuruvinda rubies are of the color of the mixture of black and white, somewhat bright and mixed with minerals, and the crystalline rubies are bright, pure and of, different colors.

3. Rubies of superior quality are bright, glossy, pure, red, and rendering red objects around, dazzling, heavy, well-shaped and of good water.

4. Gems that are dim, slightly bright, with lines, mixed with minerals or with gravel, or broken are not good ones. These are the faults of gems.

5. A gem of the color of the bee, the neck of the peacock or the tip of flame, if found in the head of a serpent has no value.

6. A king who wears such a gem will never suffer from the attacks of poison and disease. There will be rainfall in his country every day in the year and the king's enemies will meet with ruin—all this through the virtues of the gem.

7. The price of a ruby weighing a pala is 26,000 kārṣāpaṇas, and the price of a ruby weighing three karshas[1] [$\frac{3}{4}$ of a pala] is 20,000 kārṣāpaṇas.

8. If the weight be two karshas ($\frac{1}{2}$ a pala) the price is 12,000 k. panas; if the weight be a karṣa, the price is 6,000 k. panas, and if the weight be 8 Mashas, the price is 2,000 k. panas.

9. If the weight be 4 Mashas, the price is 1,000 k. panas, and if it be 2 Mashas, the price is 500 k. panas. For rubies of

intermediate weight, the price shall be ascertained by proportion. The price of rubies which fall a little short of being superior rubies is as follows.

10. If the fault be a defect in color, the price shall be reduced to one-half; if the gem be not bright and glossy, the price shall be reduced to one-eighth, and if the gem possess very few good qualities but many faults, the price shall be reduced to one-twentieth.

11. If the gem be wholly red black and full of wounds and if the good qualities be very few, the price shall be reduced to a two-hundredth part. Thus has been described the valuation of rubies by the ancient writers.

REFERENCE

1. 16 Mashas = 1 karsha.
   4 Karshas = 1 pala.

CHAPTER 83

On Emeralds

Emeralds of the color of the parrot, the leaves of the bamboo, the bark of the plantain and the flower of Śirīṣa (Acacia Śirīṣa) and of good quality will conduce to prosperity if they are worn by men on occasions of worship of the Devas and the Pitṛs.

Notes : Emeralds are to be valued in the same way as rubies. According to Budhabhata, the five chief gems are diamonds, pearls, rubies, emeralds and sapphires. Sapphires must be examined in the same way as rubies. Mahānīla is a gem which when put into milk turns it blue. The price of a ruby weighing a Māṣa is the price of a sapphire weighing a Swarna.[1]

Vaidurya (the cat's-eye gem) is of the color of the tail of the peacock, the leaves of the bamboo or the wing of the king-fisher. It is to be valued in the same way as sapphires.

Kurketana gems are bright, glossy, pure, yellow and heavy. The usual test of its superiority is to cover the stone with gold leaf and put it in fire. The gem will become black but will not lose its gloss. The whole Earth might be given for this gem.

Crystal gems are white like the stem of the lotus or the conch-shell.

Corals are glossy, pure and red. The wearer will become wealthy and will be freed from poison.

Rudhiraksha gems are green in the middle, white all round, as bright as sapphire, of the shape of the fruit of the Pilu tree (Carea Arborea). It will make the wearer wealthy and well-served. For further particulars regarding gems, the reader is referred to the works of Buddhabhaṭa.

REFERENCE

1. Swarna = 1 Karsha = 16 Mashas = 80 Raktikas = about 175 grains Troy.

CHAPTER 84

On Lamps

1. A lamp whose flame turns from right to left, whose light is dim and small, and emits sparks and which dies out even when the oil and the wick are pure indicates evil. A lamp whose flame is quivering, spreading and attended with noise and which dies out in the absence of the fly or the wind also indicates evil.

2. If the flame be close and united, long, still, bright, without noise, beautiful, turning from left to right and of the color of gold, it indicates approaching prosperity. In other respects all that has been said in the case of fire applies here also.

CHAPTER 85

On Tooth-Brush

1. Tooth-brush may be made of the twigs of spreading creepers, creepers, shrubs and trees. A description of all their effects will be long and elaborate. We shall therefore confine ourself to twigs which are to be chewed to secure certain special ends.

2. Twigs of unknown trees shall be rejected, and twigs with leaves, those of an even number of joints, those which are split or dry at the ends and those with no bark ought not to be chewed.

3. The twigs of Vikaṅkata[1], Śriphala[2], and Kāśmarī[3], if chewed, will give a person Brahminical splendour. The twigs of Kṣema will secure to a person a good wife. The twigs of the banyan will increase a person's wealth and stock of grain. The Arka twig will increase the splendour of his appearance. The Madhuka twig will give him a son. The Kakubha will add to his joy.

4. The twigs of Śirīṣa and Karañja if used as tooth-brush will make a person wealthy and prosperous. Those of Plakṣa will bring him money. Those of Aśvattha will make him respected by the people and renowned among his own castemen.

5. The twig of the Badarī if chewed as a tooth-brush will make a person healthy; that of the Bṛhatī[4] will give him a long life; that of the Khadira and Bilva will increase his wealth; that of the Atimukta and Kadamba will bring him the object of his desire.

6. The twig of the Nīmba if chewed as a tooth-brush will bring wealth to a person; that of the Karavīra will bring him good meals; that of the Bhāṇḍīra[5] will bring him much food; that of the Śamī, Arjuna and Śyāmā will destroy his enemies.

7. The twig of Aśvakarṇa, Bhadrataru[6] and Chataru-

shaka if chewed as a tooth-brush will bring a man dignity ; those of Priyangu,[7] Apamārga, Jambu and Daḍima will make a person beloved of all people.

8. Facing the north or the east, a person shall chew the tooth-brush and cleanse his teeth, for a year, firmly placing before his mind his object of desire. He shall, after its use, wash the tooth-brush with water and throw it in a pure spot.

9. If the tooth-brush when thrown away after its use be seen to stick to the ground with one end while the other end points to him and in a Santa (benefic) quarter (vide stanza 12, next Chap.) prosperity is indicated ; if it should stick for a time and then fall, the person will get good meals and if it fall otherwise the person will suffer miseries.

REFERENCES

1. Vikaṅkata : Flacourtia Sapida.
2. Śriphala : the Bilwa tree.
3. Kāśmarī : the plant Gmelina Arborea.
4. Bṛhat : the Egg plant. The other trees occurring in this Chapter have already been explained. *Vide* Glossary of Botanical terms—pages 274 to 280 Part II.
5. Bhāṇḍira : Rubia Munjistta.
6. Bhadrataru : the plant Trapa Bispinosa.
7. Apamārga : the plant Achyranthes Aspera.

CHAPTER 86

Omens through Birds and Beasts

Section I

1. Ṛṣabha has written a treatise on omens embodying the views of the Devas Śukra, Indra, Bṛhaspati, Kapiṣṭhala and Garuḍa and of the Ṛṣis Bhāguri, Devala and others.

2. Śridevavardhana, the Maharaja of Avanti (Ujjain) has written a treatise on omens embodying the views of Bhāradvāja.

3. There are also treatises on omens by the seven Ṛṣis ; numerous treatises are also found on the subject written in ancient and modern languages. Then there are the treatises of Garga and others who have written works on Saṁhita. There are also treatises written by writers who have written works on Yātrā.

4. Having examined all the above treatises I proceed to write clearly this brief treatise on omens for the enlightenment of my pupils.

5. Omens indicate to travellers the good or evil effects of their *karma* (deeds) in a former birth.

6. Omens are creatures dwelling in villages and forests, in waters, in land, in the sky, moving by day or by night or by both day and night. Their sex shall be ascertained by their sound, gait, look and speech.

7. It is often difficult to ascertain the sex of the creature and the Ṛṣis have laid down general rules for the purpose in the following two stanzas.

8. The male creatures are generally those possessing large, high and broad shoulders, large neck, fine breast, short but deep sound and uniform gait.

9. The female creatures are those possessing a small neck, head and breast ; also small face, legs and strength ; and also, a shrill but soft sound. Other creatures belong to neither sex.

10. In the present treatise on omens I shall confine myself

to matters relating to travels. What are domestic animals and what wild shall be ascertained from a general knowledge of creatures.

11. The effects of omens occurring in roads affect the traveller and those of omens occurring in armies affect the king. Omens occurring in towns affect the king or the village deity, and omens occurring before a gathering of men affect the leader; if there be no leader and if the persons be all of equal rank those of superior caste, education or age will be affected by the omens.

12. Dividing the circle of horizon into eight equal quarters beginning from the east and going round, corresponding to the eight Yamas (a yama is 3 hours) from sunrise to sunrise, the quarter which corresponds to a particular yama of the Sun in his daily motion is known as Dīpta (malefic). The quarter next before it just quitted by the Sun is known as Angari and the quarter next after Dīpta is known as Dhumīnī. The other five quarters are known as Śānta (benefic). The first three, viz., the Angari, the Dīpta and Dhumīnī quarters relate to bad events past, present and future respectively according as the omen occurs in such quarters.[1]

13. Omens occurring in the three 5th (opposite) quarters from the Dīpta quarters relate to good events past, present and future. If the omen occur in one of the remaining two quarters, the effects are good or bad according as the place more approaches the Śānta or the Dīpta quarter.

14. Effects of omens occurring in low places will be felt soon ; those of omens occurring in high places will be felt late. The increase or the decrease will follow the increasing or the decreasing character of the place occupied by the omen.

15. If the hour, the lunar day, the Nakṣatra, the wind and the sun be malefic, the omen is known as Deva Dīpta (*a*) and the effects will be of an increasingly evil character. If the gait, place, sound and motion of the omen as well as the memory (of the Astrologer) be bad, the omen is known as Kriya Dīpta (*b*) and the effects will also be of an increasingly evil character.

Notes

(*a*) That is if, at the time of occurrence of an omen, the

hour be that of a malefic planet, the lunar day be a malefic one, the Moon pass through a malefic asterism, the wind blow hard and the Sun occupy a malefic quarter.

(*b*) That is, if at the time, the gait of the animal or bird be bad or directed towards bad places, if the place occupied by the omen be bad, if the person's memory fail, if the sound of the animal or bird be hoarse and if it should strike its legs or wings or scratch its face and do the like.

16. If the character of the omen be the opposite of what has been described above, the omen is known as Deva Śānta or Kriya Śānta respectively. Creatures subsisting on leaves and fruits are known as Saumya (benefic) ; and those subsisting on flesh and excrement are known us Raudra (malefic) ; and creatures subsisting on rice and other grains are known as Saṅkīrṇa (mixed).

17. Creatures found in storied houses, temples, palaces of kings, places of marriage and the like, in beautiful spots and on trees where there may be honey, juice, milk, fruits or flowers indicate good luck.

18. If day-creatures be seen to occupy the tops of hills by day, the effect will be strong ; if night creatures be seen to occupy waters by night the effects will be strong. The effects will be of increasing strength according as the creature is a hermaphrodite, a female or a male.

19. Creatures remarkable for speed, genius, strength, place occupied, merriment, nobleness of mind or good sound are strong when in their own places ; the same rule applies to useful animals. If the character of the creatures be otherwise or if they be injurious and if they do not occupy their own places, they are weak.

20. The cock, the elephant, the parili, the peacock, the vanjula, the musk-rat, the duck and the kutapoori are strong in the east.

21. The jackal, the owl, the haritala pigeon, the crow, the ruddy goose, the bear, icheumon, the dove, as well as moans, cries and disagreeable sounds are strong in the south.

22. The ram, the swan, the osprey, the francoline partridge, the cat; as well as festivities, music and laughter are strong in the west.

23. The crane, the deer, the rat, the antelope, the horse, the cuckoo, the blue jay and the hedgehog as well as the sound of sweet-bells and of the conch-shell are strong in the north.

24. Wild creatures shall not be treated as domestic if they are found in towns, and domestic creatures shall not be treated as wild if they are found in woods. Similarly, day creatures shall not be confounded with night creatures and *vice versa*.

25. Creatures afflicted with the Dvandva (copulation) disease, frightened animals and those that go about seeking for fight or prey as well as creatures separated by a river and rutting animals shall not be treated as omens.

26. The fox, the goat, the ass, the deer, the camel, the antelope and the hare shall not be treated as omens in the Śiṣira season (from middle of January to middle of March). The crow and the cuckoo shall not be treated as omens in the Vasanta season (from middle of March to that of May).

27. The pig, the dog, the wolf and the like shall not be treated as omens in the month of Bhādrapada (middle of August to middle of September) nor shall the Abjada, the cow and the curlew be treated as omens in the Sarat season (middle of September to the middle of November); nor the elephant and the Cātaka (Cuculus Melanoleucus) be treated as omens in the month of Śrāvaṇa (July—August).

28. The tiger, the bear, the monkey, the leopard, the buffalo, and the serpent, as well as the young of animals other than human shall not be treated as omens in the Hemanta season (from middle of November to middle of January).

29. The space between the eastern and the south-eastern points of the horizon shall be divided into 4 equal parts by three points. These points are known respectively as those of Kośādhyakṣa, Anālajivi and Tapoyukta.

30. The space between the south-eastern and southern points of the horizon shall be divided similarly by three points known respectively as those of Śilpi, Bhikṣu and Vivastrā Stri and the three points between the southern and the south-western points of the horizon are known as those of Mataṅga, Gopa and Dharmāsamasrayā.

31. The space between the south-western and western points shall be similarly divided by three points known as those

of Stri, Suti and Taskarā; and the three points between the western and the north-western points of the horizon are known as those of Śaunḍika, Śākuni and Hiṁsra.

32. The space between the north-western and northern points of the horizon shall be similarly divided by three points known as those of Viṣaghātaka, Gosvāmi and Kuhakagna; and the three points between the northern and north-eastern points of the horizon are known as those of Dhanavān, Ikṣanaka and Mālākāra.

33. The space between the north-eastern and eastern points of the horizon shall be divided equally by three points known as those of Vaiṣanava, Caraka and Vājirakṣaka. These twenty-four points together with the eight points of the compass give us thirty-two quarters in all.

34. The eight points of the compass beginning from the east and going round are known as those of the king (E), the first prince (S. E.), the commander of armies (S), the messenger (S.W.), the headman (W.), a spy (N.W.), a brahmin (N.), and an elephant driver (N.E.)

Again, the four points of the compass are known as those of the Kṣtriyas (E.), the Vaiśyas (S.), the Śūdras (W.) and the Brāhmaṇas (N.)

35. The omen in a particular quarter indicates that the person who observes it whether he be going or seated will soon meet with the person presiding over such quarter.

36. If the sound of the creature be broken, timid, low, caused by pain, harsh, feeble or dull, it indicates evil. The natural sound of a joyous animal indicates prosperity.

37. The jackal, the cuckoo, the Rala, the Chuchu, the icheumon, the lizard, the sow, the Kokila, and the male of animals and birds in general indicate good luck when on the left side.

38. The vulture, the dog, the monkey, the Śrīkarṇa, the musk-rat, the peacock, the Śrīkaṇṭha, the Pippīka, the Ruru, the hawk and the females of animals and birds indicate good luck when on the right side.

39. Hissing sound, clapping of hands, auspicious music, and the sound of the conch-shell indicate good luck when on

the left side. Other auspicious sounds indicate good luck when on the right side.

40. The Madhyama, Ṣḍja and Gandhāra notes indicate good luck; the Ṣḍja, Madhyama. Gāndhāra and Ṛṣbha notes also indicate good luck.

Notes.—The Gāndhāra note is found only in Deva Loka. The niṣāda, Panchama and dhaivata notes indicate evil.

41. If the sound of the sky-lark, the ram, the peacock, the mungoose and the king-fisher be heard or if the names of these creatures be heard mentioned or if the blood-sucker be seen in front of a person there will be misery.

42. If the names of the leech, the snake, the hare, the hog or the iguana be heard mentioned prosperity is indicated; but the sound and the appearance of these creatures indicate evil. On the other hand, if the names of the monkey and the bear be heard mentioned, evil is indicated, while both the sound and the appearance of the creatures indicate prosperity.

43. If an odd number of animals, birds and the mungoose be seen to move from left to right prosperity is indicated and according to Bhṛgu the blue jay and the mungoose indicate good luck if found to move from right to left in the afternoon.

44. Chikkra, Kūṭapūrī and Pirilī indicate good luck if found to move from left to right by day, and the hog, the iguana and the snake indicate good luck if found to pass on the right side.

45. The horse and articles of white color indicate good luck when in the east; corpse and flesh indicate good luck when in the south; Virgins and curdled milk indicate good luck when in the west; and the cow, the Sādhus and the Brāhmaṇas indicate good luck when seen in the north.

46. Persons living by the use of the net and by dogs indicate evil when seen in the east. Those who live by weapons and by acts of torture indicate evil when seen in the south. Liquor and hermaphrodites indicate evil when seen in the west. And wicked men, seats and ploughs indicate evil when seen in the north.

47. On auspicious occasions and on occasions of the meeting of persons, of battle, of return journey and of search after articles lost, the omens that pass in the reverse order to

that mentioned for Yātrā (journey) generally indicate good luck. We shall however state the exceptions, and noteworthy points.

48. On the several occasions mentioned above, omens connected with the deer, the Ruru and the monkey appearing by day shall be treated as in Yātrā and omens connected with the blue jay, the Vañjula and the dog appearing at the beginning of day shall also be similarly treated.

49. Omens connected with the Naptṛka, the owl and the icheumon appearing at the end of night shall be treated in the same way as in Yātrā. In matters connected with women, omens described for men apply in the reverse order.

50. On occasions of visits to the king, of return-journey and of entry into mountains, woods and rivers, the omens mentioned for Yātrā apply.

51. Omens on the left side stated to be auspicious for Yātrā are auspicious for other occasions if they are found in front; and omens on the right side stated to be auspicious for Yātrā are auspicious for other occasions if they are found behind.

Two birds flying one on each side of a traveller form an omen known as parigha. It is Kriyadīpta in nature and points to the death of the person starting on a journey.

52. If these omens be of gentle sound and of agreeable motion they indicate the gain of wealth and are technically known as Sakunadwara.

53. According to some the term Śakunadvāra is applied to omens that remain on the right and left sides, that are of the same genus and whose sound and motion are agreeable.

54. If an omen be favorable and another be unfavorable bad luck is indicated to the traveller. He shall be guided by the more powerful omen of the two.

55. If a person starting on a journey should first note an omen stated to be auspicious for return journey and then note one stated to be auspicious for onward journey success of object is indicated. Similarly, if a person starting on a return journey should first note an omen stated to be auspicious for onward journey and then note one stated to be auspicious for return journey, good luck is indicated.

56. If an omen should first be found to be auspicious and if the same should then stop the journey, the person who proceeds nevertheless will either suffer death by his enemy or will engage in fight or suffer from disease.

57. Dīpta (malefic) omens proceeding from left to right indicate fear; and if such omens appear at the commencement of a work such work will suffer injury at the end of a year.

58. If the lunar day, the wind, the sun, the Nakṣatra the places and Ceṣṭā (motion) be unfavorable, wealth, army, strength, limbs, friends and business will suffer respectively.

59. If the malefic omens occur when the clouds roar, there will be fear of injury from strong winds. Malefic omens accurring during twilight hours indicate injury from weapons.

60. If the creatures be found in funeral piles, hair or skull there will be death, imprisonment or suffering from torture respectively and if the creatures be found on thorns, wood, or ashes there will be quarrel, suffering from hard work and grief respectively.

61. If malefic omens be found on objects hollow and weak or on stones, new fear or failure of objects is indicated; but if the omens be benefic good luck is indicated.

62. If the creatures be found to pass stool there will be failure of object; if they be found to eat anything, there will be success of object. Again, if a creature be seen to move away crying from a person, it indicates good luck to the traveller; but if it be found coming towards him, it indicates that the person might return from his journey.

63. If the sound of the creature be found to be bad, there will be quarrel; if the place occupied by the creature be bad, there will be fight. If the cry of the creature be loud at the beginning and weak at the end there will be theft of property.

64. If the omen be bad and found to remain crying in the same place, the village in the neighbourhood will meet with ruin after seven days, and the chief town, the country and the king will also meet with run after a month, six months, and one year respectively.

65. If the creatures be those that eat the flesh of their own kind, other than snakes, rats, cats and fish, there will be misery.

66. Except in the case of an ass and a mare for the generation of a mule and the case of a man and a woman of different castes joining in sexual union, if a creature of one species be found to copulate with a creature of another species the country will meet with ruin.

67. If the creature be found to pass near the feet, breast or head of a person there will respectively be imprisonment, torture and fear; if it be found to drink water there will be immediate rain; if it be found to eat grass there will be theft of property; if it be found to eat flesh the person will get wounded, and if it be found to eat rice there will also be imprisonment.

68. If the creature be seen in any of the eight quarters beginning from the Dīpta (malefic) quarter and going round, there will respectively be a meeting with offenders, wicked men, ministers, kings, preachers of Puranas, old men, cruel men and violent men.

69. If the omen be the approach of an object with excellent fruits and the like there will be gain of wealth and strength. If the same object be found bright, mild and with the eyes turned to the ground, the person will do wicked deeds.

70. If the omen be the cry of an inauspicious creature, in one of the corners (S. E., S. W., N. E., N. W.) reciprocated by the cry of a creature on the left side of a person there will be intimacy with a woman of the class belonging to such corner.

71. If the omen be the cry of a creature in a Śānta (benefic) quarter reciprocated by the cry of a creature on the Dīpta (5th malefic) quarter, there will be success in fight and a meeting with persons belonging to the Śānta quarter. If the reverse be the case there will be misery.

72. If the omen be the cry of a creature before a person, reciprocated by the cry of a creature on his left there will be fear of troubles from kinsmen; but if the cry of such creature be reciprocated by the cry of a creature on the right side there will be fear of troubles from the person's enemies; and if all the three creatures be heard to cry together there will be death.

73. An omen occurring on the top of a tree indicates the arrival of an elephant; if it occur in the middle of a tree, the arrival of a horse is indicated, and if in the foot of a tree the arrival of a chariot is indicated; if the omen occur in a long object, the arrival of human bearers is indicated; if in one of the productions of water, the arrival of a boat is indicated, and if the omen occur on a headless object, the arrival of a palanquin is indicated.

74. An omen occurring in waggons, in high places, and in shadows, indicate the gain of an umbrella. Omens occurring in the east and S. east, in the south and S. west, in the west and north-west and in the north and north-east take effect after a day, three days, five days, and seven days respectively.

75. The lords of the eight quarters beginning from the east are respectively Indra, Agni (fire), Yama (god of death), Nirṛti, Varuṇa (god of rain), Vāyu (the wind), Soma (the Moon) and Eesana (Śiva). The four prime quarters (E., S., W., N.) are masculine and the four sub-quarters (S. E., S., W., N. E.) are feminine.

76. Omens occurring in the eight quarters beginning from the east refer to wood in general, the palm, split bamboo, cloth, productions of water, arrows, leather, and shawls, and to letters of advice regarding them. Omens occurring in any of the thirty-two points of the horizon indicate dealing or business with the persons referring to them.

77. Effects of omens appearing in the eight quarters beginning from the east will occur respectively in place of physical exercise, fire, indistinct sound, quarrel, water, fetters, mantras and cows. The four prime quarters—E., S., W. and N.—are respectively red, yellow, black and white, and the color of a sub-quarter is a mixture of the colors of the two adjacent prime quarters.

78. Omens appearing in the eight quarters beginning from the east, take effect respectively in caves, water, hill places of sacrifice and the abodes of shepherds; these are also places of meeting, fear, loss and the like referred to in connection with several quarters.

79. When the question refers to women, omens appearing in the several quarters beginning from the East point to women

who are big, young, of defective organs, dirty, dressed in black cloth, mean, tall, and widowed respectively.

80. The four prime quarters beginning from the East refer to silver, gold, sick patients and to women and also to sheep, carriage, sacrificial rite and cow-shed. The eight quarters beginning from the east refer to the banyan tree, the red tree, the Rodhra, the bamboo, the mango, the Khadira, the Bilva and the Arjuna trees respectively.

REFERENCE

1. The three quarters are sometimes spoken of as Dīpta quarters.

CHAPTER 87

On the Circle of Horizon

Section II

1. If the omen be the cry of a creature in the eastern quarter[1] when such quarter is benefic there will be a meeting with an officer of the king and the gain of presents, precious gems, wealth and excellent articles.

2. If the omen be the cry of a creature in the next (2nd) benefic quarter there will be gain of gold and of a desired object. And if in the 3rd benefic quarter there will be gain of weapons, of wealth and of arecanut.

3. If the omen be the cry of a creature in the 4th benefic quarter there will be meeting with a person of the twice born class and with a Brāhmaṇa who performs the fire ceremony of Agnihotra, and if in the 5th benefic quarter (S. E.) there will be a meeting with a servant or an ascetic and a gain of gold and metals.

4. If the omen be the cry of a creature in the 6th benefic quarter there will be a meeting with a prince and the gain of a desired object, and if in the 7th quarter there will be the gain of a woman, of virtue, of mustard seeds, and barley grain.

5. If the omen be the cry of a creature in the 8th benefic quarter, there will be recovery of property lost and the gain of an object of desire by a traveller.

6. If the omen be the cry of a creature in the 9th benefic quarter (S), a person will successfully perform his journey and there will also be the gain of peacocks, buffaloes and pigeons. If in the 10th benefic quarter, there will be a meeting with musicians as well as prosperity and joy.

7. If the omen be the cry of a creature in the 11th benefic quarter, there will be meeting with fisher men and gain of fish, of partridge and the like, and if in the 12th benefic quarter

there will be meeting with an ascetic and the gain of good meals and fruits.

8. If the omen be the cry of a creature in the 13th benefic quarter (S. W.) there will be a gain of women and the arrival of a horse, ornaments, a messenger and a news letter; and if in the 14th benefic quarter, there will be a meeting with leather work-men and the gain of an article made of leather.

9. If the omen be the cry of a creature in the 15th benefic quarter, the names of monkeys and ascetics will be heard mentioned or there will be a meeting with these; and if the 16th benefic quarter, there will be a gain of fruits, flowers and of articles of ivory.

10. If the omen be the cry of a creature in the 17th benefic quarter (W) there will be a gain of the gems of the sea, of Vaidurya, and of articles set with gems; and if in the 18th benefic quarter there will be a meeting with hillmen, hunters and thieves and the gain of meals.

11. If the omen be the cry of a creature in the 19th benefic quarter there will be a meeting with persons afflicted with windy complaints and there will also be a gain of sandal wood and of agaru; and if in the 20th benefic quarter there will be a gain of weapons and books as well as a meeting with persons dealing in them.

12. If the omen be the cry of a creature in the 21st benefic quarter (N. W.) there will be a gain of the bone of the white cuttle fish, of cāmara, and of woollen shawls, and there will also be a meeting with a person of the Kāyastha[2] caste or with a scribe; and if in the 22nd benefic quarter there will be a gain of earthen ware and a meeting with conjurers.

13. If the omen be the cry of a creature in the 23rd benefic quarter there will be a meeting with friends and the gain of wealth; and if in the 24th benefic quarter there will be a gain of cloths and horse and a meeting with a close friend.

14. If the omen be the cry of a creature in the 25th benefic quarter (N) there will be a gain of curdled milk, rice and fried grain and a meeting with Brāhmiṇas; and if in the 26th benefic quarter there will be a gain of wealth and meeting with the chief of a party of men.

15. If the omen be the cry of a creature in the 27th benefic

quarter there will be a meeting with a prostitute, a Brahmachāri and a servant and there will also be the gain of dried fruits and flowers ; and if in the 28th benefic quarter, there will be a meeting with a painter and a gain of cloths.

16. If the omen be the cry of a creature in the 29th benefic quarter (N. E.) there will be a meeting with an idol-worshipper and a gain of grain, gems and cows ; and if in the 30th benefic quarter there will be a gain of cloth and a meeting with a prostitute.

17. If the omen be the cry of a creature in the 31st benefic quarter there will be a meeting with a washerman and the gain of the productions of water ; and if in the 32nd benefic quarter there will be a meeting with an elephant-driver and the gain of wealth and elephants.

18. The division of the circle of horizon into 32 equal parts was also mentioned in connection with house-building. The eight spokes (radii) and the centre form nine more places where omens indicate various effects.

19. If the omen be the cry of a creature in the centre there will be a meeting with kinsmen and friends and sexual union with an excellent woman ; if it be the cry of a creature in the eastern spoke, there will be a meeting with a king and the gain of red silk cloths.

20. If the omen be the cry of a creature in the S.E., spoke, there will be a meeting with a weaver, a carpenter a sculptor and a horse driver and there will also be a gain of wealth through them or the gain of horses.

21. If the omen be the cry of a creature in the southern spoke, there will be a meeting with virtuous persons and the gain of virtue.

22. If the omen be the cry of a creature in the south-western spoke, there will be a meeting with a cow, a player and a Kapalika, and there will also be the gain of a black-gram, horse-gram and the like and meals.

23. If the omen be the cry of a creature in the western spoke, there will be meeting with husbandmen and the gain of the productions of the sea, of crystal, of fruits and of liquor.

24. If the omen be the cry of a creature in the north-western spoke, there will be a meeting with a porter, a carpenter, and an

ascetic and there will also be the gain of the flowers of the Tilaka, the piper-betel and of the Punnāga.

25. If the omen be the cry of a creature in the northern spoke, there will be gain of wealth and there will also be a meeting with a devout person and with a person dressed in yellow robes.

26. If the omen be the cry of a creature in the north-eastern spoke, there will be a meeting with a female devotee and the gain of iron, cloths and bells.

27. Omens occurring in the eight quarters on the South, in the 2nd, 6th, 3rd, 7th, and 8th quarters on the West and in the 2nd quarter on the North are not favorable for journey. Omens occurring in the other quarters are auspicious for the purpose.

28. Inside the circle, omens appearing in the south-western and north-western spokes are not favorable for journey ; and those appearing in the other spokes and in the centre are auspicious for the purpose.

29. We have till now been describing the effects of omens in the several quarters when they happen to be benefic and we shall now proceed to describe the effects of omens in the same quarters when they are malefic. If the omen occur due East, there will be fear from the king and a meeting with the enemy.

30. If the omen occur in the 2nd malefic quarter there will be injury to gold and suffering to goldsmiths ; if in the 3rd malefic quarter there will be loss of wealth, quarrel and fight.

31. If the omen occur in the 4th malefic quarter there will be fear of injury from fire ; if it occur due S. E., there will be fear from robbers, and if in the 6th malefic quarter there will be loss of wealth and the death of princes.

32. If the omen be the cry of a creature in the 7th malefic quarter, there will be miscarriage of pregnancy, and if in the 8th malefic quarter there will be the death of dealers in gold and of sculptors as well as fight.

33. If the omen be the cry of a creature due South, there will be fear from the king and death by plague ; if in the 10th malefic quarter, the Dombas (wandering tribe) will suffer miseries.

34. If the omen be the cry of a creature in the 11th malefic quarter, fishermen and fowlers will suffer, and if in the 12th

malefic quarter, there will be injury to meals and ascetics will suffer.

35. If the omen be the cry of a creature due south-west, there will be quarrel, bloodshed and fight, and if in the 14th malefic quarter, there will be injury to articles of leather and workmen in leather will suffer miseries.

36. If the omen be the cry of a creature in the 15th malefic quarter, ascetics will suffer miseries and the sense of hearing will suffer injury ; if in the 16th malefic quarter, there will be suffering from hunger ; if due west, there will be suffering from heavy rains and if in the 18th malefic quarter, dogs and thieves will suffer miseries.

37. If the omen be the cry of a creature in the 19th malefic quarter there will be injury from violent winds ; if in the 20th malefic quarter, dealers in books and weapons will suffer ; if due north-west, books will suffer injuries and if in the next (22nd) malefic quarter there will be fear from poison, thieves and wind.

38. If the omen be the cry of a creature in the 23rd malefic quarter, there will be destruction of wealth and a quarrel with friends ; if in the 24th malefic quarter, horses will be killed and priests will suffer.

39. If the omen occur due North, there will be theft of cows and blows from weapons ; if in the 26th malefic quarter, parties of men will suffer and there will be destruction of wealth if in the 27th malefic quarter, there will be fear of injury from dogs and out-castes, servants and prostitutes will suffer miseries.

40. If the omen be the cry of a creature in the 28th malefic quarter, cloths of various colors will suffer as well as painters ; if it occur due north-east, there will be fear of injury from fire and virtuous women will suffer from calumny.

41. If the omen be the cry of a creature in the next (30th) malefic quarter there will be grief and the death of women ; if in the 31st malefic quarter, washermen and person dwelling on the banks of rivers will suffer miseries.

42. If the omen be the cry of a creature in the last (32nd) malefic quarter, elephant-drivers will suffer miseries as well as elephants. Again, if the omen occur in the eastern malefic spoke (with the circle) a person will lose his wife.

43. If the omen occur in the south-eastern malefic spoke, there will be fight and injury from fire and the death of horses, and sculptors will suffer. If it occur in the southern malefic spoke, there will be destruction of works, of charity, and if in the south-western malefic spoke, there will be fear of injury from fire and parties of men will be killed.

44. If the omen be the cry of a creature in the western malefic spoke, servants will suffer; if in the north-western malefic spoke, asses and camels will be killed and mankind will suffer from cholera and poison.

45. If the omen occur in the northern malefic spoke, there will be destruction of wealth ; and if in the north-eastern malefic spoke, the creatures of the village and shepherds will suffer, and if it occur in the malefic centre, the person himself will suffer troubles.

REFERENCES

1. Of 32 points into which the circle of horizon is divided. Vide last chapter.
2. A person born of a Kṣatriya father and a Śūdra mother.

CHAPTER 88

On Ominous Cries

Section III

1. The Indian Cuckoo, the hog, the Śaśaghna, the Vañjula, the peacock, the Śrīkarṇa, the Brahmani duck, the blue-jay, the Aṇḍīraka, the wag-tail, the parrot, the crow, the dove, the sky-lark, the wild-cock, the osprey, the Hārītala pigeon, the vulture, the monkey, the Pheṇṭa, the cock, Pūrṇakūṭa and the sparrow are day birds and animals.

2. The Jackal, the Piṅgala, the Chippikā, the flying fox, the owl and the hare are night birds and animals. If the day birds be found to move at night or if the night birds be found to move by day, either the country will suffer or the king will meet with ruin.

3. Horses, men, serpents, camels, leopards, lions, bears, iguanas, wolves, the mungoose, the deer, the dog, the goat, the cow, the tiger, the swan, the spotted antelope, the stag, the jackal, the hedge-hog, the cuckoo, the cat, the Indian crane and the pigeon are both day and night animals.

4. The Bhāṣṣa, the Kootapura, the Karabaka and the Karāyika are birds of the species known as Pūrṇakūṭa. The Piṅgalikā, the Pecikā and the Hakkā are owls of species known as Ulūkaceṭī.

5. The Kapotakī and the Śyāmā are doves of the same class. The Vañjulaka and the Khadirachañchu are fowls of the same class. The Chachhundarī and the Nṛipasutā are rats of the same class. The Vāḷeya and the Gardhabha are asses of the same class.

6. Srotobheri, Taṭakabheri and Ekaputraka are birds of the same class. The Kalahakārikā, and the Ralā are also birds of the same class. The Ralā is a bird two inches high and sounds like a Bhringara (a golden pitcher) at night.

7. The Durbalaka and the Bhāṇḍīka are birds of one

species. If these birds be found to pass on the right side, they indicate good luck to the people of the Eastern countries. Chikkāra is a species of animal and Kṛākavāku and Kukuṭa are fowls of the same species.

8. Girtākukuṭa is also known as Kulālakukuṭa and Kuḍya-matsya (the wall-fish) and Gṛahagodhikā are different names for the house lizard.

9. Divya and Dhanvana are animals of the same species ; Kroḍa and Sūkara are different names for the hog ; Go and Usrā are different names for the cow and Svan and Śārameya are dogs of the same species.

10. Thus birds and animals bear different names in different countries. The animals shall first be identified from their names and their cries shall then be interpreted as stated below.

11. If the Vañjula bird be heard to sound as *Tittiḍ*, such sound is inauspicious ; but if it be heard to sound as *Kilkili* the sound is auspicious. The other than natural sounds of the hawk, the parrot, the vulture and the crow are inauspicious.

12. If the dove be seen to conceal itself in a carriage or a seat or a bed or enter a lotus flower, it indicates evil. The effects are felt after different periods in the case of different species of this bird.

13. If the dove be wholly white, the effects will be felt after a year; if it be of various colors, the effects will be felt after 6 months and if of crimson color with a slight admixture of black, the effects will be felt that same day.

14. If the cuckoo be heard to sound as *cicit*, it indicates good luck; if as *śūlīśūl*, there will be gain of wealth; if as *Cacca*, it indicates evil and if as *cikcik* there will be gain of a desired object.

15. If the Hārītāla pegeon be heard to sound as *gugu* there will be prosperity; if in any other way, it indicates evil. The sound of the sky-lark always indicates prosperity.

16. If the female crane be heard to sound as *kiṣ-kiṣ* or as *kaha-kaha* there will be prosperity; but if the sound be *kara-kara*, there will also be prosperity but without gain of wealth.

17. If the same bird be heard to sound as *koṭuklī* there will be prosperity; if as *Kaṭuklī*, there will be rain; but if the sound of the bird be as *koṭiklī* or as *gum* there will be evil.

18. If the Divyaka be seen on the left side, there will be prosperity. If it be seen a cubit above the ground there will be gain of a desired object and if it be seen above the height of a man, the person will become master of the whole country surrounded by the sea.

19. If the cobra be seen to move towards a traveller there will be a meeting with the enemy, imprisonment, slaughter and ruin; if it be seen to move on the left side, there will be failure of a work attempted but safe journey to and fro.

20. If the wag-tail be seen on a lotus or on the heads of horses, elephants or snakes there will be gain of a kingdom; if seen in pure places and on meadows, there will be prosperity and if seen on ashes, bones, wood, husk, hair or grass, there will be grief for a year.

21. If the francoline partridge be heard to sound *kili kilkili* there will be prosperity and not otherwise; if at night the hare be seen to go crying on the left side there will be good luck.

22. If the monkey be heard to cry as *kilkili* the traveller will not meet with success. According to some, if the wild cock be heard to cry as *cuglu* or like a monkey, the traveller will meet with success.

23. If the blue-jay be seen to move to the right of a person with worms, insects or bone in its mouth or to fly round in the sky, the traveller will soon gain wealth.

24. If the crow and the blue-jay be seen to pass to the right fighting, the jay suffering defeat, the traveller will be killed and if the reverse be the case, there will be success.

25. If the blue-jay be heard to sound as *keka* like the Pūrṇakuṭa on the left side, there will be success; but if *krakra* be the cry, it indicates evil; but the appearance of the blue-jay always indicates success to the traveller.

26. If the Undira be heard to sound as *tee*, it indicates good luck and if the cry be *ṭiṭṭiṭṭee*, it indicates evil. If the Phenṭa be seen on the right side, it indicates good luck. The sound of this bird signifies neither good nor evil.

27. If the Śrīkarṇa be heard to sound as *quaqua* on the left side, it indicates good luck; but if the cry be *cik-cik* the effects will be indifferent; if otherwise, the sound signifies nothing.

28. If the Durbali be heard to sound as *ciril-virilv* on the left side, there will be the gain of a desired object and if be seen to move from left to right, there will be immediate success of work.

29. If the Durbali be seen to move from left to right crying *cik-ciki* there will be prosperity but not success of work; if it be seen to pass from right to left, there will be slaughter, imprisonment and fear.

30. If the Sārikā be heard to sound *Krakra* or fearlessly as *tre-tre*, the traveller will soon get wounded and there will be much shedding of blood.

31. If the Phenṭaka be heard to cry as *ciril-virilv* on the left side, there will be prosperity; if the sound be otherwise there will be evil.

32. If the cry of the ass be long and on the left side, it indicates good luck. If the sound be Om, a person proceeding on a journey will meet with success; otherwise, the cry is malefic.

33. If stag and the deer be heard to sound as *Aa* and if the spotted antelope be heard to sound as O there will be good luck; if otherwise there will be misery.

34. The cock crows as *Kuku* except when it sounds fearfully at night and also when ill, the long natural and high sound heard in the morning indicates prosperity to the country, the town and the king.

35. The Chippikā sounds in various ways. The *Kulu-kulu* sound is auspicious; other sounds are inauspicious. The sound of the cat is always auspicious to a traveller; if the cow be seen to sneeze, it indicates the death of the person proceeding on a journey.

36. The owl is often seen flying after its mate setting up the joyous cry of *huṁhum* or *gugluk*. The sound is benefic. If the sound be *gurulu* or *kiskisi*, it is always malefic. If the owl be seen to sound frequently as *balabala*, there will be quarrel; but if the sound be *ṭaṭaṭṭaṭa*, there will be misery. All other sounds are malefic and do not indicate good luck.

37. If the crane with its mate be heard to sound together,

it indicates good luck. But if one of them be heard to sound alone or if they be heard to sound one after the other, such sound is not auspicious.

38. If the Piṅgalā be heard to sound as *ciril-virilv* good luck is indicated. Any other sound is inauspicious.

39. If the Piṅgalā be heard to sound as *Isee* it stops the journey. If it be heard to sound as *kusukusu,* there will be quarrel. I shall now state what has to be done to make this bird foretell future events.

40. The tree in which the bird Piṅgalā may happen to dwell shall be visited by a person who has bathed either in the evening or in the twilight hours; the person shall first worship Brahma and the other Devas. He shall then adorn the tree with a fine new cloth and with Sandal paste.

41. At mid-night the person shall take his station alone to the north-east of the tree and pronouncing the mantras given below within its hearing call upon the bird to divine his thoughts and indicate the issue; he shall solemnly call upon the bird to do so in the name of every thing holy excepting the names of the Devas.

42. "O thou giver of prosperity, I entreat thee to divine my thoughts; thou art praised as knowing all languages."

43. "I mean to leave only after being informed by thee and I will question thee from the north-eastern corner early in the morning."

44. "O thou giver of prosperity, I call upon thee to indicate by signs, the issue of the object I have in view."

45. If immediately after this, the bird be heard to sound the *ciril-virilv* there will be success of the undertaking, but if the sound be either *dis* or *kuca-kuca* there will be much mental suffering.

46. If the bird be mute, then also, there will be success. The effects described for the numerous points of the Circle of Horizon apply here also; and if the bird be seated in the top-most branches, the effects will fully come to pass; if in the middle branches, one-half of the effects will alone come to pass and if in the lower branches very little of the effects will come to pass.

47. All that has been said for the thirty-two points of the outer-circle, the eight spoke lines and the centre apply to the sound of the house-lizard in these positions. Again, if the blind mouse be heard to sound as *ciccid*, the sound is malefic, but if the sound be *ṭiṭṭid* it is benefic and indicates good luck.

CHAPTER 89

On Omens Connected with the Dog

Section IV

1. (*a*) If the dog be seen to pass urine on a man, a horse, an elephant, a pot, a saddle, on milk trees, on heaps of unburnt brick, on an umbrella, a bed, a seat, a wooden mortar, on a banner, a chamara or ground covered with tender grass or flowers and to go before the traveller, it indicates success; if it be seen to pass urine on wet cow-dung, the person will get good meals, and if on dry cow-dung he will get miserable meals or sugar and cakes.

(*b*) Again, if the dog be seen to pass urine on poisonous trees, on thorny trees, dry-wood, stones, dried trees, bones, or cremation ground and to scratch over the parts and to go before the traveller, if indicates evil; if it be seen to pass urine on a bed or on the unused vessels of a pot-man and the like it indidates disgrace to virgins; if it be seen to pass urine on used vessels or on shoes, it indicates disgrace to the traveller's wife and if it be seen to pass urine on a cow, there will be a mingling of castes.

(*c*) Again, if the dog be seen to approach the traveller with a slipper in its mouth, the traveller will gain his object; if it be seen with its mouth full of flesh, there will be a gain of wealth; if with a raw bone in its mouth, there will be good luck; if it be seen to approach with a burning torch or a dry bone in its mouth, there will be death; if with a dead torch, the person will receive blows; if it be seen to approach dragging with it the head, hands, feet, face or other limbs of a person, there will be gain of lands; and if it be seen to approach with a cloth, the bark of a tree and the like, there will be danger. According to some, if a dog be seen to approach with a cloth in its mouth, there will be good luck.

(*d*) Also, if the dog be seen to enter the house with a dry-bone in its mouth, the head of the family will die. If it be seen to enter with fetters, creepers, leather-straps, ropes and the like, he will suffer imprisonment. If it be seen to shake its ears, to get on the person of the traveller and to lick his feet, he will meet with obstacles. If it be seen to stop the traveller, he will suffer attack. If it be seen to scratch the body, he will meet with opposition and if the dog be seen to lie with its head raised up, there will be evil.

2. If one or more dogs be seen to bark at the Sun from the middle of a village, there will be a change of Rulers.

3. If the dog be seen to bark at the Sun in the morning from the South-east quarter there will be immediate fear from destructive fire and from robbers; if it be seen to do so at noon, there will be death from fire and if in the evening, there will be fight and bloodshed.

4. If the dog be seen to bark at the Sun towards sunset, farmers will soon suffer. If it be seen to bark turning to the Northwest within six ghatikas after sunset, there will be suffering from winds and robbers.

5. If the dog be seen to bark at mid-night turning to the North, Brāhmaṇas will suffer and cows will be carried away by robbers; and if it be seen to bark at dawn of day turning to north-east, virgins will suffer from disgrace, there will be fear from destructive fire and a miscarriage of pregnancy.

6. If, in the rainy season, the dog be seen to bark aloud from a heap of rubbish, from the king's palace, the temple or the top of a house, there will be abundent rain; and if it be seen to do so in any other season there will be death, fear from destructive fires and suffering from diseases.

7. If, in the rainy season when there is no rain, the dog be seen to plunge frequently into water or to drink it or to shake it off from its sides, there will be rain within 12 days.

8. If the dog be seen to bark at the mistress of the house with its head on the thresh-hold while its body remains without, the master of the house will suffer from disease; but if it be seen to do so with its body within the gate and its head without

it, the mistress of the house will suffer disgrace.

9. If the dog be seen to scratch the walls of the house there will be house-breaking by robbers; if it be seen to dig the ground in the cow-shed, cows will be robbed away and if it be seen to scratch the places where grain is stored up, there will be gain of grain.

10. If the dog be seen to eat something miserable with a weeping eye and a pitiable look, the master of the house will suffer grief; and if it be seen to play with cows there will be plenty, prosperity, health and joy.

11. If the dog be seen to kiss or smell the left knee, there will be gain of wealth; if it be seen to kiss the right knee, there will be quarrel with women; if it be seen to kiss the left thigh, there will be sensual enjoyment and if it be seen to kiss the right thigh there will be enmity between friends.

12. If the dog be seen to kiss the feet, the traveller will be stopped in his journey; but a person who does not travel will gain the object of his desire. If the dog be seen to kiss the shoes of a person, that person will soon begin to travel.

13. If the dog be seen to kiss both the arms, there will be suffering from enemies and robbers and if it be seen to conceal in a heap of rubbish, flesh, bones, or any catables, there will be immediate fear from destructive fires.

14. If the dog be seen to bark first in the village and then in the village cremation ground, the chief person of the village will die and if it be seen to bark towards a traveller, it stops his journey.

15. If the dog be seen to howl with the sound of the letter *Oo* on the left side there will be gain of wealth; if with the sound of the long vovel *O* on the left side, there will also be gain of wealth; if with the sound of the letter *au* on the left side, there will be ridicule; and if it be seen to howl in any sound from behind, the traveller will meet with obstacles.

16. If dogs be seen to cry frequently uttering the sound *Śankha* as if beaten with a stick or if they be seen to run in a curve, the ruin of the village is indicated and there will also be deaths.

17. If the dog be seen to show its teeth, and lick its mouth-corners there will be good meals ; if it be found to lick its

mouth, there will be obstacle even though good meals may be within reach.

18. If dogs be frequently seen to crowd and bark together in the middle of towns and villages, the head-man will suffer miseries ; a wild dog shall be treated simply as a wild beast.

19. If dogs be seen to bark near trees there will be rain ; if they bark near Indra's banner, the minister will suffer ; if they bark in the middle of the house, the master of the house will suffer from windy complaint and if they be seen to bark from the gates of towns, the towns will suffer.

20. If the dog be seen to bark from a bed, the master of the bed will suffer miseries in his travel ; if it be seen to cry from behind, there will be fear and if it be seen to go round men from left to right and then bark, there will be trouble from enemies.

CHAPTER 90

On the Cry of the Jackal

1. All that has been said of the dog applies also to the Jackal. There are however a few special points to be noticed. The Jackal becomes ruttish in the Śiśira season (from middle of of January to that of March) when its acts signify nothing. If the jackal be seen to cry *hū-hū* first and *ṭā-ṭā* next, the cry is benefic. All other cries are malefic.

2. Kakka is the natural cry of the jackal known as Lomāśikā ; it indicates good luck, All other cries indicate evil.

3. The cry of the jackal in the east and in the north indicates good luck ; if the cry be towards a Śānta (benefic) quarter the person will be respected everywhere. If the cry be towards the smoking quarter and be malefic in tts nature, the lords of such quarter will suffer miseries.

4. In whatsoever quarter the Jackal may be, if its cry be towards a Dīpta (malefic) quarter, there will be prosperity. The cry at noon indicates great evil : the cry of the jackal in the South and towards the Sun indicates misery to the town and army.

5. If *Yāhi* be the cry of the jackal there will be injury from fire. If *tata* be the cry, there will be death. If *Dhig—Dhig* be cry, wicked deeds will be committed ; if the cry be that of the jackal with a flaming mouth, the country will meet with ruin.

6. According to some, the cry of the jackal of the flaming mouth does not indicate evil. The mouth of the jackal appears bright as the Sun or fire owing to its water.

7. If a jackal facing the South be seen to cry in answer to the cry of another jackal there will be death by hanging. If it be found to do so facing the West, there will be death by drowning.

8. If from 1 to 7 jackals be seen to cry together, there will

respectively be freedom from cares, the receipt of good intelligence, gain of wealth, gain of an object of desire, cares of the mind, misery to the chief person, and the gain of a carriage.

9. If 8, 9 or more jackals be seen to cry together, such cry signifies nothing. If the group be found to cry in the South, just the reverse of the effects excepting the 5th and 6th will occur.

10. If the cry of the jackal be found to fill man with a thrill of fear, and to cause the horse to pass urine and dung there will be miseries.

11. The cry of the jackal which stops at the sound of man, the elephant or the horse indicates prosperity to the town and to the army.

12. If *bhebha* be the cry of the jackal there will be fear. If the cry be *bho-bho* there will be danger ; if it be *phipha*, there will be death or imprisonment and if *hūhū* be the cry, there will be prosperity.

13. If a benefic jackal while crying *ā-au* should hear another cry as *ṭā-ṭā* and begin to cry so in response or if it be found to cry beginning with the sound *ṭe-ṭe* and ending with *the-the* such cries signify nothing except that the animal is in rut.

14. If the cry of a jackal be at first found to be loud and disagreeable and again as in response to the cry of another jackal there will be prosperity, gain of wealth and the return of a friend from his travels.

CHAPTER 91

On Omens Connected with Wild Animals

1. If wild animals be found to stay, wander or to come and go within the limits of towns, present, past and future fears are indicated respectively ; and if they are found to wander on all sides of the town, such town will meet with ruin.

2. If, when wild animals enter the limits of towns, their cry is responded to by the cry of country animals, villages and towns will suffer miseries ; if their cry is responded to by the cry of other wild animals, towns and villages will be beseiged ; but if such cry is responded to by both wild and country animals, women will be put into prison by the enemy.

3. If wild animals be found at the gates of towns, such towns will be beseiged by the enemy ; if they be found to enter the towns, such town will meet with ruin ; if they be found to give birth to their young, the people will suffer miseries ; if the animals be found to die within towns, there will be fears of various kinds, but if they enter the houses there will be imprisonment.

CHAPTER 92

On Omens Connected with the Cow

1. If the cow appear weak and dejected the king will suffer miseries ; if it walk striking the ground with its heels there will be diseases. If they eyes be found full of tears or if it found to fear its own master or to cry at the sight of thieves, there will be death.

2. If cows be found to cry when unmolested there will be ruin ; if they cry at night there will be fear ; but if the ox be found to cry at night there will be good luck. If cows be found to be tormented by flies or dogs, there will be immediate rain.

3. If cows while coming home with the cry of *bambhā* be found to be in pursuit of bullocks there will be an increase of cows in the cow-shed. If cows be found wet or with their hairs on end, or happy there will be an increase of wealth. The same remarks apply to buffaloes.

CHAPTER 93

On Omens Connected with the Horse

1. If either the part just behind the saddle or the side of a horse be accidently burnt, evil is indicated. If otherwise there will be good luck. If all the parts of the body be burnt, there will be misery. If the part be seen to burn or to smoke, the effects will be felt in 2 years.

2. If the organ of generation catch fire, the master's harem will suffer miseries. If the belly catch fire, the treasury will suffer ; if the buttocks or the tail catch fire there will be defeat by the enemy. If the facc and the head c atch fire, there will be success.

3. If the mane, the saddle—back and the shoulders catch fire, there will be success. If the legs catch fire, there will be imprisonment. If the forehead, breast, eyes or legs catch fire and smoke, there will be defeat ; but if they burn only there will be success.

4. If the nasal pit, the part above it, the head, the part just below the eyes and the eyes catch fire and burn at night, there will be success. If horses which are green, red, black, of different colors or blue catch fire in any part of their body, there will be the gain of a desired object.

5. If the horse be found to refuse to eat or drink or to fall its legs striking with each other or to perspire for no apparent cause or to quake, drop blood from the mouth or to smoke or not to sleep at night and on the contrary if it be found to sleep by day or be dull or listless with its eyes closed or to stick its head to the ground, there will be misery.

6. If the horse be seen to get upon another horse when the latter carries a saddle or a man or if the king's horse, apparently healthy, bc found to meet with a serious accident, there will be misery.

7. If the horse be found to raise up its head and neigh or if it be found to neigh sweet and loud as if out of joy with food in its mouth, the enemy will meet with ruin.

8. If near a horse that neighs there be found a vessel full of grain or curdled milk, a Brāhmiṇ, a temple-image, sandal paste, flowers, fruits, gold and the like or any agreeable object, there will be success.

9. A horse that is satisfied and feels happy with its food and drink, bit of the birdle and saddle trappings and that casts a side-look indicates good luck.

10. If the horse be found to strike the gound frequently with its left leg, its master will travel to foreign lands. If, during twilight hours, he be found to neigh turning to a dīpta quarter the master will suffer imprisonment or defeat in fight.

11. If the horse be found to neigh much during sleep or to flap its tail, there will be travel. If it be found to drop the hairs of its tail or to neigh pitiously or fearfully or to eat dust, there will be misery.

12. If the horse be found to lie on its right side like a box stretching its right leg, there will be success. All that has been said about the horse applies also to other animals used for riding.

13. If when the king begins to get on his back, the horse be found to be quiet and obedient and to neigh turning to another horse or touch his right side with his mouth, immediate good fortune is indicated.

14. If the horse be found to pass excerment or urine often, or to refuse to move even when whipped or to get frightened for no apparent cause or to shed tears, the master will suffer miseries.

15. Thus have been described omens connected with the horse. We shall now proceed to treat of omens connected with the elephant—the cutting, breaking &c of the tusk especially.

Notes.—All that has been said about the horse applies also to the elephant. The author now proceeds to state certain special points connected with the latter.

CHAPTER 94

On Omens Connected with the Elephant

1 to 6. Stanzas I to 6 are identical with stanzas 20, 21, 22, 23, 24, and 25, of chapter (79.).

7. If the cut be white, smooth glossy and emitting good scent, there will be prosperity. All that I now proceed to state about the breaking of the tusks applies also to its dropping down, becoming thin, and loss of color.

8. The (Gods), the (demons), and (men) reside respectively at the root, the middle and the end of the tusks of the elephant. The effects of omens connected with these parts will therefore be great, moderate and small and they will come to pass soon, after a short time and after a long time respectively.

9. If the right tusk be found to break, the king, the country and the army will suffer miseries ; and if the left tusk be found to break, the master, his wife, son, family, priest, the driver and the wood-men will suffer miseries.

10. If both the tusks be found to break, the king's whole family will meet with ruin ; but if the breaking occur in a benefic Lagna, lunar-day or Nakṣhatra and the like there will be an increase of prosperity. If it occur otherwise, there will be an increase of misery.

11. If the elephant be found to break the middle of its left tusk by striking it against milk trees, fruit or flower trees or the banks of rivers, the ruin of the enemy is indicated and if the right tusk be found to break, there wll be misery.

12. If the elephant be found to walk unsteadily, if its ears cease to move, on a sudden, if the animal be of dejected appe-rance, or if it be found to put its trunk to the ground or to breathe softly and long, if the eyes the full of tears, if the animal be found to sleep always or to be restive or to refuse to eat properly or to pass excrement, urine, often there will be misery.

13. If the elephant be found to attack and break at pleasure ant-hills, trunks of trees, decayed trees, shrubs or branches, if the eyes be of rutting apperance, if the animal be prepared to start on a journey, if while being adroned with trappings he be often found to throw out drops of water or to cry or if it begin to rut at the time or coil its trunk round its right tusk, there will be success.

14. If the elephant, while in water, be found to be dragged away by a crocodile, the king will meet with ruin ; but if he be found to drag the crocodile to the bank, there will be prosperity.

CHAPTER 95

On the Cawing of the Crow

1. In the case of the people inhabiting the Eastern countries, the crow on the right side indicates good luck ; but the crow of the crane kind indicates prosperity when on the left side. In other countries the case is otherwise. The limits of provinces shall be learnt from a general knowledge of the country.

Notes :—Countries to the South and East of the river Saravati are Eastern countries.

2. If the crow be seen to build its nest in a dead tree in the month of Vaiśākha there will be plenty and properity in the country ; but if it be seen to build its nest in a dry throny tree, there will be famine and fear in the land.

3. If the crow be seen to build its nest in an eastern branch of the tree in the Śarata season there will be rain at the beginning of the season; if it be seen to do so in a western branch in the rainy season there will be much rain; if in a northern or southern branch there will be moderate rain in the middle two months of the two seasons; and if it be seen to build its nest on the top of a tree there will be abundant rain.

4. If the crow be seen to build its nest in a southeastern branch there will be rain here and there; if in a south-wetern branch, the yellow and green leaves will grow and if in a north-western or north-eastern branch there will be prosperity.

Notes :—The commentator adds that if the crow be seen to build its nest in a north-western branch there will be an increase of rats.

5. If the crow be seen to build its nest in reeds, dirbha grass, shrubs, creepers, crops, temples, palaces of kings houses or in low ground, the country will suffer from thieves, drought and disease and will meet with ruin.

6. If the crow be seen to lay two, three or four eggs, there

will be prosperity: if five eggs, a foreign prince will begin to reign: if it be seen to lay six eggs or only one egg or no eggs at all, there will be no prosperity.

7. If the young ones be of the color of the fragrant substance known as Coraka, there will be fear from thieves; if of different colors there will be death; if white, there will be fear of injury from fire and if of defective limbs, there will be famine.

8. If a swarm of crows be found to enter a village and cry for no apparent cause, the people will suffer from hunger and if they be seen to fly round and round there will be suffering from anger; if they be seen in swarms there will be quarrels.

9. Crows, that are seen to harass men with their beaks, wings and legs, will increase a person's enemies; if the crow be seen to fly at night; the people will meet with ruin.

10. If the crow be seen to fly round and round from left to right, there will be fear of troubles from one's own kinsmen: if it be seen to fly round turning from left to right there will be fear of troubles from strangers; if it be seen to turn round in haste and fear, there will be a whirlwind.

11. If the crow be seen with its head raised and flapping its wings, a person will meet with danger in his travels; if it be seen to steal away grain, there will be suffering from hunger; and if the feathers of the crow be seen in an army there will be fight and theft.

12. If the crow be seen to throw ashes, bones, hairs or feathers, the husband will meet with troubles in his bed and if it be seen to carry gems, flowers and the like there will be the birth of sons and daughters.

13. If the crow be seen with its mouth filled with sand, grain, wet-earth, flowers and the like, there will be gain of wealth; and if it be seen to drag away vessels from places frequented by men of various class there will be fears of various kinds.

14. If the crow be seen to strike with its legs vehicles, weapons, shoes, umbrellas, shadows of men or the men themselves there will be death; if it be seen to go round a person or to throw flowers on him as if by way of worship, the person

will be respected and if it be seen to pass excrement on a person, there will be gain of food.

15. A person will gain that object which is brought to him by the crow and he will lose that which is carried away by the crow. If such object be of yellow color, there will be gain or loss of gold; if it be an article made of cotton, there will be gain or loss of cloth and if of white color, there will be gain or loss of silver.

16. If, in the rainy season, the crow be seen to caw from milk trees, from the Arjuna tree, the Vañjula tree, the banks of rivers, sand banks, there will be rain; and in other seasons, if the crow be seen to bathe in dust or in water, the sky will be overcast with clouds.

17. If two crows be see n to cry fearfully from a tree there will be fear of great danger and if they be seen to cry turning to water or the clouds there will be rain.

18. If the crow be seen to move its wing fearfully and strike with its feet the branches of trees there will be fear of injury from destructive fires; if it be seen to throw into the house a red substance, a burnt substance or straw or a piece of wood, there will also be fear of injury from fire.

19. If the crow be seen to cry from the house turning to the East, South, West, or North, the master of the house will respectively suffer from kings, robbers, quarrels and loss of cows, if such quarter be a dīpta one.

20. If the crow be seen to cry turning to the East when such quarter is benefic, there will be meeting with an officer of the king, or a friend and there will also be a gain of gold, Śālya rice and cooked rice prepared in sugar.

21. If the crow be seen to cry turning to the Southeast when such quarter is benefic there will be a meeting with a person living by fire and the gain of a woman and of precious metals; if it be seen to cry turning to the benefic South, there will be a gain of black gram, horse-gram and excellent meals and a meeting with singers.

22. If the crow be seen to cry turning to the (benific) South west, there will be meeting with a messenger and the gain of articles of luxury, curdled milk, oil flesh and good meds and

if it be seen to cry turning to the (benefic) west, there will be the gain of flesh, liquor, grain and the gems of the sea.

23. If the crow be seen to cry turning to the (benefic) north-west, there will be the gain of weapons, of lotus, twining creepers, fruits and meals; and if it be seen to cry turning to the (benefic) north, there will be the gain of food, horse and cloths.

24. If the crow be seen to cry turning to the (benefic) noth-east, there will be the gain of ghee and of oxen. The same remarks apply to the crow found seated in the several parts of a person's house.

25. If the crow be seen to pass close to the ears of a person at the commencement of a journey, there will be good luck and the gain of a desired object; and if the crow be seen to come flying and cawing towards the traveller he will return from his journey.

26. If the crow be first seen to cry on tha left side and then on the right side of a traveller, he will be robbed of his money and if the reverse be the case, there will be the gain of money.

27. If the crow be seen to cry and follow the traveller on the left side, there will be gain of wealth; in the case of the people of eastern countries, the crow must follow the traveller on the right side instead of on the left.

28. If the crow be seen to fly crying towards the traveller on the left side, there will be obstacles in the way; but if the person be not a traveller, he will meet with good luck.

29. If the crow be seen to cry first on the right side and then on the left, there will be the gain of a desired object; if it be seen to cry turning to the traveller or fly before him there will be immediate gain of wealth.

30. If the crow be seen to cry turning to the traveller and fly away behind him on the right side, the person will soon get wounded, also if the crow be seen to stand on one leg and cry turning to the Moon, the person will get wounded.

31. If the crow be seen to stand on one leg turning to the Sun and scratch its wings with its beak, the chief person will suffer at the hands of his enemies.

32. If the crow be seen to cry in a field full of crops, there will be the gain of e field with crops in it; but if such crow be malefic in character, the traveller will meet with grief before crossing the boundary.

33. If the crow be seen to cry in trees in which there are fruits and flowers and which are covered with glossy and tender leaves and are fragrant milky, juicy, without wounds, erect and beautiful, there will be the gain of wealth.

34. If the crow be seen to cry in places covered with ripe crops and full of grass, in houses, temples, palaces of kings, the mansions of the rich, green spots, graneries and places where there are benefic objects, there will be the gain of wealth.

35. If the crow be seen to cry seated in the tail of a cow or a snake-hole there will be the sight of a serpent; if it be seen to cry from the back of a buffalo there will be fever that very day; and if from a bush, there will be an imperfect gain of an object of desire.

36. If the crow be seen to cry from a heap of rubbish or from a bone on the left side the person will meet with obstacles in his attempt to gain an object; and if it be seen to cry from an elevated space, a burnt place, or a place struck by lightning, there will be slaughter.

37. If the crow be seen to cry from a good spot with thorny trees in it there will be success of an undertaking, but quarrels at the same time; if it be seen to cry from a thorny tree, there will be quarrels and if from a place overgrown with creepers, there will be imprisonment.

38. If the crow be seen to cry from a tree whose end has been cut off, there will be suffering from sword cut if from a dried tree, there will be quarrel; if from a dung hill either before or behind, there will be the gain wealth.

39. If the crow be seen to cry from the body or the limbs of a dead person there will be deaths; and if it be seen to cry breaking a bone with its beak, there will be a fracture of bones.

40. If the crow be seen to cry holding in his mouth a string, a bone, a piece of wood, a thorn or any weak substance, there will respectively be suffering from a snake, from diseases, from tusked animals, thieves, creepers and fire.

41. If the crow be seen to cry holding in its mouth a white flower, an impure substance or flesh, there will be gain of wealth to the traveller; if it be seen to cry with its hoad raised and striking its wings on its sides, there will be obstacles in the way.

42. If the crow be seen to cry holding in its mouth a string, a strap of leather, or a twining creeper, there will be imprisonment and if it be seen to cry from a stone, there will be a meeting with a new traveller who has suffered much from foot journey.

43. If crows be seen to exchange food with one another there will be great happiness; if the male and the female crows be heard to cry together there will be the gain of a woman.

44. If the crow be seen to cry from a well-filled water pot on the head of a woman, there will be the gain of a woman or wealth; if it be seen to strike the pot with its feet, the person's son will meet with danger; and if it be seen to pass excrement into the pot, there will be the gain of meals.

45. If, when an army begins to encamp in a place, the crow be seen to cry striking its wings on its sides, the army will meet with success in some other place; and if it be seen to cry without moving its wings, there will be only fear and nothing serious will happen.

46. If the crow, accompanied by a vulture and a heron, be seen to enter an army without fighting there will be good luck and if they happen to be at strife there will be fight between the enemies.

47. If the crow be seen to cry from the back of a pig there will be imprisonment; if it be seen to cry from the backs of two pigs covered with mire, there will be the gain of wealth if from the back of an ass or a camel, there will be prosperity. Accordicg to some, if the crow be seen to cry from th back of an ass there will be imprisonment.

48. If the crow be seen to cry from the back of a horse, there will be gain of a vehicle: if it be seen to cry following another crow, there will be blood-shed. The same remarks apply to other birds.

Notes :—These must be carnivorous birds such as the owl, the vulture, the hawk and the like.

49. The crow in the several points of the compass indicates the same effects as those described for other cminous birds.

50. If the crow be heard to cry *kā* from its nest, the cry signifies nothing; but if it be heard to cry *kara* there will be hilarity of mind; and if *kā* be the cry, there will be a meeting with an intimate friend.

51. If *kara* be the cry of the crow, there will be quarrel; if *kuru-kuru* be the cry there will be joy; if *kata-kata* be the cry there will be gain of rice prepared in cvrdled milk; if *ke ke* or *ku ku* be the cry, there will be gain of wealth to the traveller.

52. If *khare-khare* be the cry of the crow there will be a meeting with a foot passenger. If *kha-khā* be the cry, the traveller will meet with death; if *khala-khalā* be the cry there will be an obstacle to journey and rain that same day.

53. If *kā kā* be the cry of thc crow, there will be obstacles; if *ka ka-tee* be the cry there will be injury to meals; if *kava-kava* be the cry there wlll be joy; and if *kagaku* be the cry there will be imprisonment.

54. If *kara kav* be the cry of the crow there will be rain; if *gud* be the cry there will be fear, if *vat* be the cry there will be gain of cloths; if *kalaya* be the cry there will be a meeting of the Śudras and the Brāhmiās.

55. If *phat* be the cry of the crow there will be gain of frnits; if *phala* be the cry, there will be the sight of serpents; if *tat* be the cry, there will be suffering from blows; if *stree* be the cry, there will be the gain of women; if *gat* be the cry there will be the gain of a cow; and if *put* be the cry there will be the gain of flowers.

56. If *Ṭākuṭāku* be the cry of the crow there will be fight; if *guhu* be the cry there will be injury from fire; if *kate-kate* be the cry, there will be fight; and such sounds as *takuli*, *ciṇṭichi*, *ke ke ka* and *pnrancha* indicate bad luck,

57. If two crows bc seen to cry together or to move together, the effects will be the same. All the above remarks apply to omens connected with other birds ; and all that has been said about the dog applies also to wild tusked animals.

58. If the creatures of land and water be seen to change

their nature in the rainy season there will be abundant rain and if they do so in any other season, there will be great fears. If there be no honey in the hives, the country will be wasted ; and if bees black at the head be seen to disappear, there will be deaths.

59. If ants be seen to throw their eggs in water there will be no rain and if they be seen to ascend a bank and approach the foot of a tree with their eggs, there will be immediate rain.

60. Effects of omens ocurring at the commencement of a work will come to pass that same day. Omens shall be observed at the time of commencement of a work, a journey or re-entry into the house after a journey. Sneezing is said never to indicate good luck.

61. The learned in the science say that a king who observes omens carefully and regulates his acts according to their indications enjoys prosperity :—that he will succeed in all his attempts, that he will successfully afford protection to his subjects and that he will gain all his objects and will be in the enjoyment of good health.

62. According to some, the cry of a creature beyond the distance of akrośa signifies nothing. If a person meets with a bad omen once, the evils may be escaped by his performing the *Prāṇāyāma* 11 times ; if he meets with it a second time he shall perform the Prāṇāyāma 16 times ; and if he meets with a bad omen a third time, he shall return from his journey.

Notes :—Akrośa=the range of the voice in calling or halloing.

CHAPTER 96

Supplementary to Omens

1. A person learned in the science of omens shall make predictions taking into account the direction, place, motion, sound, week day, the Nakṣhatra, the Muhūrta, the rising sign, Navāṁsa and the fixed, moveable and the double nature of signs and their strength or weakness.

2. In the case of person who do not proceed on a journey, omens are divided into two sorts—the stable and the unstable. Omens pointing to the king, the messenger, the spy and foreign lands as well as those connected with troubles and kinsmen are known as unstable.

3. Omens pointing to death by hanging, abduction of a women, meals, thieves, fire, rain, festivals, sons, torture, quarrels and fears are known as stable omens if the sign occupied by the Moon at the time be a fixed one and they are known as unstable omens if the sign occupied by the Moon at the time of their occurrence be a moveable one.

4. Omens occurring in hard and firm places, in stone house, in temples, in land and in waters are known as stable ; and omens occurring on weak or moving objects are known as unstable—the latter omens point to gain.

5. Omens occurring when the rising sign, the Nakṣhatra, the Muhūrta and the Dik are watery ones and those occurring in water and on new and full Moon periods and which are at the same time *dīpta* (malefic) and attended with sound point to gain ; also it the creaturcs of water be Śānta (benefic) there will rain.

6. Ominous cries occurring in the direction, rising sign, Muhūrtas and places appropriate to fire and when the Sun ia Dīpta (malefic) point to injury by fire. Ominous cries of a malefic character occurring in thorns and leafless creepers when

the Karaṇa at the time is Bhadra and when the rising sign is either Capricorn or Aquarius point to thieves.

7. If the creatures of the village, malefic in character and in their tone and motion, be found to cry from thorny trees and an either side of the south-western quarter when the rising sign is either Aries or Scorpio there will be quarrels.

8. If creatures, malefic in character, be found to cry with their necks bent to the ground and from one of the four corners when the rising sign is Cancer or when the rising sign or Navāṁsa is either Taurus or Libra there will be a meeting with a woman and the woman will be one of the class belonging to the particular corner.

9. If the omen occur in an old lunar day, in one of the prime quarters, and when the rising sign is a malefic one and if the creature be of the male kind there will be a meeting with a man and if the omen be of the hermphrodite kind there will be a meeting with a harmaphrodite.

Notes.

If the omen be one of a creature of the female sex and if it occur in one of the corners or on an even lunar day when the rising sign or Navāṁśa is that of Taurus there will be a meeting with a person of the class belonging to the north-eastern quarter.

10. If the omen be malefic in character and occur whe Leo is the rising sign or Navāṁsa or when the Sun occupies the rising sign, the chief person will proceed on a journey to foreign lands.

11. At the time of commencement of a work if the rising sign be old when counted from the sign occupied by the Sun, the work will end well and if be an even sign the attempt will fail

12. If the omen be malefic in character and occur when the Sun occupies the 12th horse from the rising sign, the person concerned will loss his right eye ; and if at the time, the Sun occupy the rising sign and be aspected by malefic planets the person will lose both his eyes ; if at the time, the Sun occupy sign Leo and be aspected by malefic planets the person will become lame or deaf or an idiot.

13. If at the time of occurrence of an omen malefic planets occupy the sixth house and be aspected at the same time by other malefic planets, the person concerned will receive a wound in the part of body which corresponds to such sixth house.

14. If, at the time of query, the rising sign or Navāṁsa be a movable one the name of the person with whom there will be a meeting will consist of two syllables ; if the rising sign or Navāṁsa be a fixed one the name will consist of four syllables and if it be both movable and immovable the name will be a combination of two names and will consist of there or five letters.

15. If the powerful planet be Mars the letters will be of the group *ka*, *kha*, *ga*, *gha*, *nga* ; if the powerful planet be Venus the letters will be of the group *ca*, *cha*, *ja*, *jha*, *nga ;* if the planet be Mereury the letters will be those of the group *ṭa*, *tha*, *da*, *dha*, *na* ; if the planet be Jupiter the letters will belong to the group *ta*, *tha*, *da*, *dha*, *na*, if the planet be Saturn, the letters belong to the group *pa*, *pha*, *ba*, *bha*, *ma ;* if the planet be the Moon the letters belong to the group, *ya*, *ra*, *la*, *va*, *sa*, *śa*, *ṣu* *ha* and if the planet be the Sun, the letters belong to the group of vowels from *a* to *an*.

16. Also in the cases of the planets from the Sun to Saturn, the names will be the Devas *Agai*, *Varuṇa*, *Subrāmania*, *Viṣnu*, *Indra*, *Indrāni* and *Brahma* respectively. The particular name required shall be determined from the number of syllables it consists of.

17. If at the time of query, relating to the age of a person, the lord of the rising sign be the Moon, Mars, Mercury, Venus, Jupiter, the Sun or Saturn, the age will respectively be that of infancy (1 to 4), boy-hood (5 to 8), period succeeding investiture with the thread (9 to 12), youth (13 to 32) middle-age (33 to 50), old age (51 to 70) and dotage (above 70).

CHAPTER 97

On Effective Periods

1. In the case of the Sun, the effects will occur after a fortnight ; in the case of the Moon, after a month ; in the case of Mars after the same period as that stated for the retrograde motion of planets ; in the case of Mercury the effects will occur before his disapperance and in the case of Jupiter a year.

2. In the case of Venus, the effects will occur after 6 months ; in the case of Saturn after a year and in the case of Rāhu after 6 months. If the matter refers to a Solar eclipse the effects will occur after a year and in the case of solar spots known as Tvāṣṭa and Kīlaka the effects will be felt that same day (vide stanzas 6 and 7 of CH III Part I).

3. Effects of Phenomena connected with the appearance of dark comets will occur after three months ; those of phenomena connected with the appearance of white comets will occur after seven days ; effects of halos, rainbows during twilight hours and color of the twilight sky and of clouds will be felt after seven days.

4. Effects indicated by "abnormal changes of temperature, by the appearance of fruits and flowers out of season, by the flaming horizon and by portents relating to the motion of unmoving bodies and to the refusal to move of moving bodies and to abnormal births will be felt atter 6 months.

5. Effects indicated by portents relating to the completion of an event without an agent, to earth quakes, to severe calamities, to malefic symptoms such as those connected with homa fire and by portents relating to the drying of a wet substance and to the course of rivers will occur after 6 moths.

6. Effects of portents connected with pillars and the like, with graneries, the temple-images-their speech, weeping quaking and swetting, cattle-fight and fight between the people of a

house during twilight hours and the appearance of the rainbow at night and lighting will be felt after three weeks.

7. Effects of portents connected with the increase of worms, rats, flies and snakes and of those connected with the sound of birds and animals and with the fioating of a lump of earth on water will be felt after three months.

8. Effects indicated by dogs and the creature of the village bearing their young in the woods, by the entry of wild animals into the village and the several abnormal phenomena connects with bee-hives, town gates, and Indra Dvaja will be felt after a year or a longer period.

9. Effects connected with swarms of the jackal and the vulture will be felt after 10 days. Those of phenomena connected with mysterious musical sound will be felt that same day. Those of phenomena connected with disagreeable sounds will be felt after a fortnight and also effects of phenomena connected with ant-hills and openings on the surface of the earth will also be felt after a fortnight.

10. Effects of protents relating to the appearance of fire where there is no fire and the shower of ghee, oils, serum of flesh and the like will be felt that same day ; and the effects of casual words of women and children will be felt after a month and a half.

11. Effects of portents relating to umbrellas, piles of bricks, the sacrificial post, fire, and seeds will be felt after three months. According to some, effects of portents relating to umbrellas, gates and towers will be felt after a month.

12. Effects of portents relating to the friendly union of creatures of deadly natural enmity, to sounds heard in the sky and to the union of the cat and the mungoose with the rat will be felt after a month.

13. Effects of the appearance of cloud-castles will be felt after a moth and effects of protents relating to juice, gold, flag-staff, hoses and to dust storms and smoke will also be felt after a month.

14. Effects of phenomena occurring in the eight constellations from Aśvinī will be felt after 9, 1, 8, 1, 1, 6, 3, and 3 months respectively and the effects of those occurring in the constellation of Āśleṣa will be felt that same day.

15 Effects of phenomena occurring in the ten constellations from Maghā will be felt after 1, 6, 6, 3, ½, 8, 3, 6, 1 and 1 months respectively. Effects of those occurring in the constellations of P. Āṣaḍa and U. Āṣaḍa will be felt after four months and the effects of those occurring in the constellation of Abhījīt will be felt that same day.

16. Effects of phenomena occurring in the remaining 6 constellations from Śrāvaṇa will be felt after 7, 8, 1½, 3, 3 and 5 months respectively.

17. If the effects be not felt soon after the periods mentioned, they will be felt with greater severity after double the period, if no steps be adopted for their expiation by the gift of gold, gems and cows and by the performance of expiatory ceremonies with the help of *Brāhmiṇs.*

CHAPTER 98

On the Constellations

1 & 2. The number of Stars of the various constellations from Aśvini are 3, 3, 6, 5, 3, 1, 5, 3, 6, 5, 8, 15, 5, 1, 1, 5, 4, 3, 11, 2, 8, 3, 5, 100, 15, 8 and 32 and these numbers also represent the various stellar periods.

3. In matters connected with marriage these numbers represent years after which the effects indicated will be felt. Recovery from fever and the like will begin after so many days.

4 & 5. The following table contains the names of the Devas presiding over the several constellations

The residing deities of the 28 constellations beginning with Aśvini are the Divine Physicians, Yama, Agni, Prajapati, the Moon, Rudra, Aditi, Jupitar, Sarpa, the Manes, Bhaga, Āryaman, Savitṛ, Tvaṣṭṛ, the Wind, Indra—Agni, Mitra, Indra, Nirrti, Water, Viśve—devas, Brahman, Viṣṇu, Vasu, Varuṇa, Ajaikapāt, Ahirbudhnya and Pūṣan, respectively.

6. Of these 28 constellations, those of U. Phālguni, U. Āṣāḍa and U. Bhādrapada together with the constellation of Rohiṇī are known as (Dhruva) stable asterisms. Coronation of kings, expiatory ceremonies, planting of trees, the building of towns, acts of public utility, the sowing of seeds and acts of permanent effects shall be commenced when the Moon passes through the stable asterisms.

7. The constellations of Mūla, Ārdrā, Jyeṣṭhā and Āśleṣā are knwon as (Tīkṣṇa) sharp asterisms. Punishment, mesmerism, exorcism, imprisonment of person, acts of torture, of separation or of union shall be commenced when the Moon passes throgh the sharp asterisms.

8. The constellations of P. Phālguni, P. Āṣāḍa, P. Bhādrapada. Bharaṇī and Maghā are known as (Ugra) severe atsterisms. Acts of digrace, destruction, deceit, imprisonment, poison,

burning, beating with weapons and the like shall be done when the Moon passes through the severe asterisms.

9. The constellations of Hasta, Aśvnī, and Puṣhya are known as (Laghu) light asterisms. Sales, acts of sexual love, acquisition of knowledge, wearing of ornaments, arts, sculpture, medicine purchase of carriage and the like shall be commenced when the Moon passes through the light asterisms.

10. The contellations of Anurādhā, Citra, Revatī and Mṛgaśirsa are known as (Mṛdu) soft asterisms. Acts of friendship, sexual union, the purchase of cloths, and the wearing or making of ornaments, any auspicious deeds and music shall be commened when the Moon passes through the soft asterisms.

11. The constellations of Kṛittikā and Viśākhā are known as (Mṛidu Tīkṣṇa) soft and sharp asterisms and they produce effects of mixed character. Śravaṇa, Śrāviṣṭa, Śatabhiṣak, Hasta and Svāti are asterisms through which when the Moon passes shall be commenced works of a moving character.

12. A person shall get shaved when the asterism of Hasta, Chitra, Śrāviṣta Svāti, Mṣga Śiras, Śrāvaṇa, Śatabhiṣak, Revatī, Aśvini, Jyeṣṭhā, Puṣya, may happen to rise or in the Mūhurta of such asterisms or when the Moon passes through them, or when the asterism is a benefic one for the person—when it is an even one or the ninth one from the asterism occupied by the Moon at the time of a person's birth.

13. A person who has just bathed and is wet, one that proceeds on a journey, a person who has dressed and adorned himself, one who has got himself rubbed oil, one who has taken his meals and a person who has received blows in a field of battle shall not get themselves shaved. Shaving is prohibited in twilight hours, hours of night, on Tuesdays, Saturdays and Sundays, on Riktā (*a*) Tithies, on the ninth lunar day and when the Karṇa is Bhadra.

14. When directed by the king or with the consent of the Brāhmiṇas or on the occasions of marriage or pollution, or when a person is released from jail, or at the commencement of sacrificial rites, a person may get shaved on any day in the month.

15. When the Moon passes through the constellations of

Hasta, Mūla, Śravaṇa, Mṛgaśīsaṣa and Puṣya a person shall perform deeds befitting a male.

16. The various ceremonies of purification, religious rites, the practice of austerities and the wearing of the Sacred belt shall be commenced when the Moon passes through the osterism of Hasta, Revati, Svāti, Anurādhā, Puṣya and Citra and when Jupiter is in conjunction will Mercury, Venus or the Moon.

17. The ceremony of boaring the ear shall be performed when the rising sign is that of a benefic planet and not occupied by malefic planets, when benefic planets occupy the 11th and 3rd house, when Jupiter occupies the rising sign or when the Moon passes through the asterism of Puṣya, Rohiṇī, Citra, Śrāvaṇa or Revatī

18. All works commenced when the 12th house, the Kendras, and the 8th house are not occupied by planets, when malefic planets occupy the 3rd, 6th and 11th houses and when Jupiter or Venus occupies the rising sign or one of the Kendras, will end successfully. House-building or entry into a house shall be commenced when the rising sign is benefic to the person or when it is a fixed sign.

REFERENCE

1. Riktā Tithi vide Stanza 2 next Chapter.

CHAPTER 99

On Lunar Days and Half Lunar Days

1. The lords of the 15 lunar days are respectively (1) Brahma, (2) Vidhātā, (3) Hari, (4) Yama, (5) Moon, (6) Subramaṇya, (7) Indra, (8) Vasu, (9) Sarpa, (10) Dharma, (11) Śiva, (12) Saviā, (13) Manmatha (14) Kali and (15) Viśvadeva.

2. The New-Moon day is sacred to the Pitṛs. A person shall commence works suited to the Devas presiding over particular lunar days. The 1st, 6th and 11th lunar days are known as Nanda; the 2nd, 7th, and 12th lunar days are known as Bhadra; the 3rd, 8th and 13th lunar days are known as Vijaya; the 4th, 9th, and 14th lunar days are known as Riktā and the 5th, 10th and 15th lunar days are known as Pūrṇa.

3. Works directed to be done in particular Nakṣatras shall be done on lunar days sacred to the lords of the Nakṣatras. The same remarks apply to Karaṇas and Mūhūrtas.

4. The lords of the seven karaṇas—Bava, Bālava, Kavlava, Taitila, Gara, Vaṇija and Viṣṭi, are Indra Brahma, Mitra, Aryama, Bhū, Śrī and Yama.

Notes—Karaṇa is half a lunar day. The seven Karaṇas mentioned above are known as Moveable, and when eight times repeated occupy the space from the second-half of the first day in the Moon's increase to the first-half of the 4th day in its wane.

5. The four Dhruva (fixed) Karaṇas are Śakuni, Catuṣpada, Nāga and Kiṁstughna and they begin from the second half of the 14th day of the wanting moon. These are sacred to Kali, Vṛṣa, Sarpa and Vāyu.

6. In a Bava Karaṇa shall be done deeds of an auspicious, a moveable or a fixed character as well as deeds for the promotion of a person's health or comfort. In a Bālava Karaṇa shall

be done acts of charity and acts of help to Brāhmināś. In a Kaulava Karaṇa shall be done joyful deeds and those for the acquisition of friends and in a Taitila Karaṇa shall be done deeds liked by the public at large and also houses shall be built.

7. In a Gara Karaṇa lands shall be tilled, seeds sown, houses built and the like. In a Vaṇija Karaṇa, works of a fixed nature shall be done as well as dealings with merchants. In a Viṣṭi or Bhadra Karaṇa, auspicious deeds shall not be done but acts aimed at the ruin of enemies and those connected with poison may be done.

8. In a Śakuni Karaṇa a person shall do acts for the increase of his health and comfort, shall take medicine and shall learn or repeat the Mūla mantras (magical formulae.) In a Catuṣpada Karaṇa a person shall do deeds connected with cows, Brahmins, the Pitṛs and the king. In a Nāga Karaṇa a person shall do works of a fixed nature, cruel deeds, acts of stealth and wicked deeds. In a Kiṁstughna Karaṇa, a person shall do any work for the increase of his health and comfort as well as suspicious deeds.

Notes—A Muhūrta is 48 minutes. The 12 hours of day and 12 hours of night are each divided into 15 Muhūrtas. The 15 day-Muhūrtas are sacred respectivaly to (1) Rudra, (2) Sarpa, (3) Mitra, (4) Pitṛ, (5) Vasu, (6) Vara, (7) Viśvadeva, (8) Vidhi, (9) Brahma, (10) Indra, (11) Indrāgni (12) Daitya, (13) Varuṇa, (14) Āryaman and (15) Bhaga. The 15 night—Muhūrtas are sacred respectively to (1) Īśvara (2) Ajapada, (3) Ahirbhudhnya, (4) Puṣya, (5) Nasaṭya (6) Yama, (7) Vanhi, (8) Dhata, (9) Śaśi (10) Aditya, (11) Guru, (12) Achyuta, (13) Arka, (14) Tvāśṭa and (15) Vāyu. Of the 15 night—Muhūrtas, the 1st, 2nd, 6th and 7th shall be rejeeted for all auspicious purpose.

CHAPTER 100

On Marriage Lagnas

1. Marriages shall take place when the Moon passes through the asterism of Rohiṇī, U. Phālguni, U. Āṣāḍa, U. Bhadrapada, Revatī, Mṛgśiras, Mūla, Anurādhā, Maghā, Hasta or Svāti, when the rising sign is Virgo, Libra or Gemini, when the benefic planets occupy other than the 7th, 8th and 12th houses, when Moon occupies, the 2nd, 3rd or 11th house, when the malefic planets occupy, the 3rd, 6th, 8th and 11th houses, when Venus does not occupy the 6th house and when Mars does not occupy the 8th house, and,

2. When the rising sign is other than the 2nd, 9th, or 8th house from the Lagna in the horoscope of the bridegroom or the bride, when at the time the course of the Sun of benefic, when the Moon does not occupy the same sign with the Sun, Mars, Saturn or Venus, or when she is between two malefic planets, when the Yoga is neither the Vyatipāta nor that of Vaidhṛti, when the Karaṇa is other than Virṭi, when the lunar day is other than a Rikta one, when the week day is other than that of a malefic planet, when the Āyaṇa is other than the Dakṣināyaṇa, when the month is other than that of Caitra or Pauṣa and when the rising Navāṁśa is a human Navāṁśa.

CHAPTER 101

The Moon in the Asterisms

1. A person born when the Moon passes through the asterism of Aśvinī will be fou d of ornaments, will be of fine appearance, of amiable manners, skilled in work and intelligent.

A person born when the Moon passes through the asterism of Bharaṇī will be successful at work, truthful, free from diseases, able and free from grief.

2. A person born when the Moon passes though the asterism of Kṛttikā will be a glutten, found of the wives of other men, of bright appearance and of wide-spread fame.

A person born when the Moon passes through the asterism of Rohiṇī will be truthful, will not covet the property of other men, will be of cleanly habits, of sweet speech, of firm views and of fine appearance.

3. A person born when the Moon passes through the asterism of Mṛgsīraṣa will be of no firm views, will be able, timid, of good speeeh, of active habits rich and will indulge in sexual pleasures.

A person born when the Moon passes through the asterism of Ārdrā will be insincere, of irascible temper, ungrateful, troublesome and addicted to wicked deeds.

4. A person born when the Moon passes through the asterism of Punarvasu will be devout and of patient habits, will live in comfort, will be good natured, quiet, of wrong views, sickly, thirsty and pleased with trifles.

5. A person born when the Moon passes through the asterism of Puṣya will have a control over his passions, will be generally liked, will be learned in the Sāśtrrs, will be rich and will be found of doing acts of charity.

A person born when the Moon passes through the asterism of Āśleṣa will not be attensive to the work of other men, will be a promiscuous eater, will be sinful, ungrateful and skilled in deceiving other men.

6. A person born when the Moon passes through the asterism of Maghā will have numerous servants, will worship the Devas and the pitṛs, and will be engaged in important works.

A person born when the Moon passes through the asterism of P. Phalgunī will be of sweet speech, will be liberal in his gifts, will be of wandering habits and will serve under kings.

7. A person born when the Moon passes through the asterism of U. Phalgunī will be generally liked, will earn money by his learning and will live in comfort and luxury.

A person born when the Moon passess through the asterism of Hasta will be of active habits, full of resources, shameless, merciless, a thief and a drunkard.

8. A person born when the Moon passes through the asterism of Citra will wear clothes of various colors, and flowers and will be of beautiful eyes and limbs.

A person born when the Moon passes through the asterism of Svāti will be of a mild and quiet nature, will control his passions and desires, will be killed in trade and merciful, will be u able to bear thirst, will be of sweet speech and will be disposed to do acts of charity.

9. A person born when the Moon passes through the asterism of Viśākhā will be jealous of another's prosperity, will be a niggard, will be of bright appearance and of distinct speech, will be skilled in the art of earning money, will be disposed to bring about enmity between persons.

A person born when the Moon passes through the asterism of Anurādhā will be rich, will live in foreign lands, will be unable to bear hunger and will be inclined to move from place to place.

10 A person born when the Moon passes through the asterism of Jyeṣṭhā will have very few friends, will be cheerful, virtuous and of irascible temper.

A person born when the Moon passes through the asterism of Mūla will be haughty, rich, happy, not disposed to injure other men, of firm views and will live in luxury.

11. A person born when the Moon passes through the asterism of P. Āṣāḍha will have an agreeable wife, will be proud and will be attached to friends.

A person born when the Moon passess through the asterism of U. Āṣāḍha will be obedient, will be learned in the rules of virtue, will possess many friends, will be grateful, will return favours received and will be generally liked.

12. A person born when the Moon passes through the asterism of Śrāvaṇa will be prosperous and learned, will have a liberal minded wife, will be rich and of widespread fame.

A person born when the Moon passes through the asterism of Dhaniṣṭhā will be liberal in his gifts, will be rich, valient, will be found of music and will be a niggard.

13. A person born when the Moon passes through the asterism of Śatabhiṣhak will be harsh in his speech, will be truthful, will suffer grief, will conquer his enemies, will thoughtlessly engage in works and will be of independent ways.

A person born when the Moon passes through the asterism of P. Bhadrapadā will suffer from grief, will place his wealth at the disposal of his wife, will be of distinct speech, will be skilled in earning money and will be a niggard.

14. A person born when the Moon passes through the asterism of U. Bhadrapadā will be an able speaker, will be happy, will possess children and grand-children, will conquer his enemies and will be virtuous.

A person born when the Moon passes through the asterism of Revatī will possess perfect limbs, will be of aimable manners, will be deeply learned, will never covet the property of other persons and will be rich.

Notes :—The effects described in this Chapter will *fully* come to pass if the Moon be powerful.

CHAPTER 102

On the Division of the Zodiac

1. Sign Aries consists of the asterisms of Aśvinī, and Bharaṇī and the first quarter of Kṛttikā. Sign Taurus consists of the last three quarters of Kṛttikā, the asterism of Rohiṇī and the first two quarters of Mṛgaśīrsa.

2. Sign Gemini consists of the last two quarters of Mṛga-śirṣa, the asterism of Ārdrā and the first three quarters of Punarvasu. Sign Cancer consists of the last quarter of Punarvasu and the asterisms of Puṣya and Āśleṣa.

3. Sign Leo consists of the asterisms of Maghā and P. Phalgunī, and the first quarter of U. Phalgunī. Sign Virgo consists of the last three quarters of U. Phalgunī, the asterism of Hasta, and the first two quarters of Citra.

4. Sign Libra consists of the last two quarters of Citra, the asterism of Svāti, and the first three quarters of Viśākhā. Sign Scorpio consists of the last quarter of Viśākhā and the asterisms of Anurādhā and Jyeṣṭhā.

5. Sign Sagittari consists of the asterisms of Mūla and P. Āṣaḍha and the first quarter U. Āṣaḍha. Sign Capricorn consists of the last three quarters of U. Āṣaḍha the asterism of Śrāvaṇa and the first two quarters of Sravishta.

6. Sign Aquarius consists of the last two quarters of Śrāviṣṭha, the asterism of Śatabhiṣaj, and the first three quarters of P. Bhadrapadā. Sign Pisces consists of the last quarter of P. Bhadrapadā and the asterisms of U. Bhadrapadā and Revatī.

7. Signs Aries, Leo, and Sagittari begin respectively with with the asterisms of Aśvinī, Magahā and Mūla and the several signs end with the first, second, third of fourth quarters of the odd asterisms succeeding the said three asterisms.

CHAPTER 103

On Marriages

1. If at the time of marriage the rising sign be occupied by the Sun or Mars, the woman will become a widow; if it be occupied by Rāhu, the son will die; if by Saturn, there will be poverty; if by Venus, Mercury or Jupiter, the woman will remain chaste: and if by the Moon, the woman will die early.

2. If at the time of marriage, the 2nd house from the ascendant be occupied by the Sun, Saturn, Rāhu or Mars there will be much suffering from poverty; if it be occupied by Jupiter, Venus or Mercury the woman will become rich and will not become a widow and if the 2nd house be occupie by the Moon, she will get many sons.

3. If at the time of Marrigage, the 3rd house from the ascendant be occupied by the Sun, the Moon, Mars, Jupiter, Venus or Mercury the woman will have many sons and will become rich : if the 3rd house be occupied by Saturn, the woman will be liked by all and if it be occupied by Rahu, she will die early.

4. If at the time of marriage, the 4th house from the ascendant be occupied by Saturn, the woman will not have much milk ; if it be occupied by the Sun and Moon, the woman will not be generally liked ; if it be occupied by Rāhu, he husband will have another wife, if it be occupied by Mars she will have very little wealth ; and if it be occupied by Venus, Jupiter or Mercury, the woman will be happy.

5. If at the time of Marriage the 5th house from the ascendant be occupied by the Sun or Mars there will be death of sons ; if it be occupied by Jupiter, Venus or Mercury, the woman will get many sons ; if by Rāhu, she will die early, if by Saturn she will be afflicted with serious diseases ; and if it be occupied by the Moon she will get daughters.

6. If at the time of Marriage, the 6th house from the ascendant be occupied by Saturn, the Sun, Rāhu, Jupiter or Mars, the woman will be liked by all for her good nature and she will show due respect to her father-in-law and others ; if it be occupied bp the Moon, she will become a widow ; if by Venus, she will become poor, and if by Mercury she will become prosperous and quarrelsome.

7. If at the time of Marriage, the 7th house from the ascendant be occuipied by Saturn, the woman will become a widow ; if it be occupied by Mars, she will suffer imprisonment ; if by Jupiter ; she will suffer from torture ; if by Mercury she will suffer miseries ; if by Rāhu, she will suffer loss of wealth ; if by the Sun she will suffer from diseases ; if by the Moon, she will travel to foreign lands and if by Venus, she will die early.

8. If at the time of Marriage, the 8th house from the ascendant be occupied by Jupiter or Mercury, there will be separation between husband wife ; if it be occupied by the Moon Venus or Rāhu the woman will die early ; if by the Sun she will escape widowood ; if by Mars she will be afflicted with diseases ; and if by Saturn she will become rich and will be liked by her husband.

9. If at the time of marriage the 9th house from the ascendant be occupied by Venus, the Sun, Mars or Jupiter, the woman will be charitable ; if it be occupied by Mercury she will be free from diseases ; if by Rāhu or Saturn she will barren ; and if by the Moon, she will bear daughters and will be of a wandering nature.

10. If at the time of Marriage, the 10th house from the ascendant be occupied by Rāhu, the woman will become a widow ; if it be occupied by Saturn and the Sun, she will be inclined towards sinful deeds ; if by Mars, she will die early ; if by the Moon, she will become poor and unchaste, and if by any of the other planets she will be rich and liked by all.

11. If at the time Marriage the 11th house from the ascendant be occupied by the Sun. the woman will get many sons ; if it be occupied by the Moon, she will become rich ; if by Mars, she will get sons : if by Saturn, she will become very wealthy ; if by Jupiter, she will be of long life ; if by Mercury, she will

live in plenty ; if by Rāhu she will die before he r husband and if by Venus she will become wealthy.

12. If at the time of marriage the 12th house from the ascendant be occupied by Jupiter, the woman will become rich ; if it be occupied by the Sun, she will become poor, if by the Moon, she will lose her wealth ; if by Rāhu, she will become unchaste ; if by Venus, she will be chaste : if by Mercury she will get many sons and grand-sons and if by Mars, she will be found of liquor.

13. The most excellent hour for marriage is the hour in the evening when cows are being driven home, and the sky is covered with dust raised by their hoofs striking against the ground while running. The married woman will get wealth, health and sons and will be prosperous. This hour is known as Godhuli Lagna. In the case of such hour, the character of the Nakṣhatra, the Tithi, the Yoga, the Karaṇa, or the Lagna need not be considered. Such an hour will make a person happy and prosperons.

CHAPTER 104

On the Effects of Planetary Motions

1. The truths of Science have for a long time remained scattered for want of arrangement. They will become fit for ready use if arranged and systematized.

2. The influence exercised by the planets over human affairs as they move through the signs of the Zodiac is various. I desire to describe their effects in stanzas written in a variety of metres and the learned are requested to excuse this wish in me. (*a*).

Notes.

(*a*). Each stanza of this Chapter is written in a distinct metre and contains the name of the metre also. On account of this restriction the ideas exdressd in many stanzas are curious and far fetched.

3. One who has read the works of Maṇḍavya on present subject will not like my treatise, and if he likes it at all, he will like it in just the same way as a person will like his wife whom he knows to be unchaste.

Notes.

This stanza is written in the Jaghanacapala metre which term also means a harlot.

4. When the Sun passes through the 6th, 3rd and 10th signs from the sign occupied by the Moon at the time of birth of a person (*a*) the effects will be benefic ; when the Moon passes though the 3rd, 6th, 10th, 7th, and 1st signs from the Moon, the effects will also be benefic ; when Jupiter passes through the 7th, 9th, 2nd and 5th signs or when Mars and Saturn pass through the 6th and 3rd signs or when Mercury passes through the 6th, 2nd, 4the, 10th and 8th signs from the Moon the effects will be benefic. But when Venus passes through the 7th, 6th, and 10th signs from the Moon the effects will be

malefic. All the planets produce benefic effects when they pass through the 11th house from the Moon.

5. When the Sun passes through the sign occupied by the Moon at the time of birth of a person such person will suffer from fatigue, from loss of wealth, chest-pain and foot journey. When the Sun passes through the 2nd house from the Moon the person will suffer from loss of wealth, discomfort, eye-diseases and deceit. When the Sun passes through the 3rd house from the Moon, the person will return to his place, will become rich, happy and free from diseases and will destroy his enemies. When the Sun passes through the 4th house from the Moon, the person will suffer from diseases and will be hindered from enjoying the company of an excellent wife.

6. When the Sun passes through the 5th house from the Moon, the person will suffer from diseases and enemies. When the Sun passes through the 6th house, the person will be freed from diseases, from enemies and from grief. When the Sun passes through the 7th house the person will suffer from the fatigues of foot-journey, from chest-pain, from humility and consumption. When the Sun passes through the 8th house from the Moon, the person's own beautiful wife will not be of use to him.

7. When the Sun passes through the 9th house from the Moon, the person will suffer from accidents, humility, diseases, mental pains and opposition. When the Sun passes through the 10th house from the Moon, the person will achieve great success and will gain his object. When the Sun passes thrugh the 11th house, the person will achieve success, will return to his place, will be respected, will become prosperous and will be freed from diseases. When the Sun passes through the 12th house, the person will gain his object only by the adoption of just and proper means and not otherwise.

8. When the Moon passes through the sign occupied by herself at the time of birth of a person, such person will get meals, excellent bed and clothes. When the Moon passes through the 2nd house, the person will suffer loss of respectability and of wealth and will also suffer from obstocles. When the Moon passes through the 3rd house, the person will get clothes, women, and wealth in abundance. When the Moon passes through the

4th house, the person will have no liking for mountains and will be as cruel as a serpent.

9. When the Moon passes through the 5th house from the sign occupied by herself at the time of birth of a person, such person will suffer from humility, diseases, pain of mind and obstacles in his path. When the Moon passes though the 6th house, the person will enjoy wealth, comfort and the ruin of his enemies and will be freed from diseases. When the Moon passes through the 7th house, the person will enjoy a carriage, respectability, a good bed, good meals and wealth. When the Moon passes through the 8th house the person will live in fear of evils.

10. When the Moon passes through the 9th house from the sign occupied by herself at the time of birth of a person, such person will suffer from imprisonment, pain of mind, fatigue of body and chest-pain. When the Moon passes through the 10th house, the person's orders will be carried out and he will succeed in his work. When the Moon passes through the 11th house, the person will enjoy prosperity, will get new friends and wealth. When the Moon passes through the 12th house, he will suffer from injuries received from a bullock.

11. When Mars passes through the sign occupied by the Moon at the time of birth of a person, such person will suffer from troubles. When Mars passes through the 2nd house from the Moon, the person will suffer from the king, from quarrels, from enemies and from disgrace. He will also suffer from bilious and windy complaints and from thieves.

12. When Mars passes through the 3rd house from the Moon there will be gain of objects from robbers and from children the person will become of bright appearance, his orders will be carried into effect, the will get wealth, blankets, metals, gems and the like.

13. When Mars passes through the 4th house from the Moon, the person will suffer from fever, belly-ache and blood discharges and he will also suffer miseries through association with wicked men.

14. When Mars passes through the 5th house from the Moon, the person will suffer from enemies, diseases, fears and troublesome children and his appearance will become less bright.

15. When Mars passes through the 6th house from the Moon, the person will be freed from enemies and quarrels ; he will obtain gold, corals and copper and will lead an independent life.

16. When Mars passes through the 7th house from the Moon, the person will suffer from a qurrelsome wife, from diseases of the eye and from belly-ache. When he passes through the 8th house there will be bloodshed, loss of wealth and of respectability ; and when he passes through the 9th house, the person will suffer disgrace and loss of wealth and the like ; his gait will be slow and he will become weak.

17. When Mars passes through the 10th house from the Moon, the person will obtain much wealth and when he passes through the 11th house, he will obtain success and renown and will rule over a province.

18. When Mars passes through the 12th house from the Moon, the person will suffer from various expenses, troubles, diseases of the eye, from an angry wife and from bilious compliants through he may be born in the family of Indra.

19. When Mercury passes through the sign occupied by the Moon at the time of birth of person, such person will suffer loss of wealth caused by the advice of wicked men, by tale bearers, by imprisoument and quarrels. He will besides receive disagreeable intelligence when in his journey.

20. When Mercury passes throgh the 2nd house from the Moon, the person will suffer disgrace and gain success and wealth. When he passes through the 3rd house the person will get friends and will be afraid of troubles from the king and from his enemies and he will quit his place from his own wicked deeds.

21. When Mercury passes through the 4th house from the Moon a person's kinsmen and family will increase and there will be much gain. When Mercury passes through the 5th house from the Moon, the person will quarrel with his wife and sons and will not enjoy the company of an excellent wife.

22. When Mercury passes through the 6th house from the Moon, the person will be liked by all and will gain renown. When Mercury passes through the 7th house the person's appearance will become less bright and there will be qurrels.

When Mercury passess, through the 8th house the person will get sons, suceess, cloths and wealth and will become happy and powerful.

23. When Mercury passes through the 9th house from Moon the person will meet with obstacles to his work. When Mercury passes through the 10th house from the Moon the person's enemies will meet with ruin and the person will get wealth, will enjoy the company of his wife and will be dressed in flannel.

24. When Mercury passes through the 11th houses from the Moon the person will get wealth, eomfort, sons, women, friends and conveyance, will be happy and will receive good intelligence. When Mercury passes through the 12th house from the Moon, the person will suffer disgrace from his enemies, will suffer from diseases and will not enjoy the company of a good wife.

25. When Jupiter passes through the sign occupied by the Moon at the time of birth of a person, such person will lose his wealth and intelligence, will quit his place and will suffer from many quarrels. Mhen Jupiter passes through the 2nd house from the Moon, the person will have no enemies and will enejoy wealth and women.

26. When Jupiter passes through the 3rd house from the Moon, the person will quit his place and will meet with obstacles in his work. When Jupiter passes through the 4th house from the Moon, the person will suffer from troubles caused by his kinsmen, will become patient and resigned and will delight in nothing.

27. When Jupiter passes through the 5th house from the Moon, the person will get servants, prosperity, sons, elephants, horses, bullocks, gold, towns, houses, women, cloths, gems and good qualities.

28. When Jupiter passes through the 6th house from the Moon, the person will be so much afflicted at heart that he will take no delight in the agreeable faces of beautiful women, in the music of the peacock and the cuckoo and in houses made pleasant by the frolic of children playing like the young of the deer.

29. When Jupiter passes through the 7th house from the

Moon, the person will enjoy a good bed, the company of an excellent woman, weath, good meals, flowers, conveyance and the like and he will be of good speech and intelligence.

30. When Jupiter passes through the 8th house from the Moon, the person will suffer from imprisonment, diseases, heavy grief, the fatigue of journey and serious illness. When Jupiter passes through the 9th house from the Moon the person will become efficient at work and influential and he will get sons, success in work, wealth and grain.

31. When Jupiter passes through the 10th house from the Moon, the person will quit his place and suffer loss of health and wealth. When Jupiter passes through the 11th house, the person will return to his country and will recover his health and wealth. When Jupiter passes through the 12th house, the person will suffer grief in his return journey

32. When Venus passes through the sign occupied by the Moon at the time of birth of a person, such person will enjoy excellent perfumes, flowers, cloths, houses, bed, meals and women. When Venus passes through the 2nd house from the Moon, the person will get sons, wealth, grain and presents from the king; will have a prosperous family, will enjoy flowers and gems and will be of bright appearance.

34. When Venus passes through the 3rd house from the Moon, the person will become influential, wealthy and respectable and will return to his place and will get cloths. His enemies will meet with ruin. When Venus passes through the 4th house, the person will get friends and will become greatly powerful.

35. When Venus passes through the 5th house, the person will become happy, will get kinsmen, sons, wealth and friends and will not suffer defeat by the enemy.

36. When Venus passes through the 6th house from the Moon, the person will suffer disgrace, will be afflicted with diseases and will be exposed to danger. When Venus passes through the 7th house the person will suffer injuries through women. When Venus passes through the 8th house from the Moon, the person will get houses, articles of luxury and beautiful women.

37. When Venus passes through the 9th house from the Moon, the person will become virtuous, happy and wealthy,

and he will get plenty of cloths. When Venus passes through the 10th house from the Moon, the person will suffer disgrace and will also suffer from quarrels.

38. When Venus passes through the 11th house from the Moon, the person will get the wealth of his friends and will also get perfumes and cloths. When Venus passes through the 12th house the person will get very few cloths.

39. When Saturn passes through the sign occupied by the Moon at the time of birth of a person, such person will suffer from poison and from fire, will quit his kinsmen, will suffer imprisonment and torture, will travel to foreign lands and live with his friends there; will suffer miseries, loss of wealth and of sons, will suffer also from the fatigues of foot-journey and from humiliation.

40. When Saturn passes through the 2nd house from the Moon, the person will suffer loss of beauty and comfort, will become weak and will get wealth from other men and he will not enjoy this wealth long.

41. When Saturn passes through the 3rd house from the Moon, the person will get wealth, servants, articles of enjoyment, camels, buffaloes, horses, elephants, asses and houses. He will become influential, happy, free from diseases and will become greatly powerful and will defeat his enemies in fight.

42. When Saturn passes through the 4th house from the Moon, the person will be separated from his friends, wealth and wife and ever suspecting evil in everything will never feel happy.

43. When Saturn passes through the 5th house from the Moon, the person will be separated from his sons and wealth and will suffer from quarrels. When Saturn passes through the 6th house from the Moon, the person will be freed from his enemies and diseases and will enjoy the company of women.

44. When Saturn passes through the 7th or 8th house from the Moon, the person will be separated from his wife and sons and will travel on foot in a pitiable condition. When he passes through the 9th house, the person will be all that was stated for for Saturn passing through the 8th house and will besides suffer from hatred, chest-pain, imprisonment and in consequence will not properly observe the daily duties.

45. When Saturn passes through the 10th house, the person will get work and will suffer loss of wealth, learning and fame. When Saturn passes through the 11th house from the Moon, the person will become cruel and will get women and wealth. When Saturn passes through the 12th house from the Moon the person will suffer much grief.

46. Though a planet might be benefic to a person, he produces benefic effects only according to the nature of the Dasa periods and the rank of the person in life, just in the same way as the quantity of rain falling into a small cup cannot but be small though the rain be excessive.

47. The Sun and Mars shall be worshipped with red flowers, sandal paste, (the fragrant flower of Mimusops Elengi), gift of copper, gold and oxen to Brāhmiṇas. The Moon shall be worshipped by the gift of a white cow. Venus shall be worshipped with white flowers and by the gift of silver, and sweet and nutritious things. Saturn shall be worshipped by the gift of black substances. Mercury shall be worshipped by the gift of gems, silver and with the Tilaka flower. Jupiter shall be worshipped with yellow flower and by the gift of yellow substances. By the worship of the planets, a person escapes all miseries.

48. Evils indicated by the motion of the planets may be escaped by the worship of the Brāhmiṇas and the Devas, by expiatory ceremonies, by the recitation of mantras and sacred texts, by the practice of austerities, by gifts to Brāhmiṇas, by the subjugation of one's passions, by moving in the company of Sadhus, and by conversing with them.

49. The Sun and Mars produce their effects when passing through the first half of a sign; the Moon and Saturn produce their effects when moving through the 2nd half of a sign. The learned have declared so.

50. Mercury produces his effects throughout the period of his motion through a sign.

51. When Jupiter passes through the middle of odd signs, be produces miseries even to the righteous and when he passes through the 6th house he also reduces the person to a condition of misery.

52. When a benefic planet is aspected by a malefic planet

or when a malefic planet is aspected by a benefic planet or when a benefic planet and a malefic planet occupy a sign together, in all the above cases the effects will be the same.

53. The good effects assigned to a planet will fail if such planet occupies his depression sign or an inimical sign or if he be an Aṣṭāṅgata planet or if he be aspected by an inimical planet—and as person can as little enjoy them as the blind can enjoy the beauties of a woman.

54. Saturn will produce effects in just the same way as the Sun—just as the Ariagiti (metre) follows the rules of the Vaitāli metre and the Magadhigadha follows the rules of Āryā.

55. If Saturn be an Aṣṭāṅgata planet or if he be about to disappear by conjunction with the Sun he will not produce miseries to the righteous.

56. The Moon partakes of the character of the planet who occupies the same house with her—just in the same way as the face assumes the character of the mind.

57. If the planets occupy malefic places a person will lose his importance i.e. become light just in the same way as the 5th letter of all the four feet and 7th letter of the 2nd and 4th feet become short—these restrictions apply to the Anuṣṭup metre (in which this stanza is written.)

58. Planets occupying benefic places always produce good effects.

59. If planets do not occupy benefic places, all that a person may do to promote his welfare will only prove injurious to him just in the same way as the ceremony of exercism of the ghost injures a person when not properly conducted.

60. A king who starts on a journey when the planets are in benefic places will gain his object though he might possess little power.

61. On a Sunday and when the Sun occupies an Upācaya Sign (the 3rd, 6th, 10th and 11th houses), shall be done any work or, business connected with gold, copper, a horse, dried sticks, bones, skin, woollen blankets, hills, the bark of trees, nails, serpents, thieves, weapons, forest, service under a tyrannical prince, sacred bath, medicine, white silk, articles for sale, shepherds, impenetrable paths, cures, stones, works of art, pure articles, well-known objects, valiant fight and works connected

with fire. The same work shall be done when the Sun occupies the rising sign.

On Mondays or when the Moon occupies the rising sign or when she occupies one of the Kendras shall be done any work or business connected with jewels, conch shells, pearls, productions of water, silver, sacrificial rites, sugarcanes, articles of food, women, milk, milk-trees, the brances of trees, crops of wet low lands, liquids, Brāhmiṇs, horses, the work of cooling, horned animals, the cultivation of lands, the summoning of a commander of armies, the king, popular favour, the demons, phlegmatic substances, elephants, flowers and cloths.

On Tuesdays shall be done any work or business connected with mineral mines, gold, fire, corals, weapons, theft, torture, forests, impenetrable places command over armies, trees of red flowers, all red substances, bitter substances, pungent substances, works of art, serpents, ropes, young men that live by dealing in these, physicians, Buddhist ascetics, working by night, white silk, cheating and foppery.

On Wednesdays, and when Mercury occupies the rising sign, shall be done any work or business connected with emeralds, lands, perfumes, cloths, plays, knowledge of science, skill in work literary performances, arts, magical formulae, metalic work, law suit, acts of ability, articles for sale, practice of austerities and Yoga practice, messengers, promotion of long life, deceit, lies, bathing, objects either long or short, dependence on other men for help and important works.

62. On Thursdays shall be done any work or business connected with gold, silver, horses, elephants, oxen, physicians, medicinal planets, the Brāhmiṇas, the Pitṛs and the Devas, umbrellas, fans, orgaments, kings, temples, alms-houses, auspicious deeds, science, beautiful objects, fruitful objects, truthful words, the practice of austerities, sacred fire and wealth.

63. On Fridays shall be done any work or business connected with painting, cloths, spermatic drugs, friendship with prostitutes, buffoonery, the pleasures of the youth beautiful places, crystals, silver, enjoyment of flowers, perfumes and the like, conveyances, sugar canes, autumn crops, cows, tradesmen, farmers, medicine and the productions of water.

On Saturdays shall be done any work or business connected with a buffaloe, a goat, a camel, black metal, a servant, an old man, any low deeds, a birds, a thief, rope works, wicked persons, pot-shreds and obstructions.

64. Thus have been described the effects of the motions of the planets through the signs of the Zodiac by Varāha Mihira in a variety of sweet metres after examining the science of prosody.

REFERENCE

1. In future we shall only employ the expression "from the Moon" to denote the sign occupied by the Moon at the time of birth of a person.

CHAPTER 105

On the Worship of the Stellar Deity

1. The asterism of Mūla forms the feet of the Nakṣatra Puruṣa. The asterisms of Rohiṇī and Aśvinī form his shanks; those of P. Āṣāḍhas and U. Āṣāḍhās form his thighs and those of P. Phalgunī and U. Phalgunī form the privity.

2. The asterism of Kṛttikā form the lip of the Nakṣatrapuruṣa. Those of P. Bhadrapadā and U. Bhadrapadā form his sides; that of Revatī forms his abdoment; and that of Anurādhā forms his breast.

3. The asterism of Dhaniṣṭhā forms the back of the Nakṣatrapuruṣa. The asterism of Viśākhā forms his arms, that of Hasta forms his hands, that of Punarvasu his fingers and that of Āśleṣā his finger nails.

4. The asterism of Jyeṣṭhā forms the neck of the Nakṣatrapuruṣa, that of Śravaṇa forms his ears, that of Puṣya his face, that of Svāti his teeth, that of Śatabhiśaj his smiles, that of Maghā his nose and that of Mṛgaśirṣa his eyes.

5. The asterism of Cittra forms the forehead of the Nakṣatrapuruṣa, that of Bharaṇī forms his head and that of Ārdrā his hairs. Thus have been described the features of the Nakṣatrapuruṣa.

6. A person shall worship Viṣṇu and the Nakṣatrapuruṣa on the 8th lunar day of the dark half of the month of Caitra when the Moon passes through the asterism of Mūla and shall fast that day.

7. At the close of the fasting, the person shall give away to a Brāhmina astronomer a vessel filled with ghee together with gold, gems and cloths to the extent of his power.

8. A person, who desires a bright and beautiful appearance, shall feed Brāhmiṇas with rice mixed with milk, ghee and sugar

and shall fast on days when the Moon passes through the several asterisms representing the features of the Nakṣatrapuruṣa begining from the feet and he shall then worship both Viṣṇu and the Nakṣatrapuruṣa.

9. A person who fasts and worships as stated above will have long arms, broad and firm breast, a moon-like face, white beautiful teeth, the gait of an elephant, eyes long like the leaves of the lotus and appearance calculated to attract the eyes of women and a body as fine as that of cupid.

10. A woman who fasts and worships as prescribed above will have a face as bright and spotless as the summer sun, eyes as soft and large as the petals of the lotus, beautiful teeth, fine ears, and hairs as black as the bee.

11. Her voice will be sweet as that of the cuckoo, her lips will be red, her feet and hands will be as soft and bright as the lotus, her waist will be thin and ben with the weight of her bosoms and her navel turning from left to right.

12. Her thighs will be like the plantain; her buttocks will be beautiful, the cavities in the loins above her hip will be fine and her toes will be close.

13. A person who observes the Nakṣatrapuruṣa vṛta (ceremony) will after his death, become a star and along with the innumerable stars of brilliant lustre, live to the end of Brahma's day (432,000.000 years after which occurs the dissolution of the Universe). At the beginning of the next kalpa, the person will first be born a famous emperor and in his next birth, he will be born either a king or a rich man or a Brāhmiṇas.

14 & 15. The twelve months beginning from Mārgaśīrṣa (November and December) are respectively sacred to Keśava, Nārāyaṇa, Mādhava, Govinda, Viṣṇu, Madhusūdana, Trivikrama, Vāmana, Śrādhara, Hṛṣīkeśa, Padmanābha and Dāmodara.

16. A person who, having fasted previously, worships Viṣṇu on Dvādasi days singing the twelve names mentioned above will be freed from the trammels of re-birth and will obtain Salvation.

CHAPTER 106

Conclusion

1. Planting the hill of my learning in the vast ocean of astrology and churning it. I have thus brought out this bright Moon of Science which sheds its light of knowledge over the whole world.

2. O ye good men, I have not omitted to mention anything contained in the old Śāstras; you may compare my work with the Śāstras and follow the rules freely.

3. If good critics discover a few merits in an ocean of demerits, it is their nature to bring the former to the notice of the world, while the nature of bad critics is just the reverse.

4. Exposed to the fire of malicious criticism, the good of a literary production becomes purified. Every attempt must therefore be made to bring a work to the notice of severe critics.

5. If, in any of the copies of this work or in the recitation of it by persons who have learned it from their preceptors, the learned happen to notice any portion either missing or erroneous or omitted, they will, it is hoped, setting aside all feelings of malice, correct the error of supply the omission.

6. By the blessing of the Sun, the Sages and the reverened preceptors worshipped by me, I have been able to write this brief treatise. Salutation to the ancient writers of Saṁhitā.

Dear reader,

The Index could not be attached with the book due to certain production problems.

Please send this card to us with your name and address for free delivery of the same.

Inconvenience caused is regretted.

From :

Stamp

To:

Sri Satguru Publications
1st Floor
40/5, Shakti Nagar
Delhi 110 007
India